Political Part
Government Regulation

Political Participation and Government Regulation

SAM PELTZMAN

The University of Chicago Press

CHICAGO AND LONDON

SAM PELTZMAN is Sears Roebuck Professor in the Graduate School of
Business at the University of Chicago.

The University of Chicago Press, Chicago 60637
The University of Chicago Press, Ltd., London

© 1998 by The University of Chicago
All rights reserved. Published 1998
Printed in the United States of America

07 06 05 04 03 02 01 00 99 98   1 2 3 4 5

ISBN: 0-226-65416-8 (cloth)
ISBN: 0-226-65417-6 (paper)

Library of Congress Cataloging-in-Publication Data
Peltzman, Sam.
    Political participation and government regulation / Sam
Peltzman.
        p.   cm.
    Includes bibliographical references and index.
    ISBN 0-226-65416-8 (cloth : alk. paper). — ISBN 0-226-65417-6
(pbk. : alk. paper)
    1. Political participation—United States.   2. Industrial laws and
legislation—United States.   3. Government spending policy—
United States.   I. Title.
JK1764.P45   1998
323′.042′0973—dc21   98-14276
                                                     CIP

CONTENTS

INTRODUCTION

I have spent most of my professional life studying the interface of the private economy and the public sector. This volume brings together ten of my articles on two broad questions: how does government work? And how do the voters and their elected representatives make decisions? The answers which emerge from these articles do not, on the surface, easily coexist. The electorate comes off as surprisingly well informed. It appropriately rewards good performance by those in office and penalizes bad. It understands its interests and votes accordingly. This is surprising because economists still have a hard time understanding why voters vote in the first place, let alone why they incur the costs of acquiring and processing information about the performance of politicians. Our traditional view is that voters should be, in Anthony Downs's phrase, "rationally ignorant" about such matters since their individual vote cannot change the electoral outcome. Readers looking for a resolution of the implied conundrum will be disappointed. Somehow the decisions of millions of rationally ignorant individuals add up to a more or less sensible collective outcome. Moreover, the broad pattern of voting by legislators emerging from my work is one of faithful representation of the interests of their constituents. Qualifications aside for the moment, we usually get pretty much what we vote for.

A somewhat different picture emerges from the articles on the operation of government, especially those on the economics of government regulation. The emphasis here is on the role of narrow interests which can parlay inherent advantages in exerting political pressure into regulatory outcomes favorable to them but costly to the broader constituency. As the last article in this volume makes clear, this emphasis owes much to my teacher and colleague, the late George Stigler, who is usually given credit for pioneering the modern economics of regulation. While I modify this Stiglerian emphasis in some important respects, a disjunction with the work on politics remains: if we get the kind of legislators we vote for, why do they then allow our interests to be sacrificed by regulators whom they appoint, oversee, and provide with budgetary sustenance?

An answer of sorts emerges from the subject matter of the two sets of articles. The articles on political participation emphasize broad issues, such as how well the macroeconomy is functioning and whether I should want my congressman to support a larger or a smaller role for government in general. The articles on regulation are about government bodies concerned with narrower issues, such as what the price of electricity should be, how many trucking firms should be granted operating certificates, or how should the control of pollution be implemented. Two aspects of this difference in the breadth of issues seem relevant here. First, the work on political participation makes clear that interest groups and the campaign contributions of their political action committees are important elements of the legislator's constituency. Since the life-or-death issues animating these interest groups are often regulatory issues, it would hardly be surprising for the legislator to give the regulators a certain amount of leeway in serving those narrow interests. Second, rational ignorance cuts more sharply on regulatory issues. The consequences of, say, a poorly functioning macroeconomy can be devastating to the voter who loses a job or has the value of savings eroded by inflation. Nothing as consequential is at stake for the typical voter in most regulatory decision making. So the risk to the typical legislator of a voter uprising over something like restrictive entry in trucking is going to be trivial next to the continued flow of PAC dollars generated by the policy.

I do not, however, want to push this reconciliation of the two bodies of work too hard. It rests heavily on the differential strength of rational ignorance as between broad and narrow political issues. And, as I hope I have made clear, I do not think our understanding of voter knowledge and motivation is as yet so far advanced that we can speak confidently about why rational ignorance should be taken more seriously in one context than in the other.

The more durable connection between the two parts of the book is personal. It comes from a lifelong interest in public affairs. My first conscious memory of this interest was the election of 1948, where the issue of whether to vote for Henry Wallace or Harry Truman aroused as much passionate discussion on my Brooklyn block as the progress of the Dodgers in the pennant race. Both Wallace and the Dodgers lost that year. So did Tom Dewey, but his voters were as few among us as Yankee fans. To my neighbors both represented the "haves" of this world who deserved a reflexive animosity. The emphasis on the redistributive aspect of politics evident in this book has deep roots.

Serious interest in the economics of politics and regulation began for me during graduate school and my early professional career in the 1960s. This was a time when scholarly interest in the subject began to flourish. The last chapter of this book elaborates some of the reasons for this and discusses George Stigler's singularly important role in this early growth. It also discusses the subsequent developments in more detail than I can go into here. What set this early work apart from its predecessors was systematic investigation of the actual effects of regulation. At the same time, important theoretical innovations in the economic analysis of politics ("public choice") were being developed by, among others, James Buchanan, Gordon Tullock, Anthony Downs, and Mancur Olson. These two streams came together in the early 1970s when, again under Stigler's influence, economists came to understand that the economics of regulation and the economics of politics were inextricably linked. Prior to these developments economists were mostly content to ignore the political context of regulation by treating the subject as a branch of applied welfare economics. The main questions were about the circumstances in which regulation of one sort or another was conceptually desirable. The untested assumption was that actual regulators were muddling their way toward the role economists had conjured up for them. That optimism, naïve in hindsight, withered in the wake of the results of the early empirical investigations of the effects of regulation.

The economics of regulation was not alone in making this passage from optimism about the role of government to disillusion about its actual effects. By the early 1970s doubt about the ability of economic policy to stabilize the macroeconomy, to eradicate poverty, and so forth was growing not only within the profession but in the public square as well. If there was anything unique about the economics of regulation at this time it was that it probably led the rest of the profession in stressing the importance of political forces in shaping the outcome of policy. The fundamental precept of public choice economics was that politicians should, like everyone else, be treated as self-interested actors. And public choice economists were showing how the incentive structure of political choice could be inconsistent with maximization of social welfare. Regulation economists, hungry for some explanation of the apparent failure of regulation to do what it ought, quickly seized on the developments in public choice.

It was in this intellectual context that much of the second half of this book was written. The closest connection to the developments I have been discussing is in my 1976 article "Toward a More General Theory of Regulation" (chapter 6). This has probably had more professional influence than any of the other articles in the book. And it is the only mainly theoretical article I have written in a long career. It was my contribution to a festschrift for George Stigler's sixty-fifth birthday which I helped organize with Gary Becker and Richard Posner. This article is sometimes described as a generalization of Stigler's seminal article "The Theory of Economic Regulation" (*Bell Journal of Economics and Management Science* 2 [Spring 1971]: 1–21). It is that, but it also reflects my qualms about some important parts of Stigler's article. Stigler had conceptualized regulation as a political contest between the regulated industry and the rest of us (the "public" or the consumers of the industry's output). He concluded that the regulated industry would usually win this contest, because the larger public typically had far too diffuse a stake in the outcome to organize effectively against the industry interest.

This conclusion had considerable appeal to a profession searching for an explanation for "regulatory failure," but it struck me as something of an overreaction to the previous view of regulation as a mainly benign antidote to "market failure." For one thing, it was inconsistent with some key features of most regulatory activity, particularly the tendency of regulators to perpetuate uneconomic services. Richard Posner had emphasized this tendency, sometimes called "cross-subsidization," in his article "Taxation by Regulation" (*Bell Journal of Economics and Management Science* 2 [Spring 1971]: 22–50). Another reservation I had about the notion that regulators would be "captured" by the regulated was the passive role it assigned to regulators and the rest of us. If the regulator were indeed the rational maximizer Stigler (and I) made him out to be, would he not seek some competition for his services rather than accept unquestioningly an inevitable triumph of the regulated industry? Would not some of us, perhaps already organized for some other purpose, form a sufficiently cohesive force to provide that competition? The mainly positive answers to such questions found in my 1976 article result in a characterization of regulation as the search for coalitions that can sustain the regulatory enterprise. Cohesive interests like the regulated industry will usually be part of the dominant coalition, but not all of it. That view of regulation led to numerous empirical implications, such as the tendency of regulation to suppress economically meaningful differences within the dominant coalition, which I think have contributed to the article's professional influence.

The integration of politics into the economics of regulation, indeed into the economic analysis of government policy more generally, has become commonplace. A larger field called 'political economy' has been created. That integration was already far along when I wrote "Current Developments in the Economics of Regulation" (chapter 8) in 1981. This article was written for a conference sponsored by the National Science Foundation and the National Bureau of Economic Research that aimed at taking stock of the flourishing literature on regulation. Most of the leading figures in the field contributed to the conference. I was flattered to be asked to write an evaluative piece. Some of what I wrote then seems incomplete in hindsight. In particular, the United States was just beginning to deregulate important industries, and neither I nor my professional colleagues had yet grasped the importance of this. However, I think that the substance of this piece remains timely. I pointed out that the traditional analysis of regulation as applied welfare economics had not died. Rather it had been supplemented by the "creeping realism" provided by the analysis of politics, especially the politics of interest groups. Environmental regulation is a good example of this. Most economists see the potential improvement in social welfare from this regulation. And the growth of this form of regulation in the 1970s hardly seemed like an example of the regulated capturing the regulator. Yet by the early 1980s the profession had learned not to take such examples at face value. While the regulated industry had indeed not captured environmental regulation, it was part of the relevant coalition, and its interests were not ignored. The instinct of regulation economists to look for this aspect of pollution regulation (and of most other types of regulation), and their ability to find evidence of its importance were already well honed by 1981. This is no less true today.

Deregulation has become an international "buzzword." Sometimes the word really means a change in regulation rather than its demise. For example, the so-called deregulation of American telecommunications led to an increased role for the Federal Communications Commission and a lesser one for the state utility commissions. It is nevertheless fair to say that the need for regulating a variety of industries has come under active scrutiny all over the world. In the United States that scrutiny led, beginning in the 1970s, to the demise of numerous regulatory restrictions in transportation, communications, and finance among others. Who, as they say, would've thunk it? The line of theory with which I am associated came to be called the economic theory of regulation, because it treated regulators as rational maximizers whose primary task was self-preservation. Yet hardly had the ink dried on the theory when many of these regulators were being put out of business The apparent irony of this development was not lost on my professional colleagues. Some time in the late 1980s—I cannot date it more precisely—I received a call from Martin N. Baily of the Brookings Institution. He recounted the developments I have just outlined and challenged me to write an evaluative piece for Brookings's annual conference on microeconomics. This was the genesis of my 1989 article "The Economic Theory of Regulation after a Decade of Deregulation" (chapter 9).

That piece makes no special claim of prescience. Neither I nor, if the truth be told, the economics profession as a whole, had anticipated the strength of the deregulatory tide that was about to roll in when the economic theory of regulation was being developed. I pointed out, however, that what distinguished the economic theory from its predecessors was its emphasis on wealth redistribution as a main feature of regulation. The rational regulator's role in the theory was to use the power at his disposal (over prices, entry, and so forth) to transfer wealth to those groups who could reciprocate with meaningful political support for the regulatory enterprise. Accordingly, if the regulator's ability to transfer wealth were compromised that support would wither. My 1989 article argues that market forces—sometimes created by the regulation itself—had eroded the wealth available for redistribution in many (though not all) of the industries that ultimately were deregulated. Accordingly, there seems to be a rough consistency between what the economic theory would finger as the leading suspect in promoting deregulation (loss of redistributable wealth) and what actually happened.

I believe that the message of that 1989 piece is, if anything, more relevant today than it was then. It is unlikely to be coincidental that the rising worldwide interest in deregulation and privatization coincides with the increasing internationalization of markets. That process makes it increasingly difficult for one country to shelter its domestic markets from competition and thereby generate the wealth that can sustain the regulatory enterprise. So the process of deregulating and privatizing industries that have traditionally heavy state involvement is likely to continue. Consider, for example, international aviation. This industry grew up with substantial regulatory barriers to entry and price competition and remains so in much of the world. Not coincidentally it came to be populated by many inefficient government-owned airlines. That made a certain amount of political sense when an overly large and overpaid work force could be partly paid for by high fares charged to tourists and business people from other countries. But it makes increasingly less sense as access to international routes and competition among international gateways grows. Therefore, I would be surprised if any significant number of today's state-owned airlines remain either unprivatized or unreformed by the end of the coming millennium's first decade.

The twin notions that wealth redistribution and coalition building underlie the success of much government policy play a prominent role in my 1980 article "The Growth of Government" (chapter 7). This article has not had the same professional impact as some of my others, but it is my personal favorite. I learned much about the history of government spending in several countries. I found in those histories and in a wide variety of contemporary data, ranging from American states to third world countries, what I still think is a remarkably consistent and somewhat surprising pattern driving the growth of government. Moreover the phenomenon with which I grapple in that article is hardly trivial. When this century began, governments all over the world were small by any measure. The federal government of that day, for example, was little more than a small army and a post office. As the century ends, governments everywhere are very much larger than they used to be. By the measure used in my article— government spending per dollar of gross domestic product—they are on the order of five or ten times the size they were when the century began. One would think that so profound a development would have elicited an outpouring of investigation by economists. However, as the first part of my article makes clear, this had not happened, nor was I satisfied with the state of what little literature there was.

My work on regulation had convinced me of the importance of the redistributive element in government activity. Why should not the same force that made for successful regulation—politically optimal wealth redistribution—operate more generally in the political economy? This question was not entirely novel. One of my influential teachers, Aaron Director, had promulgated a "law of redistribution" (summarized by George Stigler in "Director's Law of Public Income Redistribution," *Journal of Law and Economics* 13 [April 1970]:1–10) whereby governments' political success rested on redistribution from the rich and poor to the middle class. Though I did not realize it at the start of my research, my conclusion was not to be so different from his. The route to my conclusion began with the syllogism that if redistribution was important and government had grown, then the demand for or supply of redistribution must have increased. Almost every study of the distributional aspects of government programs shows that, on balance, they tax the rich and favor the not-so-rich. And in a democratic society with so many more of us than them, this seems to make sense politically. But these notions quickly run into trouble when applied to the growth of government in this century. They would suggest that governments will grow when the rich have more for the rest of us to democratically separate them from. Yet this is almost universally wrong. The United States has a more equal distribution of income today (before counting any impact of government programs) than it did in the era of tiny government. The greatest growth of government in the developed world has taken place in the relatively homogeneous and egalitarian societies of Northern Europe and Scandinavia. Indeed I found that narrowing, rather than widening, inequality preceded every important example of government growth I examined.

My resolution of this apparent paradox lay in the nature of that growth. It has been concentrated in a very few specific programs. Without universal education and social insurance, government would still be a post office and a (somewhat larger) military. I argued that these "mega-programs" could not succeed without broad-based agreement about their desirability, and that such agreement required the growth of a large and articulate middle class. A society where life spans are short and uncertain and where children are an important source of income for many families, such as America one hundred years ago, is hardly fertile ground for broad-based support of public education and social security. It is not the gap between the few very rich and the rest of us that is relevant here but rather the gap between the poor and not so poor. When that gap narrows, the political ground for a coalition in support of massive government programs becomes fertile.

At the end of my 1980 article I ventured boldly to predict a coming era of restrained government. This was based on the perception that the narrowing of income inequality which had produced the broad middle class had run its course. Subsequent trends in income inequality reinforce that perception. However, governments have generally continued to grow since 1980, more so in Europe than the United States. And the growth currently programmed into those massive social insurance programs seems to portend continuing growth. Nevertheless I am unprepared to abandon my prediction. While the reality has not yet changed, the political climate has. Optimism about the ability of government programs to solve social problems has waned. The political center of gravity has shifted from promoting more programs to restraining the growth of old ones. And the parties of the left seem to succeed only when they ratify that shift rather than reverse it. It is, I believe, hardly a coincidence that this waning of support for "big government" has occurred when income differences within the voting population have widened.

Some of these notions are echoed in my 1992 article "Voters as Fiscal Conservatives" (chapter 5). This is the last of the articles on the political process in part I of this book. The main result in that article is that voters penalize growth of government spending at both the federal and state level. More precisely, since roughly 1950 at least, they have on balance been less inclined to vote for incumbent Governors and Presidents whose administrations had above average spending growth. That result creates a dilemma which has not yet been fully resolved: If spending costs votes why has spending risen so much over the course of the twentieth century? A potential resolution lies in the time period I studied. It came after the great leap in spending during the New Deal and World War II. That particular example of spending growth hardly seemed costly politically. Indeed Franklin Roosevelt was rewarded with unprecedented electoral success. In the circumstances, it would hardly be obvious to a postwar politician that government was now big enough and that the time had come to rein in its growth. Many would have to learn this the hard way, by losing votes after raising expenditures. This line of reasoning gets some support from the record of the last two decades when, in spite of the great growth of entitlement spending, there has been a marked deceleration of the growth of total government spending.

My interest in the working of the political process arose out of my earlier work on regulation. This had convinced me that the economic analysis of any government activity, whether it be regulation or something else, like the size of a budget, could not be separated from analysis of politics. So I felt the need to delve more deeply into how the primary participants in the political process—the voters and their representatives—made their decisions. As an empirical economist I was naturally drawn to the most easily measurable aspect of this problem, votes recorded on election day and in the legislative arena; and my working hypothesis was that economic forces played an important role in voting behavior. I was hardly the first economist to look for this connection between economics and politics. Two main strands of this inquiry began before my work. One focused on how voters responded to the macroeconomy. I pursued this connection in my 1987 article "Economic Conditions and Gubernatorial Elections" (chapter 3) and in my 1990 article "How Efficient Is the Voting Market?" (chapter 4). It also appears in the 1992 piece on voter response to spending. The other path I followed centered about the issue of how faithfully legislators represented the interests of their constituents. My 1984 article "Constituent Interest and Congressional Voting" (chapter 1) and my 1985 article "An Economic Interpretation of the History of Congressional Voting in the Twentieth Century" (chapter 2) deal with this issue.

The preceding literature on voting and the macroeconomy had dealt mainly with presidential elections. Most of it showed that presidents gain politically when the economy performs well during their term in office, especially, perhaps even exclusively, during the last year of that term. My first foray into this field was to try to extend this result to gubernatorial elections. This seemed an obvious, if modest extension. If presidents get votes for robust growth of national income, should not governors be rewarded for an expanding state economy? The answer proved to be less than rhetorical. I found that a governor's electoral success was largely unaffected by growth of the state's economy. However, governors shared in the successes or failures of presidents. So, for example, a growing national economy during the term of a Republican president would help both the president and Republican governors at the polls.

That finding struck me as both odd and comforting. Odd because the voters as a group were making fine distinctions—here between the national and the state economy—of the sort that, as I mentioned at the outset, economists have difficulty understanding. But it was comforting that the distinction seemed to be a sensible one to make. A president's policies have some plausible connection to the performance of the national economy, at least over the short run. Governors have much less leeway to affect state economic conditions. I was sufficiently impressed by this apparent ability of the voters to sift information on the economy to pursue the phenomenon more systematically. I did so in the 1990 article on voting market efficiency.

The word "efficiency" in the title refers to how well a market processes information. Prices in efficient markets correctly reflect the information available to buyers and sellers. The concept is central to the modern theory of financial markets from which I deliberately borrowed it for my title. I did this to make clear that I was treating elections as a market where voters are buying the wares of candidates and vote shares are the resulting prices. The central question addressed in my 1990 article is whether those prices correctly reflect the available information, in this case about the macroeconomy. I was somewhat surprised to find that the answer for the voting market, no less than the stock market, is yes. For example, economists take great pains to distinguish expected from unexpected inflation and to emphasize that only the latter can be harmful. It does not matter, we argue, whether the inflation rate is 1 percent or 10 percent so long as the rate is what market participants expect it to be. The harm arises when we expect 1 and get 10. This is not an easy distinction to get across to students and journalists. But the voting market seems to get it. On my evidence, it responds to unexpected inflation and ignores expected inflation. Just how such a subtle distinction emerges from the aggregation of millions of poorly informed votes remains a mystery to me.

My 1984 and 1985 articles on congressional voting stepped into a professional debate about how faithfully legislators represent the interests of their constituents. I can illustrate the issues in the debate with the example of Senator Kennedy of Massachusetts. If an economist innocent of that state's political history were asked to predict how a senator from Massachusetts would vote, a likely answer would be "fairly conservatively, at least on economic issues." Underlying that prediction would be a view about the motivation of the electorate (they would vote their self-interest), some knowledge about some of their relevant characteristics (Massachusetts voters have above average incomes, and "liberal" economic policies usually transfer wealth away from such people), and a view about how competitive the electoral process is (competitive enough to give the voters the opportunity to have their interests represented). In this case, of course, all such knowledge would be useless. Senator Kennedy votes for liberal economic policies and keeps getting reelected by the Massachusetts voters. Moreover his case is not exceptional. Economists studying congressional voting had by the mid 1980s documented a broad disjunction between the apparent interests of the electorate and the voting patterns of their representatives. They had done so mostly by following the research strategy implied by my example. That is, they tried to match indexes of congressional voting patterns against measures that presumably captured the interests of the electorate, such as their per capita income. Most economists did not find a very powerful connection between such measures and congressional voting patterns. Two alternative conclusions seemed to follow from this apparent failure of a simple economic model of congressional voting. One was that the voters cared about more than their own material interests. Senator Kennedy was not, after all, fooling his voters. They kept reelecting him and voting for others with similar records. Another view was that rationally ignorant voters cut their representatives much slack. As a result a legislator could stray far from the electorate's preferences and still survive politically.

My 1984 article argued against this hasty abandonment of the simple economic model. I felt that the previous tests of the model had missed something essential about representative government. In my conception of the appropriate economic model, Senator Kennedy is not successful because he represents "Massachusetts." Rather he gets reelected by continuing to please the part of the Massachusetts electorate that voted him into office and, importantly, those who contribute to his campaign fund. Political scientists recognized this difference between a representative's district and his or her reelection constituency, but economists mainly had ignored it. In my 1984 article, I tried to measure some of these differences and use them to analyze voting patterns. For example, suppose a voter's income is related to his interest in economic policies, and suppose that Senator Kennedy wants to represent the interests of his voters. What should then matter to him is not average income in all of Massachusetts but the income of those who voted for him. I found that the economic model of politics fared much better by using in the analysis such arguably more relevant measures of constituency interest.

The point of this exercise was as much methodological as substantive. I do not believe that economists will resolve all the mysteries of politics by ever more accurate measures of constituency interest. However, we are on a slippery slope if we abandon an economic model after a few poorly crafted tests. We would then be competing in an arena with political scientists, psychologists, and so forth, where we have no obvious comparative advantage and where the odds against our contributing significantly to an understanding of politics are much longer. I followed this "Shoemaker, stick to your last" advice in my 1985 article on the history of congressional voting.

This article tries to make sense out of the profound regional differences that have colored the history of American politics. In the end I find that there are substantial regional differences that elude a simple economic explanation. But these are remarkably durable. For all of this century, and probably before, the South, for example, has tended to be more skeptical about expanding the role of the state in the economy than the North. The durability of these regional preferences turned out to be of great help to my quest for an understanding of regional voting patterns. I found that, these durable preferences notwithstanding, regional voting patterns in Congress had changed substantially over time and that a very simple economic model could explain these changes. The nub of the explanation is the fact that, on balance, federal programs have consistently transferred wealth from richer areas to poorer and from urban to rural areas. Thus the simplest economic model would have wealthy urban areas sending conservatives to Congress and poor rural areas electing liberals. This is not so successful a model at particular points in time. Today, for example, wealthy urban districts often elect liberals. It is, however, an extremely successful model for understanding the sweeping changes that have taken place over this century. Consider the American polity circa 1900. On economic policy, New England was a bastion of conservatism and the South was home to a populist activism. While this regional gap narrowed, it remained until the end of the New Deal. (Remember Roosevelt's quip that as Maine goes so goes Vermont.) Today, however, regional alignments are completely reversed. Maine is no longer rock-ribbed Republican and the solid Democratic South has very nearly disintegrated. What brought about this change? In 1900 the South was very much poorer and more rural than the rest of the country, so much so as to overwhelm its preference for conservative policies. As it became more like the rest of the country, the payoff it could expect from liberal policies fell, so the cost of exercising its conservative proclivities fell. The relative economic decline of New England moved it to the left politically by lowering the cost it bore from liberal policies.

I concluded the telling of this straightforward tale with a prediction based on the continuing decline of regional economic differences and the durability of their historic political differences. It was that the importance of those historic differences would grow over time because the cost of exercising them was vanishing. I believe the subsequent decade's experience has borne this out. The left-right gap between the North and South appears to have grown in this decade.

I hope this introduction gives the reader some idea of the context in which I wrote the articles in this book. But that risks an overemphasis on the past. So I want to conclude by discussing the future of the economics of regulation and politics. In my 1993 article "George Stigler's Contribution to the Economic Analysis of Regulation" (chapter 10), I try to do some of this by highlighting some of the unsolved puzzles emerging from the economic theory of regulation that Stigler pioneered. For example, he likened regulation to a commodity bought by the regulated industry for its benefit. This now seems to me entirely inadequate. The better analogy would be that of an arranged marriage between reluctant, even hostile, partners who eventually reach a symbiotic accommodation. We clearly have much work to do on the origins of regulation and on its life patterns. Similarly large issues remain everywhere in the economics of politics and government. I eschew trying to catalog them. But just to understand the magnitude, consider the system of redistribution our political system has erected. It levies moderately progressive taxes and provides somewhat regressive or distributionally neutral benefits. In much of my work I took this system as a given and tried to understand its implications. But the system raises at least two major puzzles. One is that most voters seem to be net losers from this system. Indeed, as I discuss above, there is evidence of political resistance to further expansion. Yet the basic system of redistribution itself remains unchallenged politically. The other puzzle arises from the large brokerage role this system creates for government. This is particularly evident in the vast system of entitlements we have created. I am taxed today to provide benefits mostly to people very much like me except that they are a bit older. In a few years, I expect to turn the tables on my neighbors' children. Put aside the very important tax distortions created by this churning. The enduring political appeal of a system in which much is done for little net effect remains to be understood.

My point in raising these issues is simply to indicate how large an intellectual challenge remains in front of us. Unfortunately, however, I sense a reluctance in the economics profession today to confront such big issues. Work on general models of regulation, for example, appears to have stopped. Instead the focus seems to be on highly specific problems—how does this or that system of regulation function, for example. There is nothing wrong in this, and the increased level of technical skill being brought to bear on specific problems is an admirable advance. However, I doubt that a steady diet of small advances can entirely sustain an intellectually vibrant economics of regulation and politics. Therefore, I hope that this proclivity for singles hitting will soon give way to an occasional swing for the fences.

PART ONE
Political Participation

ONE

Constituent Interest and
Congressional Voting

I. Introduction

This article shows that congressional voting behavior can be analyzed usefully with a simple principal-agent model. This model, in which political competition constrains legislative agents to serve the interests of those who "pay" for their services—with votes and other forms of political currency (for example, campaign funds)—is often the starting point for economic analysis of legislation. But a frequent conclusion has been that political ornithology is at least as important as the interests of constituents in explaining legislative voting behavior. Thus, "liberal democrats," for example, tend to vote alike on many specific issues where the diversity of their constituencies would seem to suggest otherwise.

This result has emerged in a number of empirical studies of voting that share a common methodology.[1] This typically starts with a statistical model such as

First published in *Journal of Law and Economics* 27 (April 1984): 181–210. © 1984 by The University of Chicago.

I want to thank Michael Hartzmark for valuable research assistance, Rodney Smith, Joe Kalt, James Heckman, George Stigler, Gary Becker, and other participants in the Economic and Legal Organization Workshop at the University of Chicago for helpful comments on an earlier draft. The financial assistance of the Procter and Gamble Foundation and the Center for the Study of the Economy and the State, University of Chicago, is acknowledged gratefully.

1. The most comprehensive example is James B. Kau & Paul H. Rubin, Self-Interest, Ideology, and Logrolling in Congressional Voting, 22 J. Law & Econ. 365 (1979). Their analysis is expanded in James B. Kau & Paul H. Rubin, Congressmen Constituents and Contributors (1981) (mimeographed, Univ. Georgia); published as Congressmen Constituents and Contributors (Boston: Nijhoff, 1982). Both study Congressional voting on a broad range of issues. Other examples covering specific issues include Jonathan I. Silberman & Gary C. Durden, Determining Legislative Preferences on the Minimum Wages: An Economic Approach, 84 J. Pol. Econ. 317 (1976); Edward J. Mitchell, The Basis of Congressional Energy Policy, 57 Tex. L. Rev. 591 (1979); Joseph P. Kalt, The Economics and Politics of Oil Price Regulation (Cambridge: Harvard Univ. Press, 1981); Joseph P. Kalt & Mark A. Zupan, The Politics and Economics of Senate Voting on Coal Strip Mining Policy (1982) (mimeographed, Harvard Univ.); published as Capture and Ideology in the Economic Theory of Politics, 74 Am. Econ. Rev. 279 (1984); and James B. Kau & Paul H. Rubin, Voting on Minimum Wages: A Time-Series Analysis, 86 J. Pol. Econ. 337 (1978).

(1) $Y = DX + CI + \text{error term}$,

where Y is the probability that a legislator will vote yes on a particular bill, say, a bill to put a price ceiling on crude oil; X is the "economic interest" of constituents in the outcome—their gains or losses from the price ceiling on oil; I is the legislator's "ideology"; and D and C are parameters. As a practical matter, neither X nor I is directly observable, so what is typically estimated is a regression such as

(2) $y = d\text{M} + cR$,

where y is a dummy equal to one for a "yes," zero for a "no" vote; M is a vector of economic characteristics of constituents, which should be correlated with X; and R is some overall rating of the "liberalism" of the legislator's voting record (ignoring party for simplicity) by a group such as the Americans for Democratic Action (ADA). This liberal pressure group's rating is just the percentage of the legislator's votes, in a selected sample, that agreed with the ADA's position.

This regression model has been employed to determine how much of the variation in Y can be explained by "interest" and how much by "ideology," where ideology is treated as a residual category. For this purpose, any characteristic plausibly related to the effects of legislation on constituents' wealth is a candidate for inclusion in M. Some of these may be issue specific and more or less clearly associated with the stakes of constituents in the outcome of the bill—for example, oil production in the district in the case of our oil price control bill. But others will be included in M simply because they are likely to capture some diversity of interest across constituencies. For example, because an oil price ceiling is unlikely to have the same effects on rich and poor districts, a per capita income variable may be included even if the direction of the effects is unclear a priori. Race and union membership variables might be included because racial and labor group interests have been articulated politically on other issues and are therefore likely to be articulated on an oil price control bill as well.

When (2) is estimated for particular votes or issues, a substantial part of the variation in y can frequently be explained by R (ideology) even when M is very broadly defined. This is often interpreted to mean that political agents are not faithfully representing the interests of their principals.[2] Of course, there are procedural and interpretive complexities in this

---

2. This result and/or conclusion appears, with varying degrees of qualification, in all the works cited in note 1 *supra,* except in Silberman & Durden, who do not explicitly introduce an ideology variable.

literature to which this brief summary does not do justice. I discuss some of these below. Nevertheless, a reader of this literature can hardly fail to note either the central importance of noneconomic variables or the "fishing-expedition" character of the empirical methodology I have just sketched. Pending some analytical advance that leads ineluctably to a different research strategy, further fishing for relevant economic variables will be hard to avoid. In this respect, this article claims no revolutionary advance over past methods. But it does claim to show that when "constituent interest" is given a more appropriate empirical characterization than it has had up to now, it plays a far larger, even dominant, role in congressional voting, and party and ideology correspondingly smaller roles, than heretofore believed.

While I retain the ideology-interest dichotomy, I also want to clarify some problems with the interpretation that legislators are shirking representation of their constituents' interests when ideology variables appear to explain legislative voting behavior. Shirking has been rationalized on grounds that individual voters have weak incentives to monitor legislative performance.[3] But this same "rational ignorance" could lead voters to use cheap summary indicators of interest, such as a candidate's party or reputation for liberalism, in selecting among them. A faithful agent will then sometimes vote against the immediate interest of his constituents to preserve the information value of his liberal voting record. In this case ideology is determined by interest. This general possibility has been recognized, but explicit attempts to allow for the possibility have not succeeded in substantially reducing the role of ideology as a residual category in explaining voting.[4] However, the larger issue—whether the ideological component in legislative voting signifies shirking or catering to voter demands—cannot be so easily settled. Voters may choose to fasten on issues unrelated to interest, such as the candidate's moral beliefs, and interest variables may reflect these sorts of constituent demands less well than "noneconomic" variables.[5] Conversely, variables ostensibly related to vot-

3. See, for example, Gordon Tullock, Toward a Mathematics of Politics (Ann Arbor: Univ. of Michigan Press, 1967).
4. See the works by Kalt, Kalt & Zupan, and Kau & Rubin cited in note 1 *supra* for attempts to explain ideology by interest variables.
5 There is, of course, no clear boundary between economic or interest and noneconomic variables. For example, voters' religious affiliations may affect their demand for legislation because of the moral (ideological) imperatives of the religion or because some poorly measured economic interest happens to be correlated with religious affiliation. Economists face this sort of ambiguity all the time when implementing theory empirically—nonpecuniary variables which "work" empirically can be interpreted as proxies for variables suggested by the economic model or as "taste" variables about which economists have nothing much

ers' material interest (income) may also be related to more general "consumer" preferences for legislation (liberalism could be a normal consumer good even if it is costly to wealthy voters).

My main goal here is to see how far an appropriate characterization of the principals' (constituents') demand gets us in explaining their agents' (legislators') behavior without invoking a residual category, such as ideology, which is unfamiliar to economists. I address only indirectly the question of whether the constituent demands are mainly for "producer" goods—votes that raise constituent wealth—or for some more general consumer good. I show that, generally, the larger and more well defined the wealth stakes in a vote, the more important are constituent characteristics in explaining their agents' behavior. That result at least suggests that the producer-goods aspects of votes is important. However, for now the reader may interpret my use of the term "economic interests" as shorthand for "characteristics related to constituents' demand for votes."

In the next section, I elaborate on the inadequacies of existing empirical characterizations of constituent demands and on the consequences for empirical analyses of voting.

II. THE ECONOMICS AND STATISTICS
OF CONGRESSIONAL VOTING MODELS

The usual procedure in modeling legislators as agents has been to treat all the residents of a legislator's district as his principals. That is, the vector M in (2) usually consists of a set of *average* resident characteristics, that is, per capita income, education, and so on. As a literal characterization of the relevant principal-agent relation, this is absurd. It implies that voters should choose among candidates randomly, or better yet not vote, since any candidate should represent the district in the same way. However, as we shall see, voters do not vote randomly. Competing candidates attract voters with systematically different incomes, education, and so on. A sensible principal-agent model would allow the agent to be sensitive to these differences in the characteristics of those who voted for him and those who did not. Accordingly, I attempt to take account empirically of differ-

---

useful to say. In a field such as the demand for legislation where the basic theory is undeveloped, considerable agnosticism about just what a particular population characteristic is really measuring seems required. Accordingly, in this paper I focus mainly on whether we can identify a set of constituent characteristics as the *dominant* source of demand for legislation. The only bound I impose is that the set contain variables already familiar to economists as important determinants of the demand for nonpolitical goods—for example, I will use income and educational attainment, but not religion.

ences in economic characteristics among a legislator's supporters and opponents.[6]

I also seek to redress past neglect of the sources of campaign funds.
Since campaign funds seem to play an important role in mobilizing votes,[7]
a legislator's decisions ought to be expected to give some weight to the
interests of contributors.

I eventually allow the data to tell how legislators weight the diverse
interests of supporters, opponents, and contributors. However, I begin
with a simple model of legislator choice in order to guide the empirical
analysis. It follows the outlines of the progenitor of currently fashionable
"median voter" models of political choice, attributable to Hotelling.[8] He
concluded that political platforms would converge to the middle of the
distribution of voter preferences. The platform would not be identical, but
each party (or seller) would serve exclusively a "hinterland" to the left or
right of the middle by offering platforms that compete for the middle and
are distinctly preferred by those in their respective hinterlands. For example, if preferences are related to income, party A might offer to benefit
the median-income voter and those richer at the expense of the poor, while
B offers to vote for redistribution from the super-median rich to the poor.

My model introduces probabilistic elements, but mainly as a convenience. I take the legislator's proximate objective to be maximization of
his expected share of the popular vote or, equivalently, his probability of
reelection. I ignore changes in the size or composition of the electorate,
so the legislator seeks votes from former supporters and opponents, and
his expected vote share in the next election (M) is

(3) $M = T(1 - m) + Rm,$

where m is his share in the last election; and R and T are fractions of those
who voted for or against him, respectively, last time and who he expects
to support him next time he runs.

For concreteness suppose income is the only relevant characteristic,
and that those who voted for the legislator have higher average incomes

6. It might be a defensible shortcut to ignore these intradistrict differences if they were
small compared with interdistrict differences, so that few voters in a high-income district
typically had below-average incomes. However, intradistrict heterogeneity is not always so
trivial. For example, the coefficient of variation of income and education within a typical
state is many times the comparable figure for state averages. So it is conceivable that a senator
from Mississippi has wealthier supporters than a senator from New York.

7. See, for example, Phillip Nelson, Political Information, 19 J. Law & Econ. 315 (1976);
and Gary Jacobson, Money in Congressional Elections (New Haven: Yale Univ. Press,
1980).

8. Harold Hotelling, Stability in Competition, 39 Econ. J. 41 (1929).

(Y_F) than those who voted against him (Y_A). Following his election, the legislator votes on a number of bills, each of which, I assume, either helps or hurts voters according to their incomes. By choosing the number of such bills to support, the legislator affects both T and R—directly because of the differing incomes of voters, and indirectly because of the effects of his votes on potential campaign contributors who have their own interests in these bills. This can be expressed:

(4) $\quad T = T[v, X(v)]$

(5) $\quad R = R[v, X(v)]$,

where v = number of votes cast for the interests of the wealthy; and X = expected campaign funds. The first-order condition for the problem, choose v to maximize M, is

(6) $\quad M_v = 0 = (1 - m)(T_v + T_x \cdot X_v) + (R_v + R_x \cdot X_v) \cdot m$.

In general, T_v and R_v will be related to Y_A and Y_F, respectively:

(7) $\quad T_v = t(Y_A)$

(8) $\quad R_v = r(Y_F)$,

with both t_{Y_A}, $r_{Y_F} > 0$. That is, the richer a voter group, the more members who benefit from a pro-rich vote and hence the more who are likely to reward our legislator in the next election. To make the problem interesting, assume that Y_F is high enough so that $R_v > 0$. Both T_X and R_X can be safely assumed positive. While in principle X_v can have any sign—that is, contributors can seek either to restrain the legislator's natural proclivity for the rich or to reinforce it—I show later that $X_v > 0$ is more likely. If $X_v > 0$, then a non-corner solution requires $T_v < 0$, and this requires $Y_A \ll Y_F$, so that past opponents are sufficiently poor to be hurt by pro-rich votes.

With this background I derive implications of changes in Y_F and in Y_A. Note first that

(9) $\quad \text{sgn } v_{y_F} = \text{sgn } m\, r_{y_F} > 0$

and

(10) $\quad \text{sgn } v_{y_A} = \text{sgn}(1 - m)t_{y_A} > 0$.

So if either the rich or the poor get richer, the legislator increases v, because his supporters will now be more pleased and fewer of his opponents displeased by such votes. Now hold average income constant and allow the spread between the two groups to widen, which means that Y_F increases and Y_A decreases. The direction of the effect of this event on v depends on the difference between two positive terms, r_{y_F} and t_{y_A}, so it is theoretically ambiguous.

Unfortunately, intuition cannot resolve the ambiguity at this level of generality. A legislator who is more sensitive to the interests of opponents than to supporters, which is one way to interpret $r_{y_F} < t_{y_A}$, risks making future campaign promises less credible, losing campaign funds, and perhaps incurring opposition in the next primary. But Hotelling's story can be recalled and modified for use here: because the winner got more than half the vote, the marginal voter (the one who was indifferent between the candidates) does not have the median income. The marginal voter's income is closer to Y_A than Y_F—that is, he is *poorer* than the median where the supporters are, on average, *wealthier*. To hold this marginal voter, the legislator may have to vote for his wealthy hinterland less often the higher its income relative to that at the competitive margin.[9] Thus, although the direction of the effect of differences in characteristics of supporters and opponents has to be left to the data, the model does suggest that the vector, **M**, in (2) should be expanded to include those differences.

The preceding discussion raises implicitly the possibility that ideology measures, such as R in (2), help "explain" voting behavior because they are correlated with relevant economic variables that have been left out of **M**, such as the difference between supporter and opponent characteristics. But any empirical counterpart to **M** will be imperfectly correlated with X, the "true" determinants of interest. Some relevant variables will be measured with error. For example, income per capita might be a proxy for income per voter strongly affected by this bill. Others will be left out en-

---

9. To illustrate this point, suppose that the winner got 55 percent of the vote with his pro-rich platform, and that the forty-fifth percentile on the income distribution is $10,000. These facts imply platforms that said, in effect:
  1. winner: "If your income exceeds $10,000, I will vote for a package of bills benefiting you"; and
  2. loser: "If your income is below $10,000, I will vote for a package of bills benefiting you."
To sidestep important problems related to dynamic adjustment of these platforms and to account for the fact that incumbents are usually reelected, assume that these are "equilibrium" platforms—they will not change unless the income distribution changes. Then assume a mean-preserving increase in the dispersion of incomes, such that something over 45 percent of votes now have incomes under $10,000. With no change in platforms, the incumbent's majority will decline or disappear. Accordingly, he has a first-order incentive to replace $10,000 in his platform with a lower number, which requires that he cast fewer pro-rich votes than in the past.

tirely. In a general study of this kind, which looks at many issues, it is unlikely that a few variables can adequately capture the nuances of economic interest in a large set of votes on diverse issues, and it would be futile and uninformative to try to do so by enlarging the set of interest variables substantially. Just what *is* gained by enlarging that set at all, as I propose to do?

The answer is that if the independent effect of ideology on voting is small (large), any substantial improvement in the correlation of **M** and X is likely to entail a large (small) reduction of the explanatory power of R. So we can infer the likely importance of ideology from the degree to which its explanatory power changes when **M** is made more accurate.[10]

To summarize the discussion so far I outline the empirical strategy pursued in the rest of the paper.

First, I treat **M** in (2) as a vector of characteristics that can be subdivided:

$\mathbf{M}_1$ = average characteristic of the population of a legislator's district, for example, per capita income in the district;

$\mathbf{M}_2$ = *difference* between the characteristics of those who voted for the legislator and the district average, for example, average income of supporters minus average income in the district; and

---

10. To see this, go back to (1) and (2) and recall that there is an interest component in any ideology measure, so R, as well as **M**, is correlated with X. To simplify and fix ideas, treat **M** and X as single indexes, let a yes vote be pro-liberal, and let it be positively correlated with X, so $D > 0$ in (1). Since R is usually just a summary of voting on many issues, the correlation of R and X is positive also. Then the estimated coefficient of ideology (c in (2)) and the true coefficient (C in (1)) are related:

(a)
$$c = C + \frac{D}{A} \cdot \phi .$$

where A is the (positive) regression coefficient of X on R (the economic component of the ADA rating).

(b)
$$\phi = \frac{r_*^2 - r^2}{1 - r^2} ,$$

r = correlation of R with **M**, and r_* = correlation of R with X. Now, since **M** is error-laden, $r_* > r$ and $0 < \phi < 1$, and c will be a biased estimate of C. In particular, if C is really zero, then $c > 0$. That is, we would incorrectly infer an effect of ideology when there is none, and the direction of that effect is the same as that of the economic variables. In this case, R is just another estimator of X whose error contains no independent information (like ideology) but "helps" in the regression because it is imperfectly correlated with the error in **M**. In this sense, the econometric deck is stacked in favor of incorrectly revising a prior form of "ideology has no effect." But note that $d\phi/dr < 0$, so as we reduce the measurement error in **M** and so increase r, c will get smaller and, in this case, approach zero.

$\mathbf{M}_3$ = characteristics of the legislator's campaign contributors, for example, the share of contributions coming from unions.

Then, instead of estimating just

$$(2') \quad y = d_1\mathbf{M}_1 + c_1R ,$$

as has usually been done heretofore, I estimate

$$(2'') \quad y = d_1\mathbf{M}_1 + d_2\mathbf{M}_2 + d_3\mathbf{M}_3 + c_2R .$$

I do this primarily to determine whether adding $\mathbf{M}_2$, $\mathbf{M}_3$ reduces the heavy weight so far accorded R in the literature—that is, is $c_2 << c_1$? The answer is yes.

Because c_2 sometimes remains significantly different from zero I also try to determine whether R is plausibly a proxy for left-out or badly measured economic variables. I do this first by treating R as a variable dependent on $\mathbf{M}$. If R is a proxy for interest, considerable explanatory power should be gained by adding $\mathbf{M}_2$ and $\mathbf{M}_3$ to $\mathbf{M}_1$.

In addition, I investigate whether any independent effect of R differs among types of votes. If R is mainly a proxy for interest, its independent effect should be larger where the economic interests are hard to discern (for example, votes on allowing school prayer) than where the wealth stakes are clear (such as tax bills). In general, both strategies yield positive results.

The following section describes how the variables meant to fill out $\mathbf{M}_2$ and $\mathbf{M}_3$ were constructed, and the remaining sections employ those variables in analyses of both ideology and voting.

III. The Characteristics of a Legislator's Constituency

The secret ballot precludes direct measurement of characteristics of those who voted for and against a legislator, so I use statistics to generate proxies. For U.S. senators it is possible to run a regression of the following form with country or city data:

$$(11) \quad S = \mathbf{a} \cdot \mathbf{M},$$

where S is the senator's share of the vote in a county of his state; $\mathbf{M}$ is a vector of economic characteristics of county residents; and $\mathbf{a}$ is a vector of coefficients. Then, if the coefficient of, say, per capita income is negative, we can infer that the senator's supporters are poorer than the average of his district.

I focus exclusively on senators in this paper only because I can implement (11) for them. For (almost) each senator sitting in the 96th (1979–80) Congress, I regressed a vector of county election returns from the election he won—in log-odds form, that is, $\ln[S/(1 - S)]$—on a short list of county economic characteristics that might at least begin to separate the population into groups with different interests on many issues. The variables I used were

1. (log of) median family income;
2. median education;
3. the percentage of population over 65,
4. black, and
5. residing in urban areas; and
6. the share of the labor force employed in manufacturing.

With a few exceptions, the regressions produce coefficients unique to each senator.[11]

The regression results are summarized in table 1.1. In spite of substantial collinearity among the characteristics, all of them are significant in half or more of the regressions. These variables seem to provide a plausible basis for distinguishing the interests of a senator's supporters and opponents. The general, though far from universal, tendency is for the wealthy, educated, and old to vote Republican, and the urban and black to vote Democrat.

To characterize differences between a senator's supporters and the average voter, I first assigned a dummy variable to each characteristic ac-

---

11. Some senators were unopposed, so their supporters cannot be distinguished from the rest of the population. In some small states there are too few counties for the regression to be reliable. These were treated as follows: (1) In the New England states, both city and county election returns are available and, at the cost of some double counting (where city and county characteristics cannot be separated), I added cities to the sample. (2) In two cases, I combined contiguous states (Delaware with Maryland, Arizona with Nevada) and ran the regression with a state dummy. (3) In two cases (Hawaii, Alaska) I simply assumed all the coefficients were zero. I also made some adjustment for the sometimes peculiar behavior of the black variable. Especially in the North, the black population tends to be concentrated in a few counties, so the variable is really something of a dummy. More generally, it tends to be highly collinear with the urbanization and manufacturing variables. To get around the resulting problems, (1) the variable is deleted if the black population is less than 1 percent of the state, on grounds that the senator from such a state can safely ignore their special interests, and (2) for other states, I ran the regression without the black variable, and if another coefficient then achieved significance, I used that coefficient rather than the one from the longer regression. This amounts to hedging one's bets on the possibility that the black coefficient may be measuring the effect of the other variable. Finally, since the variance of the error term in this regression is theoretically decreasing in the number of voters in a county, I estimated each regression in weighted form, with $(voters)^{-1/2}$ as the weight.

TABLE 1.1 Frequency of Significant Coefficients by Region in Regressions of Republican Vote Share on Population Characteristics: Senators in 96th Congress

	Number of Regressions	Characteristic (%)											
		Income		Education		Age		Urban		Race		Manufacturing	
Region		(+)	(−)	(+)	(−)	(+)	(−)	(+)	(−)	(+)	(−)	(+)	(−)
Northeast	18	67	11	56	17	22	17	0	83	11	28	17	17
North Central	24	58	13	50	25	46	4	4	71	0	62	13	71
West	22	36	32	41	0	50	32	18	45	5	55	27	23
South	25	48	16	44	0	44	16	12	44	4	60	32	36
Total	89	52	18	47	10	42	17	9	60	4	53	22	38

Note: For eighty-nine of the one hundred senators in the 96th Congress, a weighted regression was run of the form log $(GOP_i/1 - GOP_i) = f(\text{characteristics}_i)$, i = county, GOP = share of vote obtained by Republican candidate in the election won by the senator. The characteristics, from the 1970 census, are

Income = log median family income, 1969;

Education = mean years of schooling of those over twenty-five;

Age = percentage of population over sixty-five;

Urban = percentage of population residing in urban areas;

Race = percentage of population black; and

Manufacturing = percentage of workers in manufacturing.

The weight was (total votes)$_i^{-1/2}$. Coefficients from regressions are summarized as follows: If t(coefficient) ≥ 1.5 the coefficient is deemed significantly positive (+), $t \leq -1.5$ means negative (−) and all others are deemed zero. (See text for departures from this scheme.) The entries in the table are the percentages of all regressions with plus or minus coefficients in a region. The percentage of zeros is not shown. County election returns are from R. Scammon and A. McGillivray. America Votes (various years). Characteristics are from U.S. Census, County and City Data Book, 1977 (1978) (exception, education, which is from U.S. Census, Census of Population, 1970, state volumes.)

cording to its coefficient in (11). The dummies took the value $(+1, -1, 0)$ if the coefficients were significantly positive, negative, or insignificant (with $|t| \geq 1.5$ as the criterion). Then I assumed that the true difference was proportional to a transformation of this dummy.[12]

Information about campaign contributors has become available through the administration of the Federal Election Campaign Act. The data distinguish individual from interest group contributors, and they classify the latter by type. Three types—labor unions, business, and medical (mainly AMA) organizations—account for almost all interest group contributions, with labor the largest of the three. I use the labor union share of total interest group contributions as my sole measure of "contributor interest," because differences between labor and the other two groups seem more important than any differences between those two.[13] I discuss subsequently the strong correlation (.69) of this labor-share variable with Democratic party status.

IV. CONSTITUENT CHARACTERISTICS AND CONGRESSIONAL VOTING BEHAVIOR

Although I want to estimate the effect of constituent characteristics on legislative voting behavior, my first result is that these characteristics are

---

12. The differences can in principle be estimated from the regression coefficients in (11). To illustrate, let b equal coefficient of manufacturing (m). The conditional log odds that a manufacturing worker votes Republican then is the average of log odds $+ b(1 - \bar{m})$. From this we can deduce the percentage of the senator's voters who are manufacturing workers and the difference between this and $\bar{m}$. An approximation to this difference, for a Republican senator, would be

$$b(1 - s)(1 - \bar{m})\bar{m},$$

where s = senator's share of popular vote. Similar calculations can be made for the other discrete characteristics—age, urban, black. For the continuous characteristics—income and education—the approximation would be

$$b(1 - s) \cdot .64V$$

(V = population variance of characteristic) under a normal distribution. Because the technique assumes that the coefficient is valid far beyond the sample means, the estimates were frequently unrealistic—for instance, that virtually all old people supported one candidate. Accordingly, the transformations I used replace the coefficient with the dummy. Thus, the variable equals dummy $\cdot (1 - s) \cdot (1 - \bar{m})\bar{m}$ for manufacturing, and so on. The transformations reflect the fact that the senator's supporters cannot differ from the average if the population is either unanimous $(s \to 1)$ or homogenous $(\bar{m} \to 1)$.

13. The correlation of the AMA share of total interest-group contributions with the business share of labor and business contributions exceeds $+.8$. A few senators reported extremely low contributions—under \$25,000—from interest groups, and one, Proxmire of Wisconsin, reported none from any source: Proxmire is arbitrarily assigned the sample mean of the labor-share variable. The others with low interest group contributions are assigned an average of their computed labor share and the sample mean. The data for 1974 elections are from Common Cause, 1974 Federal Campaign Finances (1976); 1976 and 1978 data are

more important determinants of ideology measures than has previously been shown. That result makes it correspondingly difficult to disentangle the role of ideology and interests in legislative voting, and I do not attempt to conclude that one or the other is "really" driving voting behavior. Instead I have in mind a more specific methodological goal, which can be understood with a hypothetical example: Suppose an economist initially seeks to explain auto purchases with two variables—price and party registration—and he finds that party is clearly the more important of the two variables. An economist, unlike a sociologist or political scientist, would probably suspect that party is simply a proxy for income. Now, suppose an ordinary price-cum-income demand relationship explains the data about as well as price-cum-party, but that party provides some small marginal explanatory power. This result would sooner lead the economist to elaborate the role of income (or price) than to undertake serious analysis of the role of party preference in durable goods purchases. Had the ordinary demand function failed utterly to reduce the plausible role of political preference, some pessimism about the future of economic versus sociological analysis of car buying would be warranted. My purpose here is to see how much the role of categories like "political ideology," which are unfamiliar to economists, can be reduced by simple and fairly crude manipulation of economic categories. Thereby we will see if a similar pessimism about prospects for economic research in voting behavior is warranted.

A. A Preliminary Analysis of Ideology Measures

Because the ideology variable in voting studies is often a summary of votes on several bills (for example, the ADA index is the percentage of "correct" votes in a sample of about twenty bills), an analysis of the role of constituent characteristics in explaining ideology measures can both illustrate my empirical procedure and preview subsequent results. Therefore, I first seek to explain a senator's ADA rating with variables categorized as follows:

A. *Average* characteristics of the state population. These are statewide averages of the variables used in the analysis of popular elections (family income, education, age, urbanization, race, and the manufacturing employment share) plus the fraction of the work force unionized. (Unions are a potentially important organized interest, but lack of data precluded analysis of the role of union membership in the popular vote.)

B. Deviations of *supporter* characteristics from the average. Each aver-

from U.S. Federal Election Commission Reports on Financial Activity, 1977–78 Interim Report No. 5: U.S. Senate and House Campaigns, and FEC Disclosure Series No. 6: 1976 Senatorial Campaign Receipts and Expenditures (1977).

age characteristic, except unionization, has a supporter counterpart constructed as described in the last section. (Since manufacturing employees are the most unionized, the supporter-manufacturing variable can also be viewed as a proxy for supporter unionization.)

    C. A simple contributor interest variable—the *labor share* of total interest group contributions.

    D. Senator's party.

Most past voting studies have not used the category B and C data, and a glance at the first two columns of table 1.2 shows why it has been difficult to explain voting patterns solely with economic variables. The average characteristics alone (column 1) explain a limited, but not trivial, proportion of the variation in ADA ratings. However, knowing a senator's party (column 2) substantially increases one's information about a senator's voting pattern, so the easy conclusion seems to be that senators frequently ignore the makeup of their constituency to vote with their party colleagues. A different picture begins to emerge in column 3, where party is deleted in favor of supporter characteristics. This regression closes most of the gap in explanatory power between the first two regressions, and, with the addition of contributor characteristics (column 4), the explanatory power of the party model of column 2 is exceeded. Finally, when party affiliation is added to the whole list of interest variables (column 5), little more is gained than by ignoring it.

    These results should not be interpreted to say that interest rather than political kinship really determines voting patterns. There is much collinearity between party affiliation and the characteristics of supporters and contributors, perhaps too much for such a conclusion to be confidently drawn. The results do imply that economists unfamiliar with the workings of party loyalties can proceed *as if* such things did not matter and focus instead on who the constituents are and where the campaign funds come from.

    There is surely sufficient mystery in the results to occupy the analyst of economic interests. For example, table 1.1 shows that the wealthy and old tend to vote "conservative" (Republican), but table 1.2 implies that senators with wealthy and old constituents tend to vote liberal. Note also that most Group B coefficients have signs opposite to their Group A counterparts. This implies that the characteristics of *opposing* voters are given greater weight than those of supporters, a result which lends credibility to the Hotelling model's emphasis on the importance of the marginal voter.[14]

---

    14. To see this, write the regression model in table 1.2

(a) $$y = A\overline{X} + B\lambda(X_s - \overline{X}) + \ldots.$$

Further evidence that ideology is mainly a proxy for interest is found in table 1.3, which replicates table 1.2 on another liberalism index—that of the AFL-CIO's Committee on Political Education (COPE). Both ADA and COPE rate congressmen on a variety of issues—social, foreign, domestic economic, and so forth. The two ratings are highly correlated (.9), but COPE understandably gives greater weight to economic issues, especially those affecting labor union interests. The pattern of results in table 1.3 is, unsurprisingly, similar to table 1.2—an initially large role for party is eliminated and overshadowed by finer specification of interests. However, there are suggestive, if small, differences: (1) The interest variables tend to explain more of the COPE than of the ADA variable; (2) the weight given to union membership and union campaign funds also tends to be larger for COPE (the column labeled *TDIFF* shows *t*-ratios for a regression of the difference between the COPE and ADA ratings, and they are suggestively positive for both the union membership and contribution variables). These results go in just the direction expected if ideology is a summary measure of interest.

The data in tables 1.2 and 1.3 can also help tell us whether contributors act to offset or to reinforce the demands of the constituency. To get at this, I first calculated, from the regression in column (4), the estimated value of each senator's ADA or COPE index with the labor share variable set equal to zero. This "partial" ADA or COPE variable in effect tells how each senator would vote if he received no union contributions but nevertheless succeeded in attracting the same set of voters to the polls. The correlations between these partial variables and the labor contributions variable are $+.50$(ADA) and $+.56$(COPE). Since unions are "pro-liberal," these

---

where

X_s = value of characteristic for a senator's supporters;

$\overline{X} = wX_s + (1 - w)X_0$ = average characteristic in the state (group A variable);

w = senator's vote share;

X_0 = opposing voter's characteristic;

$\lambda(X_s - \overline{X})$ = group B variable (λ = positive constant);

A, B = regression coefficients of the group A and B variables, respectively.

This can be written

(b) $y = [wA + B\lambda(1 - w)]X_s + [(1 - w)(A - B\lambda)]X_0 + ...$

To fix ideas, let both bracketed expressions be positive, but let the first be smaller, so supporters receive less weight than opponents. In this case, A and B must be of opposite sign. Note further that the marginal voter's characteristic (X_m) is correlated positively with X_0 and negatively with X_s: if a senator draws most of his votes from the wealthy, $X_s > \overline{X}$, then $X_0 < \overline{X}$ and the voter indifferent between the senator and his losing opponent has $X_m < \overline{X}$. So the opposite signs of A and B can be interpreted to mean that X_m receives greater weight than X_s.

TABLE 1.2 Regressions of Senators' ADA Ratings on Constituency Characteristics

	B	t	B	t	B	t	B	t	B	t
	(1)		(2)		(3)		(4)		(5)	
A. Average characteristics:										
1. Log median family income	.69	3.1	.46	2.7	.64	3.3	.44	2.9	.42	2.8
2. Mean education	−.27	1.5	−.00	.0	−.40	2.6	−.32	2.6	−.23	1.7
3. Age	.37	3.1	.22	2.4	.34	3.4	.25	3.3	.24	3.0
4. Urbanization	−.25	2.1	−.21	2.3	−.19	1.9	−.06	.8	−.09	1.1
5. Race	.01	.1	−.04	.4	−.14	1.3	−.12	1.4	−.10	1.1
6. Manufacturing	−.02	.2	.08	.9	−.04	.4	−.03	.4	−.00	.1
7. Unionization	.28	2.3	.23	2.5	.30	2.9	.13	1.6	.14	1.7
B. Supporter average characteristics:										
1. Income					−.11	1.2	−.10	1.4	−.06	.9
2. Education					.04	.5	.12	1.9	.15	2.3
3. Age					.06	.7	.11	1.7	.10	1.6
4. Urbanization					.44	4.9	.27	3.7	.23	3.0
5. Race					.04	.4	−.01	.2	−.03	.4
6. Manufacturing					.06	.8	.01	.2	−.00	.0
C. Labor share of campaign contributions							.55	7.6	.46	5.0
D. Senator's party (1 = Republican)			−.57	8.6					−.18	1.6
R^2	.36		.65		.59		.76		.76	
SE	.83		.62		.69		.53		.53	

Note: See table 1.1 note for characteristics. All variables are standardized deviates (that is, deviations from mean, divided by standard deviation), so coefficients show the number of standard deviations by which dependent variable changes when independent variable increases one standard deviation. Dependent variable is average of senator's 1979 and 1980 percentage of pro-ADA to total votes on bills used by ADA to compile its rating. (The ADA counts absence or abstention as opposition, but I do not.) Independent variables are as described in text. Sample size = 100; B = coefficient; t = absolute t-ratio; R^2 = coefficient of determination; SE = standard error.

(highly significant) positive correlations imply that union contributions reinforce the already pro-liberal tendencies of the senators they support rather than offset a pro-conservative bias.

This last result helps rationalize the rather small marginal effects of party in the regressions: party labels, like brand names generally, can be cheap sources of information about which candidates are likely to best

TABLE 1.3 COPE Ratings and Constituency Characteristics

	(1) B	(1) t	(2) B	(2) t	(3) B	(3) t	(4) B	(4) t	TDIFF	(5) B	(5) t
A. Average characteristics:											
1. Log median family income	.57	2.6	.30	2.2	.48	2.6	.25	2.1	−1.6	−.14	1.9
2. Mean education	−.26	1.5	.04	.3	−.37	2.5	−.27	2.8	.5	−.14	1.3
3. Age	.32	2.8	.15	2.1	.27	2.8	.16	2.6	−1.4	.14	2.3
4. Urbanization	−.24	2.0	−.19	2.5	−.17	1.8	−.03	.4	.6	−.07	1.0
5. Race	.04	.3	−.02	.2	−.11	1.0	−.09	1.3	.5	−.06	.8
6. Manufacturing	−.04	.3	.08	1.0	−.05	.5	−.04	.6	−.1	.00	.1
7. Unionization	.43	3.6	.36	4.8	.43	4.3	.24	3.5	1.6	.26	4.0
B. Supporter average characteristics:											
1. Income					−.11	1.3	−.10	1.7	−.0	.05	.8
2. Education					.07	.8	.02	.5	−1.9	.07	1.3
3. Age					−.02	.2	.04	.8	−1.3	.03	.6
4. Urbanization					.36	4.2	.17	2.8	−1.8	.11	1.8
5. Race					.04	.5	−.02	.3	−.0	−.04	.7
6. Manufacturing					.08	1.1	.02	.4	.1	−.00	.0
C. Labor share of campaign contributions							.64	10.8	1.5	.50	7.1
D. Senators' party (1 = Republican)			−.65	11.9						−.26	3.2
R^2	.39		.76		.62		.84		.86	.41	
SE	.81		.51		.66		.43				

Note: All variables are standard deviates (see note to table 1.2). Dependent variable is average COPE rating for 1979–80. See text and note to table 1.2 for other variables. *TDIFF* is *t*-ratio of coefficient in a regression of the difference between the standardized COPE and ADA ratings on the independent variables.

serve the interests of voters or contributors. Accordingly, (1) the simple correlation between party and contributor or constituent interest variables will be high, and (2) the simple correlation of party and legislative voting patterns will be high as well. My results indicate that party membership need not be regarded as a fundamental source of these patterns. Instead, this source is a mutually reinforcing coalition of contributors and voters who happen to rally frequently to the same party banner.

B. Votes on Senate Bills, 1979–80

In each session of the 96th Congress, the Senate took some four or five hundred record votes. Here I analyze a nonrandom sample of such votes in much the same way I treated the ADA and COPE indexes: that is, I ask how far the electorate and contributor characteristics take us in explaining Senate voting and how much further party-cum-ideology takes us. To get at this, five regressions are run for each vote. The dependent variable is dichotomous (+1 = a vote *for* the position taken by a majority of Northern Democrats, 0 = vote against this position), and the independent variables are those in equations (1), (3), (4), and (5) in table 1.2 plus a regression including the ADA index. Thus, the information in the regressions increases progressively, and marginal goodness-of-fit measures tell us how much explanatory power is gained from:

1. just the *average* characteristics of a state (group A in table 1.2);
2. A plus *supporter* characteristics (B);
3. A plus B plus *contributor* characteristics (C);
4. A plus B plus C plus *party* of the senator (D);
5. A plus B plus C plus D plus senator's ADA *index*.

My motive is to see whether much is gained by going beyond (3), which is my complete set of interest variables.

My sample comprises about one-third (331) of all record votes in 1979 and 1980. It excludes certain votes entirely,[15] and includes only the decisive vote on a distinguishing issue. Important bills frequently run a gauntlet of votes on amendments. The amendments may be only tangentially related to the purported purpose of the bill, and often they engender close votes even if the final bill passes almost unanimously. For example, on March 13, 1979, the Senate voted ninety to six to maintain U.S. relations with

---

15. These are votes on (1) parliamentary procedures—votes on request for attendance of absent senators, germaneness of amendments, rules for debate, and so on; (2) confirmations of presidential nominees; (3) resolutions to ratify treaties (wherein the senate votes on several treaties with foreign governments at the same time); and (4) any vote with fewer than twenty-five votes on the losing side—where there is little variance to be "explained."

Taiwan unofficially (following U.S. recognition of the mainland Chinese government). In the previous week seven amendments to the bill were voted on, all dealing with the *degree* of support for Taiwan. I included only two of these votes: one to declare that hostile action against Taiwan would threaten U.S. security interests (it lost), and another to require Senate confirmation of the unofficial ambassador to Taiwan. Although the two issues are arguably not distinguishable, I generally included such doubtful cases.

I then put each vote into one of eight categories. These are so highly subjective that I can only set out my definitions, give some examples, and offer to interested readers a list of votes by category. The categories are evenly divided between issues where the economic stakes seem well defined and those where they are not. The economic issues are

1. budget, general interest (BGI);
2. budget, special interest (BSI);
3. regulation, general interest (RGI);
4. regulation, special interest (RSI).

Budget bills involve expenditures or taxes, while regulation bills involve constraints on expenditures, on powers of regulatory agencies or the executive, and on private sector resource allocation. (See 5 and 7 below for exceptions.) The GI-SI distinction turns on the magnitude or extent of the program. If many individuals in most states are affected, the bill is put into GI. Examples: BGI—to provide revenue sharing funds for states; BSI—to provide funds for research on rural development; RGI—to establish a gasoline rationing plan; RSI—to limit export of animal hides.

The noneconomic issues are

5. domestic social policy (DSP). These are regulatory bills on moral or ethical issues—abortion, school prayer, and busing were the most popular examples in this Congress;[16]
6. defense and foreign policy, budget (DFB);
7. defense and foreign policy, resolutions (DFR).

Bills involving spending for defense and foreign relations (for example, foreign aid funds and funds for aircraft) are in DFB, while more general congressional foreign and defense policy directives (for example, the Taiwan relations bills described above) are in DFR. Last is

---

16. They are often amendments to *B* or *R* bills, so I had to decide (guess) the primary intent of the bill. I put a bill to suspend busing during a national energy emergency into *DSP* rather than *RGI*. These issues recurred, and I treated each recurrence as a new issue. So, for instance, a bill to prohibit use of Justice Department funds to enforce school busing is also in the *DSP* sample.

8. government organization (GO). These regulate the activities of Congress or the federal bureaucracy. (Regulation of nonfederal government entities is in RGI or RSI.) Examples: income limits for senators, creation of a department for education.

Sometimes, I use a subset of the above labeled "major redistribution" votes, which appear to involve unusually large transfers of wealth. They are culled from key votes (or amendments thereto), as defined by *Congressional Roll Call*,[17] which involve changes in taxes, expenditures, or the allocation of private sector wealth of no less than $10 billion within a decade. The largest number of such votes was related to the "windfall profits tax" on crude oil, which was passed in this Congress.[18] The potential problems with my classification are obvious: for example, constituents have an economic stake in the structure of the bureaucracy and our friendship with foreign governments. I leave the usefulness of the classification to the subsequent data and to a comparison with some not-yet-existent alternative.

Tables 1.4 and 1.5 summarize goodness-of-fit statistics from logit regressions run on the 331 votes. Table 1.4 focuses on the logit analogue (2 × log likelihood, or 2LL) to the mean squared error in ordinary regressions. For each vote, I first compute 2LL for a naive "intercept-only" model: each senator's log odds of a yes vote equals the mean log odds on the vote. Then I add sets of variables (average characteristics, supporter characteristics, and so on) and compute the successive improvements in 2LL. Thus, reading across row 1 tells us that when average characteristics are added to the intercept-only model, the average improvement in 2LL for the 183 votes for 1979 is 21.8; that an *additional* average improvement of 18.2 is obtained by adding supporter characteristics to the intercept plus average characteristics model of column 1, and so on. To put these data in context, the average 2LL for the naive model is about −120 for these samples, and the statistic has an upper limit of zero (perfect fit). By adding all variables, improvement over the naive model averages 57.6 for all 1979 votes (add columns 4 and 7); that is, we are about half way toward

17. These are the votes (usually about twenty) which the publication deems most important for a particular year. The wealth changes are measured from the main bill in the case of amendments (for example, an amendment to a budget ceiling), or from the status quo for the main bill (for example, a key vote on a new tax).

18. There were several amendments to the tax formula, any of which would involve large dollar amounts. Several other amendments involved more general tax issues—for example, a bill to limit the ratio of federal expenditures to GNP. Other votes that passed the two criteria concerned: increases in defense spending, reductions in income taxes, funding of synfuels projects, and regulation of trucking (shifting the burden of proof in an entry case to the complainant).

zero, or in more familiar terms, $R^2 \approx .5$. The change in 2LL has a χ^2 distribution with degrees of freedom equal to the number of variables added: all of the average changes in rows 1 and 2 are significant at better than 5 percent, except for column 5 (party).

Table 1.5 summarizes a cruder goodness-of-fit measure. The logit regressions are used to predict a senator's vote: if the regression predicts probability of a yes vote $> .5$ for a senator, I predict a yes vote; otherwise I predict a no vote. The naive model here is "all senators vote with the majority," and it always classifies correctly a majority of senators equal to the number of votes on the winning side. The data in rows 1 and 2 show the mean marginal increases over this naive model in correctly classified votes. Since the average number of votes on the losing side is about thirty-six, the data in row 1 imply that on average the full set of variables eliminates a bit over half (22.0 in 1979—again, add columns 4 and 7) the mistakes made by the naive model.

There are two main messages in the summary data on lines 1 and 2 of the tables: (1) the vast bulk (80–90 percent) of the information contained in the full set of variables is obtainable from the interest variables (average, supporter, and contributor characteristics) alone (compare columns 4 and 7), and (2) these patterns are consistent, indeed almost identical, over the two years studied. So any expectation that, for example, party would play a larger role in the election year (1980) is unfulfilled. Instead what is most striking about the party variable is its negligible role in either year. This is further evidence that parties, as such, are not important vehicles for organizing legislative voting coalitions. While the effect of ideology (ADA rating) is not so negligible, the earlier caveat (note 10 *supra*) about the potential bias in the coefficient of that variable needs to be reemphasized. On the whole, the results seem to encourage a research strategy that treats legislators simply as agents for the parochial interests of their constituency, with party or ideology playing the role of brand names around which like-minded candidates, voters, and contributors come together.

The lower panels of tables 1.4 and 1.5 show how the patterns just described vary by type of vote. Each entry here is a deviation from the all-vote mean on lines 1 and 2. The relevant comparison is between column 4, which summarizes the impact of economic interests, and column 7, which summarizes party/ideology. The main result is on line 13: interest variables tend to do better and party/ideology worse at explaining votes on economic than on noneconomic issues (more so in table 1.4 than 1.5). The contrast is particularly striking for the major redistribution issues summarized on line 14: for no other subcategory are the interest variables nearly

TABLE 1.4 Mean Change in 2 × Log Likelihood From Additional Variables × Senate Votes, 1979–80

| | | | Variables Added to Logit Regression | | | | | |
Vote Class	Average Characteristics (1)	Supporter Characteristics (2)	Labor Share of Contributions (3)	Sum of Interests (1 + 2 + 3) (4)	Party (5)	ADA (6)	Sum of Ideology (5 + 6) (7)	Number of Votes (8)
Mean all votes:								
1. 1979	21.8	18.2	6.3	46.3	3.0	8.3	11.3	183
2. 1980	20.4	16.9	6.0	43.3	3.2	8.0	11.1	149
SD:								
3. 1979	11.2	12.3	5.8	17.8	4.3	7.8	6.7	...
4. 1980	9.9	12.1	5.9	18.6	3.9	7.5	7.5	...
Deviation from all-vote mean by vote class (1979 and 1980):								
5. Budget, general interest	−6.1***	6.0***	2.6***	2.5***	1.3***	−1.2	.2	40
6. Budget, special interest	.8	−2.6***	−1.3***	−3.2***	.4	−1.4**	−.9	84
7. Regulation, general interest	4.0**	2.2	−1.0	5.2*	−.6	−2.2*	−2.9**	23
8. Regulation, special interest	3.8***	1.1***	.6	5.4***	−.9***	−2.6***	−3.4***	75

9. Domestic social policy	−.5	−5.3***	−2.2***	−8.0***	−1.0*	9.5***	8.6***	48
10. Defense/foreign policy, budget	−4.8***	−5.0***	−.6	−10.1***	−1.1*	2.8***	1.8*	32
11. Defense/foreign policy, resolution	1.2	4.1***	1.8	8.5***	.2	6.2***	6.5***	22
12. Government organization	−3.4**	3.0*	.1	−.4	1.6***	−4.4***	−2.9***	.26
13. All economic issues minus all noneconomic issues (sum of 5–8, less sum of 9–12)	2.4***	2.0*	.3	4.8**	.1	−5.4***	−5.3***	
14. Major redistribution votes	3.0*	10.6***	1.9*	15.4***	.4	−4.4***	−4.0***	21

Notes: Lines 1–4 are averages (SDs) over the whole sample of votes in 1979 or 1980 of the *marginal* change in $2 \times$ log likelihood of logistic regressions run on votes. Column 1 shows the mean *improvement* (SD) over the naive model (the log odds for each senator is log odds at sample mean) from adding such "state average" characteristics to a model with an intercept only; column 2 is the mean improvement over 1 from adding six supporter characteristics variables; and so on. (See table 1.2 for these variables). Lines 5–14 show how much above or below the sample mean the average improvement in $2 \times$ log likelihood is for the specific subsample of votes, except that line 13 shows the difference between the means for economic and noneconomic issues. These are found by averaging the data for all budget and regulatory bills (lines 5–8) and deducting the average for all other bills (lines 9–12), respectively.

*Significant at 20 percent (two-tailed test).

**Significant at 10 percent.

***Significant at 5 percent.

TABLE 1.5 Mean Change in Number of Votes Correctly Classified from Additional Variables: Senate Votes, 1979–80

| | Variables Added to Logit Regression | | | | | | | |
Vote Class	Average Characteristics (1)	Supporter Characteristics (2)	Labor Share of Contributions (3)	Sum of Interests (1 + 2 + 3) (4)	Party (5)	ADA (6)	Sum of Ideology (5 + 6) (7)	Number of Votes (8)
Mean of all votes:								
1. 1979	10.7	6.5	1.6	18.8	1.1	2.1	3.2	183
2. 1980	11.1	6.1	1.8	19.0	0.9	2.3	3.2	149
SD:								
3. 1979	6.4	5.3	2.8	7.9	2.3	3.4	3.5	
4. 1980	6.3	5.6	2.7	7.3	2.7	2.9	3.2	
Deviation from all vote mean by vote class:								
5. Budget, general interest	−3.0***	3.5***	.4	.9	−.1	.0	−.1	40
6. Budget, special interest	−.3	−1.0**	−.2	−1.5***	.4**	−.6**	−.1	84
7. Regulation, general interest	2.1***	−.3	.0	1.9	.0	−.7	−.7	23
8. Regulation, special interest	1.4***	−.6	.3	1.0	−.3	−.6**	−1.0***	75

9. Domestic social policy	1.4	−1.8**	−.7*	−1.1	−.3	2.7***	2.4	48
10. Defense/foreign policy, budget	−2.6***	−.1	.1	−2.7***	−.1	.6	.6	32
11. Defense/foreign policy, resolution	1.7*	1.0	.3	3.0***	.4	1.4***	1.8***	22
12. Government organization	.1	1.1	−.6	.7	.1	−1.0**	−1.0*	26
13. All economic issues minus all noneconomic issues (sum of 5–8, less sum of 9–12)						−1.4***	−1.3***	
14. Major redistribution votes	2.3**	4.1***	−.2	6.2***	−.4	−1.4***	−1.8***	21

Notes: See note to table 1.4. The data here pertain to votes classified according to the rule: If the regression yields a predicted probability of a senator's voting "yes" > .5, then predict that the senator voted yes. If not, predict he or she voted "no." The naive model from which the successive marginal improvements in columns 1–7 are calculated is "every senator votes with the majority." This rule always correctly classifies a number of senators' equal number of votes on the winning side of a bill, that is, over half the senators on every bill.

*Significant at 20 percent.
**Significant at 10 percent.
***Significant at 5 percent.

TABLE 1.6 Coefficients and Absolute *t*-Ratios of Average and
Supporter Characteristics: Mean Values for All Votes, 1979–80

	Coefficients			Absolute *t*-Ratio		
Variable	Mean (1)	SD (2)	R (3)	Mean (4)	SD (5)	R (6)
1. Income A	.75	1.04	−.10	1.12	.75	−.07
2. Income S	−.22	.46	. . .	.90	.67	. . .
3. Education A	−.76	1.15	.23	1.45	.85	.19
4. Education S	−.14	.44	. . .	.89	.65	. . .
5. Age A	.53	.64	.10	1.35	.86	.07
6. Age S	.01	.41	. . .	.76	.57	. . .
7. Urban A	−.15	.53	−.11	.88	.67	−.02
8. Urban S	.68	.59	. . .	1.79	.93	. . .
9. Race A	−.23	.66	−.18	.86	.67	.19
10. Race S	.17	.51	. . .	.84	.61	. . .
11. Union A	.61	.72	.06	1.41	.84	.00
12. Manufacturing A	−.18	.60	−.07	1.08	.76	.09
13. Manufacturing S	.09	.46	. . .	.88	. . .	. . .

Note: A = average; S = supporter. Columns 1 and 2 are means (SDs) of the coefficients of the variables across all 1979 and 1980 votes in our sample ($N = 331$) from the logistic regression containing all thirteen variables—that is, contributor characteristic, party, and ADA variables are excluded. Column 3 is the simple correlation, across all votes, of the coefficients of the average and supporter characteristics. Columns 4–6 contain companion data for absolute *t*-ratio. See text and notes to tables 1.1 and 1.2 for description of variables. (The union variable is paired with the supporter-manufacturing variable, because the latter may be a proxy for differential unionization among a senator's supporters.

as powerful. This pattern of results comports well with the "investment" view of the constituents' demand for votes.[19] The strongest result that emerges from the finer categorization on lines 5–12 is the pronounced shift of explanatory power from economic to ideology variables on domestic social policy votes (line 9). This is the only one of the eight vote categories where an interest-only view of senatorial voting seems clearly inadequate.

In table 1.6 I summarize the behavior of the coefficients of the economic variables in the regression that includes only the thirteen average (A) and supporter (S) characteristic variables.[20] Since the dependent vari-

19. But there are also anomalies and puzzles: note, for example (1) the above average weight (line 11) for *both* economic and ideological variables on foreign policy resolutions, where the economic interests seem unclear, and (2) the heavier weight of the economic variables on regulatory issues (lines 7, 8) than on budget issues (lines 5, 6).

20. I excluded the contributor, party, and ADA variables to get at effects of the economic variables "gross" of any impacts they have on the remaining three variables. The independent variables are in standardized form, as in tables 1.2 and 1.3. Unionization and manufacturing are paired in the table, because unionization is especially high for manufacturing employees.

able is one if the senator voted with a majority of northern democrats, zero otherwise, a positive coefficient implies that increases in the associated variable raise the probability of a pro-liberal vote. The signs of the mean values of the coefficients (column 1) follow a pattern similar to that in the ADA and COPE regressions, with the average characteristic and its supporter counterpart tending to have coefficients of opposite sign. Since all of these coefficients range broadly on either side of zero (see column 2), I also summarize (column 3) the joint distribution of each A-S couplet by their correlation coefficients across all votes. While none are very large, the correlation is negative in every case where the mean values of the coefficients have opposite signs. This means that if the coefficient of average income is more positive than average, the supporter income coefficient tends to be more negative than average.[21] So the tendency for opposing signs of the A and S coefficients seems to be more than a statistical fluke. Whether the Hotelling story or some alternative—such as nonmonotonic interests—best explains the phenomenon remains to be seen.[22]

So above average support from manufacturing employees may be a proxy for support from union members.

21. And, by way of rough consistency, in the only case where the coefficients have the same sign on average—education—they move together across votes as well.

22. A potential example of nonmonotonic interests emerges from data implying that modest-sized cities benefit proportionately more from federal spending than major urban centers. If they do, then a senator (a) from a state with few major cities (low average urbanization) who (b) draws the urban vote in that state (high supporter urbanization) is most likely to support increased spending and taxes—which is just what the sign pattern of the two urbanization coefficients in table 1.6 implies. The empirical basis for the preceding is as follows. For each state, the census gives UR equal to the share of state population in urban areas (over 2,500 population) and MET equal to population share in standard metropolitan areas (in or near larger cities); so $NONM = UR - MET$ is a good proxy for the share of state population in small urban areas. (It is a proxy since some SMAs are of fairly modest size and some of them include some rural population.) When the ratio (XT) of federal expenditures in a state to federal taxes collected from that state is regressed on MET, $NONM$, and PCI, the log of state per capita income, (all as of 1975), we get

$$XT = 3.62 + 1.52\,NONM + .77\,MET - 1.82\,PCI,$$
$$\qquad\quad (3.6) \qquad\quad (2.7) \qquad\quad (6.2)$$

$R^2 = .59$, SE $= .18$, t-ratios in parentheses, $N = 46$ (excludes Alaska, Hawaii, D.C., Maryland, and Virginia) and $\overline{XT} = 1.07$, SD $= .27$. To understand the implications of the regression, imagine a state with average UR (and PCI), but where all of the UR are in MET. For such a state the predicted $\overline{XT} \approx 1.0$. Now suppose all the UR are in $NONM$ (outside large urban areas), then the predicted $XT \approx 1.5$. Thus net benefits flow disproportionately to states whose urban population is concentrated in small towns outside metropolitan centers. Moreover, $NONM$ and MET are strongly negatively correlated ($-.88$). If we take account of this correlation and compute the total effect of a 1-percentage-point increase in $NONM$, (a) XT rises by .36 percentage points and (b) UR falls by .5 percentage points. That is, larger

My analysis of COPE and ADA ratings revealed a complementarity between the interests of contributors and constituents, and I found this in the vote sample as well. The analogue to the test conducted on the ADA and COPE data is to compute, for each vote, the correlation between two partial predicted log odds, one holding a senator's contributor characteristics constant and the other holding constituent characteristics constant. For 82 percent of the votes, this correlation was positive, and the mean correlation coefficient was $+.23$ (standard error $= .01$). This positive correlation of interests means that when large union contributions push a senator toward a pro-union vote so do the characteristics of his constituency. The same complementarity shows up across as well as within votes: I correlated the vote-specific change in log likelihood from constituency characteristics alone (the datum summarized by adding columns 1 and 2 in rows 1–4 of table 1.4) with the marginal contribution of the contributor characteristics variable (column 3 of table 1.4) for that vote. This cross-vote correlation was also significantly positive $(+.34)$. To the extent that these marginal changes in explanatory power reflect the importance of a vote to one or another group, the implication is that bills important to constituents are also important to contributors. So, in both direction and magnitude, the pressures of constituents and contributors on senatorial voting seem to be reinforcing.[23]

Finally, I investigated whether the correlation of interests is higher where bills are more important to one or another group. The answer may provide insight into the behavior of the (presumably) better-organized contributor groups. On some bills the labor union interest may be opposed to that of otherwise pro-union constituencies. But the unions may not press that interest if it is weakly felt and the constituent interest strongly felt, because they have a larger interest in assuring the senator's reelection by a friendly constituency. Such fine tuning of the organized interest group's pressure would imply that the correlation of interests for a particular vote is higher where the issue is more important to constituents and less important to the organized contributors. This tends to be borne out by the following regression:

$$r = 272 + 8.6\,DLLCON - 2.5\,DLLAB - 3.0\,LLNAIVE$$
$$(1.9)\quad(11.5)\qquad\quad(1.2)\qquad\quad(2.5)$$

---

values of XT tend to be found in states with (a) below-average urbanization, (b) where much of the urban population resides in small towns.

23. No significant correlation appeared in similar tests in which the importance of constituent or constituent-plus-contributor interest, on the one hand, and party ideology, on the other, were correlated.

($R^2 = .30$, SE $= 204$, $N = 331$ votes, t-ratios in parentheses), where

r = correlation coefficient of log odds due to constituents with log odds due to contributors on a vote $\times$ 1000;

$DLLCON$ = increase in log likelihood ratio (over naive model) from adding constituent variables to the logistic regression for this vote;

$DLLLAB$ = increase in LL (over "constituent-only" model) from adding contributor variable to the logistic regression for this vote; and

$LLNAIVE$ = minus LL of the naive model.[24]

The significantly positive coefficient of $DLLCON$ is clearly consistent with the notion that contributors tend to refrain from asserting any contrary interests where the constituent interest is strong. The negative, albeit weaker, effect of $DLLLAB$ is also consistent with the view that contributors save their political capital for issues of special importance to themselves. The regression is hardly conclusive, but it suggests some of the subtlety of the relevant group interactions.

V. SOME EXTENSIONS
A. "Left-Out" Variables: Interest or Ideology?

While a very crude principal-agent model typically does well in explaining voting patterns, it is hardly perfect. Here I use the fact that each state has a pair of senators to hint at the likely productivity of more accurate specification of the principals' interest. My results on the popular vote imply a large common element in the characteristics of the constituencies of senators from the same state and party. When they differ in party, this common element will be smaller and perhaps dominated by intrastate differences in constituent characteristics. Accordingly, if relevant constituency characteristics have been left out of the regressions in table 1.4, the residuals should be positively correlated for senators of the same state and party and the correlation should be smaller if the senators differ in party. To test this implication, I estimated regressions for each vote of the form:

$RESIDUAL_{1j}$ = constant + intercept dummies +
$a \times RESIDUAL_{2j} + b(RESIDUAL_{2j} \times SAME$
$PARTY\ DUMMY)$

and

24. $LLNAIVE$ increases with the closeness of the vote, and conflicts between the two ordinarily compatible groups can be expected to be greater on close votes. This is borne out by the significantly negative coefficient of $LLNAIVE$.

$$RESIDUAL_{1j} = \text{constant} + a' \times RESIDUAL_{2j},$$

where j = state j; 1, 2 = senators from j, and $SAME\ PARTY\ DUMMY$ = 1 if both senators are from the same party.[25] The residuals are computed from the regression that includes only the economic interest variables.[26] Since the expected variances of the two residuals are equal, the parameters have the dimensions of a correlation coefficient (that is, $a' = 1$ means perfect correlation of residuals). If some relevant constituent characteristics have been left out, $b > 0$ and $(a + b) > 0$.

Though they are not large, all the relevant correlations tend to be positive and, as expected, greatest for senators from the same party. Specifically, the mean (standard error) of a', the correlation without regard to party, is $+.128$ (.012). For senators of the same party, the average correlation $(a + b)$ is half again as large, or $+.192$ (.017), and for those of opposite party a is only half the sample mean, or $+.060$ (.016).[27]

The possibility, discussed in Section II, that some of the explanatory power of an ideology variable could stem from its correlation with left-out interest variables, gains credibility when the residuals from the ADA regression (column 4, table 1.2) are subjected to the same analysis as the vote residuals. While none of the relevant coefficients for the ADA residuals ($a' = .149$, $a = .082$, $a + b = .212$) is significant, they are strikingly similar in value to the corresponding average for the vote sample. Thus, one reason the ADA variable "works" in the voting regressions is simply that it captures some common interests of the constituency shared by senators from the same state.

25. When the parties differ, I selected the Democrat as senator 1. The (two) intercept dummies distinguish between the remaining combinations—both senators Democrats or both Republicans.

26. To compute residuals from the logit regression, I set the actual values of the senator's vote at .999 or .001 instead of one or zero.

27. Regional patterns in ideology can be invoked to explain these positive correlations. Common social and education backgrounds could lead eastern liberals or western conservatives to deviate in the same direction from their constituents' interests. But such an interpretation is rendered less plausible, and a principal-agent model more plausible, by the very strong negative correlation ($-.647$) between a and b across votes. Common regional ideologies should imply a positive correlation: on votes where the ideological stakes are highest, common backgrounds should pull senators from the same region of either party furthest away from their constituents' interest. If differences in interest, rather than ideology, are crucial, variation in the degree of regional interest will induce the observed negative correlation between a and b. That is, on issues where differences among states are important (say, wheat price supports), senators will pair by state rather than party (a is high relative to b). On more general issues (say, personal tax rates) intrastate constituency differences, proxied by party, will be crucial and a will be low relative to b.

B. The Party as Interest Group

Because senators respond to contributor interests, party contributions could affect voting behavior, much as do union or business contributions, even if party per se does not matter much. Indeed, the small overall effect of party on voting becomes intelligible if parties are treated as just another contributor group, because parties raise only about one-fifth the total funds raised by all economic interest groups. However, for some senatorial campaigns parties play a much larger financial role.[28] This suggests the following refinement: Until now, the basic model has been

$$VOTE = A \times \text{other variables} + B \times PARTY.$$

But, if parties influence voting by fund raising,

$$B = B_0 + B_1 \times PARTY\ SHARE \text{ (of total interest group contributions).}$$

If *all* of a party's influence is due to its fund raising, B_0 should be zero.

I implemented this extended interest group model on a subsample of eighty-eight votes by adding two party share variables—share of Republican and share of Democratic committee funds in total interest group funds—to the economic, contributor, and party variables.

Table 1.7 summarizes the patterns of significant coefficients in the eighty-eight vote subsample. Since the party effect is often weak, I used a generous ($|t| > 1.0$) significance criterion which was met by the *PARTY* coefficient in fifty-six regressions (line I.1). Contrary to the simple party-as-interest-group story, *PARTY* virtually always retains significance ($B_0 \neq 0$) when the financing role is accounted for (See I.2. Also see lines II.3 and III.3, which show the number of cases where $B_0 = 0$ and $B_1 \neq 0$.) Party contributions (especially Republican) also matter in many of the regressions (lines II and III), usually those where *PARTY* retains significance. But this independent effect seems peculiar, almost perverse. Usually, and again especially for Republicans, larger contributions from a party pull a senator to the middle of the political spectrum, away from the average party position. (See line II.2: the coefficient of the Republican party share variable tends to be the same as that of the PARTY dummy where $+1 =$ DEMOCRAT.) This finding implies that voting may affect party contributions, rather than vice versa: opposing interest groups may care less than the party if, for example, a "liberal Republican" is elected, thereby forcing him to rely more on the party for his funds.

28. For example, twelve senators in the 96th Congress received over 40 percent of their total interest group funds from party committees.

TABLE 1.7 Behavior of Party and Party Share of Contributions
Coefficients: Eighty-eight Vote Subsample

Variable	Number of Significant Coefficients	Percentage of Total or Subtotal*
I. Party dummy:		
1. Alone	56	63.6
2. With share variables included	57	64.8
II. Republican contribution share (direction of effect):	46	52.3
1. Same as party	2	4.3
2. Opposite to party	31	67.4
3. Neither	13	28.3
III. Democratic contribution share (direction of effect):	33	37.5
1. Same as party	8	24.2
2. Opposite to party	14	42.4
3. Neither	11	33.3

Note: The data summarize results from the following two regressions run on
each of eighty-eight votes:

(a) $VOTE = A \times$ other variables $+ B \times$ party $(+1 = DEMOCRAT)$

and

(b) $VOTE = A \times$ other variables $+ B_0 \times$ party $+ B_1 \times REPSHARE + B_2 \times DEMSHARE$.

RESHARE or *DEMSHARE* = share of total interest group contributions to senator from
Republican or Democratic party committees. (*REP(DEM) SHARE* = 0 for Democratic
(Republican) senators.) Line 1.1 shows number of regressions of type (a) above in which
the coefficient B is significant ($[t] > 1.0$); line 1.2 shows number of regressions in which
B_0 coefficient in type (b) regression is significant. Lines II and III show number of times
B_1 and B_2 are significant. Lines II.1 and III.1 show number of significant B_1 and B_2 coefficients with signs consistent with that of B_0 (where B_0, B_2 have the same sign, and B_0, B_1
opposite signs). Lines II.3 and III.3 show number of regressions in which B_1 or B_2 is significant, but B_0 is not.
*Percentages refer to number of regressions ÷ 88 (the subsample size) except for lines
II.1–3 and III.1–3, which are percentages of numbers of regressions shown on lines II and
III, respectively.

VI. SUMMARY AND CONCLUSIONS

The tendency for legislators to shirk serving their constituents' interests in
favor of their own preferences (ideology) seems more apparent than real.
Ideology measures can explain much legislative voting behavior statistically. But they turn out to be proxies for something more fundamental:
liberals and conservatives tend to appeal to voters with systematically
different incomes, education, and occupations, and to draw contributions

from different interest groups. And these systematic differences prove, by and large, capable of rationalizing voting patterns without much need for relying on explanations that involve shirking.

When I classified issues by degree of wealth redistribution, the economic variables did best—and ideology worst—on issues involving the greatest redistribution of wealth (many of these were related to the windfall profits tax on crude oil, which was passed in the Congress I studied). On more run-of-the-mill economic issues, economic variables retained above-average explanatory power. Only on social policy issues (abortion, school prayer, and so on), where the wealth stakes are unclear, did ideology play a prominent role. One way to read this result is that, if shirking is at all important, it is subject to the law of demand: less is bought the higher the price (wealth gain or loss to the principals). The obvious challenge to future research is to see whether what now appears to be shirking on social issues is explicable by constituent demand (for example, by the religious composition of voters in the case of school prayer).

Economists have come to view the principal-agent model as an embarrassing legacy of their analysis of private markets, which, after some respectful acknowledgment, needs to be jettisoned before progress can be made in understanding political markets. The main message of this article is that this judgment is premature. Economists can shift their major analytical energies toward a simple principal-agent model and relegate shirking to a sideshow, just as profit maximization rather than managerial shirking remains the main analytical engine for understanding firm behavior.

An Economic Interpretation
of the History of Congressional Voting
in the Twentieth Century

This paper interprets historical change in the U.S. Congress in terms of the simplest principal-agent model. I will show that profound changes in congressional voting patterns over the course of the twentieth century can be traced mainly to corresponding changes in the economic interests of their constituents. This claim may appear, at once, modest and extravagant. Modest, because the notion that agents by and large serve their principals' interests is so familiar in nonpolitical contexts. Extravagant, because economists have found the notion difficult to apply to the behavior of political agents. I begin by outlining the empirical source of this difficulty. Then I describe the main trends in twentieth-century economic history and congressional voting behavior that are the focus of subsequent empirical analysis. The analysis reveals a much closer connection between economic and political history than might be suggested by much contemporary empirical literature on the economics of voting. I conclude by attempting to reconcile these apparently divergent results.

I. The Questionable Connection Between
Congressmen and their Constituents

Economists and political scientists have adduced a variety of explanations for why congressmen might rationally choose *not* to vote consistently for the interests of a majority of constituents (see, for example, Anthony Downs, 1957; James Buchanan and Gordon Tullock, 1962; George Stigler, 1971; Morris Fiorina, 1974). A more recent literature emphasizes the difficulty of linking empirically congressional voting patterns and constit-

First published in *American Economic Review* 75, no. 4 (September 1985): 656–675. © 1985 by American Economic Association. Reprinted by permission.

I thank Kenneth Carl and John Markson for research assistance and anonymous referees for valuable criticism and suggestions. The financial support of the Center for the Study of the Economy and the State, University of Chicago, and the Procter and Gamble Foundation is acknowledged gratefully.

uent economic interests (James Kau and Paul Rubin, 1979, 1982; Joseph Kalt, 1981; Kalt and Mark Zupan, 1984; Edward Mitchell, 1979). Because my focus is also empirical, I attempt in table 2.1 to provide the general reader with a sense of that difficulty.

Consider first who gains and who loses from federal tax-spending policy. This is summarized in panel A of the table. Here two measures of benefits and costs from federal programs are regressed on some state economic characteristics.[1] Each is scaled so that higher values imply more per capita "net benefits" (or lower tax rates). Neither measure is perfect,[2] but the regressions tell a similar story: the federal budget tends to redistribute wealth away from states with high incomes and large manufacturing sectors. Urbanization has a less clear-cut effect. City dwellers pay more taxes (line 2a), but perhaps those who dwell in small cities (i.e., outside SMSAs) receive net benefits (line 1b).

Panel B describes voting patterns in the Senate. The two dependent variables here, like those in panel A, are scaled so that higher values imply more support for federal taxing and spending. Again, despite their imperfections,[3] both measures tell a similar story: apart from the tendency for Democrats to vote for more spending/taxes (col. 7),[4] there is either no connection or a *perverse* connection between the interests of constituents and the votes of their senators. For example, holding party constant, pro-tax/spending voting is either uncorrelated (line 1a) or *negatively* correlated (1b, 2a, 2b) with the direction of benefits from those policies. Further, the

1. The particular characteristics—income, urbanization and the state's industrial mix—are chosen pragmatically. They can explain these data fairly well, and they are readily available for the much longer historical period that is this paper's main concern.

2. Both numerator and denominator of line A.1 are estimates based on sometimes arbitrary assumptions—for example, that the burden of the deficit is proportional to taxes paid. Apart from its neglect of benefits, some of the taxes attributed to a state in line A.2 are in fact paid by residents of another.

3. The variable *NTUA* is derived from an unweighted count of a senator's votes for increased spending or taxes on *all* roll calls dealing with taxing and spending. Thus, a vote to increase total taxes is weighted the same as a vote to increase the budget of the Battle Monuments Commission. The variable *ADA* is derived from votes for the Americans for Democratic Action (ADA) position on a selected sample of 20 issues deemed "important" by that organization. These issues are not limited to tax-spending matters, as with *NTUA*. However, they will usually include the more important tax-spending issues in a Congress, since the ADA has traditionally favored expansion of federal spending, especially on domestic programs.

4. My 1984 article (chap. 1) shows that in popular elections, Democrats tend to draw votes from lower-income voters. Thus, since federal tax-spending policy appears "progressive," the tendency for Democrats to be pro-spending/taxing is consistent with a simple principal-agent story.

TABLE 2.1 Federal Tax-Spending Patterns, Senate Voting Patterns, and State Economic Characteristics

				Coefficients of[a]					
Dependent Variable	HH INC (1)	MFG (2)	URB (3)	METRO (4)	SPEND/TAX (5)	1 – TAX (6)	DEMS (7)	R^2 (8)	SEE (9)
A. Measures of Benefits									
1. *SPEND/TAX* × 100									
a	-11.8 (5.5)	-1.22 (3.8)	.20 (.8)					.58	17.5
b	-12.3 (5.8)	-.88 (2.2)	.79 (1.6)	-.36 (1.4)				.60	17.3
2. 1 – *TAX*									
a	-1.36 (4.2)	-.15 (3.2)	-.09 (2.4)					.64	2.66*
b	-1.42 (4.4)	-.11 (1.7)	-.01 (.1)	-.05 (1.3)				.65	2.64
B. Pro-Spending or Pro-Liberal Voting Measures									
1. *NTUA*									
a					-.01 (.2)		18.4 (3.7)	.24	11.4
b						-.68 (1.8)	18.9 (3.9)	.30	10.9
c	.48 (.3)	.03 (.1)	-.25 (.8)	.18 (1.0)			16.0 (2.9)	.28	11.4

2. ADA

a	.65	.88	.03	−.13	−.28	26.3	.34	17.5
	(3.4)	(2.4)	(.1)	(.5)	(2.7)	(3.4)		
b					−2.08	30.7	.40	16.7
					(3.6)	(4.2)		
c						29.5	.51	15.7
						(3.9)		
Mean	13.5	22.2	65.7	57.6	106.7	83.9	.59	
S.D.	1.6	8.2	14.6	26.1	26.1	4.3	.33	

Sources: SPEND/TAX, (1 − TAX), and independent variables: *Statistical Abstract of the United States,* NTUA and ADA from data supplied by NTU and ADA, respectively.

Notes: Dependent Variables.

1. *SPEND/TAX:* Estimate of federal government expenditures in a state/estimate of federal tax burden in the state. The tax "burden" includes allocation of various nonpersonal taxes (for example, corporation income taxes) to citizens of each state: average for 1975, 1976, 1979 × 100.

2. (1 − *TAX*): One minus ratio of Internal Revenue Service collections from individual income and payroll taxes in each state to total personal income in the state (taxes may be collected in one state from residents in another). Average for 1977–79 × 100.

3. *NTUA:* 100-average rating by National Taxpayer's Union (NTU) of senators from state for 1979–80. The *NTUA* rating is the percentage of a senator's votes that favored reduced taxes or spending, or opposed increases, so higher values of *NTUA* imply more support for taxes/expenditures. The NTU uses all votes on tax-spending issues to construct its index.

4. *ADA.* Average rating by Americans for Democratic Action (ADA) of senators from a state for 1979–80. The ADA rating is percentage of times a senator votes for the ADA position on a selected sample of 20 issues. The ADA counts absence or abstention as opposition; I recalculated the *ADA* rating by ignoring these nonvotes.

Independent Variables: Col. 1. *HH INC:* Median Household Income in state (thousands), 1975; col. 2. *MFG:* Percent of nonagricultural labor force in manufacturing, 1978; col. 3. *URB:* Percent of state population in urban areas, 1970; col. 4. *METRO:* Percent of state population in standard metropolitan statistical areas (SMSAs), 1978; cols. 5, 6: see lines A.1, A.2; col. 7, *DEMS:* Number of Democrat senators from state/2, 1979–80.

[a]The *t*-ratios are shown in parentheses below coefficients.

characteristics most clearly *negatively* correlated with net spending benefits—income and manufacturing—are either uncorrelated (line 1c) or *positively* correlated (2c) with voting for larger federal spending.

The results in table 2.1 are only a suggestive introduction to the empirical literature on congressional voting.[5] But I believe that the reader will
find table 2.1 consistent with an important broad conclusion of that literature, namely that there is a large "inertial" component (often labelled
"ideology") in congressional voting: "liberal" or "conservative" voting
patterns tend to persist from issue to issue, whether or not they seem consistent with constituent interests.

My task here will be to see if this sort of inertia is evident in a much
longer historical perspective: is it just a recent anomaly or a main feature
of the history of legislation? Have long-period changes in economic circumstances had any substantial connection with historical changes in congressional voting patterns? If so, is the connection consistent with changes
in economic interests? In answering these questions, I shall try to disentangle the economic analysis of legislation from some of the idiosyncracy
of American history. A clear regional pattern underlies data such as those
in table 2.1: southern congressmen tend to be more conservative than
northerners (Kau and Rubin, 1979), while per capita income in the South
is also lower than the North. If "economic interest" is supposed to be
all that matters, this positive correlation between income and liberalism
appears perverse. But it can be consonant with a world in which economic
interest is either *important* or *unimportant*. There is a long American history of regional political division, as well as of regional economic differences, and any cross-section correlation between income and liberal voting
will reflect a mix of historical and economic forces. Accordingly, we cannot tell from the positive correlation we observe today whether economic
interest and other factors (like the legacy of the Civil War) tug strongly in
opposing directions, or whether economic interest matters little next to
"history," or whether history matters little and political redistribution is
merely a "normal" consumer good "bought" most heavily by rich constituencies. A major goal herein is to sort these possibilities out.

5. The regressions in panel A do not, for example, capture the within-state variance of
benefits or costs. For example, if taxes are sufficiently concentrated within a state, a high
tax-income ratio or low spending-tax ratio for a state may still leave a majority of residents
with net benefits from the federal budget. Also, note that even if the *total* impact of the
federal budget is progressive, this need not be true of the *additions* to the budget at issue in
congressional votes in 1980. Hence a positive correlation between "pro-spending" votes and
income is not necessarily "perverse" from the standpoint of the economic interests of constituents.

The paper is organized as follows. Section II sets out the basic economic and political history that underlies the subsequent empirical analysis. Section III describes how I measure both economic interest and voting behavior and what I think these measures tell us. Sections IV and V use these measures in empirical analyses designed to gauge the importance of economic forces in shaping the history of congressional voting. The main findings of this analysis are that: 1) voting patterns in a typical Congress reveal an interplay of economic forces and often conflicting regional cultural preferences, but these preferences seem remarkably stable over time. More importantly: 2) this "historical inertia" has not prevented a profound change in voting patterns over the course of the twentieth century; and 3) this change seems entirely attributable to a corresponding change in economic interests in redistributive legislation. Section VI reexamines some puzzles such as those in table 2.1 in light of these findings.

II. The Historical Background

One fact dominates the twentieth-century American economic history which is relevant to this paper: states and regions have become economically more homogeneous. Figure 2.1 illustrates this for three characteristics.[6] The solid lines track dispersion across states. They begin turning down c. 1920 (over a period centered on 1920) or earlier, and by 1980, have fallen by about 25 percent (urbanization) to about 70 percent (income) from their peak values. The same movements are evident when states are grouped into the nine census regions (broken lines). The generally small vertical distances between these roughly parallel lines imply that the homogenization process has been mainly a regional phenomenon.

Any economic explanation of congressional voting has to come to grips with this profound narrowing of regional economic differences and, presumably, of economic interests. However, if this would seem to imply a similar narrowing of political differences, the crude data belie such similarity. Figure 2.2 portrays the history of a few measures of state and regional political difference. The top panels focus on party membership in Congress. Any detectable narrowing of sectional differences in party membership seems confined to the most recent two decades or so, or thirty years after the onset of the economic homogenization. In addition, there is much more intraregional variability in party membership than in the economic data. Because the heterogeneity of American parties may make party membership too crude a measure of political difference, the bottom

6. See the notes to table 2.3 for explanation and sources of these variables.

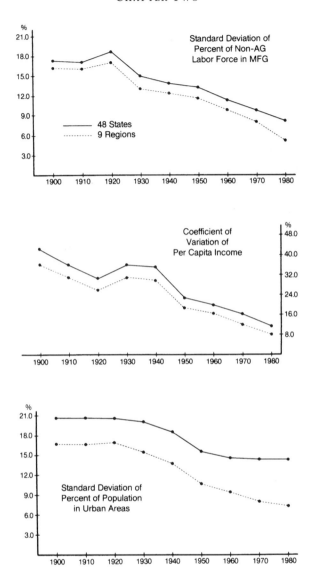

FIGURE 2.1

panels of the figure focus directly on voting behavior. The specific measure underlying these panels is the average frequency with which a state's or region's congressmen voted with the northern Democrat majority on successive samples of 25 votes taken in a session of each House. (The sample and the voting variable are described more fully in the next section.) The

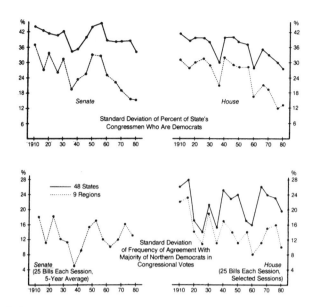

FIGURE 2.2

bottom panels of figure 2.2 show time series of the standard deviation of these frequencies across states and regions. They appear trendless. As with party membership, agreement between these political data and the economic data in figure 2.1 escapes the naked eye.[7]

I will attempt to bridge this apparent disjunction between economic and political differences in Section VI.

III. THE CALIBRATION OF ECONOMIC INTEREST AND CONGRESSIONAL VOTING

Are the data discussed in the two previous sections hiding some historically durable connection between the way congressmen vote and their constituencies' economic stake in that vote? I want to answer this with conventional, easily replicable statistical analysis, and this demands plausible empirical summaries of both the votes and the economic interests. This is a formidable demand. The dramatic growth of the size and scope of the federal government implies that the menu of issues facing Congress and the nature of the stakes may be much different today than in 1900. My

---

7. We cannot, of course, rule out the possibility that increased homogeneity has affected the content of proposed legislation. For example, rural congressmen will oppose either a 1 percent tax or a 10 percent tax on farm incomes, but the former clearly entails a smaller difference between urban and rural interests.

first task, therefore, is to show that there is enough historical consistency in both the nature of the "stakes" and the pattern of voting to motivate the reader's interest in the subsequent empirical analysis.

To get at the consistency of the stakes, I focus on the redistributive element in federal policies. I showed earlier that contemporary budget policy redistributes wealth away from high-income, manufacturing-intensive, and, possibly, large urban areas. Unfortunately, a long history of the redistributive effects of federal spending and taxes is unavailable. However, the income-progressivity feature of the redistribution seems to go back at least to 1950 (Morgan Reynolds and Eugene Smolensky, 1977). Moreover, there are enough income tax collection data for replication of the sort of regression on line A.2a in table 2.1 for most of the relevant historical period and they also show a fairly consistent pattern. I regressed the log of the income taxes/income ratio in each state in the years 1920, 1930, . . . , 1970 on the same three variables as in table 2.1 plus time dummies and obtained:

$$
\begin{aligned}
& \text{Log } (Tax / Income)_{it} \\
& = \text{Constant} + \text{coefficients} \times YEAR \text{ dummies} \\
& \quad + \underset{(5.0)}{.59} \left(\frac{Per\ Capita\ Income_{it}}{US\ Per\ Capita\ Income_t} \right) \\
& \quad + \underset{(5.4)}{.011}\ URB_{it} + \underset{(3.8)}{.006}\ MFG_{it} \\
& \qquad\qquad R^2 = .95, SEE = .32,
\end{aligned}
$$

(1)

where i = state, t = 1920, 1930, . . . , 1970.[8]

When the regression is estimated separately for each of the six years, the coefficients are not always significant, but 17 of the 18 are positive and all 18 simple correlations are significantly positive. Thus, the few available pieces of data give at least a broad hint about the nature of the stakes in political redistribution: the constituents from high-income, manufacturing-intensive, and urban areas have *generally* been asking for opposition by their congressmen to expansion of the federal budget for at least the last sixty years.[9] Accordingly, in the subsequent analysis I use the income,

8. The sample is the 48 continental states, except Delaware, which is an extreme outlier in the earlier years. Tax data are from U.S. Internal Revenue Service and comprise personal income and employment taxes. See table 2.1 for definition of *URB* and *MFG*, and see table 2.3 for sources. The t-ratios are shown in parentheses.

9. The qualifications to this conclusion would include: 1) Non-income taxes—customs and excises—were far more important revenue sources prior to World War II than today, and there is no presumption that their geographical distribution followed that of income taxes. In addition, customs duties provided net *benefits* to protected industries. 2) Other

urbanization, and manufacturing measures to summarize the diversity of interest in redistribution across congressional constituencies.

I will compare these interests with an equally simple summary measure of congressional voting behavior: the extent of support for the position taken by the majority of northern Democrats. While the details of my treatment of the Senate and House differ, nothing essential is lost if I first describe my procedure for senators and then explain why I think it results in an historically consistent measure of voting behavior.

From each Congress, from the 63rd (when popularly elected senators began sitting) to the 96th (1980), I drew a sample of 25 bills on which record votes were taken.[10] I included only votes on "economic" (i.e., non-defense budgetary and economic regulatory) issues where the winning side had less than a 2–1 margin and where over half the senators voted.[11] These criteria were meant to limit the analysis to controversial issues with potentially significant redistributive elements. Each senator's vote on each bill was then coded +1 if he voted in favor of the position taken by the majority of northern Democrats or 0 if he voted the other way. Call the dichotomous variable liberal (LIB). I then extracted the regional[12] elements of LIB on each vote from the regression

$$(2) \quad [LIB_{ij} - \overline{LIB_j}] = \sum_k B_{kj} \cdot D_{ik} + \text{error term},$$

where LIB_{ij} = ith senator's vote on the jth bill, $\overline{LIB_j}$ = average value of LIB on the jth bill, ($i = 1, \ldots , 96$ senators; $j = 1, \ldots , 25$ bills in each session of Congress), D_{ik} = dummy variable = +1 if senator i represents

---

forms of federal government activity (for example, regulation) could have different distributional implications than spending and taxes, so general opposition to expansion of government economic activity need not be in the interest of, for example, a high-income constituency. 3) One could surely lengthen the list of variables potentially related to the interest in redistribution—I intend my short list as a plausible summary, not an exhaustive summary.

10. The voting data are from tape files compiled by the University of Michigan Inter-University Consortium for Political and Social Research (ICPSR). The files give a brief narrative description of each record vote and the position taken by each congressman.

11. Today a record vote almost always attracts substantial participation, but prior to the 1930s it was not uncommon for a majority of senators to be absent without declaring a preference on a vote. I counted any expression of support or opposition—paired votes and announced positions—as a "vote."

12. Since the economic data are available by state, my goal of relating political to economic behavior suggests extracting the state, rather than regional, regularities in LIB. However, with no more than two senators from a state voting on a bill, the "standard error" of the "state" regularity is rather high. Also, the dominant role of regional differences in the interstate variance of economic variables suggests that "region" is a sensible level of aggregation for my purpose.

a state in census region k; 0 otherwise; $k = 1, \ldots, 9$ census regions, $B_{kj} =$ bill-specific regression coefficient of D_{ik}.

For each bill, I also estimated a regression with the same left-hand side variable as (2) and right-hand variables:

(3)   regional dummies $+ C_j (P_i - \bar{P}_j)$

where $P_i = +1$ if senator i is a Democrat,[13] 0 if Republican; $\bar{P}_j =$ average value of P on bill j; $C_j =$ bill-specific regression coefficient.

An important motivation for holding party effects constant, as in (3), is to control for some of the effects of the intraconstituency diversity of economic interest.[14]

The measure (denoted B_{kt}) of a region's liberal voting tendency for a session which I use in subsequent analyses is the average of each region's B_{kj} across the 25 sample votes in that session. In substance, each B_{kt} is just a count of the relative frequency of agreement with the northern Democrat majority. For example, suppose that the typical New England senator voted *LIB* 30 percent more frequently than the average senator and 20 percent more frequently than the average of his party colleagues in 1920. Then B_{kt} from (2) = +.3, while B_{kt} from (3) = +.2 for $t = 1920$. Since the average of the B_{kt} across regions is roughly zero[15] in every session, any B_{kt} measures the liberalism (*LIB*) of a region's senators *relative* to all senators in that session.

My *LIB* measure and its derivatives are replicable, but are they measuring any historically consistent political behavior? I want to suggest that

13. Senators who belonged to neither major party were assigned to one of the two main parties as follows. For each of the 25 bills in each session, I calculated the average value of *LIB* for Democrats and for Republicans. Then I correlated the third-party senator's *LIB* with the difference between the Democrat and Republican average. If the correlation was significantly positive (negative), I called the senator a Democrat (Republican). In virtually every case these correlations were so high (on the order of ±.8) that there was little doubt about where to put the ostensibly maverick senator.

14. See fn. 4. More generally, a senator's constituency is not his "state," but those parts of the electorate relevant to putting him in office and keeping him there. See Richard Fenno (1978) for a discussion of this point. My earlier article (chap. 1) shows that the economic characteristics of this "supporting electorate" differ systematically according to a senator's party. Thus, for example, the typical constituency of Democrats from rich states gains less from redistribution than that of Democrats from poor states, but not necessarily less than that of Republicans from poor states.

15. More precisely, since the number of states per region varies, a state-weighted average of B_{kt} across regions is zero. At the same time, my procedure induces a purely statistical bias in favor of positive B's for the North and negative B's for the South. The nature and size of the bias is discussed in fn. 18 below.

TABLE 2.2 Differences between Northern Democrat and Republican Positions on Income Tax and Tariff Issues, Vote Samples for 61st–74th Congresses

	Number of Votes	
Issue and Position	Senate	House
A. For Higher Income Taxes or More Progressivity		
1. Total Bills	21	11
a. % Northern Dems (ND)		
For > % Republicans (GOP)	14	10
b. % ND < % GOP	3	0
c. No significant difference	4	1
B. For Higher Mfd. Good Tariffs:		
1. Total Bills	32	21
a. % ND > % GOP	0	0
b. % ND < % GOP	30	20
c. No significant difference	2	1

Source: ICPSR File.

they measure just what the *LIB* acronym might suggest: a propensity to support progressive redistribution. This is not a controversial suggestion for the period since the New Deal, since Democrats, especially in the North, have been in the vanguard of support for expansion of the progressive tax-spending structure. But I want to argue that the same interpretation is plausible for the pre-New Deal period as well. In my sample of bills from the pre-New Deal Congresses, I found two issues recurring often enough to permit meaningful generalization. These were bills to change 1) the level or degree of progressivity of federal income tax rates, and 2) tariff rates on imports of manufactured goods. For each such bill in my sample, I computed the difference between the percentage of northern Democrat and Republican votes in favor of increased taxes or progressivity or of increased tariffs on manufactured goods. The results, summarized in table 2.2, indicate the clear preference of northern Democrats for higher/more-progressive income taxes and lower tariffs on manufactured goods. The distributive implications of the northern Democrats' income tax policy are reasonably clear. I am unaware of any evidence on the incidence of tariffs in this period. However, the first-order protective effects of tariffs in the early twentieth century would appear to be regressive: they raised incomes of individuals (owners and workers in manufacturing) who, in a society with a large, low-income agricultural sector, had above-average income. So, with some uncertainty, it seems plausible to characterize the economic policy favored by northern Democrats as consistently pro-redistributive for all of this century.

The main conclusions from this brief tour of twentieth-century economic and political data are: 1) high values of B (or LIB) connote congressional support for a progressive redistributive economic policy; 2) the main beneficiaries of such policies should be found in poor, non-urban, non-manufacturing-intensive areas.

IV. EMPIRICAL RESULTS: THE HISTORICAL CONNECTION BETWEEN ECONOMICS AND POLITICS

In light of previous discussion, I analyze the link between economics and politics in terms of three models of the process:

1. Only economic forces matter in politics.
2. Economic forces don't matter at all, that is, historical regional political differences persist in spite of economic change.
3. Both economics and history matter. Operationally, this entails estimating regressions which are variants of the general form

(4) $B_{kt} = K + \Sigma M_i \cdot ECON_{ikt} + \Sigma N_k \cdot R_k,$

where B_{kt} = the relative LIB of region (or state) k's congressmen in year t; $ECON_{ikt}$ = proxies for k's economic ($ECON$) interest in liberal (LIB) votes in t; R_k = a set of time-invariant regional (or state) dummies; K, M, N = parameters.

The overall fit and the accuracy of the parameters of regressions on various subsets of the $ECON$ and R variables will be used to draw inferences about which of the three models best describes the voting behavior summarized by the B_{kt}.

For the Senate, I have estimates of each region's B_k for each session of Congress from the 63rd through the 96th (1913–80). The $ECON$ variables suggested by the preceding discussion (income, urbanization, manufacturing intensity) are consistently available only every decade. As a compromise between the rich political data and lean economic data, I computed (a) 5-year averages of the B_k and (b) semidecadal values of the economic variables (by interpolation of the decade-end values). The economic variables, like the political variables, are each measured relative to their period means. This yields 126 observations on relative political behavior and relative economic conditions: one for each of nine regions in each of 14 periods ending 1915, 1920, . . . , 1980. Table 2.3 summarizes the results of implementing the three models with this body of data. There are two dependent variables: relative liberalism of a region's senators without regard to party in columns 1–3 and adjusted for party (i.e., the average deviation of a region's Democrats and Republicans from their party's average) in columns 4–6. Each triplet implements the three models successively. The clear result is that the eclectic model which includes both *ECON* variables and regional dummies yields the most adequate description of the voting history. The eclectic model has greater explanatory power (as measured by *SEE*), and coefficients of both the economic and regional variables tend to be estimated more precisely than in the special-purpose models. Thus, these data suggest that economic forces have combined with persistent regional differences to produce the observed Senate voting patterns.

The same conclusion emerges from analysis of voting in the House of Representatives. Here, to economize on computation costs, I sampled votes only from sessions ending in year 0 and year 6 of each decade from 1910 through 1980. However, with over 400 representatives, there are sufficient degrees of freedom to allow the state, as well as the region, to be the unit of analysis. Accordingly, for each House vote,[16] I estimated equations like (2) and (3) except that 48 state dummy variables, rather than just 9 regional dummies appear in them. Then, as with the Senate, I averaged the coefficients of the dummies over the 25-vote regressions in each session to provide my measure of the liberalism of a state's House delegation for that session. This yielded a sample of 720 observations on the measure of political behavior—one for each of 48 states in each of 15 sessions ending 1910, 1916, 1920, 1926 . . . 1980. The results of implementing the same three models as for the Senate are shown in table 2.4. Again, the eclectic models (cols. 3 and 6) fit the data significantly better than either the "economics only" or "history only" models.[17]

16. As with the Senate, I drew samples of 25 votes—on criteria like those for the Senate vote samples—from each of the sessions included in the analysis.

17. The economic variables appear to have less marginal explanatory power over the "location only" model for the Senate (compare the change in *SEE* from cols. 2 to 3 or cols. 5 to 6 in the two tables). However, this is due to the larger number of locational dummies in the House regressions, and the consequent ability to better "explain" state idiosyncracies. If the House data are, like the Senate data, grouped into regions and the table 2.3 regressions replicated exactly (i.e., with regional economic and dummy variables), the *SEE*'s are as follows:

col. 1 : .116   col. 2 : .124   col. 3 : .087
col. 4 : .086   col. 5 : .075   col. 6 : .057.

Here the gain in *SEE* from col. 2 to 3 or col. 5 to 6 is around twice that in table 2.4 and almost identical to that in table 2.3 for the Senate.

TABLE 2.3 Regressions of Political Liberalism in the Senate on Economic Characteristics and Regional Dummies; 5-Year Periods: 1910–15 to 1975–80, 9 Regions

| | Dependent Variable and Model, Liberalism (B_{kt}) | | | | | |
| | No Adjustment for Party | | | Net of Party Effect | | |
Independent Variables	ECON (1)	Region (2)	Both (3)	ECON (4)	Region (5)	Both (6)
Economic						
1. MFG	−.281 (2.2)		−.576 (1.5)	−.199 (1.9)		−.436 (1.8)
2. PCI	−.319 (3.3)		−.501 (5.1)	.018 (.2)		−.374 (5.9)
3. URB	.288 (1.3)		−.467 (1.5)	.232 (1.3)		−.195 (1.0)
Regional Dummies						
4. New England (NE) (ME, NH, VT, MA, RI, CT)		−.071 (2.2)	.138 (2.9)		.029 (1.4)	.171 (5.6)
5. Mid-Atlantic (MA) (NY, NJ, PA, DE, MD)		−.060 (1.9)	.227 (5.9)		.037 (1.8)	.223 (8.9)
6. EN Central (ENC) (OH, IN, IL, MI, WI)		−.022 (.7)	.180 (4.8)		.032 (1.5)	.166 (6.9)
7. WN Central (WNC) (MN, IA, MO, ND, SD, NE, KS)		−.064 (2.0)	−.193 (5.6)		.040 (1.9)	−.042 (1.9)
8. S Atlantic (SA) (VA, WV, NC, SC, GA, FL)		.039 (1.2)	−.128 (2.4)		−.103 (4.9)	−.207 (6.0)
9. ES Central (ESC) (KY, TN, AL, MS)		.074 (2.3)	−.210 (3.7)		−.037 (1.8)	−.222 (6.1)
10. WS Central (WSC) (AR, LA, OK, TX)		.047 (1.5)	−.148 (4.2)		−.084 (4.0)	−.219 (9.6)

	(1)	(2)	(3)	(4)	(5)	(6)
11. Mountain (MT) (MT, ID, WY, CO, NM, AZ, UT, NV)	.007 (.2)	.050 (1.6)		-.002 (0.1)	.085 (4.1)	-.060 (1.5)	.188 (6.9)
12. Pacific (PAC) (WA, OR, CA)		-.077 (1.3)	.209 (4.9)			
R^2	.24	.17	.57	.09	.38	.69
SEE	.112	.119	.087	.093	.078	.057

Notes: Dependent Variables: For cols. 1–3, the variable is derived from regression estimates of equation (2) (see text). Coefficients of the regional dummies in those vote regressions are averaged over the 25 votes in each session. Then these regional averages are further averaged over 5-year periods as follows. Since each session of Congress ends in an even-numbered year, let B_{k2}, B_{k4}, . . . , B_{k10} represent the average coefficient for region k in the 25 vote regressions for a session ending in year 2, year 4, etc., of a decade. The dependent variable for the first 5-year period in a decade is $1/2.5 (B_{k2} + B_{k4} + .5\overline{B}_{k6})$ and that for the second 5-year period is $1/2.5(.5\overline{B}_{k6} + B_{k8} + B_{k10})$. (For the period ending 1915, the calculation is $(1/1.5) (B_{k4} + .5\overline{B}_{k6})$, because I exclude data from Senates without popularly elected senators). The variable for cols. 4–6 is constructed in the same way except that it is based on regression coefficients from equation (3) which includes a party dummy. The vote data on which these variables are based come from the ICPSR files.

Independent Variables: Economic—each of these has the form $(X_{kt} - \overline{X}_t)$ where X_{kt} is an average over the states in a region in year t and $\overline{X}_t$ is a 48-state average for t (Alaska and Hawaii are excluded), and t is every 5 years from 1915 through 1980. The definition and sources of the state data are

1. MFG = percent of nonagricultural labor force in manufacturing. For 1940, see the U.S. Bureau of Labor Statistics, *Handbook of Labor Statistics;* for 1910–40, I use (gainful workers in manufacturing/all nonfarm gainful workers) from Everett S. Lee et al. (1957). I regressed the BLS data on the Lee et al. data for 1940 and 1950 ($R^2 > .95$) and used the regression coefficients and the Lee et al. data to generate estimates of the BLS measure for years prior to 1940.

2. PCI = Log of per capita personal income. For 1930–80, from U.S. Bureau of the Census, *Historical Statistics of the United States* and *Statistical Abstract . . . ;* for 1920, Maurice Leven (1925); for 1910, Lee et al.

3. URB = Percent of state population in urban areas from *Historical Statistics . . .* and *Statistical Abstract. . . .*

For the middle year of each decade, each variable is a linear interpolation of the value at the beginning and end of the decade. Regional dummies each = +1 if the dependent variable is for region k, 0 otherwise. The regions are as defined by the Census Bureau, except that, as in Lee et al., Delaware and Maryland are moved from the South Atlantic to Middle Atlantic region. All variables except dummies are in fractions of 100, for example, the coefficient of MFG in col. 1 means: "in a region where MFG is 10 percent above the national average, senators will vote LIB 2.81 percent less frequently than the average senator." The coefficients of the regional variables in col. 3 are given for $MFG = PCI = URB = 0$, for example, the coefficient for New England in col. 3 means "if New England had the national-average economic characteristics, its senators would have voted LIB 13.8 percent more frequently than the average senator." For cols. (4)–(6), these statements apply to the deviation of the average senator in a region from the average of all his party colleagues. The residuals from the regressions in cols. 3 and 6 are both serially correlated ($r = .35$). (This is partly induced by the averaging process used in generating the data, in that the dependent variable for adjacent periods shares the common term $.5B_{k6}$ (see above). Accordingly, I reestimated these regressions via *GLS.* The results were virtually identical to those reported here, except that t-ratios were smaller than those reported here (shown below the coefficients in parentheses). For example, the *GLS* t-ratios for MFG, PCI, and URB were 1.1, 4.2, and 1.4 for the col. 3 regression, and 1.0, 4.6, and 1.1 for col. 6.

TABLE 2.4 Regressions of House Voting Patterns on Economic
Characteristics and State Dummies, 15 Congresses (1910–80),
48 States

	Dependent Variable and Model Liberalism (B_{kt})					
	No Adjustment for Party			Net of Party Effect		
Independent Variables	ECON (1)	State (2)	Both (3)	ECON (4)	State (5)	Both (6)
Economic						
1. MFG	−.134		−.273	−.042		−.151
	(2.1)		(1.7)	(1.1)		(1.5)
2. PCI	−.323		−.327	.093		−.163
	(7.5)		(5.4)	(3.5)		(4.4)
3. URB	.234		−.878	.070		−.483
	(3.2)		(6.6)	(−1.6)		(6.0)
State Dummies: Regional Averages (and standard deviations)						
4. New England		−.085	.104		.042	.144
		(.12)	(.35)		(.02)	(.12)
5. Mid-Atlantic		−.002	.297		.042	.201
		(.08)	(.13)		(.01)	(.07)
6. EN Central		−.060	.124		.026	.125
		(.05)	(.09)		(.02)	(.05)
7. WN Central		−.087	−.213		.058	−.010
		(.12)	(.22)		(.05)	(.06)
8. S Atlantic		.100	−.082		.093	−.189
		(.04)	(.09)		(.06)	(.06)
9. ES Central		.115	−.144		−.057	−.193
		(.05)	(.11)		(.09)	(.12)
10. WS Central		.150	−.006		−.066	−.148
		(.02)	(.09)		(.03)	(.04)
11. Mountain		.025	.081		−.017	−.048
		(.11)	(.16)		(.04)	(.06)
12. Pacific		−.011	.168		.059	.154
		(.04)	(.14)		(.02)	(.06)
R^2	.09	.30	.45	.02	.31	.43
SEE	.205	.185	.165	.126	.109	.099

Notes: See table 2.3 and text for definitions and sources of variables. Each of the 720 observations is on a state in a session. The sessions are at 4- or 6-year intervals 1910, 1916, 1920, 1926 . . . 1980. The dependent variable is the average coefficient on a state dummy variable from 25 vote regressions like equations (2) and (3) estimated in each session. The regressions used for estimating the dependent variable for cols. 4–6 include a party dummy. The Economic variables are deviations of state variables from a 48-state average for each session. (District-level data are unavailable for the whole period.) The regressions in cols. 2, 3, 5, and 6 include 48 state dummies. Their coefficients are summarized here by region: the standard deviations of the state coefficients in a region are shown in parentheses below the regional mean of these coefficients. These means have the same interpretation as their counterparts in table 2.3—i.e., they show the difference between frequency of liberal voting in a region and in whole House (cols. 2, 3) or within a party (cols. 5, 6). I reestimated the regressions using weighted least squares, with (number of congressmen)$^{-1/2}$ as the weight, because analysis of the residuals revealed some heteroscedasticity. But the coefficients and *t*-ratios of the economic variables were virtually identical to those reported here.

It is, at this point, only convenient shorthand to describe the preceding results as showing that economic change modifies historical inertia. These results are conceptually similar to those of the previously cited literature on contemporary voting in that "noneconomic" variables—here regional dummies—have important marginal explanatory power. So, one could allude to regional differences in ideology as easily as to "historical inertia" (or "tastes" or "unmeasured variables"). Later, I provide some motivation for my shorthand by showing that there is in fact considerable inertia in the history—that is, that the coefficients of the regional dummy variables in cols. 3 and 6 of tables 2.3 and 2.4 are stable. But, however they are labeled, the statistical significance and large magnitudes of these regional differences are a challenge to future research:[18] can we find measurable regional characteristics with histories much different from those already

---

18. A very small part of these differences is due to the statistical bias alluded to in fn. 15. The bias arises because my *LIB* measure is, in part, regionally based. Since northern Democrats are a subset of northern senators, measures of how the average northern senator and the northern Democrat majority vote will tend to agree even if there are no substantive regional differences. Thus, the coefficients of the northern regional dummies will tend to be positive. However, the *magnitude* of this bias is much too small to account for the regional differences observed in cols. 3 and 6 of tables 2.3 and 2.4.

To isolate the magnitude of the bias, assume that every one of 100 senators votes randomly on every bill, so there are no substantive regional differences at all. My procedure would then select the X Democrats among the 70 (in round numbers) northern senators and use their randomly generated majority position to define a *LIB* vote. The random process generating this majority produces a mean of $.5\,X + .399\sqrt{X}$ votes in favor of that position among northern Democrats (under a normal approximation). This implies the following differences between the mean probability $(\overline{P})$ of a vote favorable to the northern Democrat majority and the corresponding regional probability;

$$P_{NORTH} - \overline{P} = .399\sqrt{X}[(1/70) - (1/100)]$$

$$P_{SOUTH} - \overline{P} = -.399\sqrt{X}/100.$$

These differences (or, equivalently, regression coefficients on regional dummies) are as follows for various values of X which span the range of twentieth-century political experience:

X	$P_{NORTH} - \overline{P}$	$P_{SOUTH} - \overline{P}$
10	.005	−.013
30	.009	−.022
50	.012	−.028
60	.013	−.031

Thus, statistical bias implies coefficients of regional dummies which average only one-tenth or so of those in cols. 3 and 6 of tables 2.3 and 2.4.

in my analysis whose inclusion would reduce the explanatory power of the regional dummies?[19]

In the next section, I use the results in tables 2.3 and 2.4 to analyze historical *changes* in voting patterns, but they also reveal interesting regularities in the average "levels" of political behavior:

1. The coefficients of the economic variables in columns 3 and 6 are "sensible" (unlike their contemporary counterparts in table 2.1): these variables, all of which we have seen to be negatively correlated with benefits from redistribution, are also negatively correlated with voting for redistribution.

2. Economics and history have tended to be opposing forces. This is revealed by comparing the regional coefficients in columns 2 and 5 (of either table 2.3 or 2.4) with their counterparts in columns 3 and 6. The latter isolate the effect of history, because economics is separately accounted for in these regressions. The coefficients in columns 2 and 5 show the *net* impact of history and some average of economic forces. Note that these "net" measures range less broadly ($\pm.10$, very roughly) than the "pure history" measures (the range in cols. 3 and 6 is around $\pm.20$). Thus, economic forces have typically dampened the effects of history. In particular, they have dampened the South's conservatism and the North's liberalism.[20]

3. Economic forces affect both the behavior of congressmen from the same party and the party composition of Congress. To see this, compare

19. My earlier paper (chap. 1) argues that differences among senators in sources of electoral and financial support can explain much of the apparent ideological inertia in contemporary voting. For example, senators from the same state will vote differently because they drew votes and funds from systematically different groups within the state. This finding suggests that we look to persistent regional differences in these sources of electoral and financial support for an economic explanation of historical inertia—for example, senators from historically conservative regions may have drawn support from the upper end of their state's income distribution. On this argument, the low voting participation of low-income blacks in the South for most of the twentieth century may help explain that region's historical conservatism. If so, the size of the regional coefficients would be reduced if we could substitute something like income per voter for income per capita in the regressions.

20. The same dampening also shows up within regions. In table 2.4, note the smaller intraregional variation (the entries in parentheses) of the net coefficients in cols. 2 and 5 vs. their pure history counterparts in cols. 3 and 6. Yet another indication of the opposition of economics and history is revealed by subtracting the coefficients in col. 3 (or col. 6) from their counterparts in col. 2 (or col. 5). This operation shows the average direction of the effect of regional economic forces in modifying history, and it almost always yields a number opposite in sign to the impact of history. For example, line 4, col. 6 of table 2.3 tells us that, *holding economic forces constant,* the typical New England senator votes liberal 17 percent more frequently than his party colleagues. But when economics is not held constant (col. 5), this excess liberal frequency is only 3 percent. The implication is that economics has, on average over the twentieth century, pulled against these senators' "natural" liberalism.

the coefficients of the economic variables in column 6 (which describe intraparty behavior) with those in column 3 (where interparty differences are not removed). The former have the same signs but are smaller absolutely than the latter. This says that, for example, higher income in a region makes both Democrats and Republicans in that region more conservative (col. 6, line 2) but it makes the average congressman still more conservative (the absolute value of col. 3, line 2 exceeds that of col. 6, line 2 in both tables). This implies an increase in the number of more conservative Republicans representing that region.[21] Apparently congressmen are at least partly constrained by the central position of their party: they move away from it to accommodate the economic interests of their constituencies but not always far enough to remain in office. This finding helps explain why narrowing of interregional differences in party composition (for example, the breakup of the "Solid South") lags behind the narrowing of economic differences: the initial changes in economic interest can be accommodated by shifts in position within a party, but their cumulation over time eventually breaks a party's hold on a region.

V. THE ECONOMIC BASIS OF HISTORICAL CHANGE IN CONGRESSIONAL POLITICS

Thus far I have shown that voting patterns in a typical Congress can be described by the interaction of economic forces and persisting regional differences, rather than by the working of economic forces alone. In this section, I examine critically the logical corollary of that description—that the only source of historical *change* in voting patterns is economic change. How well does this corollary describe the changes that have occurred over the course of the twentieth century? Are the political changes attributable to economic change substantial or trivial? Are they substantial enough to overcome or just slightly modify the otherwise persisting regional differences?

The answers are summarized in table 2.5 (for the Senate) and table 2.6 (House). These tables reveal a profound change in regional voting patterns over the course of the century, and they show that *nearly all* this change can be attributed to changed economic interests. The basic facts about

21. Compare also the sizes of the differences between the regional coefficients in cols. 2 and 3 on the one hand, with those between cols. 5 and 6 on the other. These measures of the impact of economic forces in modifying history tend to be smaller absolutely within parties (col. 5–col. 6) than within the Senate or House as a whole (col. 2–col. 3), though they go in the same direction. Again, the implication is that if economics impels toward, for example, more conservative voting, part of the impulse is reflected in the replacement of members of the more liberal party.

TABLE 2.5 Change in Frequency of Liberal Voting in the Senate, c. 1920–c. 1975, Regions

| | | | | Region and Voting Measure × 10³ | | | | | | SD Across Regions |
Liberal Voting Measure	NE (1)	MA (2)	ENC (3)	WNC (4)	SA (5)	ESC (6)	WSC (7)	MT (8)	PAC (9)	(10)
A. Within Senate (No Party Adjustment)										
1. Actual c. 1920	-225	-118	-75	-71	206	188	171	0	-58	152
2. Actual c. 1975	154	89	148	-6	-136	-139	-119	-90	135	128
3. Change (2.–1.)	379	207	223	65	-342	-327	-291	-90	193	273
(Col. 3, Table 2.3)					(r = .95)					
4. Predicted Change	290	189	109	-121	-214	-274	-230	-63	115	204
5. Residual (3.–4.)	89	18	114	186	-128	-53	-61	-27	78	100
B. Within Parties (Net of Party Effect)										
1. Actual c. 1920	-44	-30	18	50	-12	-22	-51	-13	48	37
2. Actual c. 1975	151	212	107	25	-198	-175	-167	-64	141	159
3. Change (2.–1.)	195	242	89	-25	-186	-153	-116	-51	93	153
(Col. 6, Table 2.3)					(r = .96)					
4. Predicted Change	182	121	66	-85	-147	-192	-148	-26	79	134
5. Residual (3.–4.)	13	121	23	60	-39	39	-13	-25	14	49

Note: The entries in the table are based on the measure of liberal voting analyzed in table 2.3—i.e., the frequency of agreement with the majority position of northern Democrats, for example, the -225 on line A.1, col. 1, means that New England senators voted with the northern Democrat majority 22.5 percent less frequently than the average senator (over a period centered on 1920). The entries on lines A.1 and A.2 are the average of the dependent variable in table 2.3, cols. 1–3 (×10³) for the 1915, 1920, and 1925 periods, and 1970, 1975, and 1980 periods, respectively. Lines B.1 and B.2 use the dependent variable in table 2.3, cols. 4–6. The entries on lines A.4 and B.4 are the changes in the predicted values over the relevant period from the regressions in cols. 3 and 6 of table 2.3, respectively. These are found by multiplying the change in each economic variable by its coefficient from the indicated table 2.3 regression and summing. The r = coefficient of correlation between actual and predicted change.

TABLE 2.6 Change in Frequency of Liberal Voting in the House, c. 1920–c. 1974, Regions

Liberal Voting Measure	Region and Voting Measure × 10³									*SD* Across Regions
	NE (1)	MA (2)	ENC (3)	WNC (4)	SA (5)	ESC (6)	WSC (7)	MT (8)	PAC (9)	(10)
A. Within House (No Party Adjustment)										
1. Actual c. 1920	−227	−108	−90	−13	171	230	231	−35	−144	169
2. Actual c. 1975	183	108	−54	−85	−80	−91	−35	−117	73	105
3. Change (2.−1.)	410	216	36	−98	−252	−321	−266	−82	217	253
					(r = .98)					
4. Predicted Change	340	210	121	−84	−187	−195	−247	−90	143	207
5. Residual (3.−4.)	70	6	−85	−14	−65	−126	−19	8	74	67
B. Within Parties (Net of Party Effect)										
1. Actual c. 1920	−65	−13	2	73	−23	25	−5	−28	20	39
2. Actual c. 1975	170	120	45	−10	−183	−130	−180	−58	65	129
3. Change (2.−1.)	235	133	43	−83	−160	−155	−175	−30	45	142
					(r = .98)					
4. Predicted Change	182	115	66	−46	−103	−107	−136	−50	78	114
5. Residual (3.−4.)	48	18	−23	−37	−67	−48	−39	20	−33	36

Note: See table 2.5. The same techniques used to generate data in that table are used here. Predicted and actual values come from regressions like those in table 2.3 rather than table 2.4, i.e., the House data are grouped into regions, and regressions like those in table 2.3 (using 9 regional dummies) are used to generate the coefficients of the economic variables which are then used to calculate the predicted changes on lines A.4 and B.4. The data are from 4-period averages with 1910, 1916, 1920, and 1926 comprising the first period, and 1966, 1970, 1976, and 1980 the second.

voting patterns are on the first three lines of each panel of each table (positive values denote support for liberal policies). In the early part of the century, support for liberal economic policy came mainly from the South, and opposition from the Northeast and Pacific states. Today, these alignments are exactly reversed (see panel A). Party alignments changed similarly: the number of northern Democrats grew and victory for southern Republicans became conceivable. But a profound change in the same direction also occurred within each party. This is shown on the first three lines of panel B in the tables. In the early twentieth century, regional differences within parties were relatively small (line B.1).[22] But in the sixty years after World War I, the northern members of both parties grew more liberal and the southerners more conservative (B.3). These within-party changes have accounted for a substantial part of the overall change in Congress (compare the standard deviations in col. 10 for lines A.3 and B.3) and have produced considerable regional differences within parties today.

I think that the most noteworthy finding of this paper is the remarkably close degree to which these profound political changes can be attributed to changes in economic interest. This is seen by comparing lines 3 and 4 of each panel in both tables 2.5 and 2.6. The "predicted changes" on line 4 are obtained from the coefficients of the economic variables in the regressions in col. 3 or col. 6 in table 2.3 or 2.4, and the change in those variables from the early to late twentieth century. There are 36 predicted changes in tables 2.5 and 2.6 (two voting measures for each House for each of nine regions). Only 1 of these 36 disagrees with the sign of the actual change. Only 2 deviate from the actual change by more than half the standard deviation of the actual change. None of the correlation coefficients between these actual and predicted changes is below .95.[23]

---

22. But economic differences were relatively large. The explanation for this strange pairing which is consistent with my previous results on the opposition of history and economics. Prior to World War I, the strong northern economic interest in conservative economic policy and southern interest in liberal policy clashed with opposite historical tendencies (see the pattern of the dummy variables in tables 2.3 and 2.4. cols. 3 and 6). At the level of Congress as a whole (line A.1) the economic interest dominated, but within parties the two forces offset each other (B.1).

23. The regressions in table 2.4 and associated data permit comparison of actual and predicted changes across the 48 states. These state-level data are also highly correlated (.82 for both the within-House and within-party measures). In spite of the greater "noise" in these state-level data, the positive correlation holds even after the very large regional elements are removed: the correlation of the actual with predicted *deviations* of state changes from the regional means is .37 for within-House data and .49 within-party (both are significant).

The results are similar if the longer period is divided into two subperiods of roughly equal length centered on the end of World War II. This is done in table 2.7. These subperiods have somewhat different characteristics—more stable regional party alignments and slower erosion of regional economic differences in the pre-World War II period—but the simple economic model is able to rationalize most of the political change in both subperiods: of the 72 pairs of actual and predicted changes in table 2.7, the signs agree in 63 cases. The correlation coefficient between these two variables never falls below .80 in the eight series in the table, and averages .86. The substantive message of table 2.7 is that the South's move away from liberal policies and the North's move toward them is not compressed into the recent period when regional party alignments began changing. The economic forces underlying these shifts and the political response to them are palpably evident long before this and continue to work essentially up to the present.

So far I have forced on the data a model in which economic change is the only source of political change. An alternative story would be that the noneconomic regional preferences, which I have so far assumed to have remained unchanged, have in fact changed as well. That alternative cannot be ignored in light of the seemingly massive and long-lasting political realignments engendered by the New Deal. Could not, for example, the post-New Deal rise of labor unions and ethnic and racial constituencies in the North have been responsible for the shift toward liberal politics in that region? Table 2.7 provides part of the answer—the shift was going on before the New Deal. But I sought a more formal test. Instead of *assuming* that the regional effects in the columns 3 and 6 regressions of tables 2.3 and 2.4 never changed, I added a set of post-New Deal regional dummies; each $= 1$ for an observation on a particular region for 1940 and after, 0 otherwise. The coefficients of these post-New Deal regional dummies show the extent to which regional voting patterns (net of the effects of the economic variables) *changed* from the pre- to the post-New Deal period. Test of the null hypothesis (that the set of regional coefficients changed) generates statistics with an F-distribution as follows:[24]

F(Senate)	$= 0.85$	(*d.f.* $= 9{,}105$)
F(Senate, within parties)	$= 2.09$	$(9{,}105)$
F(House)	$= 1.64$	$(9{,}114)$

24. For the House, I am testing the hypothesis that coefficients of *regional* dummies in regressions using *regional* data changed over time. My computer program could not perform a similar test on the coefficients of the 48 state dummies.

TABLE 2.7 Actual and Predicted Changes in Frequency of Liberal Voting in Congress, Two Subperiods (c. 1920–1945, 1945–1975), Regions

| Type of Change and Period | Region and Voting Measure × 10³ | | | | | | | | | Correlation of Actual and Predicted (10) |
	NE (1)	MA (2)	ENC (3)	WNC (4)	SA (5)	ESC (6)	WSC (7)	MT (8)	PAC (9)	
A. Within House of Congress										
1. Senate, 1920–45										
a. Actual Change	194	136	−10	−80	−156	−61	−138	74	77	.92
b. Predicted Change	114	34	−12	−45	−103	−42	−49	−15	67	
2. Senate, 1945–75										
a. Actual Change	185	71	233	145	−187	−266	−153	−164	116	.82
b. Predicted Change	175	155	121	−76	−11	−232	−180	−48	48	
3. House, 1915–45										
a. Actual Change	112	83	−6	−102	−63	−154	−91	128	252	.84
b. Predicted Change	131	46	−34	−38	−101	−45	−102	8	127	
4. House, 1945–75										
a. Actual Change	341	164	84	59	−274	−246	−268	−239	11	.93
b. Predicted Change	227	168	147	−49	−106	−168	−160	−81	23	

B. Within Parties

1. Senate, 1920–45

a. Actual Change	104	63	4	−80	−51	45	−23	31	31	.80
b. Predicted Change	76	15	−11	−30	−71	−27	−25	−4	38	

2. Senate, 1945–75

a. Actual Change	92	179	85	55	−134	−196	−92	−82	62	.90
b. Predicted Change	107	107	77	−56	−77	−165	−124	−22	41	

3. House, 1915–45

a. Actual Change	116	63	54	−6	−120	−143	−93	83	97	.82
b. Predicted Change	73	26	−18	−21	−55	−24	−56	3	70	

4. House, 1945–75

a. Actual Change	120	67	3	−57	−73	−23	−110	−107	−37	.86
b. Predicted Change	126	92	81	−27	−58	−92	−89	−46	12	

Note: Actual and predicted changes are computed in the same manner as in tables 2.5 and 2.6 (see their notes), but for two subperiods. Three-term averages of the relevant data are computed for an "early," "middle," and "current" period as follows. The early period is an average of 1910, 1916, and 1920 data for the House and 1915, 1920, and 1925 data for the Senate. The middle period is an average of 1940, 1946, and 1950 data for the House and 1940, 1945, 1950 for the Senate. The current period is 1970, 1976, and 1980 for the House and 1970, 1975, and 1980 for the Senate. The changes shown above as 1920–45 or 1915–45 are middle minus early data; the 1945–75 changes are current minus middle data.

TABLE 2.8 Measures of Relative Impact of Economic and Historical
Change on Political Change in Congress, World War I to Present

	Correlation Coefficient Actual Change vs. Components of Predicted Change		Beta Coefficients for Components of Predicted Change	
Type of Change	ECON (1)	HIST (2)	ECON (3)	HIST (4)
A. Within Houses				
1. Senate	.92	.43	.92	.22
2. House	.93	−.30	1.17	.39
B. Within Parties				
1. Senate	.95	.08	.99	.30
2. House	.93	.74	.71	.47

Note: Data are from the unrestricted model (see text) in which changes in both economic and historical forces are permitted to affect voting behavior; this model permits the
coefficients of the regional dummies to change between the pre- and post-1910 periods.
Accordingly, the predicted (PRED) change in voting behavior for any region has two components in this model: (a) ECON = change due solely to changes in economic variables
(i.e., holding constant any shift in the coefficient of the regional dummy). (b) HIST =
change in the coefficient of the regional dummy.
    Cols. 1 and 2 show the correlation coefficient between actual change and each compo-
nent of PRED. Cols. 5 and 6 show the contribution of each component to PRED in standard deviation (SD) units. For example line A.1 says "a region where ECON is 1 SD above
the mean will have a PRED .92 SD above the mean," etc. These beta coefficients are calculated by dividing SD of ECON and of HIST by SD of PRED. Panel A data are for
changes in behavior across all congressmen without regard to their party. Panel B refers
to changes within parties.

$$F(\text{House, within parties}) = 2.30 \qquad (9,114)$$
$$F_{.05} \approx 2.0 \qquad F_{.01} \approx 2.6$$

These numbers imply rejection of the null hypothesis at the 1 percent level
for all four regressions, but acceptance at 5 percent for two of them. So,
the evidence for ("noneconomic") shifts in regional political preferences
is weak, and this provides justification for the restricted model in which
economic change alone drives political change.

    Shifts in regional preferences seem quantitatively, as well as statisti-
cally, insignificant. We already know that the restricted model (i.e., only
economic change matters) explains virtually all of the change in political
behavior. So, the only way that changes in regional preferences could plausibly be an important source of political change would be for the unrestricted model to "reapportion" explanatory power from the economic

variables to those measuring the shift in regional preference. However, table 2.8 shows that this is not what the unrestricted model does. The data are based on the two separate elements of the change in voting behavior predicted by the unrestricted model—the *ECON* element (the sum of co-efficients of the economic variables times the changes in these variables over time) and the change in historical (*HIST*) preferences (the change in the coefficients of the regional dummies from the pre- to post-1940 period). The first two columns show that, standing alone, *ECON* is the much more *reliable* guide to the data than *HIST*; indeed the correlations in column 1 are not much lower than those previously reported for the restricted model. The last two columns show that *ECON* is quantitatively the much more important element in the change in behavior predicted by the un-restricted model.

All of this implies that what I had before merely labeled the "persistent historical" element in political behavior (i.e., the coefficients of the re-gional dummies in tables 2.3 and 2.4) really is persistent. This focuses more sharply my earlier challenge to future research: an economic expla-nation of these regional differences will have to uncover economic differ-ences among regions that *have not changed much since the beginning of the century.* The regional homogenization evident in so many dimensions of economic activity makes this a formidable challenge.

VI. A REEXAMINATION OF PREVIOUS PUZZLES

I showed (Section II) that political differences among regions in Congress have not declined along with economic differences. That seeming anomaly is restated in panel A of table 2.9. This shows simple correlations between the *dispersions* of the economic and the various congressional voting mea-sures I have been analyzing. If there is a simple connection between nar-rowing economic and political differences among states, these should be consistently positive, and they obviously are not. However, if there are persistent regional elements in political behavior, there should be a posi-tive correlation over time between the dispersions of economic variables and of voting measures *net of the persistent regional element.* Accordingly, I subtracted the appropriate coefficient of the regional (or state) dummy in tables 2.3 and 2.4 from each measure of voting behavior and recom-puted the simple correlations between the dispersions of the adjusted po-litical and economic variables. These are in panel B of table 2.9 and they are all strongly positive.

The persistent regional element has to be removed to reveal this tan-

TABLE 2.9 Correlation Coefficients between Standard Deviations of
Liberal Voting Measures in Congress and of Economic Variables;
1910 or 1915 to 1980; Across Regions or States

Standard Deviation of Liberal Voting Measure	Correlation Coefficient with SD of		
	MFG (1)	PCI (2)	URB (3)
A. Unadjusted (for Persistent Regional or State Differences)			
1. Within			
a. Senate	.10	−.14	.03
b. House: Regions	.48	.45	.53
States	.01	−.01	.01
2. Within Parties in			
a. Senate	−.86	−.85	−.80
b. House: Regions	−.67	−.74	−.67
States	−.74	−.66	−.73
B. Adjusted (for Persistent Regional or State Differences)			
1. Within			
a. Senate	.82	.76	.75
b. House: Regions	.87	.85	.84
States	.83	.87	.82
2. Within Parties			
a. Senate	.77	.86	.76
b. House: Regions	.82	.83	.85
States	.71	.76	.79

Note: Each entry is a simple correlation coefficient between a time series of standard deviations of an economic variable across regions or states and a time series of a *SD* of one of the political liberalism measures analyzed previously (see tables 2.3 and 2.4 notes). Each House time series has 15 observations and each Senate time series has 14 observations. See text for method of calculating voting measures used in panel B.

dem decline of political and economic differences because the conflict between history and economics described in Section IV has abated over time. Early in the century, the South's historical conservatism and the North's liberalism (see the regional coefficients in cols. 3 and 6 of tables 2.3 and 2.4) clashed sharply with the redistributive interests entailed by southern poverty and northern affluence. This clash made regional differences in political behavior smaller than otherwise. However, the clash and its re-

TABLE 2.10 Regressions of Senate Voting Patterns, on Economic and Political Characteristics, States, 1979

					Coefficient of				
Dependent Variable	HH INC (1)	MFG (2)	URB (3)	MET (4)	SPEND/ TAX (5)	DEMS (6)	HIST (7)	R^2	SE
1. NTUA									
a					.13	20.8	39.8	.41	10.1
					1.8	4.6	3.4		
(Table 2.1)					(−.01)	(18.4)		(.24)	(11.4)
c	−5.96	−.46	−.59	.27		16.0	92.3	.59	8.7
	3.7	2.1	2.2	2.0		3.9	5.4		
(Table 2.1)	(.48)	(.03)	(−.25)	(.18)		(16.0)		(.28)	(11.4)
2. ADA									
a					.08	32.3	95.0	.68	12.4
					.8	5.8	6.6		
(Table 2.1)					(−.28)	(26.3)		(.34)	(17.5)
c	−3.85	.08	−.52	.02		28.6	148.7	.80	10.2
	2.1	.3	1.7	.1		6.1	7.5		
(Table 2.1)	(.65)	(.88)	(.03)	(−.13)		(29.5)		(.51)	(15.7)

Note: The regressions follow the same format as counterparts in table 2.1, panel B, except for the addition of *HIST* as an independent variable. *HIST* is a vector of the coefficients of the state dummy variables in the regression in col. 6, table 2.4. That is, *HIST* measures the historical liberalism of a state's representatives (I have no state-specific data for senators) relative to their party mean over the whole 1910–80 period after accounting for economic variables. For comparison, the regression coefficients and summary statistics from the corresponding table 2.1 regression are shown in parentheses on the lines labeled (Table 2.1). See table 2.1 for definitions and sources of all variables other than *HIST*. *t*-values are shown below coefficients.

straining influence on regional political differences, has diminished with the relative economic rise of the South.[25] Interestingly, my data imply that regional political differences will *grow* in the future even as the economic element of these differences diminishes.[26]

The weak or even perverse relationship between voting and economic interest often found in contemporary Congresses (see the discussion surrounding table 2.1) can also be clarified by my results. They suggest that, for example, wealthy areas sometimes produce liberal congressmen because the pull of history can overcome the push of interest. This is more likely today, when differences in interest are smaller, than it has been in the past. If this explanation is correct, then some adjustment for history should bring the role of interest in contemporary voting into sharper focus. This adjustment is made in table 2.10 which adds history, in the form of a vector of the coefficients of state dummy variables from the column 6, table 2.4 regression, to some of the regressions in table 2.1.[27] The coefficient of this *HIST* variable (col. 7) is uniformly positive and significant, which is further testimony to the durability of these sectional differences. More important, with the addition of *HIST*, the coefficients of the economic variables change in the "right" direction from their table 2.1 values (shown in parentheses); that is, income, manufacturing and urbanization, which are negatively correlated with the benefits of redistribution, have algebraically smaller and usually negative coefficients in table 2.10.[28] Similarly, the partial correlation of liberal voting with the benefits from redis-

---

25. To see formally why the variance of political behavior (S^2) across regions need not decline along with the variance of the economic (+ any random) element (E^2) of that behavior, note that $S^2 = E^2 + H^2 + 2rEH$, where H^2 = variance of the historical (i.e., time-invariant) element across regions, and r = correlation between the historical and economic (+ random) elements across regions at time t. Then

$$\frac{dS}{dt} = \frac{1}{S}\left[\frac{dE}{dt}(E + rH) + \frac{dr}{dt} \cdot EH\right].$$

For most periods in the data, $dE/dt < 0$, but $r < 0$, so the sign of dS/dt is indeterminate.

26. In the notation of fn. 25, E^2 is now so small that, with $r < 0$, $(E^2 + 2rEH) < 0$ and $S^2 < H^2$. Therefore, if E continues to approach zero, over time S^2 will rise toward H^2. For the Senate, in the period 1970–80, $S = .128$ while $H = .185$. The latter figure is about equal to the maximum S observed in this century.

27. These coefficients describe historical preferences in the *House* and the regressions in table 2.10 describe voting in the *Senate*. This is done because I do not have comparable state-level data for the Senate. I also ran the regressions in table 2.10 with the relevant regional *HIST* of the Senate. These were qualitatively similar to those in table 2.10, but none explained the data as well as its table 2.10 counterpart.

28. The coefficient of *MET*, however, moves in the "wrong" direction, in that the crude evidence in table 2.1 implies that residents of SMSAs lose from redistribution.

tribution (lines 1a and 2a) is positive in table 2.10, while it was strangely negative in table 2.1.

VII. SUMMARY AND CONCLUSIONS

The evidence in this paper is consistent with a model in which congressional agents act as if they are maximizing a utility function like

(5) $U = F(L,W)$,

where L = the number or frequency of liberal votes cast,[29] and W = their principals' wealth per capita.

The agent's choice of L affects W via the political redistribution process, and the usual first-order conditions are

(6) $F_L/F_W = -dW/dL$,

the "price" of a liberal vote in terms of W. That price depends on the nature of redistribution—it will be positive in some constituencies and negative in others. Accordingly, (6) has an interior solution only where liberalism is a costly good (F_L, $-dW/dL$; both > 0) or a productive bad. My data imply that where liberalism seems to be a good (the North) it has historically been costly, and where it is a bad (the South) it has been productive. This amounts to invoking a "tastes" category to permit F_L to be nonzero in the same way that, say, an analyst of the market for rock music might have to invoke tastes to "explain" why some pay to hear it and others pay to avoid it. But to invoke tastes is also to challenge future research. In this case, the challenge is to uncover objective forces which can reduce the importance of my particular tastes category.

Meanwhile, I have followed the traditional path in utility analyses of choice, that of focusing on the effects of changes in constraints. The characteristics of American political redistribution suggest that, in general, the shadow price of a liberal vote ($-dW/dL$) rises with relative wealth, and, when that price rises, we expect fewer such votes to be "bought." That expectation is strongly confirmed by my data, as is the underlying assumption that the tastes in question are stable. I have shown that this conventional economic model is powerful enough to explain substantially all of the major political realignments among regions in this century. The economic convergence of congressional constituencies has gradually lowered the price of a liberal vote to northern congressmen and lowered the price of a conservative vote to southerners. This elemental fact is sufficient to

---

29. At this level of generality, one has to be agnostic about whether L generates utility for the agents or principals or both.

explain 1) why the once conservative North has become liberal and why
the opposite occurred in the South; 2) why once more-or-less homogeneous parties have become regionally divided, with northern members of
either party now more liberal and southerners now more conservative than
their party average, and 3) why Democrats have gained "market share" in
the North and lost it in the South. Since the process of economic convergence appears not to have run its course, the strong suggestion of my
results is that these political trends will continue. The seemingly paradoxi-
cal result predicted by my data is that Congress will become more sharply
divided regionally as their constituencies converge economically.

REFERENCES

Buchanan, James and Tullock, Gordon, *The Calculus of Consent,* Ann Arbor: Uni-
    versity of Michigan Press, 1962.
Downs, Anthony, *An Economic Theory of Democracy,* New York: Harper & Row,
    1957.
Fenno, Richard, *Home Style: House Members in their Districts,* Boston: Little
    Brown, 1978.
Fiorina, Morris, *Representatives, Roll Calls & Constituencies,* Lexington: Lexing-
    ton Books, 1974.
Kalt, Joseph, *The Economics and Politics of Oil Price Regulation,* Cambridge: Har-
    vard University Press, 1981.
——— and Zupan, Mark, "Capture and Ideology in the Economic Theory of
    Politics," *American Economic Review,* June 1984, *74,* 279–300.
Kau, James and Rubin, Paul, "Self-Interest, Ideology and Logrolling in Congres-
    sional Voting," *Journal of Law and Economics,* October 1979, 22, 365–84.
——— and ———, *Congressmen, Constituents and Contributors,* Boston: Nij-
    hoff, 1982.
Lee, Everett S. et al., *Population Redistribution and Economic Growth, United
    States, 1870–1950,* Vol. I., Philadelphia: American Philosophical Society, 1957.
Leven, Maurice, *Income in the Various States,* New York: National Bureau of Eco-
    nomic Research, 1925.
Mitchell, Edward J., "The Basis of Congressional Energy Policy," *Texas Law Re-
    view,* March 1979, 57, 591–613.
Peltzman, Sam, "Constituent Interest and Congressional Voting," *Journal of Law
    and Economics,* April 1984, 27, 181–210 (chap. 1 of this volume).
Reynolds, Morgan and Smolensky, Eugene, *Public Expenditures, Taxes and the
    Distribution of Income,* New York: Academic Press, 1977.
Stigler, George, "The Theory of Economic Regulation," *Bell Journal of Economics,*
    Spring 1971, 2, 3–21.
U.S. Department of Commerce, Bureau of the Census, *Historical Statistics of the
    United States,* Washington: USGPO, 1975.

————, *Statistical Abstract of the United States,* Washington: USGPO, various years.

U.S. Department of Labor, Bureau of Labor Statistics, *Handbook of Labor Statistics,* Washington: USGPO, 1967.

U.S. Internal Revenue Service, *Annual Report of the Commissioner,* Washington: USGPO, various years.

Economic Conditions and Gubernatorial Elections

The literature on the effect of economic conditions on election outcomes has so far focused mainly on presidential (Ray Fair, 1978; Allan Meltzer and Mark Vellrath, 1975; Burton Abrams and Russell Settle, 1978) or congressional elections (Gerald Kramer, 1971; George Stigler, 1973; Howard Bloom and H. Douglas Price, 1975). Typically some aggregate voting measure (for example, the incumbent party's share of the national vote) is regressed on macroeconomic measures of the putative success or failure of the incumbents' economic policy. The broad consensus of the literature is that voters reward "good" economic performance, but that they have short memories. Usually income growth in the year preceding the election dominates measures like the unemployment rate or inflation rate, but prior economic performance seems not to matter at all.[1]

The existing literature is constrained to work with small samples. For example, there have been fewer than 20 presidential elections since countercyclical monetary/fiscal policy became important. The small sample compromises the power of any test, or, where pre-1930s data are used, raises questions about the sophistication of either the voters or the research design. This paper is a modest attempt to overcome the small sample problem by focusing on post-World War II gubernatorial elections, of which there have been several hundred.

These extra degrees of freedom are not really free, because governors can have only limited effects on the economic welfare of voters. In the organization chart of the American federal system, governors and presidents share similar powers of appointment, budget making, etc., and the role of the governor's mansion as a training ground for presidential candi-

First published in *American Economic Association Papers and Proceedings* 7, no. 2 (May 1987): 293–297. © 1987 by American Economic Association. Reprinted by permission.

I thank David Barker for research assistance, and the Bradley Foundation and the Center for the Study of the Economy and State, University of Chicago, for financial support.

1. This result has motivated research on political business cycles, in which politicians respond to the voters' short memories with stimulative policies just prior to elections.

dates is well established. But, as chief executive in a small open economy without a central bank, the governor cannot conduct very powerful macro policy. That weakness does yield a benefit: We can begin to see if voters make sensible connections between policy and performance. That issue was raised by Stigler, who argued that sensible voters would ignore short-run economic fluctuations, but it has since been largely ignored. How then are we to interpret the result that voters reward good short-term macro performance when this result comes from time series including pre-New Deal or even pre-Federal Reserve data (as in Fair or Kramer)? If early presidents, like today's governors, could not plausibly "perform," the inference would appear to be that voters are not very sensible.[2] The subsequent evidence shall, however, cast some doubt on that inference.

I. DATA AND MODEL

I use a sample of 269 postwar elections which comprises essentially all gubernatorial elections to four-year terms from 1949 through 1984 in states with competitive party systems.[3] I then follow the literature and try to connect the incumbent party's share (*IPS*) of the two-party vote to economic performance (*EP*) during the governor's term. I assume that the representative voter has some normal probability (K_i) of voting for the incumbent party from which he deviates according to his estimate of the impact of the party's policies on his economic welfare (EW_i). Aggregating over voters, we get

$$(1) \quad IPS_t = K + f(EW_t),$$

I allow voters to translate *EP* into *EW* slowly according to

$$(2) \quad EW_t = (1 - w)EP_t + w \cdot EW_{t-1}, \quad 0 < w < 1.$$

That is, voters remember their estimate of *EW* at the last election and give it some weight (w) in calculating EW_t. A linear version of (1) which incorporates (2) is

2. I eschew the term "rational," since voters may be rationally nonsensical, given their putative lack of incentive to invest in information on the connection between policy and performance.

3. A shrinking number of states have two-year terms, and I excluded these elections. When a state adopts a four-year term, I included that state from the second four-year term election. I also exclude Alaska and Hawaii and all elections in states where a single party received over 70 percent of the vote for at least three consecutive elections. In effect this criterion eliminates a few southern states where Democrats have received only token opposition for some or all of the period. Over 90 percent of all gubernatorial elections occur in even-numbered years.

(3) $IPS_t = K(1 - w) + m(1 - w)EP_t + w \cdot IPS_{t-1}$,

where m and w are (assumed) constant. To implement (3) on the sample, I allow K to vary across states, but not over time. So, operationally, K is the incumbent party's long-run average share in a state. I also allow for the well-known advantage to incumbents seeking reelection. An implication of this scheme is that the performance measures used by sophisticated voters should be "unexpected" at $t - 1$; any component of performance which is predictable at $t - 1$ should be reflected in that election's IPS.

A pervasive result of my preliminary work was that voters do respond consistently to the surprises in performance rather than to the expected component. For example, cursory examination of annual real income, inflation, and unemployment series reveal considerable persistence, while growth of real income, change in inflation, and change in unemployment are approximately random walks, and these latter are what voters react to. Another pervasive result is reaffirmation of the voters' short memory. This shows up in two ways: 1) no estimate of w was ever far from zero (see table 3.1), and no performance measure going back more than a year or so before election day (with one notable exception) ever "mattered." Accordingly subsequent results focus on surprises in the election year.

II. RESULTS

Regression (1), table 3.1, is the obvious extension of the literature to these data. The incumbent party's vote share is regressed, inter alia, on the growth of real per capita income[4] in the state in the election year. This regression hints that good performance *hurts* the incumbent party, but any paradox vanishes on closer inspection. State income growth, of course, reflects fluctuations in national income, and it turns out that these are the dominant influence on gubernatorial elections. The (marginal) voter apparently understands that governors have little influence on the growth of state income, and he or she accordingly rewards (penalizes) the *party* of the incumbent *president* for good (bad) macro performance. This is shown in regression (2). Here performance is measured by national per capita income growth, and slope and intercept dummies are included which distinguish whether the incumbent party in a state is the same (= +1) or different (= −1) from the president's party. The significantly positive coefficient of the slope dummy (+.86) is a measure of the reward

---

4. Nominal per capita personal income in the state deflated by the national personal income deflator.

TABLE 3.1 Regressions of Incumbent Party's Share of Vote; 269 Gubernatorial Elections, 1949–84

Independent Variables (In % except for Dummies)	Coefficients/ t-Ratios (1)	(2)	Mean S.D.
Incumbent Party Share in	−.01	.11	55.7
Last Election	(0.1)	(1.4)	(5.4)
Incumbent Candidate = +1.0	4.4	4.0	.56
otherwise	(4.7)	(4.6)	(.50)
Per Capita Income Growth in			
(a) State	−.16		1.7
	(1.2)		(3.4)
(b) Nation		−.33	1.9
		(1.8)	(2.3)
(c) State-Nation		.03	−.25
Presidential Dummy = +1 if			
Incumbent Party is same			
as President, −1 if		−4.1	.25
different		(5.6)	(.97)
Presidential Dummy ×			
National Income Growth		.86	.70
		(3.1)	3.0
			Incumbent Party Share
$\bar{R}^2$	.24	.34	52.6
SEE	7.0	6.5	8.0
	(3)	(4)	
Incumbent Party Share in	.12	.08	
Last Election	(1.5)	(1.0)	
Incumbent Candidate	4.1	4.1	
	(4.7)	(4.7)	
National per Capita Income	−.32	−.22	
Growth	(1.7)	(1.2)	
Change in Inflation Rate	.08	.15	.09
	(0.4)	(0.8)	(2.2)
Growth of State Revenue/		−.08	10.0
State Income		(2.6)	(13.9)
Presidential Dummy	−4.0	−4.0	
	(5.4)	(5.5)	

TABLE 3.1 *continued*

Independent Variables	Coefficients/ t-Ratios		Mean
(In % except for Dummies)	(1)	(2)	S.D.
Presidential Dummy ×			
(a) National Income	.82	.86	
Growth	(2.9)	(3.1)	
	−.29	−.29	.00
(b) Change in Inflation	(1.5)	(1.6)	(2.2)
$\bar{R}^2$	.34	.36	
SEE	6.5	6.4	

Sources: Political data: Richard Scammon and Alice McGillivray, *America Votes* (various issues); Economic data: U.S. Bureau of Census, *Statistical Abstract of the United States* and Council of Economic Advisers *Economic Report of the President,* various issues.

Notes: See text for definitions of variables. *T*-ratios are shown in parentheses below coefficients. Each regression includes a vector of state-party dummy variables, but neither their coefficients nor the constant term is shown. This vector represents K in (3). The dummy for each state (or combination of neighboring states if a state has fewer than five elections in the sample) = +1 when the incumbent party in the state is Republican, −1 when Democrat, so the dummy vector allows for long-run average differences in party strength among states.

for good macro performance bestowed on the gubernatorial candidate from the president's party.[5] The regression also suggests a curious asymmetry: the negative coefficient of income growth (−.33) implies that the reward is greater if the president's party is challenging rather than defending the governor's mansion.[6] Regression (2) also implies that, once national income growth is accounted for, the difference between state and national growth doesn't matter. This result survives all subsequent refinements.[7]

Regression (3), table 3.1, adds the change in the inflation rate (I use the Personal Income deflator) and its interaction with the presidential party dummy. The previous research has used the inflation rate and obtained

5. I was also able to confirm that income dominates unemployment as a performance measure. Substituting the change in the unemployment rate for income growth produced qualitatively similar but perceptibly weaker results than regression (2).

6. Specifically, when the president's party is defending the gubernatorial mansion, a 1 percent acceleration of income growth increases his party's vote share by .53(= .86 − .33) percent. When the president's party is challenging, the increase is +1.19(= .86 + .33) percent.

7. That is, the difference between state and national growth is never significant when added to any subsequent regression. Neither is the interaction of this difference and the presidential dummy. So voters do not penalize the candidate of the president's party if local income grows more slowly than national income.

mixed results.[8] I found it insignificant in a counterpart to regression (3) not shown. However, there is considerable persistence in annual inflation rates,[9] which essentially disappears on first differencing. Thus, if voters dislike inflation, it makes no sense for them to, for example, penalize an absolutely high inflation rate if it is declining. Indeed, the change in inflation seems to be the more relevant inflation variable. The negative coefficient of the presidential party change in inflation interaction suggests that the president's party is penalized for unpleasant surprises in inflation.[10]

Governors do have one policy lever that can perceptibly affect voters' economic welfare, namely their influence on the state budget. Regression (4), table 3.1, adds the *four-year* percentage change in state general revenues divided by state personal income, and it suggests that voters penalize budgetary expansion. In this case voters' memories seem longer than for national performance: the one-year value for this variable proved insignificant. Because state revenues come from federal aid as well as taxes, I tried a refinement which distinguished the local from the federal aid component of revenues. But this decomposition did not improve on regression (4);[11] voters do not act as if federal aid is a free lunch. Since both revenues and federal aid have, until recently, been rising relative to income, these results raise obviously intriguing questions of interpretation.

III. SUMMARY

Voters in gubernatorial elections seem able to draw appropriately delicate distinctions in their response to economic conditions. They vote as if they understand that national rather than local policies have the dominant effect on their income. They also act as if they understand that national policies affect national income more than its geographic distribution. They do this, on the evidence here, by holding gubernatorial candidates of the president's party hostage to the perceived effectiveness of his macro policy and by ignoring local idiosyncracies. Voters also will get good grades from economists for correctly distinguishing expected from unexpected infla-

---

8. Fair found the inflation rate insignificant. Kramer found it significant after correcting a data error in his original article (Saul Goodman and Kramer, 1975).

9. The first-order serial correlation of the inflation rate is +.81 over my sample period.

10. The insignificant positive coefficient of the change in inflation hints weakly at the same sort of asymmetry found for income growth.

11. Specifically, since revenue/income = state's own revenues per dollar of income × (1 + federal aid/own revenues), I entered the growth rates of both components separately. Each had indistinguishably different negative coefficients. Substituting expenditures for revenues produces results similar to those in regression (4).

tion. Finally, voters do respond to the local variable that the governor can control: they penalize growth of the state budget.

My results may offer a clue about voters' seeming myopia. About two-thirds of gubernatorial elections coincide with the midterm congressional election. If (the voters believe) the president is the responsible agent for macro policy, these midterm elections give voters an opportunity to "settle up" with the president for the past two years. The signal that emerges should then alter or affirm macro policy, and the president's response to it would be monitored at the next presidential election. On this view, voters should respond to performance in each biennium and, given the usual policy lags, election year surprises would not be a bad proxy for biennial performance.[12]

Direct comparison of my results with the previous literature is complicated by the asymmetry I find between challengers and defenders. To facilitate comparisons, consider a stylized case in which the president's party is defending half the contested governors' mansions and challenging the other half. Then each extra percentage point of national income growth increases the average vote share of the candidates from the president's party by over $3/4$ of a percentage point (regression (4)). This is between Kramer's result for congressional candidates (about $1/2$ percent) and Fair's for presidential elections (about 1 percent). A similar calculation for inflation yields an extra $1/3$ point in vote share for each point of deceleration in inflation, about the same as Fair's (insignificant) result for the inflation rate itself. Some idea of the importance of these effects may be gleaned from the data in the last column of table 3.1. The standard deviations of the growth and inflation variables are both around $2 1/4$ percent. So, a simultaneous swing from 1 standard deviation below to 1 standard deviation above the mean of these variables would add about 5 points to the average vote share of party confreres of the president. Many election outcomes will survive such a swing, given the large standard deviation of the incumbent party share. However, about half these shares lie between 45 and 55 percent, where performance swings could conceivably make a difference. By comparison, it takes very large tax increases—about at the maximum of the revenue growth variable in my sample—to cost the incumbent party 5 vote share points.

Finally, it is worth asking what is gained from the extra detail provided by local election returns. Those of my results which can be compared with

---

12. In fact, preliminary results imply that there is little to choose statistically between one- and two-year performance measures.

past analyses of aggregate time-series are not spectacularly different or stronger. So the answer has to focus on refinements. For example, my results deepen the puzzle about voters' myopia by showing that it is national rather than local income that counts; voters are not merely turning the rascals out when their last paycheck is reduced. Neither this nor the added puzzle of the asymmetry between challengers and defenders could plausibly have been revealed by the less detailed data. If we lack a theory capable of rationalizing such puzzles, the larger sample at least provides the flexibility to delineate them more precisely.

REFERENCES

Abrams, Burton and Settle, Russell, "The Economic Theory of Regulation and Public Financing of Presidential Elections," *Journal of Political Economy,* April 1978, *86,* 245–57.

Bloom, Howard and Price, H. Douglas, "Voter Response to Short Run Economic Conditions: The Asymmetric Effect of Prosperity and Recession," *American Political Science Review,* December 1975, *69,* 1240–54.

Fair, Ray, "The Effect of Economic Events on Votes for President," *Review of Economics and Statistics,* May 1978, *60,* 159–73.

Goodman, Saul and Kramer, Gerald, "Comment on Arcelus and Meltzer," *American Political Science Review,* December 1975, *69,* 1255–65.

Kramer, Gerald H., "Short Term Fluctuations in U.S. Voting Behavior, 1896–1914," *American Political Science Review,* March 1971, *65,* 131–43.

Meltzer, Allan and Vellrath, Mark, "The Effects of Economic Policies on the Vote for the President," *Journal of Law and Economics,* December 1975, *18,* 781–98.

Scammon, Richard and McGillivray, Alice, *America Votes,* Washington: Elections Research Center Congressional Quarterly, various issues.

Stigler, George, "General Economic Conditions and National Elections," *American Economic Review Proceedings,* May 1973, *63,* 160–67.

U.S. Bureau of the Census, *Statistical Abstract of the United States,* Washington, various issues.

U.S. Council of Economic Advisers, *Economic Report of the President,* Washington, various issues.

How Efficient Is the Voting Market?

It is by now well established that good macroeconomic conditions benefit the incumbent president and his congressional party confreres at the polls. This result is not unanimous (see, for example, Stigler[1] or Arcelus and Meltzer[2]) and may not be universal.[3] However, the basic results in Kramer,[4] the progenitor of the modern literature on the effect of economic conditions on elections, seem to have stood the test of time. The broad consensus of this literature is that voters in presidential and congressional elections (1) reward income growth and punish unemployment and inflation, (2) probably give greater weight to income growth than to unemployment and inflation, and (3) myopically ignore any information beyond the recent past, say, prior to the election year.[5] So far, however, the data have outrun interpretation. While economic conditions seem to matter, we do not know why they matter or how plausibly to characterize the process by which voters translate information about economic conditions into voting decisions. This article tries to fill that gap. Though it extends the empirical literature to gubernatorial elections, its main concern is evaluative: do voters correctly use economic information in voting decisions?

First published in *Journal of Law and Economics* 33 (April 1990): 27–63. © 1990 by The University of Chicago.

I want to thank David Barker and Michael Ward for research assistance, Kevin M. Murphy for comments, and the Center for the Study of the Economy and State of the University of Chicago for financial support from grants from the Lynde and Harry Bradley Foundation and the Sarah Scaife Foundation.

1. George Stigler, General Economic Conditions and National Elections, 63 Am. Econ. Rev. 160 (1973).

2. Francisco Arcelus & Allan Meltzer, The Effects of Aggregate Economic Variables on Congressional Elections, 69 Am. Pol. Sci. Rev. 1232 (1975).

3. See, for example, the international studies in Models of Political Economy (Paul Whitely ed. 1980), which divide roughly 50–50 on the issue of whether electoral outcomes are significantly affected by economic conditions.

4. Gerald Kramer, Short Term Fluctuations in U.S. Voting Behavior, 1896–1914, 65 Am. Pol. Sci. Rev. 131 (1971).

5. See the survey in Kristen Monroe, Econometric Analysis of Political Behavior: A Critical Survey, 1 Pol. Behav. 137 (1979), for some details on these results.

This question presumes a standard against which voting behavior can be judged. However, the empirical literature has so far largely evaded discussion of what that standard should be. The model implicit in this literature is one of a self-interested voter in a principal-agent relationship with the party in power. This voter settles with his or her agent—the president—ex post for much the same reason that, say, an owner compensates a manager based on past performance. It is too costly to evaluate directly the agent's actions or their implications for the principal's welfare. This analogy falters, and the theoretical lacuna emerges, over the issue of how much information the voter ought to bring to bear on his decision. Since ownership can be concentrated, owners have a plausible wealth stake in correctly processing information on their agent's performance. Voters have no such stake because a vote is costly and the likelihood that one vote will alter the election is vanishingly small. This formulation, due to Downs,[6] has two implications. One is the still unresolved "paradox of not voting" (that is, a rational actor should not vote because there are no benefits). The other is the less stringent notion that voters should be ill informed: if they are foolish to vote in the first place, they should not waste (too many) more resources informing themselves about candidates. On this view, even the most whimsical use of information is "correct."

This "rational ignorance" story has implicitly or explicitly conditioned the theoretical and empirical literature on the connection between voting and the economy. The most notable example is the "political business cycle" literature[7] in which politicians exploit the voters' short memories by stimulating the economy in the election year and dealing with any inflationary consequences later. However, the empirical basis of this theory is surprisingly weak. For example, Kristen Monroe's survey finds that the voters' time horizon is "not discussed explicitly in detail in the literature. Most of the literature assumes that voters maximize short-term interests."[8] This assumption is typically implemented by regressing the incumbent's share of the vote on a short list of macroeconomic variables measured over the year prior to election. Since voters cannot be presumed to know very much, not much attention is paid to prior specification of these variables. Anything plausibly related to how well off the voters feel in the

---

6. Anthony Downs, An Economic Theory of Democracy (New York: Harper & Row, 1957).

7. See, for example, William Nordhaus, The Political Business Cycle, 42 Rev. Econ. Stud. 169 (1975).

8. See Monroe, *supra* note 5, at 162.

recent past will do.[9] So the common procedure has been limited to showing that some more or less arbitrary transformations of income-output or
inflation measures[10] are correlated with the election outcome in plausible
directions.

Such results do not, of course, "test" rational ignorance. They merely
say that voters (1) value an informed vote (contrary to the most extreme
version of the Downsian model), (2) process some macrodata, and (3) use
the data in paying off the agent whom they hold responsible—the president. However, the fact that voters use some information about the economy in settling with their agent does not answer the question, How much
information do they use? This is the question I try to answer. If this inquiry
were about the stock market or the managerial labor market rather than
the voting market, the obvious standard for the answer would be the "fully
informed" (marginal) principal whose actions cause the market to fully
reflect publicly available information. Given what is already known about
the voting market, it seems premature to rule this out a priori. So, I will try
to discover how close the settling up process in the voting market comes to
full utilization of available information. And it turns out that the voting
market is a surprisingly good aggregator of such information.

The notion that the voting market might use information more efficiently than the empirical literature or the rational ignorance story allows
is not altogether new. For example, George Stigler's critique of the relevance of short-run income growth is couched in terms of voters who can
distinguish permanent from transitory effects.[11] He argues that, because
neither party can push the economy permanently off its long-run growth
path, voters rationally concerned with permanent wealth would not reward or punish short-run deviations from this path. Similarly, Michaels
criticizes the unquestioning use of inflation measures without any attention to the link between inflation and voters' welfare.[12] These are, however,
exceptions that have so far not much altered empirical practice. In the next
section, I spell out how a self-interested voter would process the available
economic information to evaluate correctly the policy of his political
agent. Subsequent sections apply the resulting algorithm, in a variety of

    9. See, for example, Morris Fiorina, Retrospective Voting in American National Elec-
tions (1981).
    10. For example, Kramer, *supra* note 4, uses the change in unemployment, while the
level of unemployment is used in Saul Goodman & Gerald Kramer, Comment on Arcelus
and Meltzer, 69 Am. Pol. Sci. Rev. 1255 (1975).
    11. Stigler, *supra* note 1.
    12. Robert Michaels, Reinterpreting the Role of Inflation in Politico-economic Models,
48 Pub. Choice 113 (1986).

tests, to state-level election returns for presidential, senatorial, and gubernatorial elections from 1950–88—that is, the post–Full Employment Act period when a connection between policy and the macroeconomy is plausible.[13] This use of cross-sectional detail from three types of elections enables me to get at theoretical nuances that might otherwise be hidden in the aggregate data commonly used in the empirical literature.[14] But the main result is that the voting market uses information efficiently. It makes essentially every distinction suggested by economic theory (for example, between permanent and transitory income, expected and unexpected inflation), and it does not discard relevant information from early in a president's term.

I. How Should Voters Respond to Economic Information?

Many voters, probably a majority, will choose to ignore information about the macroeconomy. They are, whether by tradition or careful evaluation of candidates and party platforms, so committed to one party that economic fluctuations of the sort I will analyze will not change their vote. Accordingly, I will focus on the "marginal voter." This voter is, on other grounds, essentially indifferent between the two parties and uses macroeconomic information to choose between them. To get on with the analysis, I assume that he chooses as if he were a rational principal (say, an owner) settling with his agent (say, a manager) on the basis of all the information available to him about the agent's performance.

The way in which this voter uses information can be summarized in three by-now-familiar propositions:

1. The agent is rewarded only for permanent improvements in the voter's welfare. This is a defining characteristic of the rational principal. Operationally, it means that a voter would not reward a policy that increases welfare prior to an election but will predictably reduce it by an offsetting amount after the election. It also means that permanent changes in welfare that occur early in the agent's tenure are not ignored. Both implications are, of course, contrary to the story told by the political business-cycle literature.

2. Only new information affects the marginal voter's decision. Consider

13. An obvious extension of my results would be to test the implicit hypothesis that the connection between voting and the macroeconomy was different in, say, the pre-Federal Reserve, gold standard era.

14. For example, I am able to distinguish the effects of changes in voters' income from changes in national income.

the preceding example, where a boom just before an election at $t = 0$ does not buy votes because it is predictably followed by a bust after $t = 0$. With respect to the next election at $t = 4$, this post $t = 0$ bust is "old news" that should not affect the vote at $t = 4$. It was, by assumption, fully known at $t = 0$ and "capitalized" into the vote on that date (by neutralizing the previous boom). Since all information up to $t = 0$ has already been used to settle with the agent, the next settlement will be based on what is learned subsequently. Operationally, this implies that the voting market, like the stock market, should have no "memory."

This analogy to the memory-free stock market requires a caveat. Principals sometimes use old information deliberately, for strategic purposes, in settling ex post with an agent. A familiar example is an experience-rated insurance contract. Here the threat that future premiums will rise if there is an accident today is meant, in part, to attenuate the usual moral hazard of insurance. There is, in principle, room for strategic use of old information in the voting market. For example, a voter might like to penalize exceptionally bad policy with two votes against the incumbent rather than just one. This can be done directly (and honestly) only by delivering the negative votes sequentially, at $t = 4$ and $t = 8$. In this example, the $t = 8$ vote would use old (pre $t = 4$) information.

There are, however, at least two forces opposing the strategic use of old information in voting markets. One is the absence of any mechanism for the voter to credibly precommit to future votes. The other, more important,[15] is ambiguity about who the agent is. The previous empirical literature implies that both the president and his party are treated as macropolicy agents. My subsequent results are consistent with this. At first glance, this may not appear sensible. Why should voters reward or punish individual congressmen or governors if the only office whose policies have a credible link to the performance of the macroeconomy is the presidency? Voting for the party does make sense, however, if voters wish to provide incentives for parties to pick "good" presidential candidates and replace "bad" ones. And this aspect of voting reduces the scope for the voter's strategic use of old information. In the example where the voter is confronted by especially bad policies in the $t = 0$ to $t = 4$ interval, the voter will want to penalize those policies at $t = 4$ but not precommit against that party's candidate at $t = 8$. To do so would reduce the party's incentive to find a better candidate at $t = 8$.

---

15. The effect on an incumbent's behavior of his belief that voters have very long memories will be similar to that of a binding precommitment.

In the empirical work, I allow for the possibility that marginal voters use old information (for example, pre $t = 4$ information at $t = 8$). But the only result that would be unambiguously consistent both with rational use of information and the finding that parties as well as presidents are agents would be that old information is ignored. As long as there is sufficient competition between parties, the marginal voter cannot assume that one party will pick better or worse candidates in the future because it has done so in the past. Each election is, in this sense, a new ball game.

3. Information that cannot plausibly be related to the agent's policy is ignored. Ex post settling up with a principal is based on outcomes because it is hard for the agent to observe the policy directly. Thus, for example, owners award bonuses to managers based on, say, profits rather than a direct evaluation of the manager's day-to-day decisions. But the owner could reasonably adjust the bonus to take account of industrywide fluctuations in demand or costs. So, no bonus would be paid if, for example, profits are high only because of an industrywide boom beyond the manager's control. The marginal voter faces a similar problem of separating the informational wheat from the chaff. He observes the change in his welfare since the last election, but some of it (as when he strikes oil or drills a dry well) is unrelated to the incumbent's policy. Full use of the available information requires not punishing or rewarding the incumbent for these policy-irrelevant changes in his welfare.

There is a link between the information-processing strategy just described and the time-series properties of macroeconomic data that should be spelled out because I use it in the empirical work. If voters fully process relevant information, it should be the post $t = 0$ innovations in the data that affect the current election (at $t = 4$), because the components of the post $t = 0$ data that could be forecast conditional on $t = 0$ information should have been reflected in the last election. Similarly, post $t = 4$ changes that can be forecast from post $t = 0$ data will affect the current election. To illustrate, recall Stigler's argument for the irrelevance of post $t = 0$ income changes. It implies a time-series model in which any deviation of income from a fixed trend is only temporary. If this is the correct time-series model, the voter's best estimate of the effect of any off-trend income fluctuation on his permanent welfare is essentially zero. Accordingly, such fluctuations provide no useful new information and should be ignored. Suppose, however, that changes in income follow a random walk with drift. Then every income change (less the drift) after $t = 0$ is fully reflected in a revision of the lifetime value of wealth. The voter using income information to settle up with his agent would then rationally reward the agent for all post $t = 0$ income changes. As it happens, the random walk with drift model seems a tolerably good characterization of real income changes.[16] So there is a rational basis for the finding that income changes affect election outcomes.

Because of their central importance in the empirical literature, most of my empirical work focuses on the roles of income and inflation. Since income changes are approximately a random walk, with constant expected growth, empirically separating the effect of the expected component of income from the "surprise" component is impossible. Accordingly, with respect to income, my main focus will be on the voters' time horizon: if all income changes after $t = 0$ contain new information about lifetime wealth, all the changes, not just the most recent, should matter. The permanent income hypothesis provides a possible extension. If permanent and transitory income changes can be empirically disentangled, only the former should matter. I test this conjecture.

I will also use income data to test the proposition that voters ignore policy-irrelevant changes in welfare. This test will be based on a presumption that the main effect of economic policy is on aggregate income rather than its distribution. If that is correct, voters will reward or punish fluctuations in national income and ignore (weigh less) their personal deviations from the aggregate change.

In the case of inflation, it will be possible to see if voters respond only to new information. Conventional wisdom among economists is that if inflation is bad (see Section III), the evil resides mainly in unexpected inflation. Because nominal contracts should reflect any expected inflation, the allocation of wealth and resources should be approximately the same at any expected inflation rate.[17] This would imply that sensible voters respond only to the inflation surprises during a president's term and ignore the expected component of inflation. For example, they would reward high but unexpectedly falling inflation and penalize low but rising inflation. Indeed, sensible voters would ignore expected inflation even if it is costly.

16. See Charles Nelson & Charles Plosser, Trends and Random Walks in Macroeconomic Time Series: Some Evidence and Implications, 10 J. Monetary Econ. 139 (1982). A partial dissent to this view is John Cochrane, How Big Is the Random Walk in GNP? 96 J. Pol. Econ. 893 (1988).

17. There is a "menu cost" to positive expected inflation—prices have to be changed periodically—and a deadweight loss in the allocation of assets between noninterest-bearing money and interest-bearing assets. For a dissent, based on the latter cost, to the view that expected inflation is harmless, see Martin Feldstein, The Welfare Cost of Permanent Inflation and Optimal Short Run Economic Policy, 87 J. Pol. Econ. 749 (1979).

One reason that there is a substantial expected component in inflation lies in the unwillingness of either party to adopt policies that would markedly change inflation rates quickly. A voter who understands this reality of political competition would not penalize the incumbent for any costs of persistent inflation because the other party would have imposed them also.

Expected inflation, unlike expected income growth, has not plausibly remained fixed over time. Average inflation rates in the 1970s, for example, were much higher than in the 1950s. This time variation in expected inflation makes it possible to test the proposition that voters do not respond to the expected inflation.

To summarize, I want to see if voters act as if they correctly process available economic information. This means that they ignore information irrelevant to their long-run welfare or to the policy of their agent and that they use all the relevant information. Each step in the empirical analysis entails operationalizing these notions. In common with much of the principal-agent literature, I assume that voters use information on policy outputs (income and inflation) rather than inputs (money supply, budget deficits). That is, I do not presume that voters have done better than economists at estimating a policy production function that can ferret out the policy-related component of the output.

II. How Do Voters Respond to Economic Information?

To make the preceding discussion concrete and capable of confronting data, begin with the relation

$$(1) \quad IS_{iT} = K_i + f(W_{i0T}),$$

where

IS_{iT} = incumbent party's share of the vote in jurisdiction i in an election on date T;

K_i = the party's normal share of the vote in i; recall that voters with sufficiently strong party preferences will not change their vote in light of new information; here I am allowing for differences across jurisdictions in the strength of these party preferences;

W_{i0T} = that change in voter welfare since the last election ($t = 0$) that the voters use to evaluate the incumbent (for subsequent simplicity, I drop subscripts except where necessary); and

$f(\cdot)$ = a function converting W into the marginal voters' vote,
$\quad f' > 0.$[18]

I assume that competitive adjustments of party policies and population turnover is sufficient to make K a constant. This seems a good approximation at the aggregate level for presidential elections, where there is no obvious trend in party shares.[19] So, in each election there is a roughly equal-sized coterie of marginal voters who will move according to their estimate of W.

My analysis focuses on the kind of information voters use to estimate W. In general, let

(2) $W = g(X, Z)$.

Think of X and Z as vectors, where
$\quad X$ = new information (revealed since $t = 0$) that permanently affects the voters' welfare and is plausibly related to the incumbent's policy; and
$\quad Z$ = all other new information about voter welfare; in principle this could include temporary changes in welfare, policy-irrelevant changes, and so on (it could also include noneconomic components, but, for reasons of specialization, I mainly ignore these).

The "strong form" of the efficient-voting-market story would be that only the X, and all of the X, belong in $g(\cdot)$. Downsian rational ignorance would suggest that some of the elements of X are ignored and some of the Z are used. For example, consider a simple case where both X and Z contain only income information and the effect of the incumbent's policy is summarized by the change in national income since the last election. If voters react only to the last few months of national income information, they would be ignoring part of the relevant information set (X). If they reward the incumbent when they have struck oil, they would be (mis)using irrelevant information (some of the Z).

Another way in which voters could sloppily (or, perhaps, strategically)

---

18. Continuity is assumed here because there is no sharp dividing line between marginal voters and others. The voter who is literally indifferent between the parties and rewards or punishes the incumbent for the slightest W is rare. Instead, voters have varying degrees of attachment to a party that can, in principle, be overcome depending on the size of W. So larger values of W cause more votes to shift. The marginal voter, in this sense, is one who can be shifted if W is in the range of experience.

19. However, at the state level, a constant K may be less plausible. For example, the weakening of the Democrats in the South and the Republicans in the Northeast might imply some trend in K for those areas. For simplicity, I ignore this possibility.

process information would be to sluggishly revise W in light of the new information. To allow for this, generalize (2) further as

(3) $W_{0T} = (1 - q) \, g(\cdot) + q W_{-T0}$,

where

q = an adjustment coefficient, $0 \le q \le 1$, and

W_{-T0} = welfare change due to information revealed in the prior election period (that is, beginning T years before $t = 0$).

If voters use only new information, $q = 0$. A linear version of (1) that incorporates (3) is

(4) $\text{IS}_T = K(1 - q) + m(1 - q) \, g(\cdot) + q \cdot \text{IS}_0$,

where a constant, m, replaces $f(\cdot)$ in (1). In this formulation, the effect of old information is summarized by IS_0. For example, suppose the current incumbent had won at $t = -T$ and performed well, so $\text{IS}_0 > K$. If that information is still being used at $t = T$ (so $q > 0$), then IS_T is also greater than K, ceteris paribus. Estimates of (4) thus will provide two tests of voting market efficiency. The primary test will be whether this market distinguishes the relevant (X) information from the irrelevant (Z). A secondary (because of the previously noted theoretical ambiguity about the role of old information) test is for $q = 0$.[20] An interesting feature of (4) is that, to the extent that only information surprises since $t = 0$ matter, IS will be a random walk around the level of K. That is, changes in IS will not be permanent.[21]

To provide a point of reference, I first estimate (4) by imposing sensible behavior. That is, I estimate surprise elements of real income and inflation and include only these X in $g(\cdot)$. The primary focus here is on the voters' alleged myopia: do voters react to all of the relevant information or just

20. Also, any trends in K can show up as an estimated $q > 0$. In addition, if IS_0 measures the effect of old information with error, estimates of q will tend to be biased toward $q = 0$.

21. This means that *changes* in IS would *not* follow a random walk. If they did, the effectiveness of ex post settling up in inducing good policies would be diluted. To see why, consider the example of an initial election with $K = \frac{1}{2}$. Suppose party A randomly wins and then adopts good policies summarized by $\overline{W} > 0$, so it receives $\Delta \text{IS} > 0$ and is reelected. A random walk in ΔIS would then imply a permanent increase in the expected value of IS. This means that party A will then win every subsequent election, even if it produces a string of negative W, as long as they sum to less than $|\overline{W}|$. To avoid such an incentive to mediocrity, the agent's bonus (deviation from K) should be based on each period's performance. This is another way of saying that, so long as neither party has a monopoly of competence ex ante ($E(W) = 0$ for either party, where E is the expected value), the role of ex post settling up is to give each party the incentive continually to select its best candidate. This is best done by not permanently rewarding or punishing the success or failure of past candidates.

the most recent components? I use two alternative estimates of income and inflation surprises. The first (denoted STAT) uses the statistical properties of the relevant time series. Since it is hard to distinguish the series from a random walk, the monthly change in the log of real per capita income (DPCI) is the STAT estimate of the income surprise. For the corresponding inflation surprise, I take account of the tendency for inflation rates to change slowly. I do so by regressing the monthly inflation rate on its past value over each of the last thirty-six months. Then the coefficients of this autoregression are used to generate month-ahead forecasts; these represent expected inflation. The STAT estimate of unexpected inflation (denoted AR) is just the difference between the actual inflation rate and the rate forecast by the autoregression.[22]

The second set of estimated income and inflation surprises (denoted ECON) uses economic theory. For income, I use Robert Hall's elaboration of the permanent-income hypothesis.[23] In essence, if consumption is proportional to lifetime permanent income, all the information consumers (voters) have about their permanent-income streams up to the current period should be revealed by last period's consumption. If so, Hall argues, the residuals from a regression of current real per capita consumption on last period's value should be "white noise" and yield an estimate of this period's permanent income surprise. I ran such a regression[24] and used the residuals (denoted CON) as an estimate of the permanent income surprise for each quarter.[25]

The ECON estimate of unexpected inflation uses Eugene Fama and Michael Gibbons's implementation of Irving Fisher's decomposition of the nominal interest rate into an expected real return and an expected inflation rate.[26] In essence, Fama and Gibbons (and I) first generate a month-ahead estimate of the expected real return from a time-series model of past actual real returns and deduct these estimates from the current

22. In preliminary work, I experimented with inflation forecast periods greater than a month. For example, I used the autoregression to estimate expected inflation a year ahead from information available at the start of the year. However, the results reported subsequently were insensitive to the choice of forecast period.

23. Robert Hall, Stochastic Implications of the Life Cycle-Permanent Income Hypothesis, 86 J. Pol. Econ. 971 (1978).

24. In logs, rather than dollars, as Hall did, to preserve constant variance of the residuals. Since consumption has drifted upward, the variance of the residual from the dollar regression tends to increase over time. I followed Hall in deducting purchases of durables from total consumption. The motive for this is the large savings element in durable purchases.

25. Consumption data are unavailable more frequently.

26. Eugene Fama & Michael Gibbons, A Comparison of Inflation Forecasts, 13 J. Monetary Econ. 327 (1984).

one-month Treasury-bill rate to generate an expected inflation rate for the next month. The ECON estimate of unexpected inflation (denoted TBIL) is just the difference between actual inflation and the expected rate implicit in the bill rate.

In evaluating subsequent results, some facts about these alternative surprise estimates should be kept in mind.

1. All of them have the desirable property of looking like white noise.[27] That is, they represent new information at least to the extent that they are not predictable from past behavior of these series.

2. The variances of the AR and TBIL estimates of unexpected inflation are about the same. This means that neither model of inflation plausibly captures more of the information voters might be using to form inflation expectations.

3. Both models surely overstate this information. The inflation autoregressions and the regressions used to extract expected inflation from Treasury-bill rates are based on data series ending in the 1980s. The structure of such regressions is unknowable to the voters of, say, the 1950s. So the unexpected inflation estimates have to be treated as noisy proxies for the information potentially available to voters.[28]

4. It is unsurprising that, of the two income-surprise estimates, the consumption-based estimate is less variable.[29] This just restates a stylized fact that motivated the permanent-income hypothesis. If that story is correct, the extra variability in income changes represents economically (politically?) irrelevant noise. I will test this, but it will be more a test of the applicability of the permanent-income story than a strong test of voter rationality. There are, after all, arguments to be made for the relevance of the "noise" in income changes,[30] and it is beyond the scope of this study to evaluate them.

These facts and caveats understood, I use the estimates of inflation and income surprises to address questions about the information voters use.

27. That is, their autocorrelation functions pass a test for "white noise" series from G. E. P. Box & David Pierce, Distributions of Residual Autocorrelations in Autoregressive-integrated Moving Average Time Series Models, 65 J. Am. Stat. Assn. 1509 (1970).

28. A similar caveat applies to the residuals from the consumption autoregression. However, these residuals essentially duplicate the percentage changes in the consumption variable. So a 1950 voter who can calculate a percentage change knows about as much about Hall's algorithm as the 1988 voter.

29. The standard deviation of the annual change in per capita personal income is around $2\frac{1}{2}$ percent compared with less than $1\frac{1}{2}$ percent for the consumption residual.

30. For example, consumers may view all of a large change in income as permanent but face costs of rapid adjustment to it.

A. Are Voters Myopic?

To answer this and subsequent questions I estimate regressions of the general form

(5) $IS = A + B_1 X^j_{INC,LAG_t} + B_2 \cdot X^j_{INF,LAG_t} + \dots,$

where

    IS = incumbent party's share of the total vote in a state in some election; and

    X^j = the sum of monthly income or inflation surprises of type j (j = STAT, ECON), converted to an annual rate, over the t months (or quarters) preceding election day.

The ellipses denote "other variables," which include (a) IS_0, the incumbent party's share in the previous election; (b) a vector of dummy variables that allow for different values of K, the normal probability of voting for the incumbent party, across states; operationally, K is the incumbent party's long-run average share in a state,[31] (c) a dummy = +1 if the candidate is an incumbent; this is extraneous to my inquiry but adjusts for well-known advantages of incumbency; and (d) where appropriate, dummies to shift the intercept and sign of X when the incumbent party is not the same as the president's (see below).

For any kind of election, I estimate a set of regressions in which t is varied, by three-month increments, from three to as many as forty-eight months prior to an election. Thus, there are sixteen regressions in each set. The first regression uses data only from the three months prior to election day, the second uses the past six months' data, and the sixteenth uses the past four years' data. This generates a set of regression coefficients (the B's), each of which is an estimate of the sum of the relevant distributed lag weights from t to election day. The change in B from any t to $t + 3$ is an estimate of the marginal weight voters attach to the X in that three-month interval.[32] Thus, if voters are myopic, the B's will peak (or bottom)

---

31. Specifically, let IP = +1 if the incumbent is Republican, −1 if Democrat, and S_i = +1 for elections in state i, 0 otherwise. I include IP and all but one IP · S_i in every regression. The coefficient of IP · S_i is, then, half the long-run difference between Republican and Democrat shares in that state (as a deviation from the excluded state).

32. To see this, assume that the dependent variable, y, is generated by

(a) $y = \sum_{i=1}^{t} b_i X_i + \epsilon,$

at a small t and tend to remain there as t is increased. This procedure is repeated for each type (STAT or ECON) of X.

This procedure is clumsier than estimating a full distributed lag on the lagged macrovariables. But it is necessitated by the data. There are only about twenty independent observations on the macrodata for senatorial and gubernatorial elections, and half that for presidential elections. Thus, there are too few effective degrees of freedom to estimate the full lag structure directly.

---

where
X = economic variable (at an annual rate);
i = periods preceding the election; and
ε = random error.

Without loss of generality, assume $\Sigma b_i = 1$, variance of all X_i are equal ($= V$), and $\overline{X}_i = 0$ for all i. I will estimate

(b)
$$y = BZ + u,$$

where

$$Z = \frac{1}{T} \sum_i^T X_i \, ,$$

that is, a T-period average of the X_i. So the estimated B is

(c)
$$\hat{B} = \frac{E(Zy)}{E(Z^2)}.$$

The denominator of (c) is

(d)
$$E(Z^2) = \frac{1}{T^2}(T \cdot V) = \frac{V}{T} \, ,$$

and the numerator is

(e)
$$E(Zy) = \frac{1}{T} \sum_i^T X_i \left(\sum_i^i b_i X_i + \varepsilon \right).$$

If T happens to be chosen correctly ($= t$), then (e) is

(e1)
$$E(Zy) = \left(\sum b_i \right) \cdot V, \quad \text{and} \quad \hat{B} = \sum_i b_i = 1.$$

If $T > t$, that is, extraneous values of X_i are included in Z, then (e) is

(e2)
$$\text{(e2)} = \text{(e1)} + \text{covariance terms involving the } X_i \text{ for } i > t,$$

and the X_i for $i < t$. If these covariance terms are zero (as they would be if the X_i are white noise), (e2) = (e1). If $T < t$, that is, the lag is too short, we have

(e3)
$$E(Zy) = \frac{1}{T} \left(\sum^T b_i \right) \cdot V, \quad \text{and} \quad \hat{B} = \sum^T b_i < 1.$$

That is, B is the sum of weights up to $T < t$, and each unit increment of T increases $\hat{B}$ by the b_i for $i = T + 1$.

I estimate (5) for three time series of cross sections of state election returns: one for presidential elections, another for senatorial elections, and the third for gubernatorial elections. These comprise most contested elections at the state level for 1950–88.[33] Initially, I assume that voters are settling up with the party of the incumbent president. So, for presidential elections, (5) can be applied directly. For senate and gubernatorial elections, because the incumbent party may differ from the president's, I estimate (dropping unnecessary subscripts)

(5′) $IS = A_1 + B(PR \cdot X) + C \cdot PR + ...,$

where $PR = +1$ if the incumbent party is the same as the president's, -1 if different. Thus, B shows the gain to a candidate from the president's party or the loss to an opposition candidate from a unit increase in X, and C is the required change of intercept.[34]

Half the senate elections and a majority of gubernatorial elections occur in nonpresidential election years. These off-year elections raise two conceptual issues about lags on the X greater than two years. One arises when there is a change in administration. For example, consider a Republican senator running in 1982, two years after a Republican president, Reagan, replaced a Democrat, Carter. Do (should) the voters in 1982 use information on Carter's performance before 1980 in settling with Reagan in 1982? Some models allow this possibility.[35] However, the pre-1980 information has already been used in 1980. To use it again in 1982 would weaken the power of the 1982 signal and thereby create bizarre incentives. In such a model, if Reagan's 1980–82 performance is merely less bad than Carter's, 1982 Republican candidates would gain rather than be penalized. The sensible voter can eliminate this incentive to mediocrity by simply ignoring pre-1980 information. The preliminary evidence was consistent

33. I deleted elections with an unopposed candidate. Also, states where the winning party received over 70 percent of the vote at the beginning of the sample period are deleted until the percentage is below 70 for two straight elections. This criterion essentially excludes a few southern states in which the Republican party offered only token opposition for part of the period.

The gubernatorial sample is limited to elections to four-year terms. Two-year terms were more common early in the sample period. This limitation left some states with too few observations to estimate meaningful long-run state party shares for gubernatorial elections. In these cases, the "state" dummy variable was set equal to $+1$ for all elections in two or three contiguous states.

34. Since the regression goes through $(\overline{IS}, \overline{X})$, the intercept has to differ by party as long as $\overline{X} \neq 0$. For example, suppose X is income growth $(\overline{X} > 0)$, and the president is a Republican. A Democrat would do better than a Republican if $X = 0$, so $C < 0$.

35. For example, Ray Fair, The Effects of Economic Events on Votes for President, 60 Rev. Econ. & Stat. 159 (1978).

with this view: I estimated (5') with two alternative constructions for X in off-year elections following a change in administration. The first reversed the sign of any component of X from the tenure of the previous administration. The second constrained the weight on such components to zero. For both senate and gubernatorial elections, and for every relevant lag and type of X, the second alternative fit the data better than the first.[36]

A related issue arises in off-year elections following a victory by the incumbent administration. Should a Republican running in 1986, for example, continue to benefit from the pre-1984 policies that resulted in Reagan's reelection? The previous discussion suggests that 1986 voters would ignore the pre-1984 information. But the evidence is unclear: I estimated (5') both with and without the constraint of a zero weight on the old information for the relevant off-year elections. These two alternatives fit the data about equally well. Subsequent results are arbitrarily based on data imposing the constraint. Thus, for every off-year election, no more than the preceding two years' information is included in the X variables in (5').[37]

The results of immediate interest from estimates of (5) and (5') are in table 4.1. These show the coefficients (total weights) of various lags of the alternative estimates of income and inflation surprises for each type of

---

36. That is, the partial correlation of IS with X for LAG $t > 24$ was consistently greater under the second alternative for X.

37. So, $X_{27}, \ldots, X_{48}$ include information over two years old only for on-year elections. For off-year elections all post $t = 24$ surprises are set equal to zero. This would suggest defining, for example, X_{27} as the sum of all surprises up to $t = 24$ divided by 27. However, dividing by t results in a variable with systematically lower variance in off-year elections. To maintain homoscedasticity, I used a divisor of $\sqrt{24t}$. It can be shown that the resulting coefficients for lags of $t > 24$ in the nonpresidential elections are unbiased estimates of the sum of weights in on-year elections only if the true (sum-of-weights, t/sum of weights, 24) $= \sqrt{t/24}$. A glance at the pattern of coefficients in table 4.1 suggests that this is not a bad approximation. In general, the coefficient shown in table 4.1 for lags over $t = 24$ for nonpresidential elections ($\hat{B}_t$) is related to the true coefficient (B_t) by

$$B_t = s\hat{B}_t + (1 - s)\sqrt{\frac{t}{24}}B_{24},$$

where
$\quad s =$ share of on-year elections in the sample (this is around $\frac{1}{2}$ for senate elections and around $\frac{1}{3}$ for gubernatorial elections), and
$\quad B_{24} =$ sum of weights for $t = 24$.
If $B_t < \sqrt{(t/24)}\, B_{24}$, then $\hat{B}_t$ overstates B_t. In the extreme, where information older than two years is completely ignored ($B_t = B_{24}$), the maximum overstatement, which occurs at $t = 48$, is on the order of 20 (senate) to 30 percent. If $B_t > \sqrt{(t/24)}B_{24}$, then $\hat{B}_t$ understates B_t. For $t = 48$, the understatement would be 15 to 20 percent if information older than two years is just as important as newer information ($B_t/B_{24} = t/24$) in on-year elections.

TABLE 4.1 Income and Inflation Surprises in Voting Regressions, 1950–88 Elections, State Returns

LAG (Months Preceding Election)	Income				Inflation			
	DPCI		CON		AR		TBIL	
	B	|t|	B	|t|	B	|t|	B	|t|
A. Presidential elections, 1952–88 (N = 401):								
3	1.3	17.4	.5	3.5	−7.0	22.4	−3.3	13.5
6	1.7	9.1	.7	5.0	−4.2	8.8	−4.8	11.5
9	1.2	8.7	1.3	7.0	−2.1	3.9	−2.4	3.2
12	2.0	12.0	2.3	10.2	−1.9	3.5	−4.2	5.0
15	1.8	9.7	3.0	11.5	−4.4	5.7	−2.7	2.1
18	1.6	7.1	2.8	10.5	−5.1	6.6	−7.4	7.8
21	2.3	7.8	3.7	10.4	−.1	.2	2.4	3.1
24	2.5	9.6	5.3	13.7	−2.6	3.6	1.2	.9
27	2.0	7.4	5.1	12.4	−3.3	4.3	7.9	6.0
30	1.5	4.3	6.2	12.3	−6.5	8.2	6.7	5.2
33	3.2	10.2	7.4	14.8	−6.5	10.4	−5.1	3.7
36	1.8	6.1	9.3	20.8	−8.6	12.7	−14.0	8.7
39	2.0	7.0	9.4	17.9	−9.2	14.4	−11.2	6.9
42	2.7	7.9	8.2	17.3	−8.6	12.1	−3.2	1.9
45	2.9	8.8	7.8	17.1	−7.9	13.0	−9.3	7.0
48	3.1	10.2	10.5	17.4	−9.7	16.9	−12.6	10.7
B. Senate elections, 1950–88 (N = 566):								
3	.2	2.3	.0	.1	−1.0	2.4	−.6	2.2
6	.1	1.0	.3	1.7	−.8	2.5	−.6	2.4
9	.6	3.5	.8	4.4	−1.1	2.7	−1.1	2.6
12	.4	3.1	1.1	4.5	−2.0	3.9	−2.3	3.6
15	.6	3.8	1.1	3.8	−2.2	4.1	−1.8	2.8
18	.7	3.9	1.3	4.6	−2.3	4.1	−1.8	2.5
21	.7	3.5	1.4	4.4	−1.6	3.3	−.8	1.3
24	.9	3.9	2.2	5.4	−2.4	4.4	−2.6	2.7
27	.8	3.3	2.3	4.9	−2.5	4.4	−1.8	1.8
30	.9	3.0	2.2	4.5	−2.8	4.8	−1.4	1.5
33	1.0	3.2	2.8	5.0	−3.1	5.3	−3.5	3.2
36	.6	2.1	2.9	4.7	−3.2	5.1	−3.3	2.7
39	.7	2.1	2.8	4.2	−3.4	5.2	−3.4	2.8
42	.9	2.6	2.7	4.4	−3.4	5.1	−3.5	2.7
45	.9	2.5	2.6	4.2	−3.3	5.0	−4.1	3.3
48	1.1	2.7	3.3	4.6	−3.6	5.2	−5.2	4.1

TABLE 4.1 *continued*

					Surprise Type			
	Income				Inflation			
LAG (Months	DPCI		CON		AR		TBIL	
Preceding Election)	B	$\|t\|$	B	$\|t\|$	B	$\|t\|$	B	$\|t\|$
C. Gubernatorial elections, 1950–88 ($N = 309$):								
3	.1	1.1	.1	.4	.1	.3	−.3	1.0
6	.0	.2	.2	.7	−.3	.5	−.4	1.1
9	.7	3.2	.8	2.9	−.1	.1	−.8	1.4
12	.4	1.6	.9	2.7	−.9	1.6	−3.0	3.6
15	.5	1.9	.9	2.4	−1.3	2.1	−3.8	4.1
18	.8	2.4	1.2	3.1	−1.6	2.3	−3.7	3.8
21	.9	2.6	1.3	3.1	−1.1	1.8	−2.3	2.5
24	.9	2.8	2.3	4.0	−1.6	2.5	−3.6	3.3
27	1.0	2.8	2.6	4.0	−1.7	2.5	−3.7	3.1
30	1.1	3.0	2.5	3.7	−1.9	2.7	−3.3	2.8
33	1.3	2.6	3.1	4.2	−2.1	2.9	−4.6	3.6
36	1.1	2.7	3.6	4.4	−2.1	2.8	−5.1	3.6
39	1.2	2.8	3.6	4.2	−2.3	3.0	−5.1	3.6
42	1.3	2.8	3.4	4.1	−2.4	3.0	−5.0	3.4
45	1.4	2.8	3.4	4.1	−2.5	3.0	−5.2	3.5
48	1.4	2.9	4.1	4.3	−2.7	3.1	−5.9	3.9

Sources: For the incumbent party's share of the two-party vote (IS): *Congressional Quarterly:* for personal income, consumption, and price index (personal income deflator): *Survey of Current Business.* For Treasury-bill rates: University of Chicago Center for Research in Security Prices.

Note: Estimates of B are from regressions of the form

$$IS_i = A + B_1X_{i1} + B_2X_{i2} + \text{other variables (see text)},$$

where IS_i = incumbent party's share of the two-party vote in state i (percentage points), and X_{ij} = estimated surprise in inflation or income growth over the t months prior to election (percentage points, annual rate). Two alternative concepts are used to estimate X_i (see text for discussion). The resulting income and inflation surprises are

DPCI = change in the log of real per capital income;

AR = difference between actual inflation rate and inflation rate predicted from autoregression of monthly inflation rate on thirty-six past values of this rate;

CON = residual from regression of log of quarterly real per capita consumption minus durables on last quarter's value; and

TBIL = difference between actual inflation rate in month and expected rate implicit in one-month Treasury-bill rate.

The coefficients and $|t|$ ratios are from two alternative sets of regressions. In one set, DPCI and AR are used as income/inflation surprise estimates. In the other, CON and TBIL are the paired surprise estimates.

Each X_i is the sum of monthly (or quarterly) surprises over the t months preceding an election, expressed as an average annual rate of change. For off-year senate and gubernatorial elections, the maximum $t = 24$, so, for example, X_{27} would be the sum of twenty-seven monthly surprises for on-year elections and equals X_{24} for off-year elections (see text for further details).

election. These results are inconsistent with the notion that voters myopically weight only the most recent experience. While the estimated total weights sometimes move erratically and vary across alternative estimates of the same surprise, the peak total weight never occurs before a two-year lag and usually occurs at a four-year lag. This pattern is shown more clearly in table 4.2 and figure 4.1. These are based on smoothed data from table 4.1. The smoothing is done in two ways. One is just to convert the columns of the table to three-term moving averages. The other is to use a maximum-likelihood technique to impose a smoothness criterion directly on the marginal weights.[38] The motive for these adjustments is the implausibility of sharp discontinuities in voters' memories. For ease of presentation, the data in table 4.2 and figure 4.1 are also averaged over types of surprises.[39] The first column of table 4.2 shows a pervasive tendency for the voters' memories to be about as long as possible: essentially all of the macroeconomic information generated during a president's term affects his and his party's electoral fortunes. The rest of table 4.2 shows how the total weight voters place on this information is distributed among the four separate years. Figure 4.1 shows the same information in less summarized form, with inflation weights tilted downward to reflect the fact that they tend to be negative.

As a broad generalization, the total weights grow more or less steadily over the two years preceding election day, increase at a smaller rate in the

38. The technique minimizes a loss function that is a weighted sum of the usual least squares criterion and squared deviations of the marginal weights from piecewise linearity. This latter component of the loss function is

$$L = \Sigma \{[(b_{t-1} + b_{t+1})/2] - b_t\}^2,$$

where the b_t are estimated marginal weights in the model

$$\text{Incumbent Share} = \Sigma b_t X_t,$$

and X_t = income/inflation surprise in a three-month interval, t, with $t = 16$ intervals beginning 3, 6, . . . , 48 months before an election. That is, L expresses the notion that any b_t should not be too different from the average of the preceding and subsequent marginal weight. The loss function that is minimized to obtain the b_t then attaches some weight to L, which can range from zero (no smoothness restriction) to infinity (every marginal weight must be the same).

The technique uses an extra degree of freedom per variable. This may account for the subsequently discussed difficulty in obtaining reliable estimates for the presidential regressions. The results shown in table 4.2 for senate and gubernatorial elections are for a representative weight on L, which fits the data insignificantly worse than an arbitrarily small weight. However, the overall pattern of those results proved similar over a broad range of weights on L. I am indebted to Kevin Murphy for suggesting this approach and for help in adapting the computational algorithm to the problem at hand.

39. See note to table 4.2 for elaboration.

TABLE 4.2 Number of Months before Election to Peak Total Effect and Distribution of Effect over Time: Averages of Surprise Measures

	Month of Peak*	Percent of Peak Effect at Month:			
		12	24	36	45 or 48*
I. Ordinary least squares estimates:					
A. Income:					
All elections	45	39	65	89	100
a) President	45	41	66	89	100
b) Senate	45	44	77	89	100
c) Governor	45	31	63	90	100
B. Inflation:					
All elections	43	39	34	91	97
a) President	39	33	−8	96	91
b) Senate	45	46	52	89	100
c) Governor	45	39	59	90	100
II. Maximum-likelihood estimates:					
A. Income:					
All elections	46	33	63	87	100
a) President	45	16	47	89	96
b) Senate	45	56	90	98	100
c) Governor	48	27	52	75	100
B. Inflation:					
All elections	48	46	71	87	100
a) President	48	60	87	92	100
b) Senate	48	41	59	81	100
c) Governor	48	36	68	88	100

Note: Panel I is based on three-term moving averages of the coefficients in table 4.1. Each moving average is converted to an index with the peak value set equal to 100. Then the two income indexes and the two inflation indexes are averaged. The first column shows the month at which these averaged indexes peak and the percentage of the peak value attained by these indexes at various months preceding elections. The "All elections" data are averages of the figures shown for the types of elections. Panel II is based on a maximum-likelihood estimate of the marginal weights on income/inflation surprises over successive three-month intervals, which imposes a smoothness criterion on these weights (see text for elaboration). The sum of these weights is then treated just like the moving averages in panel I. Each sum-of-weights series is converted to an index (peak = 100), and the two income and inflation indexes are averaged. The data shown summarize these averaged indexes following the format for panel I.

*The maximum month of peak total weight is 45 for panel I because the last value of the three-term moving average is centered on this month. For panel II, the maximum month of peak total weight is 48.

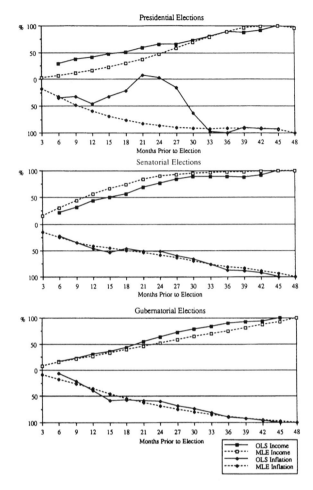

FIGURE 4.1 Total weight on income and inflation surprises over period
preceding election as a percent of peak weight.

third year, and at a still smaller rate in the fourth year. Specifically, the
central tendency is for something like two-thirds of the total weight to be
attained at two years before an election and as much as 90 percent at
three years. While there is some variation around these figures, the broad
tendency for marginal weights to be nontrivial on information from at
least the last three years of an administration's life is pervasive. It holds
for both income and inflation, for all types of elections, and is revealed by
both estimating techniques.

There is one notable exception. It concerns the pattern for inflation surprises in presidential elections. The "bottom line" here is the same as for the other elections: unexpected inflation over the course of a president's term hurts him and his party. But the estimated distribution of this burden is sensitive to the measurement technique, and the ordinary least squares (OLS) estimates are implausibly erratic. The OLS marginal weights tend to be positive going back to two years before election day; they then turn sharply negative in the third year. By contrast, the maximum likelihood estimation (MLE) technique assigns most of the burden to the first two years. There are good technical reasons to discount the MLE results in this case,[40] while the OLS alternative lacks intuitive appeal. In the circumstances, the best way to read the results on inflation in presidential elections is to focus on the broad conclusion to which both estimates point—that unexpected inflation over the last three years of an administration's life is politically costly—and to remain skeptical about further detail.[41]

That broad conclusion illustrates the major message of the data. The voting market is not myopic. It punishes unexpected inflation and rewards income growth over the whole of an administration's tenure, not just in the year or so before an election. If there is any hint of myopia in these data, it is in the typically small weight on information from the first year after election day. But, given the usual policy lags, even this is hardly inconsistent with correct processing of all the relevant information.

Two other features of table 4.1 deserve mention:

1. There is not much doubt about the statistical significance of the results just summarized, given the t-ratios of the relevant coefficients. These are especially large for presidential elections, possibly too large. The

40. Unlike the nonpresidential MLE regressions, there is substantial and significant loss of fit for minor increases in the weight on the smoothness criterion. For this reason, the MLE results for presidential elections in table 4.2 and figure 4.1 use an arbitrarily small weight (1/16 that for the nonpresidential regressions).

A glance at table 4.1 and figure 4.1 will reveal why the fit of the nonpresidential MLE regression is not sensitive to the degree of smoothness imposed on the marginal weights. The OLS weights do not show the kind of discontinuities found for inflation in the presidential elections. So the difference between the pattern of unconstrained and smoothed weights is bound to be small.

41. The need for skepticism here may be a price paid for the lack of effective degrees of freedom. My sample spans ten presidential elections, which gives ten separate observations on the macrodata. In addition to the two macrovariables, each regression includes an incumbency dummy and a presidential party dummy that vary over time but not cross-sectionally. So, with an intercept, there are five effective degrees of freedom for estimating effects of the time-varying variables, or only about one-third those available for senate and gubernatorial elections. In addition, the MLE technique costs two more degrees of freedom, one for each macrovariable.

OLS procedure assumes that each observation is independent, and this may be incorrect. Some years may be particularly "good" for one party or the other in the sense that forces not in the regression model tend to produce positive OLS residuals for the party's candidates in most states. It is unclear a priori which way such dependence across states biases the standard errors.[42] So I reestimated a few of the presidential regressions via a generalized least squares procedure. In every case, the estimated coefficients were virtually the same as in table 4.1, and the t-ratios were actually higher.[43] The proximate reason for the large t-ratios in the presidential regressions is the larger effect of the economic variables here than in the other elections: the relevant coefficients are on the order of two or three times as large. If the president is the voters' primary agent for economic policy, this distribution of punishments and rewards is sensible.[44]

2. The t-ratios in table 4.1 hint that permanent-income surprises (as measured by CON) tend to be politically more relevant than actual-income surprises (DPCI). This hint is pursued in the next section. Of the two inflation surprise estimates, the AR version tends to outscore the TBIL version, but not decisively.[45]

B. Expected Inflation and Transitory Income

If voters efficiently processed information, they would ignore expected inflation and temporary income changes because these are irrelevant to their

42. In this case, there are fewer effective degrees of freedom that assumed in the OLS procedure because each state's residual is not an independent draw. This consideration implies that the OLS standard errors are too small. However, the information about the cross-state correlation of errors can also be used to reduce remaining residual variance, but OLS discards this information. On this ground, OLS standard errors are too large. The problem of correlated residuals is less important for senate and gubernatorial elections since the incumbent party differs across states in any year.

43. The procedure allows for first-order autocorrelation in each state's time series of residuals as well as correlation of residuals across states. Because the procedure is computationally expensive, I selected four lags—12, 24, 36, and 48 months—and reestimated one of the regressions at each lag.

44. These differences may partly reflect higher participation rates in presidential election years, with those on the margin of participation more sensitive to economic conditions than regular participants. If so, the coefficients for senate and gubernatorial elections should also be larger in on-year elections. I tested this by interacting the economic variables with an on-year dummy for those elections. In general, the on-year coefficients tended to be significantly larger only for senate elections and more so for inflation than income. They did not, however, approach the magnitudes of the presidential election coefficients.

45. This does not mean that voters are discarding valuable information implicit in Treasury-bill rates. Recall that both the AR and TBIL estimates predict actual inflation about as well. Also, both are based on naive statistical models that may exclude information

permanent welfare. This can be tested with a linear version of equation (2): let any economic variable to which voters actually respond be

(6) $W = X + m \cdot Z,$

where

X = component to which voters "should" respond (unexpected inflation, permanent income).

Z = the supposedly irrelevant component (expected inflation, temporary income).

m = weight voters place on Z in arriving at W.

So, if $m = 0$, only the "right" variable would matter. If $m = 1$, voters would not be making the appropriate distinctions: only current inflation and actual income growth would matter. So far, I have constrained $m = 0$ by including only X in the regressions. But if (6) is substituted into, for example, (5), we have:

(7) $IS = A + B(X + mZ) = A + BX + BmZ.$

Thus, m can be recovered by adding Z to the regressions in table 4.1 and dividing its coefficient by that of X.

It is easier to implement this scheme for inflation than for income. I have two reasonably unambiguous estimates of expected inflation (AR and TBIL) that were the essential ingredients in my unexpected inflation estimates. Panel A of table 4.3 shows the values of m when these expected inflation estimates are added to the appropriate table 4.1 regressions. The only easily available proxy for temporary income comes from Hall's implementation of the permanent-income hypothesis. It is simply the difference between actual income growth and the CON estimate of the surprise in permanent income.[46] I added this proxy to the table 4.1 regressions, though the earlier caveat about the ambiguity in interpreting it needs to be recalled. The resulting values of m are summarized in panel B of table 4.3. All results in the table are shown for lags of two years and over since

---

used to estimate expected inflation. The AR model uses only past inflation to predict future inflation, and the TBIL model uses only past real interest rates to predict future real rates.

46. There is some weak evidence that this difference does measure a temporary component of income. The correlation of successive annual values is $-.24$ with $P = .07$ on a one-tailed test. This means that positive differences in one year tend to be partly offset by negative differences the next. Another common test for mean reversion uses the ratio of the variances of the variable calculated over one year and n years. If there is mean reversion, the latter variance should be less than n times the former. For $n = 5$, the variance ratio is around 2.5. But, with only eight nonoverlapping five-year periods, this result is merely suggestive.

this is the interval in which total weights on income and inflation surprises peak.[47]

Voters will get good grades from economists for distinguishing expected from unexpected inflation. This is clearest in the senate and gubernatorial regressions, where none of the weights on expected inflation differ significantly from zero, and all the estimates of m are much closer to zero than one.[48] The much more variable estimates in the presidential regressions need to be read in conjunction with table 4.1. The exotically high values of m cluster in the lags of under three years where, according to table 4.1, the total weight on unexpected inflation is small and sometimes positive. For the longer lags, where the total weight on unexpected inflation peaks decisively, the presidential regressions tell a story similar to the others: while the weight on expected inflation tends to be more precisely measured here, it is considerably smaller than the weight on unexpected inflation.

Voters also appear to be distinguishing permanent from transitory income. All of the point estimates of the weight on transitory income in panel B of table 4.3 are below unity. Except for the gubernatorial regressions, these weights also tend to cluster around zero. The anomalous gubernatorial election results are entirely due to regressions that employ the AR estimate of unexpected inflation. In these regressions, the weights on transitory income, though insignificantly different from zero, ranged around unity. The gubernatorial regressions using the TBIL estimate of expected inflation produced weights on transitory income similar to those found in the other elections, that is, they were closer to zero than one and statistically indistinguishable from zero. (Table 4.3 shows an average of the transitory income weights from the two sets of regressions.) In all, fifty-four regressions underlie the data in panel B of table 4.3 (9 lags × 3 kinds of elections × 2 measures of unexpected inflation), or forty-five regressions apart from the anomalous set of gubernatorial regressions. In forty-two of these forty-five, the weight on transitory income was significantly less than unity. So the data are broadly consistent with the political primacy of permanent income.

---

47. Use of shorter lags would risk confounding the effects of X and Z. For example, this year's expected inflation is partly the sum of inflation surprises over the previous year or two. So it is a proxy for relevant information about unexpected inflation.

48. The negative m's in the table mean literally that expected inflation is politically rewarded.

C. Whose Income Counts—the Voter's or the Nation's?

To a crude approximation, the president's policy affects mainly aggregate income rather than its personal distribution. If voters understood this, they would respond mainly to aggregate income surprises and ignore personal deviations from the aggregate. Voters care about these personal deviations, but they are mainly irrelevant in evaluating the *policy* of their agent. These assertions lead to the following test: since my unit of analysis is the state, let Z in (6) and (7) be the difference between the growth rate of per capita income in the state and the nation, and let the latter be X. Then, if the regression estimate of m, the weight on Z, is 1, the voters in a state respond only to their own income. If $m = 0$, they respond only to aggregate income and ignore personal deviations. This test may be too strong because the political agenda does include redistributive policies. These could affect the regional distribution of income, so some $m > 0$ would make sense. However, any such policy-induced effect on regional growth patterns ought to be small next to forces like commodity price changes or changes in the industrial distribution of demand. Thus, the "weak form" of the relevant hypothesis would be that $m << 1$.

Table 4.4 summarizes the results of this test. Most of the estimated weights are indistinguishable from zero and numerically closer to zero than one. This holds across all types of elections. The only exception is the peculiar negative weights in gubernatorial elections. Thus, the data are mainly consistent even with the "strong-form" hypothesis that voters ignore completely their own deviation from national income growth when settling with the president's party.[49] This does not imply that these personal deviations are entirely irrelevant politically. For example, voters who experience a large favorable income deviation may switch allegiance from the proredistribution party to the antiredistribution party.[50] My results do imply that any switch would occur no matter which party is incumbent.

49. Similar results are in Donald Kinder & D. Roderick Kiewiet, Economic Discontent and Political Behavior: The Role of Personal Grievances and Collective Economic Judgments in Congressional Elections, 23 Am. J. Pol. Sci. 495 (1979). Panels of voters in elections from 1956–72 were asked whether they believed (1) they were better off and (2) the nation was better off. When the respondents' vote was regressed on dummies for the answers, only the dummy for the latter was consistently significant. The authors interpreted this as the dominance of altruism ("sociotropism") over self-interest. However, Gerald Kramer, The Ecological Fallacy Revisited: Aggregate versus Individual-Level Findings on Economics and Elections, 77 Am. Pol. Sci. Rev. 92 (1983), using essentially the same argument made here, shows that the result is also consistent with sophisticated self-interest.

50. Evidence of such switching can be found in Sam Peltzman, An Economic Interpretation of Congressional Voting in the Twentieth Century, 75 Am. Econ. Rev. 656 (1985), chap. 2 of this volume.

TABLE 4.3 Estimate of Weight Voters Give to Expected Inflation and Transitory Income, Various Periods Prior to Election

Type of Election and Type of Estimate	Month before Election								
	24	27	30	33	36	39	42	45	48
A. Expected Inflation:									
1. Presidential:									
A. AR:									
m	2.23	9.15	2.50	.29	.27	.12	.22	.15	.11
$\lvert t\rvert$	8.8	11.9	11.0	5.1	7.2	3.7	5.4	3.6	3.7
B. TBIL:									
m	6.61	*	*	1.69	.06	.14	.28	.21	.14
$\lvert t\rvert$	8.3			8.5	3.9	8.4	8.6	7.9	6.8
2. Senate:									
A. AR:									
m	-.06	-.03	-.07	-.11	-.08	-.09	-.08	-.11	-.09
$\lvert t\rvert$	.7	.3	.9	1.8	1.2	1.6	1.3	1.6	1.5
B. TBIL:									
m	.06	.09	.16	.04	.05	.07	.07	.05	.04
$\lvert t\rvert$	.9	1.0	1.3	.8	.9	1.4	1.5	1.2	1.0

3. Gubernatorial:

A. AR:

m	−.14	−.13	−.14	−.16	−.13	−.13	−.12	−.14	−.12
|t|	1.1	1.0	1.2	1.6	1.1	1.3	1.1	1.3	1.2

B. TBIL:

m	−.04	−.05	−.04	−.04	−.05	−.03	−.02	−.02	−.02
|t|	.8	.9	.6	1.0	1.1	.6	.3	.5	.5

B. Transitory Income:

1. Presidential:

m	−.02	−.16	.11	−.21	.08	.19	−.16	−.04	−.20
|t|	.3	2.6	4.8	2.5	3.5	4.8	2.0	1.6	2.7

2. Senate:

m	.01	−.14	−.03	−.08	−.16	−.01	−.03	.06	.36
|t|	.4	.8	.8	.4	.7	.2	.4	.5	1.0

3. Gubernatorial:

m	.57	.47	.81	.58	.42	.50	.68	.73	.82
|t|	1.2	1.0	1.3	1.2	.9	1.3	1.3	1.2	1.2

Note: The entries are estimates of m from regressions like eq. (7), where the X and Z variables are calculated over the indicated period. The value of m shown is the quotient of the regression coefficients of Z and X. The t-ratio is for the coefficient of Z, so it is a test of the hypothesis that $Bm = 0$ (or that $m = 0$, conditional on $B \neq 0$). Two alternative sets of expected and unexpected inflation variables are used. See note to table 4.1 for definitions. Transitory income is the growth in per capita income less the residual of the regression of log consumption on its lagged value. This difference was added to regressions, including the consumption residual and unexpected inflation. Two sets of regressions were run, one using the AR estimate and the other the TBIL estimate of unexpected inflation. The average of the two resulting estimates of m and $|t|$ are shown.

*Not meaningful because estimated weight on unexpected inflation is positive.

TABLE 4.4 Estimates of Weight on Voter's Income Relative to National
Income, Various Periods prior to Election

Months prior to Election	Election					
	Presidential		Senate		Gubernatorial	
	Weight	$|t|$	Weight	$|t|$	Weight	$|t|$
Average for lags:						
12–24 months	.14	1.6	.05	.3	−.19	.8
27–36 months	.15	2.1	.02	.2	−.35	1.7
39–48 months	.15	1.9	.01	.2	−.45	2.2
Range for all lags:						
12–48 months						
Minimum	.04	.5	−.03	.1	−.47	.3
Maximum	.27	2.7	.09	.4	−.08	2.2

D. Who Is (Are) the Voters' Agent(s)?

So far, I have assumed that the only reason senators and governors are
affected by the macroeconomy is to reinforce the signal to the president.
Voters would behave this way if they understood that the president is the
only elected official whose policies can materially affect the macroeconomy. Congress as a whole may have effects, but the one senator who faces
his electorate cannot. If voters failed to make this distinction, every incumbent, not merely the president, would share the credit or blame for the
voters' good or ill fortune. Voters in senate and gubernatorial elections,
however, do make the distinction: I added income and inflation surprises
(uninteracted with the presidential party dummy) to the regressions in
table 4.1. If incumbents shared in the benefits of good times regardless of
party, the coefficients of these variables would be significantly positive and
negative, respectively. In no case was either coefficient more than two stan-
dard errors from zero, and the mean $|t|$ was less than 1.0.[51]

A more focused test is available for governors. Formally, governors and
presidents share similar executive powers. But, as chief executive in a small
open economy without a central bank, the governor cannot conduct very
powerful macropolicy. Voters who understood this would not reward incumbent governors as much as presidents for favorable income surprises.[52]

51. This is based on regressions for every lag from 24 to 48 months and both types
of surprise estimates. Essentially similar results hold if uninteracted state income growth is
substituted for national income growth.

52. The hypothesis is stated in its weak form, to allow for some macroeffect of state
taxes, which governors can influence.

Since we have just seen that the president's party gets all the credit for national income growth, the appropriate test is to add the difference between the state and national income growth (uninteracted with the presidential party dummy) rate to the gubernatorial election regressions. If the coefficient of this variable is smaller than that of the corresponding (interacted) national growth rate, voters would be rewarding the incumbent governor's party less for local income surprises than they reward the president's party for national income surprises. The evidence is consistent with this: the coefficient of the local income deviation is within two standard deviations of zero for every lag. For the longer lags (twenty-four to forty-eight months), the average (range) of the coefficient is twenty-four (9, 40) percent of the corresponding national income-growth coefficient. The average (range) of the $|t|$ ratios for these coefficients is 1.1 (.5, 1.6).[53] Thus, the results mildly suggest that incumbent governors reap some reward from superior performance of the local economy, but voters seem to understand the limits on their ability to affect it.[54]

E. How Quickly Do Voters Assimilate Information?

If voters respond only to new information, the election market should, like the stock market, have no memory. As elaborated earlier, this means that an incumbent party's share today should be independent of its share in the last election. To provide a test, the regressions summarized in table 4.1 included the lagged incumbent share. The coefficients of this variable are summarized in table 4.5, and the results are mixed. For presidential elections, the lag-share coefficient ranges modestly around a mean close to zero. For gubernatorial elections, the coefficient is consistently indistinguishable from zero. However, for senatorial elections, the lag share coefficient is consistently and significantly positive. Thus, the data are mainly, but not exclusively, consistent with the notion of complete adjustment to new information.[55] This does not mean that in the absence

53. These figures are calculated as in table 4.4. That is, regressions are run with the two income variables plus, alternately, the AR or TBIL estimate of unexpected inflation. This yields two estimates of the relative weight on the state income deviation for each lag. The average of these two is my estimate of the relative weight for each lag.

54. There is a clear implication for international comparisons: the strength of the relationship between the macroeconomy and the political fortunes of the governing party should be inversely related to the openness of the economy.

55. They are also inconsistent with a permanent change in party preferences in light of new information (see note 21 *supra*). That would imply a lag-share coefficient of unity, and all the estimates are significantly less than this.

TABLE 4.5 Coefficient of Lagged Incumbent Party Share

Lag on Income/Inflation (Months before Election)	Election					
	Presidential		Senate		Guberna-torial	
	Coeffi-cient	|t|	Coeffi-cient	|t|	Coeffi-cient	|t|
Average for lags:						
12–24 months	.0	1.4	.27	4.9	.0	.2
27–36 months	.03	1.4	.27	4.8	.0	.1
39–48 months	.04	2.5	.26	4.7	−.01	.2
Ranges for all lags, 12–48 months:						
Minimum	−.18	.2	.25	4.6	−.03	.0
Maximum	.21	4.2	.28	5.0	−.02	.4

Note: Based on regressions in table 4.1. Each of those regressions includes incumbent party share in last election as an independent variable. (For Senate election, last election refers to seat.) The coefficients and t-ratios are summarized here. Since two sets of economic variables are used and lags are increments of three months, the summary statistics are based on eight or ten regressions for each lag interval.

of new information voters act as if they toss a coin to pick a candidate. My procedure allows for party preferences.[56] Nor do my results imply that party preferences change only when there is new macroeconomic information. They do imply that, except for senate elections, any such change due to other information occurs episodically rather than gradually. In this sense, voters are separating the surprise from the predictable elements of that information as well as from the macrodata.

III. SOME INTERPRETIVE ISSUES
A. Are Voters Too Averse to Inflation?

Economists tend to be agnostic about the evils of unexpected inflation. We can point to the losses imposed on net monetary creditors, but there are also gains to debtors. To the question, "But is it bad for the country?" we have no strong answer. Table 4.1 shows that the voters are not similarly befuddled. To them, one point of unexpected inflation is at least as bad as a one point decline in income.

56. For example, in one state 70 percent of the voters might, ceteris paribus, prefer the incumbent party, while in another state only 50 percent might prefer the incumbent party. I adjust for such differences with state-party dummies. My results imply that when some voters shift from these preferences, the shift tends to be permanent.

The first path one might take to seek a reconciliation of voter behavior and the conventional wisdom of economists is to look at the voters' balance sheets. They do appear to be net creditors: for the household sector over the sample period, monetary assets less monetary liabilities have been on the order of a year's personal income.[57] So, at least the sign of the political effect of unexpected inflation makes sense. To get at plausible magnitudes, consider a household with annual income of $10,000 and equal net monetary assets. If it is like the aggregate of households, of its $10,000 net monetary assets, $2,000 will be noninterest bearing, $4,000 will be short-term interest bearing, and $4,000 will be long-term interest bearing.[58] The detail is important, because of the diverse effects of an inflation surprise. To fix ideas, I use the AR estimate of unexpected inflation, and I assume that three years before an election the inflation rate accelerates permanently and unexpectedly by 1 percent. The cash assets thus will suffer a continuing extra purchasing-power loss of 1 percent per year. The only loss for short-term interest-bearing assets will be due to the lag of short rates behind actual inflation as expected inflation catches up. But the long-term assets lose capital value when interest rates rise to reflect the higher inflation rate. A rough calculation of the sum of the three effects is a total wealth reduction of $600–$700 on the $10,000 monetary assets.[59] By comparison, a 1 percent income surprise in any month has a present value of around $1,000 to this representative household.[60] The two hypothetical surprises would have comparable effects on the variables in my

57. Based on flow of funds data. I classify demand and time deposits, currency, bonds, life-insurance reserves, pension-fund assets, and "other" financial assets as monetary assets, and all financial liabilities (90 percent of which are mortgages and consumer credit) as monetary liabilities.

58. Of course, both the total and its distribution can be different for the average voter than the aggregate of the household sector. However, the distribution across households is unavailable. For these purposes, currency and demand deposits are considered noninterest-bearing assets, net short-term interest-bearing assets are time deposits less consumer credit and "other" liabilities, net long-term interest-bearing assets are bonds, claims on life insurance and pension reserves, and "other" assets less mortgage debt. (Here, I ignore future tax liabilities for servicing government bonds.)

59. The cash assets lose $(.01)(2000) = \$20$ per year or $200 present value discounting at 10 percent. The short-term assets lose a total of $33 over 36 months if changes in short rates equal the change in expected inflation from the AR model in each month. The loss on long-term assets depends, in general, on the duration of their payment streams and the level of rates. If, to make things simple, all $4,000 of long-term assets are in ten-year zero-coupon bonds, the capital loss of a 1 percentage point rise in long rates (from any level) would be 10 percent, or $400. Then the total loss would be $200 + 33 + 400 = \$633$.

60. This is the present value at 10 percent of a $100 permanent addition to the $10,000 annual income stream.

regression,[61] so this exercise suggests a political weight on the income variable somewhat greater (10:6 or 10:7) than the inflation weight. The regressions in table 4.1 do not satisfy this. However, the larger message of this exercise is that there is a plausible link between the voters' wealth position and their strong aversion to unexpected inflation.

Another path to understanding the strength of voters' aversion to inflation may lie in policy trade-offs and the realities of political competition. Consider the results of regressing this year's per capita income growth on last year's unexpected inflation (AR method). For 1951–88 data, this yields a coefficient (t) of $-1.1(3.0)$. For Democratic (Republican) administrations, the coefficient is $-.9(-1.3)$, and these are insignificantly different. One way to read these results is that inflation impels either party to adopt restrictive policies that ultimately reduce income. Voters fully using available information would then penalize inflation surprises in part because of the future income losses they portend. In fact, the point-for-point trade-off between income and inflation in the regression is roughly consistent with the relative political weights on income and inflation in table 4.1. The obvious difficulty with this sort of explanation is its circularity: the good reason for both parties to adopt restrictive policies is the inflation aversion itself.

B. How Important Are the Economic Variables in Determining Election Outcomes?

So far, I have shown that voters respond systematically to the macroeconomy, but I have ignored the magnitude of that response. To assess the practical importance of the economic variables, I compared the actual vote share of the incumbent party to the shares predicted by two alternative models: a NO ECON model in which the economic variables are all set equal to the sample mean, and an ECON model that removes this constraint. The difference in predictions from these models is simply the estimated marginal effect on vote shares from movements in the economic variables over the relevant preelection period. For this purpose, I averaged the predicted values for all regressions summarized in table 4.1 with lags of thirty-three or more months.[62]

---

61. The inflation variable for this exercise would be an annualized sum of monthly unexpected inflation that begins at $1/12$ percent per month and tapers to zero over three years. The appropriately weighted average of $1/12$ and zero from the AR regression is about $1/40$ percent per month, or .3 percent per year. The one-shot 1 percent income shock is $1/3$ percent per year over the same period.

62. This choice of lag interval is motivated by the previous result that voters use economic information from at least the last $2\frac{1}{2}$ years of a president's term. For off-year elec-

TABLE 4.6 Measures of Accuracy with and without Economic Variables: Senate and Gubernatorial Elections, 1950–88

	Senate Elections ($N = 566$)	Gubernatorial Elections ($N = 309$)
1. RMSE (%), all elections from:		
a. NO ECON model	7.30	6.73
b. ECON model	7.07	6.39
2. Percent of all elections in which		
a. Both models agree on outcome:	93.1	90.6
(1) And both are right	72.4	65.1
(2) And both are wrong	20.7	25.6
b. They disagree:	6.9	9.4
(1) And ECON is right	4.1	5.5
(2) And NO ECON is right	2.8	3.9
3. Share of 20 election years in which:		
a. ECON RMSE < NO ECON RMSE	.70	.70
b. And is weighted by number of elections	.71	.76

Note: Panel 1: see text for description of root mean squared prediction error (RMSE), ECON and NO ECON models, and method of prediction. Panel 2 is based on predicted and actual vote shares for the incumbent party. "Right" means that predicted and actual shares are on the same side of 50.0. Panel 3: RMSE is calculated for each of the twenty sets of elections in the even-numbered years 1950, 1952, . . . , 1988. (The occasional odd-year election is included in next year's set.) Data are number of years divided by 20 in which ECON model has smaller RMSE. For 3b, the number of elections in years satisfying this criterion is divided by total number of elections. All shares are significantly greater than .5 at 5 percent.

For each election in my sample, I compute the squared prediction error from both the ECON and the NO ECON models, and I use the square root of the average of these squared errors as a measure of accuracy. The basic question is, How much is the root-mean squared error (RMSE) reduced by adding the ECON variables? The answer is that only for presidential elections do the economic variables matter much.

Table 4.6 shows that, for the nonpresidential elections, the RMSEs from the two models are within a half percentage point. The reason for this result is implicit in item 2 of table 4.6, which shows that, in about nine of every ten nonpresidential elections, the two models predict the same winner. This suggests that, given their coefficients, the economic variables do not fluctuate enough to generate predictions much different from the NO ECON model. The data also show that, when they agree, the two

tions, results essentially identical to those reported below are produced by use of a single lag of twenty-four months.

models are usually (by about 3:1) right. This reveals how important the advantages are of incumbency and the persistence of long-run party shares at the individual election level. In the comparative handful of elections where the economic variables are important enough to be potentially decisive (item 2b of table 4.6), the ECON model is modestly more successful than the NO ECON model at picking the winner. The last panel of the table shows that, even if it is small, the predictive contribution of the economic variables is more or less omnipresent rather than concentrated in a few years.

The pattern for presidential elections is markedly different in two respects. First, the economic variables are more important in the aggregate. For the whole sample of presidential election returns, the RMSE for the ECON model is 4.53 percent, or over 2 percentage points better than the 6.88 percent RMSE for the NO ECON model. Second, this improvement tends to be concentrated in a few elections. Table 4.7 summarizes this last point. For most presidential elections—all but the 1964, 1976, and 1980 elections—both models produce roughly similar results. Their RMSEs (cols. 1 and 2) are around 5 percent or less, and both models come admirably close to predicting the actual outcome. Neither is off by more than 4 percentage points (see cols. 4–8). In the three remaining elections, however, the role of the macroeconomy looms much larger. Here, the NO ECON model produces RMSEs on the order of 10 percentage points, or about twice those of the ECON model. For these elections, the NO ECON–predicted incumbent vote share is wrong by an average of nearly 10 percentage points, while the comparable error for the ECON model is under 3 percentage points.

This exercise leads to two conclusions about the role of the macroeconomy in presidential elections. One is that there are no unusual elections, only unusual economic conditions. A glance down either column 2 or 8 of table 4.7, which summarizes the performance of the ECON model, reveals roughly comparable numbers across all elections. None of the three elections that seem unusual according to the NO ECON model—the Johnson landslide of 1964 and the defeat of incumbent presidents in 1976 and 1980—remains unusual once the exceptional underlying economic conditions are taken into account. These were the rapid, noninflationary growth of the early 1960s and the "stagflation" of the 1970s. They mark, respectively, the peak and trough of professional and popular optimism about the possibilities for political management of the macroeconomy.

Another conclusion suggested by table 4.7 is that a simple economic model is no forecasting panacea. The last line of the table shows results

TABLE 4.7 Measures of Accuracy (%) with and without Economic Variables: Presidential Elections, 1952–88

| | RMSE | | | Average Incumbent Party Share | | | Absolute Error | | |
| | | | | Predicted | | | | | |
Election	NO ECON (1)	ECON (2)	Gain to ECON Col. 1–Col. 2 (3)	NO ECON (4)	ECON (5)	Actual (6)	NO ECON [Col. 4–Col. 6] (7)	ECON [Col. 5–Col. 6] (8)	Gain to ECON Col. 7–Col. 8 (9)
1952	4.7	4.9	−.3	42.7	43.3	41.1	1.6	2.2	−.6
1956	5.0	5.1	−.1	59.7	61.0	59.9	.2	1.1	−.9
1960	3.2	3.2	0	52.7	51.3	51.9	.8	.6	.2
1964	12.7	5.7	7.0	49.4	57.1	61.6	12.2	4.5	7.7
1968	5.1	3.8	1.3	43.1	49.4	47.1	4.0	2.3	1.7
1972	5.6	4.6	1.0	59.5	61.5	62.8	3.3	1.3	2.0
1976	10.0	4.9	5.1	60.0	53.7	50.8	9.2	2.9	6.3
1980	8.6	4.9	3.7	49.2	42.4	42.2	7.0	.2	6.8
1984	3.0	3.0	0	59.9	62.4	61.1	1.2	1.3	−.1
1988	3.6	4.5	−.9	53.1	51.7	54.9	1.8	3.2	−1.4
1988*	5.6	7.3	−1.7	50.8	48.7	54.9	4.1	6.2	−2.1

Note: Columns 1 and 2 are root mean squared prediction errors (see text) of the incumbent party's vote share across all states in the sample for the specified election. The number of states range from thirty-six in 1952 to forty-four in 1988. Columns 4–6 are unweighted averages across all states in the sample of predicted or actual incumbent party vote share. See text for prediction method.

*Results of out-of-sample forecast based on coefficients of regressions estimated through 1984.

of out-of-sample forecasts of the 1988 election. Both the ECON and NO ECON models essentially predict a toss-up instead of the decisive Republican victory. And the ECON prediction is furthest off. Or, consider the 1976 election, which is one of the three importantly affected by the macroeconomic background. Nevertheless, the ECON model incorrectly predicts a comfortable Republican majority. These examples suggest a circumscribed role for economic variables in forecasting presidential elections. Only if an election would otherwise be close and the economic surprises substantial are they likely to dominate the outcome. This combination of circumstances has occurred only twice (1964 and 1980) since 1952.

IV. SUMMARY

When a principal cannot directly evaluate the quality of an agent's input, the agent's compensation often depends on some measure of ex post performance. Thus, for example, compensation of chief executives of large corporations includes stock options and performance bonuses. The political market works in roughly the same way. The vote payment to the chief executive in charge of macroeconomic policy and his party depends partly on some measures of ex post performance of the macroeconomy. I have tried to determine whether the voters are using "correct" performance measures. Accordingly, I tested voter behavior in presidential, senatorial, and gubernatorial elections against some standards of "correctness" suggested by economic theory. The voters pass essentially every test, and the voting market emerges as a strikingly efficient aggregator of economic information.

For example, efficient markets are supposed to reflect all available information. In the present context, this would mean that, with due allowance for policy lags, voters would use information about the economy's performance over the bulk of the president's term. By contrast, much of the political business-cycle literature assumes that voters ignore all but the most recent information. But my results show that voters suffer no such amnesia. For both income and inflation, voters use information over at least the last three years of a president's term. The kind of income/inflation information used by the voters also seems correct, insofar as this means that voters should (1) be concerned with the permanent, rather than temporary, effects of policy; (2) ignore information that is irrelevant to their welfare; and (3) ignore information about their welfare that is not policy related. With respect to inflation, economists commonly apply the first two of these criteria to suggest that only unexpected inflation can permanently affect welfare. And my results show that voters make the correct distinction. They ignore expected inflation and penalize only unexpected inflation. Further, I show that both the sign and magnitude of this penalty make sense, given the size and composition of the voters' net monetary assets and the effect of possible lags in the policy response to inflation.

It is not so easy to make a politically relevant distinction between expected and unexpected income. The behavior of income time series suggests that all income changes are unexpected and permanent. However, I was able to make two conditional tests of my criteria: First, if the permanent-income hypothesis is correct, consumption data imply an aggregate estimate of permanent income, and this permits a decomposition of income changes into permanent and transitory components. And I showed that voters respond to the permanent component and essentially ignore the transitory component. Second, if the main effect of policy is on aggregate income, rather than on its distribution across voters, local deviations from the change in aggregate income should be ignored or weighted less heavily than the aggregate change. I found that voters clearly make this local-aggregate distinction in the predicted direction.

So the broad picture that emerges here is of self-interested voters who correctly process relevant information. Indeed, one would be hard put to find nonpolitical markets that process information better than the voting market. For example, the reader familiar with the empirical efficient-capital-markets literature will recognize the obvious analogues to my methods and the qualitative similarity of results. Thus, these results deepen the mystery with which this article began. If all voters are rationally ignorant, whence comes efficiency in the voting market?

Voters as Fiscal Conservatives

Voters penalize federal and state spending growth. This is the central result of my analysis of voting behavior in presidential, senatorial, and gubernatorial elections from 1950–1988. The composition of federal spending growth seems irrelevant. The vote loss to the president's party from an
extra dollar of defense or nondefense spending is the same. However, in
gubernatorial elections, expansion of state welfare spending exacts a dis-
proportionate political price. Deficit financing of federal or state spending
does not appear to matter politically. I conclude by discussing the obvious
question of why government budgets have grown in the face of this voter
hostility.

I. INTRODUCTION

A central fact of recent U.S. and world economic history is that public
expenditures have been growing faster than private incomes. This paper
documents the response of U.S. voters to public sector spending growth
in the period since World War II. As the title indicates, that response has,
on balance, been hostile.

This paper also follows, and extends, a literature on voters' response
to macroeconomic conditions.[1] This shows that there is ex post settlement
between principals (voters) and agents (the president and elected representatives of his party). Specifically, good macroeconomic performance—
high real income growth and low inflation—during a president's term is

First published in *Quarterly Journal of Economics* 107, no. 2 (May 1992): 327–361. ©
1992 by the President and Fellows of Harvard College and the Massachusetts Institute of
Technology. Reprinted by permission.

I want to thank Michael Ward, Nolan McCarty, and Karen Lombard for research assistance and the Center for the Study of the Economy and State for financial support from
grants from the Lynde and Harry Bradley Foundation and the Sarah Scaife Foundation. An
anonymous referee provided helpful comments on a previous draft.

1. The seminal contribution is due to Kramer (1971). See Peltzman (1990 [chap. 4]) for
a review of the subsequent literature.

rewarded politically.[2] Here I extend the evidence to the direct political effects of the fiscal policy of presidents and their state level counterparts, the governors.

This extension seems natural, indeed overdue. Fluctuations in macroeconomic aggregates are, after all, affected, perhaps even dominated, by forces beyond the reach of a president's policy. This is not the case with the federal budget. It is one policy instrument over which the president has substantial influence, and the way this instrument is used can have substantial effects on the welfare of voters. For state budgets, which receive considerable attention in this paper, governors play a similarly important role. One rationale for the voters' response to the macroeconomy is that they cannot cheaply monitor the president's policy directly. As long as the policy has some nontrivial impact on publicly (that is, cheaply) available aggregates like GNP or unemployment, the principal will optimally use the indirect outcome measure to settle with the agent. But budget information is as "public" as GNP or unemployment. It is also nontrivial. Currently, federal expenditures exceed 20 percent of GNP, and state expenditures are roughly half as large. Accordingly, the almost complete neglect of budget policy in empirical analyses of voting seems peculiar. This paper tries to fill that gap.

I focus on the direct political effects of government budgets. That is, I ask "how do the (marginal) voters respond when resources are shifted between the public and private sectors?" Most of the relevant theory implies no systematic response, because it assumes that the size of the public sector accommodates the expressed demands of voters.[3] So this paper provides a test of this assumption.

2. Economists have yet to provide a good theoretical rationale for such results. Their difficulty was outlined long ago by Downs (1957). It is that informed voting appears doubly irrational. It entails two costly activities: voting and information processing. But there are no private benefits, because a single vote cannot plausibly affect the electoral outcome. I do not dwell on this theoretical difficulty here, because the evidence seems to belie its implications. For example, I (Peltzman, 1990) have shown that the voting market processes macroeconomic information about as efficiently as, say, the stock market processes information on corporate earnings.

3. For example, in the venerable median voter model, the size of the public sector is chosen to maximize the net benefits of the median voter. Small deviations from this equilibrium would help as many voters as they would hurt. Bigger changes could be viewed as a change in the equilibrium, but these also do not imply any change in voting patterns. Half the voters would have preferred a still bigger change and half a smaller. A variety of public choice models suggest equilibria with a larger public sector than the median voter model. These include models inspired by Buchanan and Tullock (1962), based on the working of majority voting rules and interest group dominance models inspired by Stigler (1971). How-

The only similar test of which I am aware is due to Niskanen (1975), who analyzed presidential elections from 1896 through 1972. He found that, holding performance of the macroeconomy constant, increases in federal spending cost the incumbent party votes. I shall focus entirely on the arguably more interesting post-World War II period. In this "big government" era, changes in federal spending relative to GNP over the course of a president's term sometimes exceed the level of this variable in the early twentieth century. But, in spite of the difference in time period and in the method of analysis, my results confirm Niskanen's. I also examine the components of federal spending, and I find that voters do not much care how the federal government allocates its spending. Basically, every extra dollar is equally bad. I extend the analysis to non-presidential elections (for Senate and governor) and find that candidates from the president's party also lose votes when Federal spending grows. I then analyze the effect of state budget growth on the electoral fortunes of the gubernatorial incumbent's party. I find the same result as at the federal level: the voting market punishes growth of the state budget. However, here voters do seem to care how the state budget is allocated. They particularly dislike transfers to the poor (most of whom are nonvoters).

This image of the voter as a flinty-eyed fiscal conservative is sharpened by two further results. First, voters are not pacified by deficit finance. With some qualification I find that the voters' basic objection is to spending, not just the part financed by taxes. Second, voters are not easily "bought off" by election year spending. Spending just prior to an election is even more poisonous politically than in other periods.

In the next section I outline my empirical procedure and summarize the data to which it is applied. Because I am extending the literature on voting and the macroeconomy, I also summarize the main results of that literature. This is followed by the empirical results. I conclude with a brief interpretive summary.

II. EMPIRICAL PROCEDURE AND DATA

My analysis of voter response to government spending follows the same basic procedure as detailed in my (1990) analysis of voter response to the macroeconomy. I shall give only a brief outline here: the model underlying subsequent empirical work is

(1) $IS_{iT} = K_i + f(W_{ioT})$,

---

ever, none of these models implies any political penalty for the excess size of the public sector. Political agents deliver that result because it maximizes their vote.

where

IS_{iT} = incumbent party's share of the vote in jurisdiction i in an election held on date T;

K_i = party's normal share of vote in i, specified as a constant;

W_{ioT} = that change in voter welfare since the last election ($t = 0$), which voters use to evaluate the incumbent;

$f(\cdot)$ = a function converting W into a voting decision, with f' presumably > 0.

The focus here is on the marginal voter's decision, and (1) recognizes (via inclusion of K_i) that many voters may stick with their preferred party even if there are large changes in their welfare. The welfare term in (1) is then particularized to depend on economic information revealed since the previous election. Thus, the model is one of periodic ex post settling up between marginal voters and the incumbent party. The weight voters attach to the bits of information revealed in the $(0, T)$ interval is then estimated from regressions of the general form,

(2) $\quad IS_{iT} = A + BX_{i,LAGt} + \dots,$

where

X = a vector of economic data, and the LAG_t subscript denotes that X is being measured over t periods prior to election.

The value of t is allowed to vary from as little as three months to four years back from the election and the X's are constructed (as annualized rates of change) to provide B's which are estimates of the total weight voters give to information revealed in the t months before an election. For federal expenditures the effective degrees of freedom in my data preclude estimating a full distributed lag on the separate components of any X. But my procedure produces unbiased estimates of the B's.

The ellipses in (2) indicate that the relevant regressions include more than the economic data revealed since the last election. Specifically,

1. I allow for an influence from older data by including the incumbent party's share in the last election.
2. My unit of analysis is the state. I allow for different values of K, a party's normal vote share, across states with state-party dummies.
3. A dummy is included to control for well-known advantages of a candidate who is an incumbent.

Because the effects of these noneconomic variables are uninteresting for present purposes, they will be only briefly summarized.

I analyze votes in senatorial and gubernatorial elections as well as in presidential elections. The previous literature, including Peltzman [1990],

shows that candidates from the president's party share in the ex post settlement. For these non-presidential races the basic regression is (dropping
unneeded subscripts)

$$(2')\quad IS = A + B(PR \cdot X) + C \cdot PR + \ldots,$$

where

PR = dummy = $+1$ if the incumbent party in the senatorial or gubernatorial race is the same as the president's, -1 if different.

This formulation holds when the X vector contains only information plausibly affected by presidential policy.[4] When I analyze the effect of state
budgets in gubernatorial elections, uninteracted state budget variables will
be added to the right-hand side of $(2')$. Finally, I adjust the X vector for
differences in the timing of presidential and non-presidential elections.
Over half the latter occur in midterm, two years after the last settlement
with the president's party. For these midterm elections, I include only information since the last presidential election. Thus, for example, X_{LAG36}
would include data from the 36 months preceding an election in a presidential election year, but only 24 months of data for a midterm election.[5]

I implement (2) or $(2')$ on three time series of cross sections of state
election returns: one each for presidential, senatorial, and gubernatorial
elections. The data span the period 1950–1988, and they include most
contested elections at the state level in this period.[6] The dependent variable
in every regression is the incumbent party's share of the major party vote
in a state.

My main interest here is in the effect of government spending on this
vote share. However, because of the well-documented role of the macroeconomy, the X-vector always includes information about real income and
inflation in addition to budget variables. The specific form this informa-

4. The $C \cdot PR$ term allows for the different intercept accompanying the opposite signed
slope when the incumbent is not from the president's party.
5. See Peltzman (1990) for discussion of the evidence that suggested this truncation and
for details on its implementation.
6. The following elections are deleted.
    1. Gubernatorial elections to two-year terms. Two-year terms were more common
    early in the period. When a state had fewer than seven four-year-term elections
    in my gubernatorial sample, the state-party dummy was combined with that of a
    bordering state.
    2. Effectively uncontested elections. These include elections with an unopposed
    candidate. In addition, states where the winning party's vote share exceeds 70
    percent at the beginning of the period are deleted until that share falls below 70
    percent for two straight elections. This criterion essentially excludes a few
    Southern states in the early part of the period, when the Republican party
    offered only token opposition.

tion takes in this paper is a "happiness" index (hereinafter HAPI). This is just the difference between estimated permanent income and inflation surprises during the president's term. The permanent income shock is estimated, following Hall (1978), as the residual from the regression of the log of total consumption less durables on its lagged value. The unexpected inflation component of HAPI is the difference between actual inflation and an average of two estimates of expected inflation. One comes from an inflation autoregression. The other extracts expected inflation from Treasury-bill rates using a model in Fama and Gibbons (1984).[7]

The motivation for HAPI is provided by my (1990) extension of the literature on voting and the macroeconomy. Almost every macro-voting study since Kramer (1971) regresses vote shares on some subset of real activity and inflation measures. In broad summary, the results of this exercise are that (a) most any real activity measure "works"; but (b) income measures, like growth of real GNP or per capita income, tend to work better than unemployment;[8] and (c) inflation is usually, but not always, found to be politically costly. In (1990) I divided per capita income growth into permanent and transitory components and the inflation rate into expected and unexpected components. I then found that only permanent income (as proxied by nondurables consumption) and inflation surprises mattered politically. I also found that voters ignore any difference between state and national income growth in settling with the president's party or the party of the incumbent governor. So a single national income shock adequately summarizes the income information relevant for state level vote shares. This set of results is embodied in HAPI for the purposes of this paper. However, I show that the effects of budget variables are not particularly sensitive to this choice of summary measure of macroeconomic conditions.

All the federal budget variables I use are cycle-adjusted to remove the short-run feedback from real income to federal spending and taxes.[9]

7. See Peltzman (1990) for a detailed description of the permanent income and inflation surprise estimates. The average inflation surprise is multiplied by a constant in constructing HAPI. See note to table 5.1.

8. One rationalization is the below-average voter participation of the unemployed.

9. Census Bureau cycle-adjusted budget data are available quarterly from 1955.1. I estimated the earlier data from regressions on the quarterly real changes in the components of the cycle adjustment in the 40 quarters beginning 1955.1. These changes were regressed on the current and lagged real changes of the variables which entered the Census cycle adjustments model, as described in Holloway et al. (1986). The coefficients of these regressions (which consistently produced $R^2 > 0.9$) and the pre-1955 values of the independent variables were then used to extend the cycle adjustments backward from 1955.1.

III. RESULTS

A foundation for the subsequent empirical analysis is provided by the results under (1) in table 5.1. These show coefficients from a series of regressions in which HAPI is the only economic variable. The regressions are distinguished by the time period, back from election day, over which HAPI is measured. To illustrate what these coefficients mean, consider the entries in panel A under (1) for LAG 24 (3.3) and LAG 48 (7.6). These say that if, for example, a noninflationary favorable shock to permanent income of 1 percent per year is sustained over the 24 months leading up to election, the presidential candidate of the incumbent party gains 3.3 percentage points in vote share. And if the same rate of improvement is sustained over the president's whole four-year term, the vote share gain is 7.6 points. The difference between these two coefficients (4.3 = 7.6 − 3.3) gives the *marginal weight* on information generated in the first two years of the president's term. Thus, if a 1 percent per year favorable income shock is sustained over those two years, and there are no subsequent surprises, the vote share gain is 4.3 points. So the rising pattern of coefficients under (1) says that voters reward all the favorable income information generated during a president's term, not, for example, just the portion immediately prior to election day.

The data under (1) in panels B and C give corresponding results for candidates from the president's party in senatorial and gubernatorial elections. (The regression equation used here is (2′).) They indicate that these candidates share in the ex post settlement with the president, but the effects are smaller than in presidential elections.

At this point the reader should glance down the HAPI columns under (2) and (3), in which federal budget information is added to the regressions. The immediately relevant result is the basic insensitivity of the pattern of HAPI coefficients and significance levels[10] to the inclusion of the

10. The OLS *t*-ratios reported in table 5.1 and subsequently may be biased if there are "year effects," i.e., particularly good or bad years for one or the other party that produce a common pattern of residuals across states in those years. In that case the true degrees-of-freedom would be overstated (and the OLS *t*-ratios would be too large), because the state vote shares would not be independent draws. On the other hand, information about the cross-state covariance could in principle be used to reduce residual variance, but OLS does not use this information. That inefficiency biases the OLS *t*-ratios down. Peltzman (1990) reports results of applying a GLS procedure which uses cross-state residual covariance to regressions similar to those in table 5.1. These indicated that the OLS *t*-ratios are roughly correct and, if anything, too small.

To provide further insight into the magnitude of any upward bias in the OLS *t*-ratios, I first extracted the residuals from a regression of the vote share on the political variables

budget variables. That insensitivity prevailed in all the regressions discussed subsequently in this paper. All of these include HAPI. But, because electoral effects of the macroeconomy are not this paper's focus, coefficients of HAPI are generally suppressed henceforth.

A. The Federal Budget

The substantive inquiry of this paper begins with the third column under (2) in table 5.1. These are the coefficients of the change in the log of real federal expenditures over various periods preceding an election. They are consistently negative, which means that voters penalize the president's party for above-average spending growth during his term. However, the coefficients peak (in absolute value) at a lag of around two years, and for presidential elections, they get smaller for longer lags. Taken literally, this means that voters actually reward the president for spending growth in the first half of his term and punish spending growth in the second half.

These are good reasons to be wary of this strange result. They have to do with the inherently temporary nature of spending on wars and my finding (1990) that voters are generally able to distinguish temporary from permanent changes in their welfare. For my sample period the major (data) problem is the Korean War and its aftermath.[11] The war began in 1950.3. From 1950.2 real defense spending more than tripled to a peak in 1953.2. Over the next six quarters, defense spending declined by one-fourth, after which it remained roughly constant for several years. The corresponding effects on total federal spending were a near doubling from 1950.2 to 1953.2 and a decline of about one-fifth from 1953.2 to 1954.4.

(state-party and incumbency dummies). I then averaged these residuals across states for each election year and regressed the time series of these average residuals on the time series of economic variables. For presidential elections, this time-series (ten observations) regression including HAPI and adjusted federal spending growth produced the following coefficients (t-ratios) for the indicated lags:

Lag	HAPI	Federal Spending Growth
24	3.3 (2.7)	−0.5 (1.5)
36	6.4 (6.7)	−0.6 (2.0)
48	8.5 (15.2)	−1.1 (5.8)

The coefficients are typically significant and roughly similar in magnitude to their counterparts under (3) in table 5.1, while the t-ratios are anywhere from 20 to 60 percent as large. It should be emphasized that these t-ratios probably understate the "truth," because all of the information in the cross-state and time-series covariances of residuals is discarded in computing them.

11. It affects the data used for two of the ten presidential elections and four of the twenty non-presidential election years in my sample.

TABLE 5.1 Regressions of Incumbent Party's Vote Share on Happiness Index and Changes in Federal Spending

A. Presidential Elections, 1952–1988 (401 Obs.)

LAG (Months Preceding Election)	(1) HAPI Coeff	$\|t\|$	(2) HAPI Coeff	$\|t\|$	Δln Federal Spending Coeff	$\|t\|$	(3) HAPI Coeff	$\|t\|$	Δln Federal Spending Adjusted Coeff	$\|t\|$
3	1.5	12.6	0.7	4.3	−0.3	6.8	0.9	5.8	−0.2	5.6
6	1.5	13.2	1.3	11.8	−0.4	7.4	1.3	11.8	−0.3	7.1
9	1.3	10.1	1.2	9.5	−0.5	5.7	1.2	9.3	−0.5	5.5
12	2.1	11.4	2.0	11.8	−0.6	7.0	2.0	11.3	−0.5	6.5
15	2.6	12.6	2.5	13.0	−0.5	7.3	2.3	11.8	−0.7	7.2
18	2.8	13.2	3.0	16.3	−0.5	10.8	2.9	16.2	−0.9	12.3
21	1.9	7.8	3.2	14.6	−0.6	13.4	3.0	15.0	−1.3	15.2
24	3.3	12.3	3.6	14.1	−0.3	8.4	3.6	14.8	−0.8	10.3
27	3.3	10.1	4.2	14.6	−0.6	11.8	4.3	15.4	−1.4	3.0
30	3.4	10.2	3.7	12.4	−0.8	9.3	3.8	11.8	−0.9	6.2
33	5.1	15.9	5.3	17.9	−0.5	8.7	5.9	20.3	−1.4	10.8
36	6.5	21.5	6.4	22.7	−0.5	7.4	7.0	24.6	−1.0	8.6
39	7.2	22.0	7.0	21.5	−0.3	3.8	8.3	27.0	−1.2	10.5
42	6.4	20.1	6.3	20.0	−0.3	4.2	8.0	25.9	−1.5	11.5
45	6.2	21.0	6.1	20.5	0.2	2.0	7.7	25.5	−1.3	10.1
48	7.6	21.4	7.4	20.3	−0.1	1.7	8.6	26.2	−1.4	10.3

B. Senate Elections, 1950–1988 (566 Obs.)

LAG	(1) HAPI Coeff	$\|t\|$	(2) HAPI Coeff	$\|t\|$	Δln Federal Spending Coeff	$\|t\|$	(3) HAPI Coeff	$\|t\|$	Δln Federal Spending Adjusted Coeff	$\|t\|$
3	0.2	1.9	0.1	0.8	−0.1	2.4	0.2	1.5	−0.0	1.2
6	0.4	3.4	0.4	3.4	−0.0	1.9	0.4	3.6	−0.0	1.6
9	0.7	4.8	0.7	4.6	−0.1	2.5	0.7	5.0	−0.1	2.2
12	1.0	5.8	1.0	5.7	−0.1	2.3	1.0	5.8	−0.1	1.1
15	1.1	5.4	1.1	5.7	−0.1	2.9	1.1	5.7	−0.1	1.9
18	1.2	5.4	1.3	6.1	−0.2	3.5	1.4	6.1	−0.2	2.7
21	0.9	4.7	1.4	6.4	−0.2	4.9	1.3	5.9	−0.3	3.6
24	1.5	5.8	1.5	5.7	−0.1	2.4	1.6	6.2	−0.2	2.8
27	1.5	5.2	1.6	5.4	−0.2	3.2	1.8	6.0	−0.3	3.2
30	1.5	5.1	1.4	4.9	−0.2	2.6	1.8	5.7	−0.3	2.5
33	1.9	5.8	1.8	5.6	−0.2	2.2	2.1	6.3	−0.3	2.5
36	2.0	5.6	1.9	5.4	−0.2	2.3	2.2	6.1	−0.3	2.2
39	2.0	5.5	1.9	5.1	−0.2	2.0	2.4	6.0	−0.3	2.3
42	2.0	5.5	1.9	5.1	−0.2	2.0	2.4	6.0	−0.3	2.5
45	2.0	5.4	1.8	5.1	−0.2	1.9	2.3	5.9	−0.3	2.3
48	2.2	5.6	2.1	5.2	−0.2	1.6	2.5	6.0	−0.3	2.0

TABLE 5.1 continued

C. Gubernatorial Elections, 1950–1988 (309 Obs.)

| | (1) | | (2) | | | | (3) | | |
| | HAPI | | HAPI | | ΔIn Federal Spending | | HAPI | | ΔIn Federal Spending Adjusted | |
LAG	Coeff	|t|	Coeff	|t|	Coeff	|t|	Coeff	|t|	Coeff	|t|
3	0.1	0.8	0.1	0.4	−0.1	1.3	0.1	0.7	−0.0	0.2
6	0.2	1.3	0.2	1.3	−0.0	0.0	0.2	1.2	0.0	0.7
9	0.6	2.7	0.6	2.6	−0.1	1.8	0.6	2.7	−0.1	1.0
12	0.9	3.5	0.9	3.4	−0.1	1.5	0.9	3.5	−0.1	0.6
15	1.1	3.8	1.1	4.0	−0.1	1.7	1.2	3.9	−0.1	1.0
18	1.1	3.6	1.3	3.9	−0.2	2.7	1.3	3.9	−0.2	1.6
21	1.0	3.3	1.3	4.1	−0.2	2.6	1.4	3.9	−0.3	2.1
24	1.5	3.8	1.5	3.7	−0.1	1.6	1.7	4.1	−0.3	2.0
27	1.6	3.7	1.6	3.8	−0.2	2.1	1.9	4.2	−0.3	2.2
30	1.7	3.7	1.6	3.6	−0.3	2.3	1.9	4.1	−0.3	2.1
33	1.9	3.9	1.9	3.8	−0.2	2.0	2.2	4.4	−0.4	2.1
36	2.1	4.1	2.0	3.9	−0.3	2.0	2.3	4.4	−0.3	1.7
39	2.2	4.0	2.1	3.8	−0.2	1.9	2.5	4.4	−0.3	1.7
42	2.2	4.0	2.1	3.8	−0.3	1.9	2.5	4.4	−0.3	1.7
45	2.2	4.1	2.1	3.9	−0.3	1.7	2.5	4.3	−0.3	1.5
48	2.5	4.1	2.4	3.9	−0.2	1.5	2.7	4.3	−0.2	1.2

Sources: Consumption, price index (personal income deflator), federal spending: *Survey of Current Business.*

Notes: The coefficients and |t|-ratios are from regression (2) for presidential elections and (2′) for nonpresidential elections. The dependent variable is the incumbent party's share of the two-party vote in a state. The independent variables include state-party and incumbency dummies, the party's share in the last election, and for (2′) a dummy indicating whether or not the candidate is from the president's party. See text for elaboration. The coefficients shown here are for

a. HAPI: a "happiness" index = permanent income surprise − k · inflation surprise. The permanent income surprise is the residual from the regression:

$$\ln C_t = a + b \ln C_{t-1},$$

where

C_t = real per capita consumption minus durables in quarter t.

The inflation surprise is an average of two unexpected inflation estimates: one from an autoregressive model of expected inflation, the other from a model that extracts expected inflation from one-month treasury bill rates. (See text and Peltzman [1990 (chap. 4)] for elaboration.) The value of k is 1.5 for presidential elections and 2 for nonpresidential elections. (Preliminary work indicated that voters weighed unexpected inflation more heavily than permanent income growth. These values of k are the approximate relative weights at the peak values of the total weights on income and inflation. However, the fit of HAPI is basically the same for any k between 1 and 2 in any type of elections.)

b. Federal spending growth: change in the log of real per capita federal spending (national income and product accounts definition, cycle adjusted). For (3) above, federal spending is adjusted for temporary Korean War Spending as described in the text. These variables are measured as annual rates over indicated periods preceding an election. For monthly data (inflation) October of election year is the terminal month for this calculation; for quarterly data (consumption, federal spending) the third quarter is the terminal quarter.

T-Bill rate: University of Chicago, Center for Research in Security Prices.

Election returns: *Congressional Quarterly.*

Apart from the substantial temporary effects, the Korean War also engendered a regime change. Post-Korean War defense spending was more than double the pre-War value.

I took account of this history as follows: I assumed that the transition to permanently higher Cold War levels of defense spending was revealed gradually over the course of the Korean War. To implement this, I estimated "permanent" defense spending in each quarter from 1950.3 through 1954.3 by linear interpolation of the 1950.2 and 1954.4 values. To these I added 3 percent of each quarter's temporary defense expenditures—a crude estimate of the permanent flow costs of the temporary expenditures. The regressions under (3) use this Korean-War-adjusted federal spending series.[12] They reveal a stronger distaste for federal spending than the regressions under (2), but without the strange "credit" for spending in the first half of a president's term. The pattern common to all kinds of elections in (3) is for the weight on federal spending to reach a peak at around a two-year lag and remain essentially flat thereafter. This means that voters punish spending in the last two years of a president's term and basically ignore the rest.[13] I do not pursue here the reasons voters ignore the older spending data when they do not ignore corresponding macroeconomic data.

The magnitude of the voters' aversion to federal spending is of some interest. In presidential elections the peak coefficient is on the order of

12. I made no similar adjustment for the Vietnam War, because this had a far smaller impact on the data than Korea. Here real defense spending rose by around 40 percent from 1965.1 to 1968.1, which is roughly the same magnitude as the defense buildup of the 1980s. The Vietnam buildup was essentially reversed by the end of 1972, but total federal spending kept rising through this period.

13. In Peltzman (1990) I showed that voters respond only to macroeconomic surprises during a president's term and ignore developments predictable from older data. The generally stronger results for adjusted federal spending in table 5.1 are consistent with this, since the adjustment removes movements in defense spending which are arguably predictable once the Korean War began. Attempts at further refinements on this theme proved unavailing. For post-1954.2 data, the log change of real total federal spending is essentially "white noise," i.e., a series of statistical "surprises." However, the behavior of the total masks regularities in the defense and nondefense components. These are mildly positively and negatively autocorrelated, respectively. (The respective first-order autocorrelation coefficients are around 0.3 and −0.2.) I used these regularities to extract defense and nondefense surprises as well as an aggregate surprise from the data. When I substituted the latter for the series used in table 5.1, part (3) the results were essentially identical. When I used the component surprises instead of the components in regressions subsequently analyzed, I again got essentially unchanged results. The most plausible reason for the failure of these refinements lies in the data rather than in voter behavior. The regularities are so mild that the correlation between the estimated surprise and the actual change is > 0.9. So the changes are for all practical purposes new information.

TABLE 5.2 Regressions of Incumbent Party Vote Share on Various Macroeconomic Measures and Changes in Federal Spending

	(1)						(2)			
	Consumption Residual		Unexpected Inflation		Δln Federal Spending, Adj.		Δ Unemployment		Unexpected Inflation	
LAG	Coeff	|t|	Coeff	|t|	Coeff	|t|	Coeff	|t|	Coeff	|t|
A. Presidential Elections										
12	2.2	9.7	−2.0	−2.7	−.6	6.7	−4.4	9.0	−1.4	1.8
18	1.9	7.6	−8.5	11.0	−1.0	13.6	−1.1	2.5	−9.9	11.2
24	5.0	12.0	−1.8	1.9	−.8	9.5	−4.2	9.0	−5.0	5.3
30	6.3	9.1	−0.1	0.1	−.9	6.0	−4.2	6.9	−8.6	7.6
36	8.1	17.7	−7.7	8.1	−1.2	9.2	−1.9	2.8	−14.3	11.8
42	8.7	20.4	−10.1	10.4	−1.5	11.7	−6.4	7.3	−12.6	9.4
48	8.8	19.2	−12.7	17.9	−1.4	10.3	−4.3	4.1	−11.7	11.6
B. Senate Elections										
12	0.7	2.5	−3.3	4.3	−0.1	1.9	−0.6	2.1	−3.7	5.1
18	1.0	3.6	−4.2	4.5	−0.3	3.2	−1.3	4.2	−4.8	5.3
24	1.6	4.3	−3.2	4.1	−0.2	2.6	−1.9	4.7	−4.4	5.4
30	2.0	4.3	−3.2	3.7	−0.3	2.3	−2.6	5.1	−5.2	5.6
36	2.4	4.3	−4.2	4.5	−0.3	2.2	−2.1	3.5	−5.0	5.1
42	2.3	4.1	−4.9	4.8	−0.3	2.5	−3.7	4.7	−6.6	5.9
48	2.5	3.8	−5.1	5.2	−0.3	2.0	−3.7	4.3	−6.1	5.9
C. Gubernatorial Elections										
12	0.5	−1.5	2.8	2.9	−0.1	1.2	−0.0	0.0	−3.2	3.5
18	0.8	2.1	−4.2	3.8	−0.3	2.2	−1.1	2.1	−4.9	4.4
24	1.5	3.0	−2.7	3.0	−0.3	2.0	−2.0	3.0	−3.7	3.7
30	1.9	3.1	−3.0	3.0	−0.3	2.1	−2.6	3.2	−3.6	4.0
36	2.3	3.5	−3.5	3.2	−0.3	1.7	−2.2	2.5	−4.2	3.4
42	2.4	3.4	−4.0	3.4	−0.3	1.7	−3.5	3.0	−5.6	4.0
48	2.6	3.3	−4.2	3.5	−0.2	1.2	−3.5	2.9	−5.3	3.9

one-fifth the peak coefficient of HAPI. In my sample period federal spending averages a bit over one-fifth of personal income. So, my best estimate is that voters are treating the marginal dollar of federal spending as essentially worthless.[14] The judgment of voters in the nonpresidential elections seems only slightly less harsh.

Table 5.2 tests the sensitivity of the results on federal spending to the macroeconomic specification. Fewer lags are shown, to save space and eye strain. All regressions use the adjusted federal spending variable in (3),

14. That is, there is no net political reward for a one dollar increase in income matched by a dollar increase in federal spending.

TABLE 5.2 continued

A. (continued)

(2)			(3)					
Δln Federal Spending, Adj.			Δ Unemploy- ment Rate		HAPI		Δln Federal Expenditures, Adj.	
Coeff	|t|		Coeff	|t|	Coeff	|t|	Coeff	|t|
−0.8	8.7	12	−2.4	3.8	1.3	5.1	−0.7	7.6
−1.0	13.4	18	+0.4	0.8	3.0	12.2	−0.9	12.1
−0.9	10.1	24	−3.0	7.0	2.8	11.0	−0.8	11.3
−0.4	2.2	30	−2.5	4.0	3.3	9.7	−0.6	3.8
−0.2	1.1	36	+2.3	4.3	7.7	24.0	−1.4	9.7
−0.1	0.5	42	−0.7	0.9	7.8	21.7	−1.4	9.6
−0.6	3.1	48	+1.0	1.3	8.8	24.6	−1.4	10.2

B. (continued)

−0.1	1.3	12	−0.1	0.3	1.0	4.9	−0.0	0.6
−0.2	2.7	18	−0.5	1.4	1.2	4.7	−0.1	1.9
−0.2	2.7	24	−0.9	2.3	1.5	5.6	−0.2	2.3
−0.2	1.6	30	−1.2	2.6	1.7	5.5	−0.2	1.8
−0.1	1.1	36	−0.9	1.6	2.2	5.9	−0.2	1.9
−0.2	1.7	42	−1.7	2.3	2.4	5.9	−0.3	2.3
−0.2	1.5	48	−1.8	2.3	2.5	6.0	−0.3	2.0

C. (continued)

−0.1	1.4	12	0.6	1.2	1.1	3.7	−0.1	1.1
−0.2	1.9	18	0.1	0.1	1.3	3.7	−0.2	1.6
−0.3	2.0	24	−0.7	1.1	1.6	3.9	−0.3	2.0
−0.2	1.5	30	−0.8	1.1	1.9	4.1	−0.3	1.9
−0.2	0.8	36	−0.5	0.7	2.3	4.3	−0.3	1.6
−0.2	1.1	42	−1.0	1.0	2.5	4.3	−0.3	1.6
−0.2	0.8	48	−1.0	1.0	2.7	4.3	−0.2	1.2

Note: See table 5.1 for sources and definitions of consumption residual, unexpected inflation, adjusted federal spending, and HAPI. (Civilian) unemployment rate is from Citibase.

table 5.1. The results under (1) just break HAPI into its components, and they confirm that consumption growth is a political good and unexpected inflation a bad. Then under (2) I replace the consumption residual with the change in unemployment, a variable frequently used in macro-voting studies. The clear result is that periods of increased unemployment are politically treacherous for the president's party. Finally, under (3) I add the change in unemployment to HAPI. With the exception of Senate elections, the unemployment variable does not seem to reliably add information to HAPI. Thus, there seems no compelling reason to go beyond the

TABLE 5.3 Summary of Effects of Noneconomic Variables
(Average Coefficients)

Variable	Presidential	Election Senate	Governor
1. Incumbency dummy	6.3	6.0	5.1
2. Lagged vote share	0.17[a]	0.27	0.00[b]

	DEM	REP	DEM	REP	DEM	REP
3. State-party dummies	RI	UT	SC	KS	MD	DE
Top 10 states;	MA	NE	TN	WY	KY	OR
in order of allegiance	MN	ID	GA	VT	NV	CA
to each party	WV	KS	RI	UT	MT	WY
	NY	AZ	WA	NH	NC	IN
	MD	ND	WV	SD	NJ	MI
	PA	WY	MA	IN	OK	NE
	MO	OK	WI	PA	TX	KS
	GA	NH	OH	OR	UT	PA
	MI	VA	MI	ID	WV	OH

Note: Data shown are based on averages of coefficients from the 24-, 36-, and 48-month lag specifications of the regression under (3) in table 5.1. For variable 3 states are listed in rank order of their average state-party dummies. Thus, Rhode Island is the most Democratic, and Utah the most Republican state in presidential elections. In the gubernatorial election sample, state-party dummies were sometimes combined geographically due to small samples. (See footnote 5.) In these cases the coefficient measures an average party effect across two bordering states. These cases are underscored, and the state with the most elections in each pair is listed first.

For variables 1, and 2 all coefficients used in the averages are significantly different from zero except

a. only two of three coefficients are significant;

b. none significant.

simple specification of the macroeconomy in table 5.1. However, the main message of table 5.2 for present purposes is in the federal spending coefficients. These are consistently negative, and, with the exception of the presidential election results in specification (2), the coefficients follow roughly the pattern and magnitude of their counterparts in table 5.1. While an exercise like that in table 5.2 can never be complete, this one suggests that the results on federal spending growth are not just a statistical fluke.

In table 5.3, I summarize the effect of noneconomic variables. This shows that an incumbent candidate has a vote share advantage of five to six percentage points.[15] The lagged vote share coefficient has the dimension of a serial correlation coefficient, so the results indicate some modest voter inertia in Senate elections, less in presidential elections, and none in

15. This should be taken as an overestimate of a "pure" incumbency advantage. Incumbents who face certain defeat will not run, so the ones who do run are a self-selected sample.

gubernatorial elections. This inertia could result from voters' incomplete adjustment to new information or, more likely, slowly shifting party preferences. These preferences are measured as state fixed effects, and this may be unreasonable for areas like the South, where a once substantial Democratic advantage has slowly eroded.

These state fixed effects are summarized in part 3 of the table. They show the well-known east-west division in party strength in presidential elections, the tendency of Southerners to maintain support of Congressional Democrats, and a good deal of local idiosyncracy in gubernatorial elections.[16]

Is It Spending or Taxes or Both?

The notion that voters like government spending but dislike taxes has become conventional wisdom. It is a staple of popular explanations for chronic budget deficits. In professional dress, this notion appears in political business cycle models (for example, Nordhaus [1975]). Here politicians buy votes with spending increases before an election but only raise taxes later. This conventional wisdom, however, is wrong. Panel A of table 5.4 shows the results of adding the growth of total federal revenues to the regressions in part (3) of table 5.1. (Here and subsequently, I try to aid visual comprehension by showing fewer lags than table 5.1 and multiplying coefficients by 100.) For presidential elections the revenue growth coefficients move erratically on both sides of zero. The pattern of spending growth coefficients is essentially the same as in table 5.1.

The only hint that taxes have any independent negative effects occurs in the non-presidential elections. Here the revenue coefficients are consistently negative. However, they tend to be indistinguishable from zero statistically and smaller and more sensitive to the lag specification than the spending coefficients. Someone with a strong prior belief about voter aversion to taxes might conclude from these results that the political costs of spending are ameliorated by deficit finance. But there is no evidence at all for the notion that spending is politically beneficial. Here, as with presidential elections, the one statistically reliable bad is spending, not taxes.

This conclusion is strengthened in panels B and C of table 5.4. Here I

---

16. For example, the most Republican and most Democratic states in gubernatorial elections border each other. This reflects Maryland's normal proclivity for Democrats plus a couple of outsized (vote share >0.7) Republican victories in Delaware. In general, relative to the other elections, the coefficients of the state-party dummies range less broadly and tend to be less precisely estimated in gubernatorial elections. This means that, for gubernatorial elections, the states toward the bottom of each ranking do not lean very strongly toward the listed party and that the rankings are sensitive to a few outliers, as in Delaware.

look at subsets of taxes that come directly from individuals (voters) rather than businesses. These generally produce effects weaker than total taxes, while leaving the spending coefficient pattern basically the same as in panel A of table 5.1. Thus, the weak results for revenues in panel A cannot be attributed to voter ignorance, rational or otherwise, of taxes that do not come immediately from their paychecks. The broad implication of table 5.2 is that the voter's basic objection is to resource transfers from the private to the federal government sector, not to who signs the associated check.

What Kind of Spending Do Voters Dislike?

The composition of federal spending has changed substantially over time. Table 5.5 provides some perspective. It shows a shift away from defense spending to domestic transfers that is most pronounced in the 1970s. The size of these shifts is sufficiently eloquent testimony to the political pressure behind programs like social security, medicare,[17] and local government subsidies. But they leave open questions about the relevant margin: do voters prefer a smaller growth rate for these programs? Or, is their displeasure with government spending driven mainly by a desire for a smaller military?

To address these policy-relevant questions, I expand the basic regressions to allow for different political weights across spending categories. To illustrate, recall that

(2) $IS = A + BX + \ldots$

For simplicity, let X be the log change in total per capita expenditures. This is approximately

(3) $X = \sum_i W_i X_i ,$

where
X_i = log change in per capita expenditures in category i, and
W_i = share of category i in total spending.
Thus, (2) imposes a restriction that each component $W_i X_i$ receive the same political weight B. This can be relaxed by entering the $W_i X_i$ separately in an expanded version of (2) and thereby permitting each category to have a different political weight.

The results are in table 5.6. Because the effective degrees of freedom

17. Medicare, social security, and companion programs for government workers and veterans now comprise around 90 percent of personal transfers.

TABLE 5.4 Coefficients of Federal Spending and Revenue Growth: Presidential, Senatorial, and Gubernatorial Elections, 1950–1988

Revenue Concept & Lag (Mos. before Election)	Presidential Elections				Senatorial Elections				Gubernatorial Elections			
	Spending Growth		Revenue Growth		Spending Growth		Revenue Growth		Spending Growth		Revenue Growth	
	Coeff × 100	|t|	Coeff × 100	|t|	Coeff × 100	|t|	Coeff × 100	|t|	Coeff × 100	|t|	Coeff × 100	|t|
A. Total federal revenue												
12	−46	4.9	−17	2.2	−10	1.9	−14	2.0	−10	1.2	−27	2.5
18	−88	12.0	11	1.4	−21	2.7	−8	0.8	−21	1.9	−27	1.7
24	−91	11.5	55	4.8	−23	2.8	−7	0.5	−26	2.0	−22	1.0
30	−65	4.2	−73	4.8	−31	2.7	−27	1.9	−34	2.1	−21	1.0
36	−101	6.3	−5	0.3	−26	2.1	−18	1.1	−29	1.6	−13	0.5
42	−172	9.6	37	1.8	−32	2.4	−20	1.0	−29	1.5	−31	1.0
48	−141	7.8	8	0.3	−28	2.0	−9	0.4	−23	1.1	−12	0.4
B. Personal taxes												
12	−44	4.1	−11	1.7	−4	0.7	−8	1.3	0	0.0	−14	1.3
18	−119	13.8	37	5.8	−15	1.9	−8	1.0	−15	1.2	−4	0.3

24	−156	13.0	78	7.8	−22	2.1	−2	0.2	−31	2.0	7	0.5
30	−64	4.3	−61	−6.2	−24	2.0	−20	2.0	−33	2.0	−6	0.4
36	−106	6.3	1	0.1	−19	1.4	−16	1.3	−32	1.6	4	0.2
42	−166	8.1	15	1.0	−23	1.4	−19	1.2	−30	1.4	−5	0.2
48	−125	7.5	−17	1.2	−21	1.2	−15	0.9	−27	1.2	5	0.2

C. Personal income taxes

12	−35	2.8	−12	2.2	−5	1.1	−4	1.1	−3	0.4	−8	1.2
18	−147	14.1	44	7.3	−17	2.4	−4	0.7	−18	1.5	0	0.0
24	−199	14.5	86	9.9	−25	2.6	3	0.4	−34	2.3	11	1.1
30	−92	6.7	−47	7.9	−29	2.4	−9	1.4	−34	2.1	1	0.1
36	−90	6.7	−19	2.7	−23	1.8	−9	1.1	−32	1.7	5	0.5
42	−156	9.4	6	0.6	−30	2.0	−7	0.7	−34	1.7	5	0.3
48	−129	7.8	−13	0.9	−24	1.5	−8	0.7	−29	1.4	13	0.8

Note: See note to table 5.1. All regressions include HAPI (coefficients not shown) plus a spending growth and revenue growth variable. Successive panels use narrower revenue categories (from national income and product accounts). As used here, personal taxes (panel B) are the sum of personal tax and nontax receipts plus contributions for social insurance. The latter is deducted for panel C. Spending growth, here and subsequently, is adjusted for Korean War spending.

TABLE 5.5 The Composition of Federal Government Spending: Period Averages, 1950–1988

Spending Category	Period and Percent of Total			
	1950–1959	1960–1969	1970–1979	1980–1988
1. Defense	51.1%	43.6%	27.2%	25.8%
2. Nondefense consumption	10.2	11.7	11.1	9.1
3. Transfers to:				
a) Persons	19.6	24.7	36.8	38.7
b) Foreigners	3.6	1.7	1.1	1.1
c) State and local govt.	5.5	8.8	14.8	10.9
4. Interest	7.6	6.4	6.8	12.1
5. Subsidies	2.3	3.2	2.2	2.4

Note: Categories are taken from National income and product accounts.

Source: Survey of Current Business. Defense spending for 1950–1959 adjusted for temporary Korean War spending as described in text.

are severely limited,[18] I show results only for a few overlapping twofold categorizations of spending. These results do not suggest any clear differences in the way voters evaluate broad expenditure categories. For each twofold categorization, the category-specific weights are consistently negative. For each type of election the peak values of the two weights are roughly equal and occur at roughly the same time (a lag of two or more years). The broad pattern emerging from table 5.6 is that, at the margin, a dollar is a dollar. Whether it is spent on the military or civilian sector[19] or on "public" goods or private goods (transfers), the marginal dollar is equally poisonous politically.

The results in table 5.6 are necessarily crude, so the "dollar-is-a-dollar" result is tentative. In the next section I investigate the electoral impact of state government spending, where the data permit finer categorization than is practical with federal spending. That investigation produces an interesting departure from the dollar-is-a-dollar result.

18. For the ten presidential elections in my sample, there are ten corresponding sets of federal budget growth rates. An intercept and three variables that vary over time but not cross-sectionally (incumbency and presidential party dummies and HAPI) leave only six effective degrees of freedom to fit separate budget weights.

19. When unadjusted defense expenditures are used in the regressions in panel A, the defense component has a significantly lower peak weight than the nondefense component in presidential elections. It would, however, be incautious to draw substantive conclusions from this result, given the potential measurement error in unadjusted defense spending. That error tends to bias the defense coefficient toward zero.

B. State Budgets and Gubernatorial Elections

The budget-making power of a governor is similar to that of a president.[20] Here I want to see if the voters' response is similar. Accordingly, I expand the basic gubernatorial election regression (2') to include state budget variables. This expansion is

$$(2'') \quad IS_{iT} = A + B(PR_{iT} \cdot X_t) + C \cdot PR_{iT} + D \cdot S_{iT} + \dots,$$

where

X_T = a vector of national macroeconomic and budget variables applicable to all states holding gubernatorial elections in year T;

PR_{iT} = $+1$ if incumbent governor's party in state i is the same as the president's, -1 otherwise;

S_{iT} = a vector of state budget variables for i which include revenues, expenditures, and components thereof as needed.

The state budget variables come from the Census Bureau's uniform classification system for state government budgets. This system has remained essentially unchanged over my sample period. So I was able to construct cross-sectionally comparable time series of state budget data for each of the 41 states in my sample. The Census data are annual, measured over the fiscal year which ends June 30 for most states. So we can observe only four annual changes between elections, rather than the sixteen quarterly changes available for federal budget data. Also, the alignment between these annual changes and election dates is imprecise.[21] Against these technical drawbacks is one great advantage: with 41 separate state budget histories there are many more effective degrees of freedom than the federal budget data provide.

The first regression in table 5.7 provides the basic result and a link to table 5.1, part (3), panel C. Here, the annual state budget changes are matched to the 12-, 24-, 36-, and 48-month lagged changes of the national

---

20. However, governors face tighter constraints on deficit finance.

21. The fiscal year (FY) ends June 30. Therefore, the expenditure flow for FY_t (X_t) is centered on the end of the last calendar year (CY), so $\Delta X_t = X_t - X_{t-1}$ is an estimate of the change in expenditure flow from beginning to the end of CY_{t-1}. Similarly ΔX_{t+1} estimates the change over CY_t. The end of CY_t occurs around seven weeks after election day. We cannot close this gap without imposing arbitrary interpolation schemes on the budget data. Accordingly, I use ΔX_{t+1} to represent the change in the "year" preceding the election, ΔX_t to represent the change in the second year back from the election, etc. (The FY_{t+1} budget is the last one submitted by a governor before a year t election.)

TABLE 5.6 Coefficients of Components of Federal Spending Growth Elections, 1950–1988

Spending Classification and Lag (Mos. before Election)	Presidential Elections				Senatorial Elections				Gubernatorial Elections			
	Coeff ×100	$\|t\|$	Coeff ×100	$\|t\|$	Coeff ×100	$\|t\|$	Coeff ×100	$\|t\|$	Coeff ×100	$\|t\|$	Coeff ×100	$\|t\|$
A. Defense, adjusted (D) and Nondefense (ND)	D		ND		D		ND		D		ND	
12	−35	2.1	−118	2.6	3	.3	−8	1.4	−19	1.5	6	0.6
18	−66	6.7	−147	8.9	−11	1.2	−21	2.4	−28	1.9	−5	0.4
24	−51	4.7	−169	8.0	−20	1.9	−23	2.2	−31	1.9	−17	1.0
30	−160	8.7	−83	6.1	−33	2.3	−24	2.1	−39	2.0	−26	1.6
36	−123	8.9	−82	6.4	−33	2.2	−21	1.6	−36	1.7	−20	1.0
42	−145	10.7	−164	10.8	−36	2.2	−29	2.0	−36	1.6	−24	1.1
48	−143	10.4	−150	8.8	−34	2.0	−22	1.4	−30	1.3	−14	0.6
B. Public (PUB) and private (PVT) goods = defense, adjusted + foreign transfers + nondefense consumption	PUB		PVT		PUB		PVT		PUB		PVT	
12	−55	6.5	41	1.2	−3	.3	−14	1.1	−20	1.7	20	1.0
18	−79	10.1	−184	7.2	−12	1.3	−41	2.6	−28	2.0	−9	0.4

24	-64	7.2	-211	7.0	-21	2.2	-38	2.2	-32	2.2	-26	1.0
30	-184	11.5	-110	7.2	-38	2.8	-34	2.3	-45	2.4	-37	1.7
36	-145	10.5	-57	3.5	-36	2.3	-24	1.2	-44	2.1	-19	0.7
42	-135	9.4	-175	9.7	-36	2.2	-40	1.9	-42	1.9	-27	0.9
48	-148	10.3	-174	8.4	-35	2.1	-27	1.2	-37	1.6	-15	0.5

C. Domestic transfers (TFR) and nontransfers (NTF); TFR = transfers to persons and state and local governments. NTF excludes interest.

	TFR		NTF		TFR		NTF		TFR		NTF	
12	-13	0.6	-52	6.9	-15	1.4	-0	0.1	15	.9	-18	1.7
18	-80	4.6	-73	10.0	-33	2.5	-10	1.2	-3	.2	-25	2.0
24	-83	3.6	-59	6.9	-26	1.8	-18	2.0	-11	.6	-28	2.1
30	-94	6.5	-160	10.8	-27	2.1	-32	2.6	-26	1.4	-38	2.2
36	-41	3.0	-132	10.4	-21	1.3	-32	2.3	-13	.6	-41	2.1
42	-124	7.6	-121	8.6	-34	2.0	-32	2.1	-18	.7	-38	1.8
48	-116	6.5	-124	8.9	-26	1.4	-32	2.1	-11	.4	-33	1.5

TABLE 5.7 Coefficients of State Budget Variables: Gubernatorial Elections, 1950–1988

Independent Variables (Annualized Growth Rate)	Years Preceding Election							
	1		2		3		4	
	Coeff × 100	$\|t\|$	Coeff × 100	$\|t\|$	Coeff × 100	$\|t\|$	Coeff × 100	$\|t\|$
1. HAPI	100	3.7	169	4.2	242	4.6	273	4.4
Federal spending	−5	0.6	−25	1.9	−29	1.6	−24	1.2
State spending	−16	2.3	−16	1.7	−24	2.3	−25	2.3
−|distributed lag|	[−16	2.2]	[−19	2.1]	[−25	2.3]	[−28	2.5]

(All subsequent regressions are distributed lags on state budget variables. They include four-year lag of HAPI and federal spending, but these coefficients are not reported.)

Independent Variables (Annualized Growth Rate)	1		2		3		4	
2. State spending	−10	1.1	−10	0.8	−13	0.8	−12	0.8
State revenues	−14	1.5	−12	0.9	−18	1.0	−24	1.1
3. State spending less highways	−10	1.3	−16	1.5	−33	2.4	−39	2.5
State revenues	−9	1.0	−2	0.1	4	0.2	5	0.2
4. State spending less highways	−8	1.1	−12	1.4	−26	2.7	−32	3.1
5. State spending from:								
a) own sources	−11	1.4	−11	1.0	−16	1.2	−20	1.4
b) federal aid	−41	2.4	−48	2.2	−56	2.0	−56	1.8

Note: Dependent variable in all regressions is the vote share of incumbent governor's party. In regression 1, state spending growth over the 12, 24, 36, and 48 months preceding election are included with corresponding lag values of HAPI and federal spending growth. (See note to table 5.1 for description of these variables; see associated text for other variables in these regressions.) Figures in brackets are sums of coefficients from the regression.

$$\text{Vote Share} = A + B_1 \cdot HAPI_{48} + B_2 \cdot \text{Federal spending growth}_{48} + \sum_{t=1}^{4} C_t \cdot \text{state spending growth} + \dots,$$

where t = number of years before election and the numbers in brackets are partial aggregates from the four separate values of C_t. This same distributed-lag regression form is used in all subsequent regressions in this and succeeding tables. All data refer to partial aggregates of distributed lag coefficients over the indicated period preceding election. The state budget totals used here are General Expenditure and General Revenue. These exclude receipts and spending for state-owned utility systems and liquor stores and for insurance trusts (employee retirement and unemployment compensation). The regressions use changes between fiscal years in the log of real per capita budget variables. For the year preceding election, the rate of change is measured from the fiscal year ending the June 30 preceding election to the next fiscal year. See text and footnote 17 for elaboration.

Regression 5 uses the identity: state spending = spending from own sources plus federal aid, and the resulting approximation.

$$\text{Total spending growth} = w \cdot \text{own sources growth} + (1 - w) \text{federal aid growth},$$

where w = own sources share of total spending. The coefficients are for the two terms in the approximation. Source for state budget data is U.S. Bureau of Census, *State Government Finances* (various years). Fiscal year 1989 data are estimated from the projected 1988–1989 growth rate of state general fund revenues and expenditures in *Statistical Abstract of the U.S.* [1989], p. 277. This state specific growth rate is applied to each expenditure category whenever a 1989 estimate is required.

macro and budget variables. The coefficients of these two variables (blown up here by 100) essentially duplicate their table 5.1 counterparts, and this pattern prevailed in every subsequent variation. Accordingly, only state budget coefficents are reported subsequently. Because there are sufficient degrees of freedom, it is possible to estimate a full distributed lag specification on state expenditures. The sum of weights from such a specification (with macroeconomic and federal spending terms measured over four years) are shown in brackets. These basically duplicate the results from the cruder technique used heretofore. This insensitivity to estimation method also proved robust. I report only results from the distributed lag specification subsequently.

The interesting result in the first regression in table 5.7 is that voters dislike state as well as federal spending. The next two regressions grapple with the issue of whether it is spending or taxes that they dislike. This is a fine point, given state constitutional (and capital market) limits on state deficit finance. But the evidence suggests that spending is the primary bad. This is not evident in regression 2, where the negative reaction to budget growth is reflected in two imprecisely measured coefficients. These results, however, are arguably affected by "measurement error" in total expenditures. The error arises because my data include capital expenditures. Accordingly, large capital expenditures can create predictably temporary bubbles in the data, much like war spending does at the federal level. The most important source of these temporary bubbles in state spending is highway expenditures.[22] To obtain a better proxy for growth of permanent state spending, I deleted highway spending from the total. The result, in regression 3, is that spending bears all the negative political weight. This is roughly consistent with the results for federal spending. At both federal and state levels, voters seem to focus their displeasure on the growth of permanent expenditures rather than explicit taxes.[23]

---

22. These currently account for roughly two-thirds of state capital spending compared with under 10 percent of total spending. The tendency for highway spending to engender large increases and then decreases in total state spending is sprinkled through my data. However, it is most prevalent in the 1950s and 1960 when most of the interstate highway network was built. Overall, the data imply that 36 percent of a year's growth in highway spending is offset in the three following years.

23. This interpretation is offered tentatively. It cannot be distinguished from one in which voters do not make permanent-transitory distinctions, but simply confine their dislike to nonhighway spending. As with federal spending, further attempts to separate statistically predictable from surprise elements of state spending proved unrewarding. The problems here were similar to those encountered with federal spending. (1) The estimated "surprise" tends to be highly correlated with actual spending growth, so the coefficients are not much different. (2) The predictable elements tend to be episodic (like constructing a highway) and not easily modeled as a conventional time-series process.

TABLE 5.8 Allocation of Aggregate State Expenditures: Fiscal Years, 1950–1988 (Percent of Total)

Expenditure Category	1950	1955	1960	1965	1970	1975	1980	1988
1. Education	28.5%	29.7%	32.7%	36.1%	39.8%	38.9%	38.5%	37.0%
a) Higher education	8.9	8.7	10.7	13.1	14.2	12.8	12.2	12.1
2. Welfare	19.5	15.1	13.6	13.4	17.0	18.4	19.4	19.5
3. Highways	22.0	27.9	26.5	24.3	17.4	12.6	11.0	9.4
4. Health and hospitals	8.1	8.7	7.7	7.2	7.0	7.3	7.8	8.1
5. All other	22.0	18.6	19.5	19.1	18.8	22.7	23.3	26.0

Source: U.S. Bureau of the Census. State Government Finances.
Note: Detail may not add to 100.0 because of rounding.

A substantial and growing share (around one-fourth currently) of state spending is financed by federal grants. In regression 5 in table 5.7 the federal contribution to state spending growth is separated from the rest. The results imply that a dollar of federal aid, more specifically election-year federal aid, costs the governor more votes than a dollar of state-financed spending. This intolerance for shifting the expenditure burden to others seems peculiar, even after allowing for the margin of error in the result. Some insight is offered by the next set of results that explores voter reaction to the detail of state spending.

Some background on this detail is provided in table 5.8. This shows how state expenditures have been allocated among the four categories that account for the bulk of expenditures. Education is, and has been, by far the biggest of these four. Its dominant role has hardly been affected by the recent relative decline in the school-age population.[24] The other notable trends are the decline of the highway share following the substantial completion of the interstate highway network, and the revival of welfare spending over the last two decades.[25]

If voters are treated as rational principals, they should be sensitive to

24. State expenditures for elementary and secondary education are predominately (over 90 percent recently) transfers to local school districts. These have been providing an increasing share of local school spending.

25. State welfare spending includes only need-based expenditures. The largest share (about one-half) of these payments today, and the source of most of the recent growth, is for medical care of the indigent (Medicaid). About half the remainder goes for categorical assistance programs like aid to families with dependent children. Thus, the distributional implications of state welfare spending differ substantially from the entitlement programs that dominate federal transfer payments. As indicated in the note to table 5.7, the state counterparts to these entitlement programs are excluded from my data.

TABLE 5.9 Distribution of State and Local Expenditure Benefits and of Voters by Income Quartile, 1970

| Spending Category | Income Rank and Share of Benefits (Percent) | | | | Inequality Index |
	0–25	25–50	50–75	75–100	
1. General expenditures[a]	14.6%	20.0%	26.0%	39.3%	19.3
2. Elementary/ secondary education	13.2	24.6	31.6	30.7	13.5
3. Higher education	1.5	8.5	25.4	64.6	69.8
4. Public assistance	61.6	26.0	8.7	3.9	89.8
5. Highways	11.9	21.7	29.6	36.8	18.0
6. Total expenditures	18.6	21.5	26.0	34.0	8.5
7. Voters	19.9	22.7	27.7	29.7	
(Total taxes	8.5	18.0	26.6	47.1	34.6)

Note: Expenditure and tax distributions are from Reynolds and Smolensky [1977]. They allocate 1970 state and local expenditures (national income and product accounts basis) to household income classes. I estimated quartile income and tax/benefit cutoffs by linear interpolation of income classes. A similar procedure is followed for voters. These data are for the 1970 general election from *Statistical Abstract of the U.S.* [1971], p. 365. Voters and voting age population are allocated by income of their families. The open-ended class here comprises 40 percent of the voting age population. I assigned the classwide average voting probability to each member. This procedure probably understates the number of voters from the wealthiest quartile, because voting participation increases with income.

The Inequality Index is the sum of the absolute difference between quartile expenditure (tax) and voter shares. Higher values imply more concentrated benefits or taxes.

a. These are a subcategory of total state and local expenditures. It includes health and hospitals plus "all other" from the state expenditure breakdown in table 5.8.

the distributional implications of expenditures. Table 5.9 provides some relevant background for a single year (1970) near the middle of my sample period. It shows an estimated distribution of benefits from state and local[26] budgets—and a distribution of voters—by income quartile. The distribution of expenditures is modestly regressive and follows closely the distribution of voters: the richest half of households accounts for roughly 60 percent of both expenditure benefits and voters. (Net benefits, however, are progressive.) This benefit pattern holds approximately for three of the five spending categories. The exceptions are higher education and public assistance, which are mirror images of each in terms of their allocation across income classes. Note, however, that public assistance benefits are the more concentrated across voters, because the heaviest recipients have the lowest voting participation. The "inequality index" (just the sum of

26. The data are adapted from Reynolds and Smolensky (1977). State level data are unavailable.

TABLE 5.10 Coefficients of Components of State Expenditure Growth: Gubernatorial Elections, 1950–1988

	Years Preceding Election (Coeffs × 100)							
	1		2		3		4	
Expenditure Components	Coeff	$\lvert t \rvert$	Coeff	$\lvert t \rvert$	Coeff	$\lvert t \rvert$	Coeff	$\lvert t \rvert$
1. Elementary/secondary ed.	30	1.4	25	0.7	−6	0.1	−29	0.6
Higher Education	7	0.3	−12	0.3	−18	0.3	−22	0.3
Welfare	−40	1.1	−77	1.8	−97	1.9	−98	1.8
Health	−36	0.6	−27	0.3	−13	0.1	−33	0.3
Highways	−9	0.6	0	0.0	8	0.3	17	0.5
All others	−31	1.8	−26	1.0	−34	1.2	−31	0.9
2. Higher Education	14	0.6	5	0.2	6	0.2	−4	0.1
Welfare	−28	1.1	−57	1.8	−69	1.8	−71	1.7
Other[a]	−8	0.9	−8	0.6	−22	1.4	−27	1.6
3. Welfare	−26	1.1	−56	1.8	−67	1.8	−69	1.7
Other[a]	−5	0.7	−6	0.5	−18	1.5	−24	1.8

Note: Data are from regressions of the general form vote share = $\sum_{t=1}^{4} C_t^i (W_t^i X_t^i)$ + other terms including four-year macroeconomy and federal spending variables, where X_t^i = change in log of expenditure category i's share of the tth year preceding election; W_t^i = category i's share of total expenditures at the start of t; C_t^i = regression coefficient.

This regression produces four coefficients per expenditure category, one for each lagged value of expenditure growth. These are summed over the indicated interval to yield the total weights reported here. To illustrate the meaning of these total weights, consider the entry under 3 for welfare in regression 1 (−97). This says that a 1 percent increase in total state spending in each of the three pre-election years will reduce the incumbent party's vote share by 0.97 percentage points, if the increase is devoted entirely to welfare.

a. Excludes highway spending.

absolute differences of benefit and voter shares) in the last column of the table summarizes these patterns.

Table 5.9 suggests that a randomly selected majority of self-interested voters would reserve their strongest displeasure for higher education and, especially, welfare spending. These categories provide the slimmest benefits for most voters. The results in table 5.10 are consistent with half of this suggestion, the one about welfare spending. The table shows weights for various expenditure categories (see discussion of equation (3)). The first regression uses the finest categorization of my data. The only result close to standing out from a welter of otherwise imprecisely estimated coefficients is a negative voter response to growth of welfare spending. This result is common to the two subsequent regressions. Regression 2 shows that even though it does not benefit many voters, higher education growth is not politically costly. The contrast between this negative result and the result for welfare suggests that the marginal voters are not a random subset of the population. It suggests that the wealthy, better-educated, and presumably better-informed voters who benefit from higher education populate the relevant margin in numbers sufficient to neutralize opposition.

While the relevant standard errors are large enough to suggest caution, the main message in table 5.10, summarized by regression 3, seems to be that voters distinguish welfare spending from everything else. They dislike spending generally, but dislike welfare spending about three times as much as other kinds. This helps illuminate the odd aversion to federal grants in table 5.8. Federal grants are not unconditional; they are designed to subsidize the "price" of specific programs. And over my sample period the largest single chunk of federal subsidies has gone to welfare. These have typically accounted for 40 to 50 percent of federal aid.[27] Thus, one can interpret voter distaste for federal subsidies as mirroring their dislike of the welfare expenditures engendered by these subsidies.

The voters' valuation of marginal state expenditures cannot be deduced directly from table 5.10.[28] However, a comparison of table 5.10 and the results for presidential elections in table 5.1 is suggestive. Note, for example, that the peak weight on state welfare spending in table 5.10 is around one-tenth the peak weight on the happiness index in presidential elections in table 5.1, and recall that state expenditures are also around one-tenth of private incomes. This suggests that extra welfare spending is worthless to the marginal voter.[29] A similar exercise for nonwelfare spending suggests a value of around 70¢ per $1 of such spending. These calculations have to be regarded as tentative, because the voters in presidential and gubernatorial elections are different.[30]

Some Extensions

So far, I have proceeded as if every governor's budget elicits the same voter response. But the underlying principal-agent framework suggests other-

27. The exception is the 1960s when highway subsidies peaked and the welfare share declined to about one-third.

28. The reason is that a governor is not the agent primarily held responsible for private income gains.

29. To see this, suppose that private incomes (I) rise by ΔI. This raises HAPI by ($\Delta I/I$), and the agent held responsible for this rise (the president) is rewarded by $[(b_p/I) \cdot \Delta I]$, where b_p is the relevant coefficient of HAPI. A ΔW increase in state welfare spending raises the welfare component of regression 3 in table 5.10 by ($\Delta W/S$), where S is total state spending. The responsible agent (the governor) is penalized by $[(b_{wg}/S) \cdot \Delta W]$, where b_{wg} is the coefficient of the welfare term in table 5.10. If $b_{wg} = 0.1 \, b_p$ and $S = 0.1I$, then the penalty for converting ΔI into ΔW just offsets the reward for ΔI. So voter utility after the conversion is the same as if $\Delta I = 0$.

30. Most gubernatorial elections are in off-years when turnout is systematically lower. So more voters evaluate the president than governors, and these extra voters may have different sensitivity to economic information than the rest.

wise. Consider an election pitting a Big Government candidate against an advocate of fiscal austerity. The ensuing budgetary policy and electoral consequences thereof ought to depend on who wins. Above-average budget growth should, for example, allow a winning Big Government candidate to retain his or her electoral majority.

The political market, however, does not function so simply. I have no practical way to categorize the platforms of the candidates in the 300-odd gubernatorial elections in my sample. So I use party labels and the well-known tendency for Democrats to draw lower income voters than Republicans. Table 5.9 shows that state fiscal systems are progressive, and this implies that Democrats' constituencies should be more tolerant of spending growth than Republicans'.

The first hint of difficulty is that the corollary of this does not hold: the simple correlation between spending growth and an incumbent party dummy is essentially zero in my sample. The same result holds for all spending categories. None of the correlations exceed 0.1, not even for welfare or higher education where the parties' redistributive interests seem in sharpest conflict.

The more intriguing results are in table 5.11 which shows how voters respond to the budgets of Democratic and Republican governors. Here there is a dramatic difference, precisely opposite to naive expectations. The first regression shows that Democratic governors are hurt more by budget growth than Republicans are. Indeed, only Democratic governors are hurt. The second regression shows that the party difference tends to hold for both welfare and nonwelfare spending, but it is sharply defined only for the latter category. The safest conclusion is that voters always dislike welfare spending, but are especially severe on Democrats who expand the nonwelfare budget. This party difference in the voter response to spending sheds light on the lack of any corresponding difference in actual spending patterns. It suggests an equilibrium in which the voters are neutralizing the Democrats' higher demand for spending by imposing a higher political price on them.[31]

---

31. Further exploration of the role of state politics proved unrewarding. I examined several commonly used measures of a state's "liberalism" (the ADA rating of its congressional delegation, George McGovern's share of the vote in 1972, one minus Barry Goldwater's share in 1964) for a link to the voter response to state spending. There was no evidence that the response was more muted in the more liberal states. I also examined the interaction with the long-run growth rate differential between state spending and income. The notion here is that voters in states with higher long-run budget growth are more tolerant of budget growth. There is mild support for this in the data, but it disappears when the party interaction is added.

TABLE 5.11 Coefficients of State Expenditures by Party of Incumbent Governor: Gubernatorial Elections, 1950–1988

Variable and Party	Years Preceding Election							
	1		2		3		4	
	Coeff	$|t|$	Coeff	$|t|$	Coeff	$|t|$	Coeff	$|t|$
1. Total expenditures								
(a) Republicans	−0	0.0	3	0.2	−8	0.5	−12	0.8
(b) Democrats	−17	1.8	−32	2.4	−49	3.4	−55	3.8
Difference [(a) − (b)]	16	1.1	35	1.9	41	2.0	44	2.0
2. Components								
(1) Welfare								
(a) Republicans	−11	0.2	−43	0.8	−38	0.7	−69	1.2
(b) Democrats	−39	1.2	−82	1.7	−110	1.8	−79	1.1
Difference	28	0.5	39	0.5	72	0.8	11	0.1
(2) Nonwelfare								
(a) Republicans	9	0.8	13	0.9	5	0.3	7	0.3
(b) Democrats	−15	1.6	−26	1.7	−42	2.5	−50	2.8
Difference	24	1.6	39	1.8	48	1.9	56	2.1

Note: Data are from regressions of the form,

Vote share $= \Sigma_t\, C_t \cdot X_t + \Sigma_t\, D_t \cdot (IP \cdot X_t)$ + other terms (see notes to tables 5.5 and 5.8),

where

X_t = expenditure growth in year t preceding election;

IP = +1 if the incumbent party is Republican, −1 if Democrat.

For any t the coefficient for Republicans is $C + D$. For Democrats it is $C − D$, and the difference is $2D$. These values are accumulated over the indicated period prior to election to yield data shown. (Differences may differ from line (a) − line (b) due to rounding.) In regression 2 the X_t are decomposed into weighted components. (See note to table 5.10.) Total and nonwelfare expenditures exclude highway spending.

So far, I have imposed a linear voter response to budget growth. This may be too restrictive. My central result implies only that voters dislike budget growth at the rates typically observed in my data. This does not mean that voters would like the state to wither away or even stop growing. My data cover a sufficiently broad range[32] to motivate investigation of the empirical weight of this qualification. The results of this are in table 5.12. Here I use linear splines to allow for different voter responses to different expenditure growth rates. The first regression allows a different response on either side of zero. Taken literally, the regression says that the voters like zero growth best, since deviations on either side cost votes. What the

32. The standard deviation of the annual growth rate of state spending over a four-year term is roughly 4 percent, around an average of 4.5.

TABLE 5.12 Coefficients of State Expenditure Growth by Growth Rate:
Gubernatorial Elections, 1950–1988

	Years Preceding Election							
	1		2		3		4	
Growth Rate	Coeff	|t|	Coeff	|t|	Coeff	|t|	Coeff	|t|
1. (a) Negative	39	1.6	36	1.3	30	0.9	39	1.1
(b) Positive	−19	2.2	−20	1.8	−39	3.2	−46	3.9
Difference [(a) − (b)]	59	2.1	56	1.7	69	1.8	85	2.2
2. (a) ≤ 4.5 percent	4	0.2	1	0.1	−4	0.2	0.4	0.2
(b) > 4.5 percent	−17	1.5	−21	1.5	−48	3.0	−58	3.8
Difference	20	0.9	22	0.9	44	1.5	54	1.8
3. (a) ≤ 4.5 percent, Democrats	7	0.4	2	0.1	4	0.1	30	1.0
(b) > 4.5 percent, Democrats	−33	2.2	−59	2.9	−93	4.1	−100	4.7
Difference	39	1.5	61	1.8	96	2.4	130	3.1

Note: Data are from estimates of linear splines that allow different slopes for growth rates above or below indicated cutoffs. Regression 3 imposes the additional restriction that coefficients for Republican governors = 0. See note to table 5.8 for explanation of basic regression form and handling of distributed lag weights.

Expenditures exclude highway spending.

voters have actually received is roughly 4½ percent real per capita growth on average. The next regression uses this dividing line, and the results say that only above-average growth is penalized. The last regression uses the same dividing line, but imposes the further restriction suggested by table 5.9 that spending is costly only for Democrats. This produces the same general result as regression 2 in sharper form. The safest conclusion from table 5.10 is that the marginal political cost of spending growth is increasing and that governors have little to fear from modest spending growth.[33]

Table 5.13 makes the same point less formally. It details the fate of the gubernatorial administrations in the extremes of the spending distribution. The two groups hardly differ at all in party composition, in the willingness of incumbents to seek reelection or in the ultimate obscurity of most of the governors. But the difference in their electoral fate is palpable.

33. The results of a similar exercise with federal expenditures were mixed, but hinted at the same pattern as table 5.12. Specifically, I constructed linear splines on federal expenditures growth around 3 percent (the approximate mean) and reestimated the regressions under (3), table 5.1. For presidential elections there was no pattern consistent with the difference between the coefficients on the two branches of the spline. However, for both senatorial and gubernatorial elections, all these differences followed the pattern in table 5.12. That is, above-average federal spending growth provoked the stronger negative voter response. These differences were typically about 1 to 1.5 standard deviations from zero.

The free-spenders win less than half as frequently as the abstemious, and their average vote share is five points less. This result is, however, driven more by the penalty for spending than by any special reward for stinginess. The vote share and win frequency for the stingy governors are statistically indistinguishable from the full-sample averages (53.1 vote share and 0.62 win frequency for the incumbent party). This is consistent with the asymmetric payoff function estimated in table 5.12. I comment below on the interesting time pattern in table 5.13.

IV. CONCLUSIONS

The main message of this paper is that government has grown faster than the voters wish. This is true at both the federal and state level. In retrospect, there is an obvious reason for the voters' fiscal conservatism. Federal and state fiscal systems are progressive, and voters are wealthier than nonvoters. Thus, well-informed self-interested voters could be expected, on balance, to oppose marginal expansion of government budgets.

If these results occasion any surprise, it is because political economists resist the notion that significant numbers of voters are well informed. While there seem to be good theoretical reasons for this skepticism, my results suggest that they are not good enough. The voting market clearly uses publicly available budget information, even the relatively obscure information about state budgets. And this market seems to use this information sensibly. For example, it seems able to distinguish temporary perturbations of the budget growth path (due to war spending or a one-shot highway project) from permanent changes. It reflects the fact that expenditures transfer resources from the private sector whether they are financed by taxes or not. It tends to cast the most jaundiced eye toward the kind of spending (welfare) with the slimmest benefits for most voters. And this market does not discard much information. In most regressions budget information from two or three years preceding election, not just the immediate pre-election period, carries political weight.

In short, there seems to be an agency problem in politics similar to the widely discussed agency problem in corporate governance. The principals are tolerably well informed. The market registers this information. But the agents are still able to dissipate some of the principals' wealth. The obvious questions are why they want to and how they are able to dissipate this wealth.

It would be unhelpful to try to catalog the myriad ways in which political agents might derive utility from public spending. However, one is worth discussing, because it can be addressed by the data. This stems from

TABLE 5.13 The Electoral Fate of the Twenty Most Profligate and Twenty Most Abstemious Gubernatorial Administrations: 1950–1988 Election Sample

Governor	Party	State	Election Year	Annual Expenditure Growth Rate, Prev. 4 Yrs[a]	Election Outcome Gov. Runs Again?	Election Outcome Party's Vote Share (Percent)
			A. The 20 biggest spenders			
1. Earl Wright	R	WY	50	22.9	N	56.1
2. James Duff	R	PA	50	18.9	N	51.2
3. John Bonner	D	MT	52	18.2	Y	49.1
4. Vail Pittman	D	NV	50	18.0	Y	42.4
5. Richard Hughes	D	NJ	69	17.4	N	39.2
6. William Lane	D	MD	50	16.2	Y	42.7
7. Elbert Carvel	D	DE	52	15.6	Y	47.9
8. John Dempsey	D	CT	70	15.6	N	46.2
9. Richard Ogilvie	R	IL	72	13.6	Y	49.2
10. Chester Bowles	D	CT	50	13.5	Y	49.0
11. Raymond Shafer	R	PA	70	12.9	N	43.0
12. Harold Levander	R	MN	70	12.7	N	45.7
13. Kenneth Curtis	D	ME	70	12.5	Y	50.1
14. Mills Godwin	D	VA	69	12.4	N	46.4
15. C. A. Robins	R	ID	50	12.1	N	52.6
16. Norbert Tiemann	R	NE	70	11.8	Y	44.8
17. Hulett Smith	D	WV	68	11.6	N	49.1
18. Marvin Mandel	D	MD	70	11.6	Y	67.0
19. Nelson Rockefeller	R	NY	66	11.6	Y	53.9
20. Bert Combs	D	KY	63	11.5	N	50.7
Mean or share (S.D)	0.6 = D				0.5 = Y	48.8 (5.8)

[Win proportion = 0.35]

B. The 20 stingiest spenders

#	Name	Party	State		[a]		
1.	J. Hugo Aronson	R	MT	56	-7.3	Y	51.4
2.	John Fire	R	PA	54	-6.6	N	46.2
3.	Adlai Stevenson	D	IL	52	-4.0	N	47.4
4.	Richard Riley	D	SC	82	-2.0	Y	69.8
5.	Albert Quie	R	MN	82	-1.9	N	40.6
6.	John Evans	D	ID	82	-1.8	Y	50.6
7.	Len Jordan	R	ID	54	-1.8	N	54.2
8.	Richard Thornburgh	R	PA	82	-1.3	Y	51.4
9.	Hugh Carey	D	NY	78	-1.0	Y	53.0
10.	Lamar Alexander	R	TN	82	-1.0	Y	59.6
11.	James Thompson	R	IL	82	-0.9	Y	50.1
12.	Mike O'Callaghan	D	NV	78	-0.8	N	41.4
13.	William Janklow	R	SD	82	-0.8	Y	70.9
14.	John Brown	D	KY	83	-0.8	N	55.3
15.	Edmund Brown	D	CA	82	-0.8	N	49.4
16.	Reubin Askew	D	FL	78	-0.7	N	55.6
17.	Raul Castro	D	AZ	78	-0.6	N	54.0
18.	Charles Russell	R	NV	54	-0.5	Y	53.1
19.	Scott Matheson	D	UT	80	-0.4	Y	55.4
20.	Robert Graham	D	FL	82	-0.4	Y	64.7
	Mean or share (S.D)	0.55 = D				0.6 = Y	53.7*
							(7.7)

[win proportion = 0.75*]

*Significantly greater than panel A.

a. Real per capita, nonhighway spending.

Keynesian pump-priming: voters may not like extra federal spending, but they do like extra private income. If the one leads to the other, there may be a net political benefit and, consequently, no real agency problem. The facts, however, suggest otherwise. My data reveal no significant feedback between federal growth and my summary index of macroeconomic conditions.[34] The weak feedback there is goes in the right direction, but not enough to begin resolving the agency problem.[35]

The larger question is how political agents can persistently dissipate voter wealth; that is, why has government grown so much (and why is it fiscally progressive)? I have no good answer, only a challenge to future research. I can, however, use my data to offer some possibilities.

One is that the political costs of growing budgets are too weak to compel much restraint. Consider an incumbent president or governor running for reelection. According to table 5.3, they begin with a five or six point vote share advantage over their rival. Table 5.1 implies that this advantage will be offset by an extra 3+ percent per year of federal spending growth sustained over most of the president's term. Table 5.12 suggests that a poorly situated governor (a Democrat inheriting an annual spending growth path of 4½ percent) can sustain 4+ percent per year extra spending growth over his or her term without dissipating the incumbency advantage. Both spending growth figures are on the order of a standard deviation of the respective data. Or, look at table 5.13. It suggests that incumbent governors have to be in the upper tail of the spending distribution to offset their incumbency advantage. These exercises suggest that incumbents can indulge in nontrivial spending growth before they risk a close call next election day. Of course a nonincumbent who inherits defense of such profligacy is not so well situated. But this may trouble the retiring incumbent less than it does his or her heir presumptive.

Another line of inquiry concerns the role of learning. My sample period begins in the aftermath of an unprecedented—and politically successful—peacetime expansion of government spending. It ends at a time of renascent political conservatism. My results say that intervening budget growth paths were too great ex post. But to a faithful agent in 1950 who

34. Recall that my federal spending variable is net of built-in fiscal stabilizers.

35. I regressed annual growth rates of the happiness index on distributed lags of up to four years' federal spending growth. None of the individual coefficients and none of their sums were significantly different from zero. The best-fitting model ($\bar{R}^2 = 0.02$) was the simple regression of this year's HAPI on last year's federal spending growth. It implied a 0.06 increase in HAPI per 1 percent extra spending growth. Table 5.1 implies that an increase in HAPI of three or four times this amount is needed to offset the political cost of the extra spending growth.

could not know these results, these growth paths may have seemed right ex ante. And there is enough noise in the data for the required Bayesian updating to have taken a while. A glance at some broad trends supports this view. From 1950 to 1980 the annual real per capita federal spending growth rate exceeded 4 percent. Since then it has been under 2 percent. There has been a similarly sharp reduction in aggregate state spending growth.[36] This marked slowdown of budget growth suggests that the voting market may finally have overcome the agents' ignorance. The time pattern in table 5.13 seems consistent with the importance of learning. The politically unsuccessful extreme spending growth in panel A seems concentrated in the late 1960s, when a number of domestic spending initiatives (Great Society, War on Poverty, Revenue Sharing) stimulated state spending. The more successful abstemiousness in panel B is concentrated about a decade later, in the wake of tax reduction initiatives (Proposition 13 in California) and a general disillusion with the efficacy of government programs that culminated in the 1980 presidential election. This pattern suggests that a lot of learning occurred within a relatively short interval. If the learning story is correct, we can expect future budget growth to be both slower and less variable than it was before 1980, as political agents seek to avoid the political damage from extremely high spending growth rates.

REFERENCES

Buchanan, James, and Gordon Tullock, *The Calculus of Consent* (Ann Arbor: University of Michigan Press, 1962).

Downs, Anthony, *An Economic Theory of Democracy* (New York: Harper, 1957).

Fama, Eugene, and Michael Gibbons, "A Comparison of Inflation Forecasts," *Journal of Monetary Economics,* XIII (1984), 327–48.

Hall, Robert, "Stochastic Implications of the Life Cycle–Permanent Income Hypothesis: Theory and Evidence," *Journal of Political Economy,* LXXXVI (1978), 971–87.

Holloway, Thomas, Jane Reeb, and Ivy Dunson, *Cyclical Adjustment of the Federal Budget and Federal Debt: Updated Detailed Methodology and Estimates,* Bureau of Economic Analysis Staff Paper 45 (Washington: Bureau of Census, 1986).

Kramer, Gerald H., "Short Term Fluctuations in U.S. Voting Behavior, 1896–1914," *American Political Science Review,* LXV (1971), 131–43.

Niskanen, William, "Bureaucrats and Politicians," *Journal of Law and Economics,* XXVIII (1975), 617–44.

Nordhaus, William, "The Political Business Cycle," *Review of Economic Studies,* XLII (1975), 169–90.

36. From $4^1/_2$ percent annually in 1950–1980 to half this subsequently.

Peltzman, Sam, "How Efficient is the Voting Market?" *Journal of Law and Economics,* XXXIII (1990), 27–64 (chap. 4 of this volume).

Reynolds, Morgan, and Eugene Smolensky, *Public Expenditures, Taxes and the Distribution of Income* (New York: Academic Press, 1977).

Stigler, George, "The Theory of Economic Regulation," *Bell Journal of Economics and Management Science,* II (1971), 3–21.

PART TWO

Government and Regulation

Toward a More General Theory of Regulation

George Stigler's work on the theory of regulation is one of those rare contributions—rare for the rest of us, though not for him—which force a fundamental change in the way important problems are analyzed. Stigler's influence will be clear in this article. There is perhaps no more telling evidence of this influence than that its basic motivation was my dissatisfaction with some of Stigler's conclusions. (It was a dissatisfaction that Stigler shared, since I can report that we simultaneously reached one of the conclusions elaborated here—that regulatory agencies will not exclusively serve a single economic interest.) My intellectual debt to Stigler is so great that this article emerges as an extension and generalization of his pioneering work.

What Stigler accomplished in his *Theory of Economic Regulation* was to crystallize a revisionism in the economic analysis of regulation that he had helped launch in his and Claire Friedland's work on electric utilities.[1] The revisionism had its genesis in a growing disenchantment with the usefulness of the traditional role of regulation in economic analysis as a *deus ex machina* which eliminated one or another unfortunate allocative consequence of market failure. The creeping recognition that regulation seemed seldom to actually work this way, and that it may have even engendered more resource misallocation than it cured, forced attention to the influence which the regulatory powers of the state could have on the distribu-

First published in *Journal of Law and Economics* 19, no. 2 (August 1976): 211–240. © 1976 by The University of Chicago.

This study has been supported by a grant from the National Science Foundation to the National Bureau of Economic Research for research in law and economics. The paper is not an official Bureau publication since it has not yet undergone the full critical review accorded Bureau publications, including review by the Bureau's Board of Directors. The views expressed herein are those of the author and do not necessarily reflect the views of the National Bureau of Economic Research.

1. George J. Stigler, The Theory of Economic Regulation, 2 Bell J. of Econ. & Man. Sci. 3 (1971); and George Stigler & Claire Friedland, What Can Regulators Regulate? The Case of Electricity, 5 J. Law & Econ. 1 (1962).

tion of wealth as well as on allocative efficiency. Since the political process does not usually provide the dichotomous treatment of resource allocation and wealth distribution so beloved by welfare economists, it was an easy step to seek explanation for the failure of the traditional analysis to predict the allocative effects of regulation in the dominance of political pressure for redistribution on the regulatory process. This focus on regulation as a powerful engine for redistribution shows clearly in such works as Jordan's *Producer Protection* and Posner's *Taxation by Regulation.*[2] The common role of regulation in this literature is as a fulcrum upon which contending interests seek to exercise leverage in their pursuit of wealth. A common, though not universal,[3] conclusion has become that, as between the two main contending interests in regulatory processes, the producer interest tends to prevail over the consumer interest.

In one sense, Stigler's work provides a theoretical foundation for this "producer protection" view. However, its scope is much more general. It is ultimately a theory of the optimum size of effective political coalitions set within the framework of a general model of the political process. Stigler seems to have realized that the earlier "consumer protection" model comes perilously close to treating regulation as a free good. In that model the existence of market failure is sufficient to generate a demand for regulation, though there is no mention of the mechanism that makes that demand effective. Then, in a crude reversal of Say's Law, the demand is supplied costlessly by the political process. Since the good, regulation, is not in fact free and demand for it is not automatically synthesized, Stigler sees the task of a positive economics of regulation as specifying the arguments underlying the supply and demand for regulation.

The way he does this abstracts almost completely from pure allocation questions. The essential commodity being transacted in the political market is a transfer of wealth, with constituents on the demand side and their political representatives on the supply side. Viewed in this way, the market here, as elsewhere, will distribute more of the good to those whose effective demand is highest. For Stigler, the question of which group will have the highest effective demand translates very quickly into a question of numbers. In this view, "producer protection" represents the dominance of a small group with a large per capita stake over the large group (consumers)

---

2. William A. Jordan, Producer Protection, Prior Market Structure and the Effects of Government Regulation, 15 J. Law & Econ. 151 (1972); and Richard A. Posner, Taxation by Regulation, 2 Bell J. of Econ. & Man. Sci. 22 (1971).

3. Richard A. Posner, *supra* note 2, is an important exception.

with more diffused interests. The central question for the theory then becomes to explain this regularity of small group dominance in the regulatory process (and indeed the political process generally). The way the question is posed already foreshadows one of the results of the theory. For in Stigler's model, unlike most market models, there are many bidders, but only one is successful. There is essentially a political auction in which the high bidder receives the right to tax the wealth of everyone else, and the theory seeks to discover why the successful bidder is a numerically compact group. The answer lies essentially in the relationship of group size to the costs of using the political process.

To summarize the argument briefly, the size of the dominant group is limited in the first instance by the absence of something like ordinary-market-dollar voting in politics. Voting is infrequent and concerned with a package of issues. In the case of a particular issue, the voter must spend resources to inform himself about its implications for his wealth and which politician is likely to stand on which side of the issue. That information cost will have to offset prospective gains, and a voter with a small per capita stake will not, therefore, incur it. In consequence the numerically large, diffuse interest group is unlikely to be an effective bidder, and a policy inimical to the interest of a numerical majority will not be automatically rejected. A second major limit on effective group size arises from costs of organization. It is not enough for the successful group to recognize its interests; it must organize to translate this interest into support for the politician who will implement it. This means not only mobilizing its own vote, but contributing resources to the support of the appropriate political party or policy: to finance campaigns, to persuade other voters to support or at least not oppose the policy or candidate, perhaps occasionally to bribe those in office. While there may be some economies of scale in this organization of support and neutralization of opposition, these must be limited. The larger the group that seeks the transfer, the narrower the base of the opposition and the greater the per capita stakes that determine the strength of opposition, so lobbying and campaigning costs will rise faster than group size. The cost of overcoming "free riders" will also rise faster than group size. This diseconomy of scale in providing resources then acts as another limit to the size of the group that will ultimately dominate the political process.

In sum, Stigler is asserting a law of diminishing returns to group size in politics: beyond some point it becomes counterproductive to dilute the per capita transfer. Since the total transfer is endogenous, there is a corollary that diminishing returns apply to the transfer as well, due both to the opposition provoked by the transfer and to the demand this opposition exerts on resources to quiet it.

Stigler does not himself formalize this model, and my first task will be to do just this. My simplified formal version of his model produces a result to which Stigler gave only passing recognition, namely that the costs of using the political process limit not only the size of the dominant group but also their gains. This is, at one level, a detail, which is the way Stigler treated it, but a detail with some important implications—for entry into regulation and for the price-output structure that emerges from regulation. The main task of the article is to derive these implications from a generalization of Stigler's model.

A STIGLERIAN MODEL OF REGULATION

I begin with the presumption that what is basically at stake in regulatory processes is a transfer of wealth. The transfer, as Stigler points out, will rarely be in cash, but rather in the form of a regulated price, an entry restriction, and so on. I shall ignore that detail here, and the resulting model applies to any political wealth redistribution. A particularization to price and entry regulation comes later. I treat the relevant political process as if control of the relevant taxing power rests on direct voting, though this too is meant only for simplification. Though appointment of a regulatory body may lie effectively with a legislature, a committee thereof, or an executive, the electorate's receptivity to these intermediaries ought to be affected by the performance of their appointees. With Stigler, I assume that beneficiaries pay with both votes and dollars. However, again as a simplification, I assume that the productivity of the dollars to a politician lies in mitigation of opposition. A more general model might make "dollars" (broadly defined to include, for example, employment of former regulators) a source of direct as well as indirect utility to the regulator. In this model, though, direct political support—"votes"—is the object sought directly by the regulator. More particularly, he seeks to maximize net votes or a majority in his favor. There is no presumption that the marginal utility of a majority vanishes at one. Greater majorities are assumed to imply greater security of tenure, more logrolling possibilities, greater deference from legislative budget committees, and so on. The crucial decision that the regulator (or would-be regulator) must make in this model is the numerical size of the group he promises favors, and thus implicitly the size of the group he taxes. At this stage, I retain Stigler's presumption that the agency confers benefits on a single victorious group, and the essential purpose of the model is to elaborate the limits on this group's size.

To put this formally, the regulator wants to maximize a majority M, generated by

(1) $M = n \cdot f - (N - n) \cdot h$,

where

    n = number of potential voters in the beneficiary group
    f = (net) probability that a beneficiary will grant support
    N = total number of potential voters
    h = (net) probability that he who is taxed (every non-n) opposes.

Note that, because both gainers and losers face transaction and information costs, f and h are not either zero or unity, but depend on the amount of the group member's gain or loss. There are similar costs facing the regulator, so he cannot exclude nonsupporting beneficiaries. At this stage, I assume that gains and losses are equal per capita within groups. This nondiscrimination assumption serves both to simplify the problem and to force Stigler's result of a single politically dominant economic interest, but the assumption is subsequently dropped. I also assume that ignorance does not lead to perverse or biased voting. If a beneficiary, for example, does not know enough to vote for his benefactor, his voting decision is not biased for or against the benefactor. Either he does not vote, or he decides how to vote by tossing a fair coin. In either case, the f in equation (1) will be zero, and M will be the (same) difference between votes for and votes against. With nonparticipation by the ignorant, f (or h) is simply the probability that a beneficiary (or loser) votes, while with random voting by the ignorant f is the difference between the probability of a favorable and unfavorable vote by the beneficiary.

The probability of support may now be specified as

(2) $f = f(g)$,

where g is the per capita net benefit, and is

(3) $g = \dfrac{T - K - C(n)}{n}$,

with

    T = total dollar amount transferred to the beneficiary group
    K = dollars spent by beneficiaries in campaign funds, lobbying,
        and so on, to mitigate opposition
    C(n) = cost of organizing both direct support of beneficiaries and
        efforts to mitigate opposition. This organization cost

increases with n, but we place no restrictions on the shape of
the marginal cost curve.

It is assumed that equation (2) holds for any subset of the electorate, in
the sense that any coalition of size n faces the same costs of organization
and has members with the same responsiveness to benefits. Thus, the number of votes in support depends on n in two offsetting ways: a larger n
provides a broader base for support, but dilutes the net gain per member
and so the probability of a member's support.

As a further simplification I assume that the regulator chooses K as
well as T. The process could be modeled with the benefited group itself
determining the appropriate K, but in doing so it would be motivated by
the same forces affecting a regulator who would ask K as a price for con-
ferring the benefit. Thus, I treat it as a detail whether the beneficiaries
"bid" a K and "ask" a T, or whether the regulator asks a K and bids a T.

The transfer is assumed generated by a tax at the rate t on the wealth
(B) of each member outside the benefited group, so

$$(4) \quad T = t \cdot B(N - n), \text{ or } t = \frac{T}{B(N - n)}.$$

For application to problems of regulation, B can be thought of as a typical
consumer's surplus and t a regulated price if producers are beneficiaries, or
B might be a producer's surplus and t the difference between the surplus-
maximizing price and the regulated price where consumers are beneficiaries. At this level of generality, though, I simply treat B as a negative function of t.[4] Opposition is assumed generated by the tax rate and mitigated
by voter education expenditures per capita (z), so

$$(5) \quad h = h(t, z),$$

$$(6) \quad z = K/(N - n).$$

In keeping with Stigler's model, I assume that, in the relevant range, benefits are subject to decreasing returns so that

$$(7) \quad f_g > 0, f_{gg} < 0$$

---

4. This treatment is less innocent than it appears. It implicitly rules out a "pure" transfer—that is, one with no allocative effects. There may be forms of wealth whose supply is
totally inelastic with respect to taxes, but, as a general matter, these cannot be presumed to
suffice the demands of the political process—or even yield costless taxes, once tax administration and evasion costs are allowed for. The general proposition that every tax affects the
wealth base being taxed has important implications for the evaluation of the whole range of
government redistributive policies. See Gary Becker's comments on this article (Gary S.
Becker, Comment, 19 J. Law & Econ. 245 [1976]).

(unless specified otherwise subscripts will denote partial or, where appropriate, total derivatives from here on). A complementary assumption is made for z:

(8) $h_z < 0, h_{zz} > 0$

(opposition is measured in positive units), and there are assumed to be increasing political costs to taxation:

(9) $h_t > 0, h_{tt} > 0.$

In this characterization of the political process, then, officeholders or candidates to replace them must pick the size (n) of the group they will benefit, the amount (K) they will ask that group to spend for mitigating opposition, and the amount (T) they will transfer to the beneficiary group. The necessary conditions for these choices to yield the maximum majority, the presumed goal for the office seeker, are

(10) $M_n = 0 = -(g + m)f_g + f - h_t \left(\dfrac{tB}{B + tB_t} \right) - h_z \cdot z + h,$

(11) $M_T = 0 = f_g - h_t \left(\dfrac{1}{B + tB_t} \right),$

(12) $M_K = 0 = -f_g - h_z,$

where
    $m = C_n$, the marginal cost of group organization.
Combining equations (10)–(12) and making use of the definitions yields the following solution for n:

(13) $\dfrac{n}{N} = 1 - \left[\dfrac{f_g(g + a)}{f + h - f_g(m - a)} \right]$

where
    a = average cost of organization (C/n).
If there are no organization costs (a = m = 0), the ratio is less than one because of diminishing returns ($f_g g < f$). Diseconomies of scale in organization (m > a) tend to reduce the ratio further. Since we have ruled out net gains to regulation, it is hardly a surprise that a political wealth maximizer must benefit a subset of the population, so subsequent analysis will deal more formally with the forces affecting the size of this subset.

Before some of these forces are elaborated it is worth dwelling on equation (11) for a moment. This condition—essentially that the marginal political return from a transfer must equal the marginal political cost of the

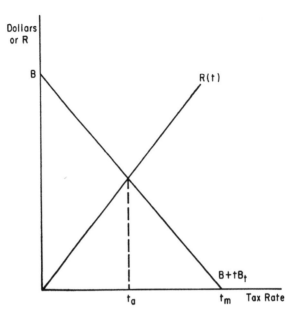

FIGURE 6.1

associated tax—has an important subsidiary implication. Since both f_g and h_t are positive, an interior maximum can occur only if the term $(B + tB_t)$ is also positive. This term is the marginal product of t in raising revenue from a member of the losing group. That it must be positive implies that these losers must be taxed less than the interests of the winners would dictate (a revenue-maximizing tax—that is, $B + tB_t = 0$).

This result is portrayed in figure 6.1. The function R(t) is (h_t/f_g). With diminishing returns in g and increasing costs in t, R_t is positive and increasing in the relevant range. The marginal revenue from t, $(B + tB_t)$, is decreasing in t, and the revenue-maximizing tax is t_m where this marginal revenue is zero. However, with R(t) positive at *any* t > 0, t_m cannot be a political equilibrium. The equilibrium, from equation (11), must occur at something like $t_a < t_m$.

Thus we have an important first principle of regulation: even if a single economic interest gets all the benefits of regulation, these must be less than a perfect broker for the group would obtain. The best-organized cartel will yield less to the membership if the government organizes it than if it were (could be) organized privately. This principle is independent of organization or campaigning costs, but rests on the heed the political process must pay to marginal opposition. (Condition (11) holds even if K and C are assumed zero.) It suggests that what the "capture" literature treats as an ad hoc detail—that "the political process automatically admits powerful outsiders to the industry's councils"[5]—is in fact integral to regulatory processes. The principle also suggests that failure of regulation to maximize cartel profits need not, as Posner has suggested, arise as an efficient substitute for other forms of taxation.[6] Even if more efficient substitutes exist and are used, a rational regulator will still tax cartel profits to secure his own position.

This logic may be pushed a step further. It will pay the rational regulator to exploit differences within the group that, taken as a whole, either wins or loses. The ability to do this may be constrained by "due process" considerations, but not typically to the point that a uniform tax must be levied or gain transferred to each member of a group. Therefore, the regulator's-choice problem is not limited to selecting the appropriate size of an interest group to benefit or tax; it includes selection of an appropriate structure of benefits and costs. Once we drop the simplification of uniform taxes (prices), the identification of regulation with any single economic interest can no longer be maintained as a general proposition.

To see this, consider the following restricted problem: the regulator has decided on the total wealth that must be transferred to one economic interest (say producers) from another, so that both T and n are data. However, he desires minimization of opposition (O) from consumers by exploiting differences among them in per capita wealth or the responsiveness of wealth to taxes (that is, differences in the height and elasticity of their demands) or in their voting sensitivity to taxes. Assume that the $(N - n)$ consumers can be separated into 2 groups of size P_1 and P_2 respectively so that the last term in equation (1) may be written

(14) $O = P_1 h_1 + P_2 h_2$.

(Subscripts denote groups here.) To simplify still further, treat z as fixed and equal for both groups. Minimization of equation (14) then involves forming the Lagrangian

(15) $L = P_1 h_1 + P_2 h_2 + \lambda(T - t_1 B_1 P_1 - t_2 B_2 P_2)$,

where the term in parentheses is the constraint that the sum of subgroup taxes is fixed, and setting the first partials with respect to t_1, t_2 and λ equal to zero. The resulting expression for the opposition minimizing t_1 is

---

5. George J. Stigler, *supra* note 1, at 7.
6. Richard A. Posner, *supra* note 2.

(16) $\quad t_1 = \dfrac{B_2 + \dfrac{TB'_2}{P_2 B_2} - \dfrac{h'_2}{h'_1} B_1}{B'_1 \left(\dfrac{h'_2}{h'_1}\right) + B'_2 \left(\dfrac{P_1 B_1}{P_2 B_2}\right)} .$

(Primes denote derivatives.) The denominator is negative, but only the last two terms in the numerator are negative. This means that a negative t_1 cannot be ruled out. Thus if one group of consumers has sufficiently large per capita demand (B_2), sufficiently low demand elasticity (B'_2) and tax responsiveness (h'_2) relative to the other group, the latter may become part of the winning group (get a subsidized price). On a similar argument, some producers may be taxed even if most are benefited. The regulator's constituency thus cannot in general be limited to one economic interest.

The structure of equation (16) shows that t_1 is affected not only by some obvious characteristics of that group (its wealth and voting response to t_1) but also by characteristics of the other group. I shall return to this subsequently, for equation (16) hints at some important implications for the structure of prices emerging from regulation—for example, that this will be the result of forces pushing both for and against profit-maximizing price discrimination.

I want now to return to equations (10)–(13) and discuss some forces affecting the size of the winning group. The Stigler model leads, after all, to more than the near truism that n/N is less than one; it more nearly asserts that the ratio is close to zero. So let us examine the effect of three variables whose importance the Stigler model asserts—support, opposition, and organization costs.

In general, if x represents a variable affecting choice of n (and T and K), we want to determine the vector of total derivatives: [dn/dx, dT/dx, dK/x]. This can be found by solving

(17) $\quad [M_{ij}][di/dx] = -[M_{ix}],$

where

$\quad [M_{ij}]$ = matrix of cross partial derivatives, i, j = n, T, K
$\quad [M_{ix}]$ = vector of the cross-partials of M_i w.r.t.x.

I now treat three simple cases:

1. A parametric shift in the support function, f, (which leaves f' unaffected). From equations (10)–(12) we obtain

(18) $\quad \begin{bmatrix} M_{nf} \\ M_{Tf} \\ M_{Kf} \end{bmatrix} = \begin{bmatrix} 1 \\ 0 \\ 0 \end{bmatrix},$

and from equation (17) and the second order condition for a maximum M (that $[M_{ij}]$ be negative definite), we obtain the following sign condition:

(19)   sign dn /df = sign C_{nn} ,

where

   C_{ij} = cofactor of M_{ij}.

Since $C_{nn} > 0$ by a second-order condition for a maximum, dn/df > 0—that is, an increase in the probability of support for a given g increases the size of the winning group. Or, as Stigler might wish to put it, the difficulty of translating the transfer into votes leads the regulator to concentrate benefits. For the other variables we have

(20)   sign dT /df = sign C_{nT} ,

and

(21)   sign dK /df = sign C_{nK} ,

which are uncertain and negative respectively. The underlying reasons may be seen by writing out the co-factors

(22) $C_{nT} = [M_{TK} \cdot M_{nK} - M_{Tn} \cdot M_{KK}]$,

(23) $C_{nK} = [M_{Tn} \cdot M_{TK} - M_{nK} \cdot M_{TT}]$.

$M_{TK} > 0$, because an increase in K reduces opposition and makes an increase in T more attractive. $M_{nK} < 0$, because an increase in K also dilutes the net gain and makes concentration of the transfer on a smaller group more attractive. M_{TT}, M_{KK} are both negative, because of diminishing returns. This leaves M_{Tn}, whose sign is ambiguous: an increase in n dilutes the gain to the winners, which would induce an increase in T. But the increase in n also concentrates the opposition, and this pushes for a reduction in T. The only restriction that can be imposed (from the second-order conditions) is $(M_{Tn} + M_{Kn}) < 0$, which is enough to imply $C_{nK} < 0$ and dK/df < 0, but is insufficient to predict the sign of C_{nT}. If buying off a more concentrated opposition is sufficiently important to render $M_{Tn} \leqslant 0$, then dT/df < 0.

2. A parametric shift in the opposition function, h. This yields precisely the same result as a shift in support (the vector of the relevant cross-partials is the same as the right-hand side of equation (19)), and this symmetry between the effects of support and opposition is perhaps one of the chief insights of Stigler's model. If a more effective political support technology (a rise in f) induces a more numerous winning group, a more effective opposition technology must lead the regulator to permit a larger

group to *escape* taxation as well. Some losers will then be made winners when there is a rise in opposition. This is better stated in the reverse. The difficulty of translating a tax into political opposition (a low h) induces the regulator to tax the many and thus to concentrate his favors on a few. Hence the filtering of information through the noise of a political process that forces consideration of many programs simultaneously acts unambiguously, as Stigler intuited, to restrict the size of the winning group. This filtering must be done by both winners and losers, and this makes it simultaneously unattractive to spread the benefits and attractive to spread the losses over large numbers.

3. A parametric shift in the cost of organizing a group for political support. Stigler argues that the cost of organizing support (for example, the cost of overcoming the "free rider" problem) also restricts n. However, on closer inspection, this is not obvious. Consider a rise in the C(n) of (3) which, for simplicity, leaves marginal cost unchanged. Then, focusing only on dn/dC, we obtain

$$(24) \quad \text{sign } dn/dC = \text{sign}(M_{nC}C_{nn} + M_{TC}C_{Tn} + M_{KC}C_{nK}).$$

This will be ambiguous for reasons apart from ambiguity about C_{Tn}. Stigler's argument focuses essentially on M_{nC}, which is indeed negative and induces a smaller n. However, because of diminishing returns to per capita gains, a rise in C will lead to an offsetting decrease in K ($M_{KC} < 0$). On balance, this fall in K requires a rise in n ($C_{nK} < 0$). That is, if K is reduced, restoring optimum effectiveness of lobbying and education efforts requires concentration of these efforts on a smaller group of losers. To obtain Stigler's result, one must conjecture that this sort of secondary effect is outweighed by the initial impulse to concentrate gains to offset the effect of increased organization costs.

It is well to summarize the results of this formalization of Stigler's model:

1. With a few ambiguities, the thrust of imperfect information about both the gains and losses of regulatory decisions and of costs of organizing for political favors is to restrict the size of the winning group.

2. But this winning group will not obtain even a gross gain through political action as great as is within the power of the political process to grant it.

3. Moreover, even if groups organize according to an economic interest (producers v. consumers), political entrepreneurship will produce a coalition which admits members of the losing group into the charmed circle.

I now apply these principles specifically to price-entry regulation and derive implications for the price-profits outcome and the demand for new regulation.

THE POLITICS OF PRICE-ENTRY REGULATION

A generalization of the Stiglerian model of political transfers just discussed would be to write the politician's objective function as:

$$(25) \quad M = M(W_1, W_2),$$

where W_i = wealth of group i, and where $M_i > 0$, but where we assume no intergroup dependencies, so that $M_{12} = 0$. This is then maximized subject to a constraint on total wealth (V):

$$(26) \quad V = W_1 + W_2 = V(W_1, W_2),$$

where $V_i > 0$, but where $V_{12} < 0$. That is, the total wealth to be distributed is limited: market failures aside, one group's wealth can be increased only by decreasing the other's. Let us now suppose that the two groups vying to achieve benefits or mitigate losses from the political process are consumers and producers, and that the process is constrained to provide these gains and costs through the setting of a maximum or minimum price together with control of entry. In this case, we can specialize the majority generating function (25) as

$$(27) \quad M = M(p, \pi),$$

where

p = price of the good
π = wealth of producers, $M_p < 0$ and $M_\pi > 0$.

The implicit assumption here is that the powers of the state are sufficient on the one hand, to enforce competition, so that any $\pi > 0$ translates into political support, and on the other, to ban sale of the good or price it out of existence, so that any consumer surplus provides some votes or stills some opposition. A somewhat more elegant, though not necessarily more insightful, formulation would define equation (27) with respect to an anarchistic reference point. I retain the Stiglerian assumption that the political returns to higher π or lower p are diminishing ($M_{pp} < 0$, $M_{\pi\pi} < 0$).[7] I will

---

7. $M_{pp} < 0$ is not, of course, strictly implied by diminishing returns, and we shall see later that so strict a condition is unnecessary. If we have the simple function $M = M(S)$, where S = consumer's surplus, rather than p, and $S = \int_p^{p'} Q(p)dp$, where $Q(p)$ is the demand curve, and $Q(p') = 0$, then diminishing political returns requires $M_{SS} < 0$. However, this is related to M_{pp} by

$$M_{pp} = M_S \cdot S_{pp} + S_p^2 \cdot M_{SS}$$

also assume no intergroup political effects (such as envy or vindictiveness), so $M_{\pi p} = 0$. The relevant constraint here is given by cost and demand conditions, summarized by the profit function

(28) $\quad \pi = f(p, c),$

where $c = c(Q) =$ production costs as a function of quantity (Q), and where over the range we shall be interested in, $f_p \geq 0$ and $f_{pp} < 0$, and, of course, $f_c < 0$. The formal problem for a successful regulator then is to maximize (I assume sufficient competition for the regulator's office) the Lagrangian

(29) $\quad L = M(p, \pi) + \lambda(\pi - f(p, c)),$

with respect to p, π and λ, which yields

(30) $\quad -\dfrac{M_p}{f_p} = M_\pi = -\lambda.$

This says that the marginal political product of a dollar of profits (M_π) must equal the marginal political product of a price cut ($-M_p$) that also costs a dollar of profits (f_p is the dollar profit loss per dollar price reduction). This result requires $f_p > 0$ (since $-M_p$, $M_\pi > 0$); which is merely a concrete application of the result in equation (11). That is, political equilibrium will not result in the monopoly or cartel-profit maximizing price ($f_p = 0$). The solution is shown graphically in figure 6.2, where equation (27) is represented as a series of iso-majority curves (M_iM_i) obeying the assumed signs for first and second derivatives. Political equilibrium occurs at tangency (A) between the profit hill and an iso-majority curve. On this formulation, pure "producer protection" can be rational only in the absence of any marginal consumer opposition to higher prices (M_iM_i are all horizontal) and pure "consumer protection" requires no marginal support for higher profits.

This analysis says nothing about whether A in figure 6.2 is anything more than trivially different from either the top or bottom of the profit hill. To make the analysis meaningful, we must either derive the appropriate political power function (the shape of the M_iM_i) or focus on the effects of changes in the underlying economic constraints. In the remainder of the article I take the latter tack. That is, I set aside the question of who gets what share of the spoils to focus on the implications of the result

---

where

$$S_p = -Q < 0 \text{ and } S_{pp} = -Q_p > 0.$$

Thus M_{pp} may be positive even if $M_{ss} < 0$, but $M_{pp} < 0$ is sufficient for $M_{ss} < 0$.

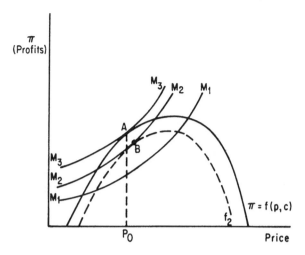

FIGURE 6.2

that the spoils will in fact be shared. For example, note one implication of equation (30) for entry in regulation. *Either* naturally monopolistic *or* naturally competitive industries are more politically attractive to regulate than an oligopolistic hybrid. The inducement to regulate is the change in the level of M_iM_i occasioned thereby. For an oligopoly with a price already intermediate between the competitive and monopoly price, the political gain from moving to A will be smaller in general than if the preregulation price is either at the top or bottom of the profit hill. This may help explain such phenomena as the concurrence of regulation of ostensible "natural monopolies" like railroads, utilities and telephones with that of seemingly competitive industries like trucking, airlines, taxicabs, barbers, and agriculture. It may also rationalize the twin focus of antitrust on reducing concentration and protecting small businessmen, and the delay until comparatively recent times in applying the Sherman Act to less than the most concentrated industries. However, the model does not explain the dilatoriness of the government in regulating a gamut of unconcentrated retail and manufacturing markets.

There is also implicit here a connection between regulation and productivity and growth. Reduction in costs or growth in demand will increase the total surplus (the height of the profit hill in figure 6.2) over which a regulator might have control and, pari passu, the political payoff for its redistribution.[8] I have seen this point made before only in connec-

---

8. This is easiest to see for a constant cost competitive industry where demand increases. In that case, the no-regulation majority is unaffected by the increased demand (p and π are the same) but the gain to regulating the industry and moving to a majority max-

tion with welfare programs,[9] and it deserves a systematic test. However, the association of new regulation with industries where demand and/or productivity is growing rapidly is frequent enough to be suggestive (electricity and telephones in the early 20th century, trucking and airlines in the 1930s and 1940s, natural gas in the 1950s, automobiles and drugs in the 1960s).

Some interesting implications for the pattern of regulatory choice can be derived from a more formal treatment of the interaction between productivity and growth and rational political choice. Consider a market already subject to regulation and in a political equilibrium such as A in figure 6.2. Then consider the effects on this equilibrium of a parametric shift, dx, in either the cost or demand function. To obtain the effect of the shift on the $p = \pi$ configuration generated by regulation, we must solve

$$(31) \quad [L_{ij}] \begin{bmatrix} dp/dx \\ d\pi/dx \\ d\lambda/dx \end{bmatrix} = -[L_{ix}],$$

where i, j denotes p, π or λ. In the case of a (marginal) cost shift, we obtain

$$(32) \quad \frac{dp}{dx} = \frac{-\lambda f_{px} + f_x \cdot f_p \cdot M_{\pi\pi}}{-(M_{pp} - \lambda f_{pp}) - f_p^2 M_{\pi\pi}}.$$

The denominator is positive by a necessary condition for a maximum, so the sign of equation (32) depends on that of the numerator, which is positive.[10] This is hardly surprising, since a rise in marginal cost leads to the same result without regulation. However, the insight provided by equation (32) is that the price increase has distinct "political" and "economic" components. The first term in the numerator $(-\lambda f_{px})$ is essentially a "substitution effect" akin to that facing an unregulated firm. A rise in marginal cost makes a higher price profitable. The second term is a "political wealth" effect: the surplus to be disposed of has shrunk, and this forces the regulator to reduce his purchases of political support. However, the usual marginal conditions familiar from consumer theory are applicable here. The regulator will, in general, not force the entire adjustment onto one group. In particular, consumers will be called on to buffer some of the

---

imizing (p, π) is increased. I demonstrate below that a similar result obtains for more complicated cases.

9. See W. Allen Wallis, Causes of the Welfare Explosion, in James Tobin and W. Allen Wallis, Welfare Programs: An Economic Appraisal (Washington: American Enterprise Inst., 1968), 33, 54.

10. $\lambda < 0$, from (30); $f_x = -c_x < 0$; $f_p > 0$, since profits are below a maximum; $M_{\pi\pi} < 0$ by assumption; and

$$f_{px} = -Q_p c_{Qx} > 0.$$

producer losses. To see this more clearly, abstract from the substitution effect by assuming a change in fixed cost only, so $f_{px} = 0$. Then the profit hill in figure 6.2 shifts down by a constant to f_2, leaving the profit-maximizing price unchanged, but increasing the political-equilibrium price and buffering the fall in profits that would otherwise occur. Of course, as is the case in consumer choice, one cannot rule out "inferiority" of price decreases or profit increases.[11] But the "normal" purely political component of the response to cost changes involves consumers shielding producers from some of the effects of cost increases and producers sharing some of their gains from cost reductions.

The case of a shift in demand is more complex, because the demand function enters indirectly into the M function: M_p depends on the relationship between price and consumer surplus, which depends on the height of demand. Formally, a change in demand, dy, yields

$$(33) \quad \frac{dp}{dy} = \frac{-\lambda f_{py} + M_{py} + f_y \cdot f_p M_{\pi\pi}}{-(M_{pp} - \lambda f_{pp}) - f^2 M_{\pi\pi}}.$$

Again, the first term of the numerator is a profit-maximizing "substitution" effect which is positive,[12] and the last term a political wealth effect which is, in this case, negative ($f_y > 0$). The middle term represents the effect of the demand shift on political "tastes"—that is, on the slope of the $M_i M_i$ in figure 6.2, but this effect is ambiguous.[13] For example, if a rise in consumer income raises the payoff to price reductions, $M_{py} < 0$, and

---

11. Such inferiority is in fact essentially ruled out here by the absence of intergroup dependencies. This plays the same role here as utility independence does in ruling out inferior goods in consumer choice theory. The closest analogy to the conventional consumer choice problem would be where the regulator always sets a marginal price equal to (a constant) marginal cost and then merely allocates the resulting surplus among producers and consumers by fashioning a suitable two-part or declining-marginal price scheme. In this case, the surplus is the regulator's "income" which can be used to purchase the "goods" producer or consumer support at a price of $1. If the utility (votes) of the two goods is independent, declining marginal utility will assure that both are normal.

This analogue helps illuminate the attraction of regulation to markets with growing productivity and demand. The increased surplus, which is the regulator's income, generates a larger utility (vote) gain from moving from either corner (monopoly or competition) to the vote maximum, again so long as there are diminishing political returns to both producer and consumer wealth.

12. Ignoring, as usual, any offsetting changes in the slope of demand.

13. In particular

$$M_p = M_S \cdot S_p = -QM_S$$

where S again denotes the underlying consumer surplus. So

$$M_{py} = -QM_{SS}S_y - M_S Q_y.$$

Since M_S, Q_y and $S_y > 0$, while $M_{SS} < 0$, the sign of M_{py} is ambiguous.

the political-wealth effect is reinforced. Ignoring this taste change, the results are symmetric with those of a cost change. Consider a rise in demand such that $f_{py} = 0$.[14] The political wealth effect will nevertheless induce a price reduction because the diminishing political returns to both profit increases and price decreases make a combination of the two the best strategy for political "spending" of more wealth.

What emerges from this discussion is more a working hypothesis than an a priori conclusion about the nature of price and profit adjustment under regulation. *If* the political wealth effect is empirically important, it will be manifested in attenuation of price changes when demand changes and in their amplification when costs change and vice versa for profit changes. In the case of the latter, the wealth-effect components of the counterparts to equations (32) and (33) may be written

$$(34) \quad \frac{d\pi}{dx} = \cfrac{f_x}{1 + f_p^2 \left(\cfrac{M_{\pi\pi}}{M_{pp} - \lambda f_{pp}} \right)},$$

$$(35) \quad \frac{d\pi}{dy} = \cfrac{f_y}{1 + f_p^2 \left(\cfrac{M_{\pi\pi}}{M_{pp} - \lambda f_{pp}} \right)}.$$

These are both smaller absolutely than what would obtain under pure producer protection (which yields simply f_x or f_y). We can then summarize the interaction between cost and demand changes and regulatory utility maximization as follows: Define variables π' and p' as the *difference* between regulated and profit maximizing profits and prices respectively. The purely political effects of changes in underlying economic conditions are then for dp'/dx and $d\pi'/dx > 0$; dp'/dy and $d\pi'/dy < 0$. Among the empirical implications of these forces would be:

1. Regulation will tend to be more heavily weighted toward "producer protection" in depressions and toward "consumer protection" in expansions. Thus, for example, it is not useful to view events like the Robinson-Patman Act and the National Recovery Act (NRA) as "inconsistent" with the intent of antitrust legislation; this intent is endogenous. Similar arguments apply to the structure of taxes (the corporate-personal tax mix

14. This requires an appropriate change in the slope of the demand curve, since

$$f_{py} = (P - C_Q) \cdot Q_{py} + Q_y.$$

So some $Q_{py} < 0$ is required for $f_{py} = 0$.

should offset changes in the share of GNP earned by capital), tariffs (more free trade when demand grows or costs fall), and so on.

2. Government intervention and regulation are both normal goods. Though this generalization has exceptions, the difference between the no-regulation iso-majority curve and the regulatory equilibrium (that is, the incentive to regulate) grows with the level of demand. As a further generalization, the income elasticity of producer protection ought to be less than that of consumer protection. This follows from the negative wealth effect of demand growth on equilibrium price, which makes for an increased consumer share of the total surplus as demand (income) increases.

3. The tendency of regulation to change prices infrequently, sometimes called "regulatory lag," ought to be stronger when demand changes than when costs change. This follows from the opposing wealth and substitution effects in the case of a shift in demand (but not in the case of a cost change). Here failure to change a price can be interpreted to mean that the opposing effects offset one another.

4. Some reexamination of studies, such as Stigler and Friedland's, which show regulation to be ineffective, is called for. In the first place the result ought to be sensitive to the dynamics of supply and demand. In a growing, technologically progressive industry, producer protection ought to yield to consumer protection over time, even if, on average, there is no effect. (Stigler and Friedland's data do show some secular trend toward lower prices.)[15] Secondly, deviations about the zero mean effect should be systematic: high-cost, low-demand markets will have prices elevated by regulation and low-cost, high-demand markets will have prices reduced. Finally, as a generalization of 2. above, entry of regulation is not exogenous. It should occur first in the low-cost, high-demand markets. This last point indicates some of the complexity engendered by the interaction of the static and dynamic aspects of the model: whether entry of regulation into any market raises or lowers prices depends on whether the market was initially competitive or monopolistic. Once that initial adjustment has been made, subsequent cost and demand changes will govern any redistribution from the initial position.

5. If regulation is evaluated against a zero-profit (fair rate of return) benchmark, we might be tempted to conclude that positive profits imply a "captured" regulator and thereby expect a positive correlation between prices and profitability. In fact the observed correlation ought to be nega-

---

15. George J. Stigler & Claire Friedland, *supra* note 1, at 7. Their estimate is that regulation had no effect on electricity rates in 1912 and lowered prices by about 10 per cent in 1937.

tive. Whatever its source—increased demand or lower costs—an increase in the profit hill of figure 6.2 generates a political incentive to move toward a combination involving higher profits and lower prices. Thus, quite apart from any private profit-maximizing incentives toward this configuration, the most profitable regulated firms ought to have the lowest prices. More precisely, the gap between the profit-maximizing and regulated price will be positively correlated with the gap between the former and the "fair-rate-of-return" price.

6. The model also yields predictions on the bias of regulation. Briefly, elastic demand and economies of scale create a bias favorable to consumers. The reason is that these sorts of demand and cost conditions enhance the consumer surplus gained while mitigating the producer surplus lost due to a price reduction. To see this formally, first introduce a parameter, w, into the slope of the demand curve at equilibrium, so that a positive dw implies a less elastic demand. By appropriate reformulation of the right-hand side of equation (31), we obtain the vector

$$(36) \quad -\begin{bmatrix} L_{pw} \\ L_{\pi w} \\ L_{\lambda w} \end{bmatrix} = -\begin{bmatrix} M_{pw} - \lambda f_{pw} \\ M_{\pi w} \\ -f_w \end{bmatrix} = -\begin{bmatrix} M_{pw} - \lambda f_{pw} \\ 0 \\ 0 \end{bmatrix},$$

where we set $f_w = 0$ (that is, assume that the less elastic demand passes through the initial price quantity combination). Both M_{pw} and $-\lambda f_{pw}$ are positive: a less elastic demand reduces the consumer surplus and vote productivity of a price reduction, while it enhances the profitability and vote productivity of a price increase.[16] The signs of the relevant total derivatives then become

(37) $\text{sign } dP/dw = \text{sign } L_{pw} > 0,$

(38) $\text{sign } d\pi/dw = \text{sign } f_p \cdot L_{pw} > 0.$

That is, a less elastic demand induces the regulator to "relocate" toward the northeast on any iso-majority curve in figure 6.2.

For the scale-economies case, introduce a parameter, v, into marginal cost and assume that a negative dv leaves profits at the old equilibrium

---

16. Again starting from $M_p = -QM_S$, we get $M_{pw} = -QM_{SS} \cdot S_w$, and $S_w > 0$, so with $M_{SS} < 0$, $M_{pw} > 0$. Since

$$f_p = (P - C_Q)(Q_p + w) + Q$$
$$f_{pw} = (P - C_Q) > 0,$$

and with $\lambda < 0$, $-\lambda f_{pw} > 0$.

unchanged. That is, if there is a lower marginal cost in the neighborhood of equilibrium, it is sufficiently higher at lower outputs to leave total costs unchanged. This sort of characterization of increased scale economies implies the vector

$$
(39) \quad -\begin{bmatrix} L_{pv} \\ L_{\pi v} \\ L_{\lambda v} \end{bmatrix} = -\begin{bmatrix} M_{pv} - \lambda F_{pv} \\ M_{\pi v} \\ -f_v \end{bmatrix} = -\begin{bmatrix} \lambda Q_p \\ 0 \\ 0 \end{bmatrix}.
$$

The term λQ_p is positive. The diseconomies of smaller outputs when $dv < 0$ make a price increase less profitable (and so a price decrease more attractive politically). This renders the derivatives, dP/dv and $d\pi/dv$, both positive, so more scale economies induce a move to the southwest on any iso-majority curve.

Pending a systematic test of the empirical relevance of these propositions, I point out potential pitfalls. The long history of "pro-producer" regulation of agriculture (price supports, marketing restrictions, and so on) seems consistent with the model, given the conventional wisdom about low supply and demand elasticities in this sector. However, the cartelization of airlines, trucking, railroads, and taxicabs where there are either constant or decreasing costs is obviously troublesome. A more general problem is how to distinguish the political incentives here from corresponding profit-maximizing incentives which push in the same direction if we want to use the result to predict the behavior of established regulators rather than the entry pattern in regulation.[17]

7. Finally, I note an implication for the theory of finance. Regulation should reduce conventional measures of owner risk. By buffering the firm against demand and cost changes, the variability of profits (and stock prices) should be lower than otherwise. To the extent that the cost and demand changes are economy wide, regulation should reduce systematic as well as diversifiable risk.

There is no obvious risk pattern among currently regulated firms: electric, gas, and telephone utility stocks rank among the least risky while airline stocks are among the most risky. However, in one case of *new* regulation (of product quality), I found that both total and systematic risk

17. As an example of the kind of entry pattern that can be predicted, consider a competitive industry with inelastic demand and supply. The political equilibrium here is closer to the monopoly equilibrium than it is with elastic demand and supply. Hence such an industry is more likely to attract regulation than one with elastic demand and supply. Similarly a natural monopoly with elastic demand and supply makes an inviting target for regulation.

of drug stocks decreased substantially after regulation.[18] A crude test on railroad and utility stock prices shows the same pattern, though the effect is weak. I correlated annual (December to December) changes in the log of the Standard and Poor's or Cowles indexes of railroad and utility stock price indices[19] with those of the industrial index (which I treat as a diversified portfolio of stocks of unregulated firms) for equal periods spanning the onset of regulation. I took 1887 as the first year of railroad regulation and 1907 as the start of utility regulation. (New York began regulating that year.) The indexes of systematic risk (estimated as the regression coefficient on industrial stock price changes) were, with standard errors in parentheses,

	Before Regulation	After Regulation
Railroads	.74	.56
(1871–86, 1887–1902)	(.24)	(.17)
Utilities	.67	.60
(1871–1906, 1907–42)	(.12)	(.10)

The total risk of these stocks relative to industrials (the ratio of standard deviations of annual changes) were

	Before Regulation	After Regulation
Rails	1.16	.85
Utilities	.97	.84

All of the differences go in the right direction, but none are significant. The main point of this exercise is simply to hint what further research might be useful.

THE STRUCTURE OF REGULATED PRICES

I have argued that the rational regulator will not levy a uniform tax nor distribute benefits equally. Rather, he will seek a structure of costs and benefits that maximizes political returns. This search for political advantage will in turn lead the regulator to suppress some economic forces that might otherwise affect the price structure. For example, the cost of serving a group of customers or their elasticity of demand will have a different

18. See Sam Peltzman, The Benefits and Costs of New Drug Regulation, in Regulating New Drugs 205–206 (Richard L. Landau ed.) (Chicago: Univ. of Chicago Center for Policy Study, 1973).

19. Standard and Poor's Trade and Securities Statistics: Security Price Index Record (1971).

impact under regulation than it will in an unregulated market because of the absence of political constraints in the latter case. The substitution of political for economic criteria in the price formulation process has several interesting implications which I shall elaborate. It is at the heart of the pervasive tendency of regulation to engage in cross-subsidization—that is, the dissipation of producer rents on sales to some customers by setting below-cost prices to others. We shall see that this cross-subsidization follows a systematic pattern in which high-cost customer groups are subsidized by low-cost customers. Further, this pattern of price discrimination emerges from a process in which conventional profit-maximizing price discrimination as well as other economic forces leading to price differences is attenuated.

A convenient starting point for this analysis is the problem first set out in equations (14)–(16), where the regulator seeks a tax structure to minimize opposition. Here I want to consider the effect on the resulting tax structure when a change occurs of the type that would ordinarily lead the gainers to seek a change in only one of the two tax rates. As an example, suppose per capita wealth rises for one group only. In the price-regulation analogue of this problem, this would lead to a rise in one group's demand, and a profit-maximizing monopolist might then raise that group's price, but not the other group's price. Under regulation, however, no such specialization of a tax increase will be tolerated, because this would violate the basic principle that opposition from the two groups must be equated at the margin.

This point can be demonstrated formally with the same framework used previously. Specifically let there be a parameter shift, dx, in the wealth of group 1 only. Then trace the effects of this shift on t_1 and t_2. These effects are obtained by solving

$$(40) \quad \begin{bmatrix} dt_1/dx \\ dt_2/dx \\ d\lambda/dx \end{bmatrix} = -[L_{1x}, L_{2x}, L_{\lambda x}] \begin{bmatrix} L_{11} & L_{12} & L_{1\lambda} \\ L_{21} & L_{22} & L_{2\lambda} \\ L_{\lambda 1} & L_{\lambda 2} & L_{\lambda \lambda} \end{bmatrix}^{-1}$$

where the subscripts 1, 2 on the right-hand side refer to t_1 and t_2. This has the following relevant solutions:

$$(41) \quad \text{sign} \frac{dt_1}{dx} = \text{sign} [-L_{1x} \cdot L_{2\lambda}^2 - L_{\lambda x} \cdot L_{22} \cdot L_{\lambda 1}],$$

$$(42) \quad \text{sign} \frac{dt_2}{dx} = \text{sign} [L_{1x} \cdot L_{\lambda 1} \cdot L_{2\lambda} - L_{\lambda x} \cdot L_{11} \cdot L_{\lambda 2}].$$

The sign of equation (41) is ambiguous, since the first term in brackets is positive while the second is negative. The first term reflects the ability of the regulator both to maintain revenues and to limit opposition by raising taxes on the now wealthier group-1 individuals, while the second term is a political wealth effect which induces lower tax rates. The more interesting result is that the sign of equation (42) is unambiguously negative. This occurs first because of the incentive to substitute higher taxes on group 1, which creates the ambiguity in equation (41) and which in equation (42) requires an offsetting decrease in t_2 to maintain equilibrium. This incentive to a lower t_2 is reinforced by the political wealth effect. The analysis assumes no interdependencies between the two groups' political responsiveness or wealth (that is, L_{12} is assumed to be zero). Thus what emerges here is that the regulator's striving for minimum opposition by equating opposition at the margin leads him to spread effects of economic forces which are local to all groups. This common element in the tax structure is provided by the wealth effect which leads the regulator to buy more of both relevant "goods" (less opposition from group 1 and from group 2).

This result can be applied to the regulation of prices by suitably generalizing the analysis of a single price summarized in figure 6.2. That is, assume that there are two separable groups of buyers, so that the majority generating function (27) is

(43) $M = M(p_1, p_2, \pi)$,

with M_1, $M_2 < 0$. The distinction between the two groups is economic rather than political, in that I assume only that there are cost and/or demand differences. Thus customers whom the regulator might wish to single out for benefits can be scattered among both groups, and p_1 and p_2 can be regarded as averages from another price structure conditioned by political forces. I suppress this structure here only to highlight the difference between a regulated and unregulated market's response to common economic forces. The cost/demand differences also give rise to the new profit function

(44) $\pi = f(p_1, p_2, c)$.

With no loss of generality, I assume that it costs nothing to produce the product for group 2, so c = cost of production for group 1. Otherwise the properties of equation (44) and its simpler counterpart (28) are the same ($f_1, f_2 \geqslant, f_{11}, f_{22} < 0, f_c < 0$). Again, to make the problem nontrivial, I rule out cross-group effects, so

$$M_{12} = M_{1\pi} = M_{2\pi} = f_{12} = 0.$$

We may now proceed to trace out the implications for the structure of regulated prices if there is a change of the sort that would lead, in an unregulated market, to a change solely of one group's price. As an example, let group 1's demand increase, so that, with independent demands and costs, the profit-maximizing or short-run competitive price would rise for that group alone. The general problem now facing the regulator is to choose the set (p_1, p_2, π, λ) which maximizes the Lagrangian

(45) $L = M(p_1, p_2, \pi) + \lambda(\pi - f(p_1, p_2, c))$.

(Note that we are dropping the restriction in equations (14)–(16) and (40)–(42) of fixed "tax receipts"—here profits—transferred to winners.) The first-order conditions for a maximum here are similar to equation (30); specifically

(46) $-\dfrac{M_1}{f_1} = \dfrac{M_2}{f_2} = M_\pi = -\lambda.$

So both p_1 and p_2 will be held below the profit-maximizing level ($f_1, f_2 > 0$). Now let there be a parameter shift, dy, in group 1's demand, and let us see what effect this has on p_1 and p_2. Consequently, we solve

(47) $\begin{bmatrix} d_1 \\ d_y \end{bmatrix} = -[L_{iy}][L_{ij}]^{-1},$

where i, j = p_1, p_2, π, λ. The left-hand side of equation (47) is a vector of total derivatives; the first term on the right is a row-vector of partial derivatives, and the second term is a matrix of partial derivatives. To present the results in a manageable fashion, I define the following variables, and indicate their signs:

$$A = [(\lambda F_{22} - M_{22}) - f_2^2 \cdot M_{\pi\pi}] > 0$$

(by second-order conditions for a maximum);

$$B = f_1 \cdot M_{\pi\pi} \cdot (M_{22} - \lambda f_{22}) > 0$$

(by second-order conditions and $f_1 > 0$);

$$C = f_2 \cdot M_{\pi\pi}(M_{11} - \lambda f_{11}) > 0$$

(by second-order conditions and $f_2 > 0$). I then show the results for the signs of dP_1/dy and dP_2/dy by components.

(48)
$$\text{sign } \frac{dP_1}{dy} = \text{sign:}$$

$$M_{1y} \cdot A? \qquad \text{(``taste'' shift)}$$
$$-\lambda f_{1y} \cdot A > 0 \qquad \text{(``substitution'')}$$
$$-f_y \cdot B < 0 \qquad \text{(``political wealth''),}$$

(49)
$$\text{sign } \frac{dP_2}{dy} = \text{sign:}$$

$$-M_{1y} \cdot f_2? \qquad \text{(taste shift)}$$
$$+\lambda f_{1y} \cdot f_2 < 0 \qquad \text{(substitution)}$$
$$-f_y \cdot C < 0 \qquad \text{(political wealth).}$$

The results in equation (48) are similar to those in equation (33), where we analyzed the effects of a shift in demand on a single price. There is a change in consumer surplus with ambiguous effects on the responsiveness of group 1 to price reductions (that is, its "tastes" for price reductions). There is a substitution effect, showing that it is "cheaper" for the regulator to collect transfers in the form of higher prices to the higher demand group. Finally there is a political wealth effect, showing that the regulator will use the expanded opportunity locus to shield group 1 from the full substitution effect.

The more interesting result is equation (49), since group 2 would be unaffected in an unregulated market. Apart from the ambiguous "taste" effect, there are two forces under regulation leading this group to benefit from the higher demand of group 1. First, there is the converse of the substitution effect. If it is now more attractive to tax group 1, then for any given tax receipt, the price to group 2 will be lower. Second, there is the same wealth effect that assists group 1. The regulator distributes the gains made possible by the higher demand partly in the form of higher profits,[20] partly in the form of a lower price to group 1 *and* partly in the form of a lower price to group 2. *All* the margins in equation (46), not just one or two, require adjustment when one group's demand increases and thereby increases the wealth available to the regulator.

This result is illustrated in figure 6.3, where I focus on the structure of prices. Each of the curves labeled M_i is a locus of price combinations consistent with a constant level of support or opposition from consumers. These are negatively sloped, indicating that the regulator can maintain the fixed support level by trading lower prices to one group for higher prices to another. The M index increases toward the origin, since lower prices

---

20. The result for the wealth component of $d\pi/dy$ is a more complex analogue to equation (35) with the same properties.

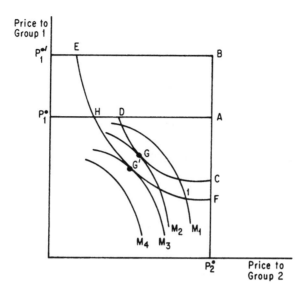

FIGURE 6.3

are preferred by both groups. For simplicity, I assume diminishing political returns to price reduction, so the M are convex from above. The point
A is the combination of profit-maximizing prices, but the rational regulator wishes to set lower prices than these. The frontier DGC shows the p_1,
p_2 combinations which yield the desired level of producer wealth. It is
negatively sloped since f_1 and f_2 are both positive (or zero at D and C
respectively), and concave from above, since both f_{11} and f_{22} are negative.
The equilibrium at G is defined by the first two conditions in equation
(46). Consider now the special case where the regulator desires to keep
profits fixed and the group-1 demand increases. If p_1 at G exceeds marginal
cost, the profit frontier will shift outward over a range of prices in the
neighborhood of G. That is, with 1's higher demand, the same profit can
be generated by a lower p_1 holding p_2 constant, or by a lower p_2 holding
p_1 constant. (For simplicity, I have assumed that the p_1 at C also exceeds
marginal cost, so that the frontier shifts out over the entire relevant range.)
It is this shift to EHG'F that produces a "wealth effect" toward a lower
p_1, p_2 set, though there will also be a change in the slope of the frontier
which will offset the incentive toward a lower p_1.

The implication here is that, not only will the average level of prices
under regulation be below what it would be in pure monopoly, but the
structure of relative prices will depart from that in either pure monopoly

or competition. The important contribution of politics is to suppress economically important distinctions and substitute for these a common element in all prices. On the demand side, this means that regulators will tax
profits by attenuating profitable price discrimination. Discrimination is
not eliminated, because there is a force—the substitution effect—unifying
the interests of a discriminating monopoly and the regulator.[21] It is countered by the wealth effect, so the empirical importance of this effect will
determine that of the unique political effect on the price structure. Equations (48) and (49) do shed this further light: the term f_y is proportional
to the difference between price and marginal cost. So, the political element
in pricing should be most prominent the more profitable the regulated
firm.

Except that this last result does not hold, the case of a change in costs
is similar to that of a change in demand. Specifically, a rise in the marginal
cost of serving group 1 leads, in addition to the conventional substitution
effect raising p_1/p_2, to a wealth effect raising both p_1 and p_2.

This incentive to reward or tax all customers for the peculiar characteristics of some has interesting implications for the structure of regulated
prices. Not only will profit-maximizing price discrimination be discour-
aged, but a peculiar form of price discrimination will replace it. This is
usually referred to as "cross-subsidization" and, to the extent that this is
not just another name for ordinary price discrimination, it connotes a
structure in which an unprofitably low price for some is paid for from
profits on sales to others. This sort of phenomenon seems difficult to reconcile with the producer protection view of regulation. Why, after all,
would a surface transportation cartel wish to perpetuate unprofitable passenger train or short-haul rail freight service? So far such questions have
received no satisfactory answer, and the phenomenon tends to be viewed
as "a process of ad hoc pacification" of vocal consumer groups.[22] Our
model suggests that the process is in fact systematic: holding demand constant, the higher-cost customers will receive the lower price-marginal cost
ratios. Their peculiarly high costs will be spread among all customer
groups by a rational regulator. Thus we need not appeal to ad hoc judgments about the political power of, say, train passengers or short-haul

21. In the case of a pure change in 1's elasticity of demand—that is, a change in the
slope but not the height of demand—the relevant total derivatives of P_1 and P_2 are opposite,
because only a substitution effect is at work.

22. George W. Hilton, The Basic Behavior of Regulatory Commissions, 62 Am. Econ.
Rev. pt. 2, at 47, 49 (Papers & Proceedings, May 1972).

freight users to explain the pattern of cross-subsidization. Instead, the model implies that we should observe either a higher level of costs (say for short hauls compared to long hauls) or more rapid increases in costs (for passengers compared to freight) for the subsidized group. More generally, the model sheds light on the tendency of regulation to produce rate "averaging" across dissimilar customer groups—for example, charging similar electricity rates to rural and urban customers (which benefits the former) or similar auto insurance rates to rural and urban customers (which benefits the latter). The common element in these price structures is their suppression of cost differences.

I used this sort of model to rationalize differences in the price structure under government ownership and regulation. This required an assumption that purely political forces will be more prominent in the former regime.[23] It will take further empirical work to show whether the political impulse to uniform treatment of customers also affects regulated rates systematically. I can illustrate some of the promise and pitfalls by application to the airline rate structure. Keeler estimated price-marginal cost ratios for standard coach service in 29 regulated city-pair markets as of 1968.[24] He found that the most prominent cost difference in airline service is distance related. Since major elements of cost are constant per flight, the per-mile marginal cost falls continuously with a flight's distance. My model would imply that effective Civil Aeronautics Board (CAB) regulation would convert this cost structure into a price structure whereby price/marginal cost rises continuously with distance—that is, the fare-distance taper would be less severe than the cost-distance taper. One immediate problem is that profit-maximizing discrimination would imply a similar price structure, since ground alternatives are more competitive over shorter distances. However, especially for standard coach service, where individual business travel tends to predominate over family and vacation travel (for which airlines offer discounts), the viability of ground alternatives is restricted. Gronau estimates that, for plausible values of time, airlines will essentially monopolize the relevant market for distances over 600 miles.[25] This implies that a profit-maximizing fare structure would have price/marginal cost ra-

23. Sam Peltzman, Pricing in Public and Private Enterprises: Electric Utilities in the United States, 14 J. Law & Econ. 109 (1971).

24. Theodore E. Keeler, Airline Regulation and Market Performance, 3 Bell J. of Econ. & Man. Sci. 399 (1972).

25. Reuben Gronau, The Effect of Traveling Time on the Demand for Passenger Transportation, 78 J. Pol. Econ. 377 (1970).

tios rising substantially more sharply with distances up to 600 miles than beyond. My model implies no such break, or at least a continual increase in this ratio in the over 600-mile-segments.

To sort these forces out, I regressed the log of Keeler's estimate of price/marginal cost (P − MC) on two distance variables: the log of distance if the city pair is less than 600 miles apart and zero (that is, one mile) otherwise (D_1), and log of distance if the distance exceeds 600 miles, zero otherwise (D_2). From Gronau's results, profit maximization implies that the coefficient of D_1 is positive, while that of D_2 is zero. Political support maximization implies that both coefficients are positive, and, in the extreme, equal. The result is

$$P - MC = -.66 + .17D_1 + .17D_2$$
$$(3.71) \quad (4.49)$$

$$R^2 = .69 \quad \text{S.E.} \times 100 = 8.46$$

(t-ratios in parentheses). If the log of per-mile cost is regressed on D_1 and D_2, the corresponding coefficients are both −.26. This association of a continuous increase in P − MC with a continuous distance economy is strong support for the political-support maximization model against simple profit maximization. The CAB essentially ignores the strength of ground competition for a particular flight and simply spreads the same part (about ⅔) of *any* flight's distance-related economy among all fares.

Now the pitfall: Keeler has recently updated his cost estimates to 1974.[26] There has been no important change in airline technology: per-mile costs still fall continuously with distance (the 1974 elasticity is −.22). There has been, though, a major change in the fare structure. For the 1974 data, the P − MC distance relationship is

$$P - MC = .41 - .01D_1 - .01D_2$$
$$(.23) \quad (.68)$$

$$R^2 = .33 \quad \text{S.E.} \times 100 = 4.17.$$

The CAB has recently espoused the desirability of cost-based fares, and, more importantly, it has implemented them: the fare and cost-distance gradients are now essentially identical. To get there, the CAB has permitted fares on the longest flights in the sample to rise by under 30 per cent between 1968 and 1975, while those on the shortest have more than dou-

26. See Staff of the Subcomm. on Administrative Practice and Procedure of the Senate Comm. on the Judiciary, 94th Cong., 1st Sess., Civil Aeronautics Board Practices and Procedures 58 (Comm. Print 1975).

bled. By 1974, much of the price discrimination, at least on coach service, had vanished.[27] This implies that the CAB has been sacrificing producer and, in terms of my model, political wealth to the ghost of Pareto. I will not pretend that my model offers any insight into this recent behavior, however well it seems to explain matters up to 1968.[28] Perhaps, though, it does help explain recent congressional and executive initiatives to reduce the CAB's regulatory powers.[29]

The intra-group equilibrium aspects of the model reveal some implications for entry—both of regulators and of regulated firms. First there is a clear incentive for regulators to limit entry (or seek the power to do so) quite apart from considerations of the producer interest. This stems directly from the fact that the politically appropriate price structure is invariably discriminatory (in the economic sense) when costs differ among customers. The proverbial "cream skimming" entrant must be prevented from

27. The range of the $P - MC$ variable was .47 in 1968 and .16 in 1974.

28. The promise and pitfalls of the model are also illustrated by surface freight rates. The cost structure here is similar to air—a negative cost/mile-distance taper. This is most pronounced for rails, and they have experienced the most profound effects of the resulting political incentives: short-haul rates sometimes below marginal cost, regulatory inhibitions on elimination of such services and, recently, bankruptcies among short-haul specialists. This all appears consistent with the basic model, except that a simple extension should have firms and consumers treated similarly. That is, the firms in this industry happen to be crudely separable by an economic criterion—average length of freight haul. Maximization of political support from producers would then appear to require spreading some of the profit effects of high-cost short-haul service to the long-haul specialists. Indeed the Interstate Commerce Commission (ICC) has the power to do this by regulating divisions of joint rates. However, it has obviously not been sufficiently diligent in its use of the power to prevent striking differences in the prosperity of long- and short-haul specialists, differences which appear superficially greater than those that might be expected without regulation of rates and exit. This suggests two problems: (1) Why are the ICC's incentives to weld a coalition so much stronger in the case of consumers and producers? (2) What accounts for the difference between the ICC and CAB willingness to endanger the consumer coalition by permitting economic efficiency criteria to intrude in the rate structure?

There is finally a problem of appropriate units. A prime example of cost-based cross-subsidization is first-class postage. The rate here ignores distance-related costs entirely and so results in price/marginal cost *declining* with distance. The model can only hint at why weight happens to be the relevant unit for the Postal Service and distance for the ICC and CAB. One way by which a regulator can suppress cost differences is to ignore them entirely. However, in deciding which kinds of differences to ignore, he must also take account of the implications for profits. Hence my conjecture would have to be that weight-related costs are more important than distance-related costs in determining first-class postal service profits and vice versa for transportation. A further implication would then be that price/marginal cost in first-class postal service would be negatively related to marginal cost/pound, holding distance constant.

29. See Staff, *supra* note 26; and U.S. President, [proposed] Aviation Act of 1975, H. R. Doc. No. 94–278, 94th Cong., 1st Sess. (1975).

serving the low-cost customers and thereby preventing the regulator from spreading the low costs to others. On the other hand, we can expect the regulator to be more tolerant of entry which dampens the enthusiasm of producers for demand-based price discrimination. The regulator seeks to suppress the full effects of differences in the elasticity of demand, and his way can be eased by permitting entry into low-elasticity market segments. This last argument has more force in industries, like banking, where the primary regulatory control is over entry rather than price. In these cases, the regulator uses the entry control to produce indirectly the desired price structure. A testable implication would be that more entry is permitted in banking, say, the larger the gap between interest rates on small and large loans.

The obverse of the previous argument is that entry of regulation is more attractive the more disparate the price structure. This is independent of the preregulatory market structure. Competitively determined, cost-based price differentials create an opportunity for political gain through entry and/or price regulation designed to suppress the effects of cost differences, just as discriminating monopoly invites political suppression of the effects of demand elasticity differences.

In summary, the same forces that make regulators seek a broad-based coalition operate on the price structure. Opportunities for increasing producer wealth by price discrimination are not ignored, but they are never fully exploited. To do this would narrow the consumer base of the coalition. The uniquely political contribution to a price structure is to force a more uniform treatment of consumers than the unregulated market by weakening the link between prices and cost and demand conditions.

CONCLUDING REMARKS

This article is concerned more with the design than the implementation of a research strategy. Much of the recent work in the theory of regulation has focused on political power relationships: which groups will have the muscle to extract gains from their regulatory process. I have largely begged this issue. In my general model, every identifiable group contains winners and losers, and even where all the winners are in one group they end up short-changed. This sort of result can hardly illuminate the nature of the underlying power relationships, but that shortcoming is purposeful.

In the way I have chosen to model the regulatory process, these power relationships play a role analogous to tastes in consumer choice theory. They shape the regulator's utility function. It has proved a highly rewarding research strategy for consumer choice theorists precisely to beg questions of taste formation and concentrate instead on the behavioral effects of changes in constraints in a regime of stable tastes. With some qualification, there is an analogous history in production theory. I am suggesting here that the theory of politics has something to learn from this experience. Even if we can do no more than derive the most general properties of political power functions, there is much to learn about political behavior in a world where the constraints do change. And the specific contribution of economics to this venture will be enhanced if the constraints are those already familiar to economists. I have tried to show here how the most familiar sort of supply-demand apparatus can be converted into a constraint on regulatory behavior. Once this is accomplished the equally familiar analytics of supply-demand changes yield refutable implications about a wide range of regulatory behavior: when regulation will occur, how it will modify the unregulated price structure, even how it will change the division of the gains over time (with no change in relative political strengths).

Of course, no student of George Stigler can view the derivation of refutable implications as more than a first step. The usefulness of the model developed here awaits tests of these implications, of which the present article is nearly devoid. The limited progress we have made in exploring political "tastes" is my main ground for optimism about the fruitfulness of a return to a more familiar theoretical mode.[30]

30. Some specification of power relationships is unavoidable. It is implicit, as Stigler has pointed out to me, in the choice of groups for which the model's regulator acts as broker. For example, why not posit a political redistribution between electricity producers and peanut vendors? Also, most of the results of the model are driven by "normality" of the political-wealth effect. Normality, in this context, is a specific assumption about power (inter)relationships.

SEVEN

The Growth of Government

I. INTRODUCTION

By conventional budget and gross national product (GNP) measures, government's role in the allocation of resources has increased considerably over the last century, and the growth shows no sign of abating. As a result, governments everywhere in the developed world have moved from a sometimes trivial to a now uniformly considerable role in shaping national expenditures. My task will be to try to explain this growth and size. To do so, I am going to equate government's role in economic life with the size of its budget. This is obviously wrong since many government activities (for example, statutes and administrative rules) redirect resources just as surely as taxation and spending, but the available data leave no other choice. My operating assumption has to be that large and growing budgets imply a large and growing substitution of collective for private decision in allocating resources. But the main intellectual problem I want to explore is the sources of this substitution generally.

I first review the facts about the growth of government and some standard explanations. Since none of the explanations seems very satisfactory, I then present my own explanation, which focuses on the incentives to use a political mechanism to redistribute wealth. Finally, I confront my theory with some relevant data. The main result is counterintuitive: greater equality of private incomes increases the demand for political redistribution.

II. TRENDS IN THE SIZE AND GROWTH OF GOVERNMENT

Table 7.1 presents a few scraps of historical data on the ratio of government budgets relative to GNP in four developed countries. The data are meant only to illustrate the extent and durability of government growth.

First published in *Journal of Law and Economics* 23 (October 1980): 209–287. © 1980 by The University of Chicago.

The author wishes to thank Gerald Dwyer, Bart Taub, and William Pelletier for their valuable assistance. The support of the Walgreen Foundation, the Center for the Study of the Economy and the State, and the National Science Foundation is gratefully acknowledged.

TABLE 7.1 Trends of Government Spending/GNP, United States and Three European Countries, 1860–1974

Country and Year		Approximate Ratio × 100	Percentage Change from Previous
United States	1870	12	
	1880	8	−30
	1900	8	0
	1920	13	+60
	1940	18	+40
	1960	27	+50
	1974	32	+20
United Kingdom	1860	10	
	1880	10	0
	1900	10	0
	1922	23	+130
	1938	23	0
	1960	30	+30
	1974	45	+50
Germany	1880	3	
	1900	6	+100
	1925	8	+30
	1935	12	+50
	1960	15	+25
	1974	15	0
Sweden	1880	6	
	1900	6	0
	1920	8	+30
	1940	12	+50
	1960	24	+100
	1974	27	+15

Sources: United States and United Kingdom: See Section V *infra.* Germany and Sweden: Brian R. Mitchell, European Historical Statistics: 1790–1970, (1975).

Note: All figures are generously rounded. The numerator for the United States and United Kingdom is spending by all levels of government and for Germany and Sweden *central* government receipts *excluding* social security taxes. For Germany and Sweden 1960 and 1974 total government/GNP ratios are 35, 41 and 32, 49.

Since important sectors of government (for example, social security, local governments) are sometimes excluded, these data cannot be used to compare the size of government across countries. The data do show that government budgets have grown faster than GNPs since at least 1900, and that they may have grown more slowly before. A more precise date for the transition from decline to growth of government would center around World War I and its aftermath. Since then, without any important exception or reversal, the government/GNP ratio in these data has increased on the order of three- or four-fold.

More comprehensive data for two decades ending in the mid-1970s are summarized for the United States and the major developed economies in table 7.2. They show the extent and growth of government spending at all levels relative to gross domestic product (GDP) according to international income accounting conventions. While these data are still less comprehensive than we would like (see note to table 7.2), they seem to reveal the following broad patterns.

(1) The relative size of the government sector in the typical developed country expanded by over one-third in the two decades, from just over a quarter to around two-fifths of the GDP.

(2) The growth accelerated markedly in the last decade, which accounts for about three-quarters of the total growth.

(3) This accelerated growth is evident both in direct consumption and in transfers. However, transfers have been growing two or three times faster per year than government consumption throughout the period.

(4) The higher recent growth rates also seem slightly more variable across countries, so that the spread among the sizes of their public sectors has widened. The growing importance of transfers, which vary more than consumption, provides an arithmetic explanation for this widening dispersion.

(5) The U.S. government sector has been a comparative laggard. Essentially, the rest of the world has caught up to the United States in public consumption. And despite doubling the share of its GDP going to transfers, the United States has made only a modest dent in the rest of the world's lead in transfers. More specifically, the locus of the United States's lag is its defense sector. By 1974 only Australia and Japan had smaller public sectors than the United States.

III. SOME EXPLANATIONS FOR THE TRENDS AND THEIR DEFICIENCIES

The literature on the size of government uses two modes of analysis for explaining the trends just described. The first focuses on specific historical events as the primary cause, whereas the second focuses on a market for "public goods." Both types of analysis demonstrate considerable variety which this brief summary cannot hope to reflect adequately. This is especially true of the first type, which prevails in studies of particular countries and time periods where questions of the generality of the analysis tend to be deemphasized.

One widely known example of the historical mode of analysis is Peacock and Wiseman's study of the growth of British government, which develops what has come to be called the "displacement-concentration" hypothesis.[1] Briefly put, the government/GNP ratio tends to be a constant until it is displaced upward by a national crisis—war, in the specific case at hand. This displacement is not completely offset at war's end, first, because the expanded bureaucracy is now better able to assert its interests and, second, because the war concentrates power at the national level. This concentration of power limits the restraint on taxes provided by competition among localities.

A glance at the British and American data underlying table 7.1 (see figures 7.1 and 7.2 in Section V) indicates some of the attraction of this generalization. The British variable fluctuates around .10 from 1880 to World War I, when it leaps to a high over .5. From 1920 to World War II, the ratio fluctuates around .20 to .25, when it is again displaced upward and then declines only to a range between .3 and .5. The U.S. data also show a ratcheting effect of the two wars, but much less pronounced than for Britain.

This hypothesis has been evaluated critically elsewhere,[2] but a few simple facts can illustrate its problems. Consider the sixteen countries summarized in table 7.2. Half were active combatants for most or all of World War II (Australia, Canada, Germany-Austria, Italy, Japan, the United States, and the United Kingdom). The rest did not enter the war or were defeated quickly. The first group ought to have (a) larger public sectors just after the war and/or (b) more rapid growth since then. In fact, the 1953 government/GDP ratios are nearly the same (28.2 for the combatants versus 29.7 for the rest), and the non-combatants' ratios have grown significantly *more* rapidly since then (the difference in mean growth rates to 1974 is 22.2 percent, $t = 2.09$). From today's vantage, participating in a major war seems ultimately to limit the size of government.

The displacement-concentration hypothesis implies that high and increasing centralization of government produces large and growing governments. This notion plays an important role in Niskanen's interesting contributions to the "specific-event" literature.[3] I put Niskanen in this cat-

1. Alan T. Peacock & Jack Wiseman, The Growth of Public Expenditure in the United Kingdom (Princeton: Princeton Univ. Press, 1961)

2. D. Davies, The Concentration Process and the Growing Importance of Non-Central Governments in Federal States, 18 Public Policy (1970).

3. William A. Niskanen, Bureaucracy and Representative Government (Chicago: Aldine, Atherton, 1971), and his Bureaucrats and Politicians, 18 J. Law & Econ. 617 (1975).

TABLE 7.2 Size and Growth of Government Expenditures/GDP, U.S. and 16 Developed Countries, 1953–1974

Expenditure Category and Country	Year (Ratio × 100)					Percentage Change from Previous Ten Years	
	1953–54 (1)	1958–59 (2)	1963–64 (3)	1968–69 (4)	1973–74 (5)	1963–64 (6)	1973–74 (7)
Total Government							
United States	27.0	27.5	28.0	31.1	32.2	4%	15%
Avg. of 16 countries	28.9	29.9	31.7	35.8	39.4	10	24
SD of 16 countries	4.1	4.3	4.8	5.9	7.2	9	12
CV of 16 countries	14.1	14.2	15.0	16.6	18.3		
Total Government Less Defense							
United States	14.7	17.6	19.6	22.1	26.5	33	35
Avg. of 16 countries	24.4	26.2	28.2	32.6	36.7	17	30
SD of 16 countries	4.7	4.5	4.6	5.9	7.0	13	14
CV of 16 countries	19.1	17.1	16.3	18.2	19.0		
Government Consumption							
United States	21.5	20.8	20.5	22.4	21.2	–4	3
Avg. of 16 countries	17.2	17.2	18.2	19.8	20.9	7	15
SD of 16 countries	2.7	2.4	2.5	3.4	3.6	12	11
CV of 16 countries	15.8	14.2	13.7	17.4	17.1		

Transfers							
United States	5.5	6.7	7.5	8.7	11.0	36	46
Avg. of 16 countries	11.9	12.9	13.8	16.2	18.8	23	38
SD of 16 countries	4.3	4.2	4.3	4.9	5.9	23	23
CV of 16 countries	36.4	32.5	31.0	30.2	31.6		

Sources of Data: Organization for Economic Cooperation & Development, National Accounts of OECD Countries, various years for all countries except United States. United States data from Council of Economic Advisors, Economic Report of the President (1976).

Notes: Numerator for columns (1)–(5) is current revenue of all levels of government plus net borrowing if any (that is, any net lending to other sectors is not deducted). The data are classified according to the United Nations' new System of National Accounts (SNA) in which receipts and expenditures of separately incorporated nationalized industries are excluded from the government sector. However, subsidies and loans made by governments to nationalized industries are included.

Government consumption includes purchases of goods and services, gross capital formation, and wages paid to government employees. Transfers include subsidies, social security benefits, and interest on debt. (This breakdown is unavailable for Switzerland.)

The sample includes: Australia, Austria, Belgium, Canada, Denmark, Finland, France, Germany, Italy, Japan, the Netherlands, Norway, Sweden, Switzerland, the United Kindom, and the United States. These countries have adopted the new SNA at different times. Where a particular series could not be reconstructed from the previous SNA, it was spliced to the series from the new SNA.

The denominator is gross domestic product at market prices (that is, includes indirect taxes), which is essentially equal to GNP. The ratios in columns (1)–(5) are averages for the two years indicated. "SD of 16 countries" is the standard deviation of the level or percentage change for the 16 (or 15) country sample, and "CV of 16 countries" is the coefficient of variation.

The years 1975–1976, the last for which I have data, show a marked acceleration of government growth. The first two figures under "Total Government" for these years would be 34.8 (U.S.) and 43.0 (16 country averages). The growth from 1973–1974 is on the order of 40 or 50% that of the entire preceding decade. Although none of the qualitative conclusions is thereby affected, I exclude 1975–1976 because they may atypically bear the brunt of the effects of the most pronounced worldwide recession since the 1930s.

egory because, even though he develops a general model of bureaucracy, he ultimately relies on a few specific events exogenous to his model to explain the size and growth of government.

Niskanen's model contemplates a bureaucracy that values larger budgets and always has some power to extract budget dollars from a legislature that values bureaucratic output. An important constraint on the bureaucracy's ability to gain unproductive budget dollars is competition among bureaucrats and among jurisdictions. Thus, institutional developments that weaken competition imply growing budgets. Among these developments, Niskanen cites centralization of governmental functions, the consolidation of governmental functions into fewer bureaus, and enhancement of bureaucratic tenure (civil service). He gives these factors greater weight than increases in the "rational ignorance" of legislators, another source of a bureau's monopoly power.

A primary difficulty with this theory, one which Niskanen explicitly recognizes, is its treatment of centralization of bureaucratic power as an exogenous event. An obvious alternative is that the same forces generating growth of government generally produce conditions facilitating that growth. This may help explain the temptation to fall back on discrete events, like wars, to rationalize subsequent growth of government. Another difficulty stems from the model's sketchy outline of the relationship between politicians and bureaucrats. Politicians do not benefit directly from bureaucratic budgets, and Niskanen presents evidence that they lose votes from marginal budget expansions.[4] (This is meant to corroborate the model's implication that bureaucracies are able to "overexpand.") But the estimated size of this loss—the elasticity of votes lost by an incumbent president with respect to federal revenues during his term is about .6—is easily large enough so that modest reductions of expenditures would have changed the results of some recent elections. In that case, one has to wonder how "rational" it is for politicians to "ignore" bureaucratic expansion.

However, there are clear factual problems with the general-concentration hypothesis taken on its own terms. The evidence that high or rising concentration of government functions is essential for large or growing government is weak at best. One measure of concentration is the fraction of all government revenues collected nationally. It is, to be sure, imperfect, because national policies can affect incentives to tax locally.[5] For

4. Niskanen, Bureaucrats and Politicians, *supra* note 3.
5. Although Thomas E. Borcherding, The Sources of Growth of Public Expenditures in the United States, 1902–1970, in Budgets and Bureaucrats: The Sources of Government

TABLE 7.3 Regressions of Size and Growth of Government on Centralization Measures, 1953–1973, (16 Developed Countries)

Dependent Variable	Centralization 1953	Centralization 1973	Growth of Centralization	R^2 SE
(1) Government Spending/GDP	.097			.09
1953–1954	(1.161)			4.2
1973–1974		.218		.22
		(1.965)		6.7
(2) Growth of Government/GDP	.121		.275	.05
1953–1954 to 1973–1974	(.343)		(.571)	17.1

Source: Organization for Economic Cooperation and Development, National Accounts of OECD Countries, Variables (all × 100):

Centralization: Current Revenues of National Government/Current Revenues of All Levels of Government in year indicated or closest year for which data are available. Series spliced to current SNA where appropriate.

Growth of Centralization: log change of centralization over 20-year period (or extrapolated to 20 years, where required).

Government Spending/GDP: see table 7.2.

Growth of Government/GDP: log change of Government Spending/GDP over 20-year period.

the United States, the broad trend of this measure supports Niskanen, in that centralization is now higher than in 1900 (about .60 versus .35). However, most of the increase took place in World War II, which is fifteen to twenty years after the persistent growth of the government/GNP ratio began. Growth since 1950 has been accompanied by a mild (about .10) decline in the centralization ratio. A comparison of the developed countries' recent experiences also yields weak support for the role of centralization. What seems most impressive about (measured) centralization is its temporal stability in the face of the considerable worldwide expansion of public sectors in the past two decades. Only Canada has experienced a larger change than the United States (also toward decentralization), and nowhere else has the centralization ratio changed by more than .10. Thus, increased centralization can hardly have played a crucial role in recent growth. The role of centralization is shown a bit more systematically in the regressions of table 7.3 which relate the size and growth of the government/GDP ratio to the level and change in centralization. The simple correlation of levels is weakly positive, and in 1973, even significant. However,

Growth 53–54 (T. E. Borcherding ed.) (Durham, N.C.: Duke Univ. Press, 1977), summarizes evidence that this is unimportant, at least for the United States.

neither the extent of centralization nor the small changes in centralization seem to explain much of the growth of government. The meager support these results provide for the centralization hypothesis still has to confront the potential endogeneity of both the level and growth of the centralization variable. The "special-event" explanations of centralization may not be adequate; for example, of the eight full-time combatants in World War II, five rank among the *least* centralized half of our sample in 1953 (or 1973). Centralization of political power can clearly occur without a major war.

In its application to the problem at hand, the "public goods" model is more an analytical framework than the expression of a single widely accepted theory of government expenditure. The common strand of the literature is the treatment of expenditures as the implicit or explicit outcome of a market for government services. That is, demand and cost conditions for publicly provided goods determine expenditures. A vast empirical literature, much of it concentrated on cross-sectional analyses of local government finance,[6] fits this mold, even though much of it is so ad hoc that even this very general categorization is risky. The prototypical procedure goes back at least to Brazer.[7] It consists of regressing aggregate or individual service expenditures on a list of variables which shift the constituents' demand for them (for example, personal income, education) and the government's cost of providing them (for example, wage rates, population densities). A somewhat more theoretically sophisticated branch of this literature tries to take account of the political process that mediates this market or the indivisibilities that the traditional normative theory of government implies will characterize publicly provided services. But these factors have little impact on empirical practice. For example, the well-known collective choice model[8] in which politicians cater to the preferences of the "median voter" is sometimes cited.[9] However, there is no overall con-

6. See Roy Bahl, Studies in the Determinants of Public Expenditures: A Review, in Sharing Federal Funds for State and Local Needs (F. J. Mushkin & J. F. Cotton eds.) (Washington, D.C.: Brookings Inst., 1968).

7. Harvey Brazer, City Expenditures in the U.S. (Nat'l Bureau Econ. Research, Occasional Paper No. 66, 1959).

8. Howard R. Bowen, The Interpretation of Voting in the Allocation of Economic Resources, 58 Q. J. Econ. 27 (1943); Anthony Downs, An Economic Theory of Democracy (New York: Harper & Row, 1957); Gordon Tullock, Towards a Mathematics of Politics (Ann Arbor: Univ. of Michigan Press, 1967).

9. See, for example, Theodore C. Bergstrom & Robert P. Goodman, Private Demands for Public Goods, 63 Am. Econ. Rev. 280 (1973); and Thomas E. Borcherding & Robert T. Deacon, The Demand for the Services of Non-federal Governments, 62 Am. Econ. Rev. 891 (1972).

sensus that, say, median income is a better proxy for this demand than average income.[10] Similarly, discussions of the "publicness" of government services often serve to rationalize inclusion of, say, a population variable and help in the interpretation of its effect.[11]

For present purposes, an adequate summary of this literature would be an equation like

$$E = bY + cP + dN + A',$$

where (all variables are logs)

E = real per capita (N) government spending;
Y = real per capita income;
P = relative price of a unit of public services;
A' = all other factors;
b, c, d = elasticities with $b > 0$ if public goods are normal, $d < 0$ if there are "publicness" scale economies, and the sign of c is dependent on the price elasticity of the demand for public goods ($c < 0$ if this elasticity > 1).

It is sometimes argued that government shares with other service industries a labor-intensive production function,[12] so P will increase with wage rates. Since wage rates increase with Y over time and cross-sectionally, it is adequate to write this as

$P = E + hY$
h = constant, $0 < h < 1$
F = "other factors."

Then, focusing on the government/income ratio, our equation would be

$$e = E - Y = (b + ch - 1)Y + dN + A$$
$$A = A' + cF$$

It is clear that secular population growth could hardly explain the secular growth of e since d is supposed to be negative. In fact, it turns out that $d \approx 0$ is the better summary of the empirical results, at least for aggregate expenditures.[13] Thus, we have to focus on the coefficient of Y if this model yields insights about e. The simplest explanation, which goes by "Wagner's Law," is that $b > 1$. However, this law remains to be enacted: Borcherd-

10. See James L. Barr & O. A. Davis, An Elementary Political and Economic Theory of the Expenditures of Local Governments, 33 S. Econ. J. 149 (1966), for an explicit test of the median voter model.

11. Again see Bergstrom & Goodman and Borcherding & Deacon, *supra* note 9.

12. See William J. Baumol, The Macroeconomics of Unbalanced Growth: The Anatomy of Urban Crisis, 57 Am. Econ. Rev. 415 (1967).

13. See the summary in Borcherding, *supra* note 5.

ing's survey of the empirical literature finds $b = .75$ a more plausible central tendency.[14] If so, there remain the price effects (ch) as a potential source of secular growth in e. Again, I rely on Borcherding's survey for an estimate of $c \approx +.5$. To get at h, note that real GNP increased at 3.2 per cent annually from 1929 to 1974, the private-goods and services deflator at 2.5 per cent, and the government-goods and services deflator at 3.9 per cent. These percentages imply an h around .4 to .5 $\left(\dfrac{3.9 - 2.5}{3.2}\right)$. Rounding up, we get $ch \approx .25$ and the whole coefficient of $Y \approx 0$. On this admittedly crude summary of conventional income and price effects, e should thus be a constant over time or across space. In fact, simple cross-sectional data are roughly consistent with trivial total income effects. For example, note the following elasticities (t-ratios) from regression estimates of the equation for e for our sixteen-nation sample:

	1953–1954	1973–1974
Income	.035	.059
	(.464)	(.297)
Population	.0003	−.075
	(.0089)	(1.916)

The one result here that is distinguishable from zero (the last population elasticity) makes growing government more rather than less intelligible, given secular population growth.

A cross section of U.S. states yields similar results. In table 7.4, per capita budget measures are regressed on per capita income and population for 1942, 1957, and 1972 (lines 1–3). The income elasticities here are a little below unity, but the shortfall seems mainly due to transitory components of income. The temporal transitory components can be reduced by averaging over time. When we do this (lines 4 and 5), the income elasticities move closer to unity. Other income components may be transitory across space: one state may temporarily gain some income lost by another. As a crude correction for this, I aggregated states into census regions. The regressions on the census region data (lines 6 and 7) yield income elasticities of almost precisely unity, just what our crude summary of the literature would lead us to expect and what we found for the cross-nation sample. The state and local data, in whatever form, also yield the negative but numerically trivial population elasticity alluded to above.

The main purpose of this brief summary and extension of the empirical public-goods literature is to establish a foundation for the subsequent em-

14. *Id.*

TABLE 7.4 Regressions of State and Local Per Capita Expenditures or Receipts on Income and Population (1942, 1957, 1972, U.S. 48 States)

Dependent Variable (Per Capita)	Coefficients/t-ratios of				R^2	SE	N
	Income per Capita	Population	1957	1972			
1. Revenue, includes federal aid	.802[1]	−.056	.382	.927	.957	.153	144
	14.87	−4.49	6.92	9.70			
2. Revenue, excludes federal aid	.870[1]	−.035	.297	.696	.974	.149	144
	16.55	−2.84	5.53	7.48			
3. Expenditures	.860[1]	−.054	.540	.980	.979	.148	144
	16.40	−4.41	10.06	10.55			
4. Revenue, excludes federal aid: average of 3 years' data	.946	−.035			.677	.116	48
	9.72	−2.06					
5. Expenditures: average of 3 years' data	.897	−.048			.659	.116	48
	9.25	−2.83					
Census Regions							
6. Expenditures	1.029	−.046[2]	.553	.877	.994	.092	27
	12.12	−1.90	6.56	5.97			
7. Expenditures: average of 3 years' data	1.072	−.022[2]			.846	.086	9
	5.54	−.53					

Sources: Expenditures and Revenue: U.S. Bureau of the Census, Census of Governments; and *id.*, Governmental Finances, various years. Income and Population: *id.*, Statistical Abstracts of the U.S. (1978).

Notes: All variables are in logs, except: 1957 = +1 for 1957, 0 otherwise; 1972 = +1 for 1972, 0 otherwise.
[1]Significantly different from unity.
[2]Population per state in region.

pirical work on the size and growth of government relative to income. The main virtue of the "public-goods" framework is precisely its suggestion that the government/GNP ratio is a variable of prime analytic interest. When the framework is given empirical content, it suggests that this ratio ought to be roughly a constant across space and time. This is the happily fortuitous counterpart of the unit income elasticity and near-zero population elasticity. We are then left with the mystery, which we shall try to resolve, of why this ratio has in fact grown over time and varies considerably across space.

A cursory glance at recent history may help explain why "public-goods" models have not resolved that mystery. The public-goods paradigm characteristically is concerned with collective decisions about classically indivisible "community goods." It seems reasonable to expect broad community agreement to expand these provisions with community income. That agreement, however, ought to be less broad for much of what government today in fact does. For example, about half of the typical developed country's public spending today goes for direct transfers, the community-wide benefits of which are dubious. Similar doubts arise about many public-consumption expenditures. For example, the human-capital literature makes clear that there is a large private element in the returns from public provision of education (about one-quarter of government consumption in the United States). And historical evidence indicates that these private returns elicited a considerable private supply which has not clearly been enhanced by subsequent public provision.[15] Whatever the community-good element in public education, a large indirect transfer is clearly involved in the typical public financing arrangements for it.

Such considerations suggest the riskiness of ignoring redistributive elements when analyzing the size or growth of government, and in the remainder of this paper I will focus on these elements. In doing so, I am not denying the importance of the collective-good aspects of public activity. However, my basic working hypothesis is that incentives to redistribute wealth politically are the more important determinants of the *relative* size and growth of the public and private sectors. This hypothesis entails deemphasis of governments' direct cost of collecting and redistributing resources. This does not have the same empirical basis as our deemphasis of public goods, in that evidence on the effect of, for example, modern communications and record keeping on tax-collection costs is lacking. Ac-

15. For example, E. G. West, Education and the State: A Study in Political Economy (London: Inst. of Econ. Affairs, 1965).

cordingly, most of the empirical analysis focuses on groups of govern-ments where differences in tax-collection costs are plausibly minor. In the case of less developed countries where such differences may be large, col-lection costs are given an explicit role in the analysis.

In the next section, I elaborate a model of the incentives to political redistribution of income, which shows how these incentives are related to the distribution of income that would prevail in the absence of political redistribution.

IV. THEORY OF THE EQUILIBRIUM SIZE OF GOVERNMENT

I treat government spending and taxing as a pure transfer. This is, of course, only meant to focus issues, and the literal-minded reader can inter-pret spending as an increment over expenditures of a purely public-goods character. I also assume that the amount of spending is determined en-tirely by majority-voting considerations. This assumption also should not be interpreted literally, since it is meant only to highlight an important difference between political and private resource allocation. What is essen-tial here is simply that popular support contributes to the viability of pub-lic policies, so that more such support is better than less. Part of this sup-port may eventually be traded for other goods—monetary gain, relaxed relationships with the bureaucracy, and so forth—but I eschew develop-ment of a multifaceted objective function for simplicity. In particular, there is no need to confine the analysis to democratic systems. As long as suppressing dissent is costly to a dictator, he ought to be sensitive to the popular support for his policies. In the empirical work I touch on the question whether redistributive considerations are more important in democratic governments.

My analysis of the democratic case can best be understood as a two-step process. The first consists of a search for a politically "dominant" redistributive program, which, speaking loosely, yields the greatest benefits for the greatest number. Once that policy is described, I take a large second step by assuming that competition among politicians will lead them to converge on that policy in their platforms and implement it upon election. Hence, I brush past the rather formidable problems connected with the uniqueness and stability of political equilibrium.

What then is meant by a "politically dominant" policy? I am going to assume that political preferences are motivated purely by self-interest. A voter will favor only those policies which promise to benefit him; social altruism plays no role. Any redistributive policy creates gainers and losers, and thus, in my scheme, potential supporters and opponents. But we need to know more than who gains or loses from a policy if we want to find the policy that will attain the widest support; the per capita stakes will also be important. To illustrate, consider a proposal whereby all of J. Paul Getty's wealth would be confiscated and redistributed equally to everyone else. This policy would maximize the number of beneficiaries, but it is unlikely to dominate alternative policies. Getty and those closely linked with him would oppose it, since they would do no worse. Perhaps Rockefeller and a few other wealthy individuals would favor it, more out of gratitude for being spared Getty's fate than for the trivial share of Getty's wealth they receive. However, most of the beneficiaries would oppose this proposal, for they could surely do better by waiting for a politician to come along and propose the expropriation of both Getty and Rockefeller. Indeed, they would continue to withhold support until a candidate came along who proposed a policy that maximized their benefits.

Of course, the identity of "they" is changing in this scenario: Rockefeller is converted from a beneficiary to a loser in the second round of this political competition. The outline of a politically dominant policy should, however, be clear. It is the policy that maximizes the difference between the number of beneficiaries perceiving the policy as the best deal and losers perceiving it as the worst deal. In a world of certainty and homogeneous beneficiaries, those perceptions should be identical among individuals. We assume neither certainty nor homogeneity. In the more general case, beneficiaries, for example, are more likely to perceive a policy as "best" the greater the per capita gains it promises, and the policy which receives most support will be the one that maximizes the *product* of the number of beneficiaries and the fraction of these perceiving it to be the best deal.

My first task will be to formalize this description of the politically dominant policy, so that we can say something about its characteristics and, crucially, about the forces which shape it. Given our twin assumptions that political competition leads actual policy to converge on the dominant policy and that incentives to redistribution drive the size of government, we can then derive predictions about the forces that shape the size of government. Important among these, I will argue, is the distribution of income.

A. Full Information

As a convenient starting point, I assume a world of fully informed voters. Each voter understands costlessly the details of a proposed policy and its implications for his well being. He does *not* know with certainty what other proposals may be offered, nor does he necessarily ignore nonredistributive issues (for example, the charisma or ethics of candidates). All that will matter is that, having understood the nature and consequences of a policy, he is more likely to vote for the candidate offering it the more it would materially benefit him. The purpose of assuming full knowledge is both methodological and substantive. It helps to show where the political system is driven when knowledge becomes less costly, and it helps isolate the effects of ignorance, which I consider subsequently.

There are two relevant pools of voters: those whom the policy proposes to tax (let their number be Q) and those who will be paid (P). Let us first focus on the P's, and the political support they will offer for a policy. In line with our previous discussion, this support will be $P \cdot F$, where F is the fraction of the P's who prefer this particular policy to all others that they may possibly face (that is, "pie-in-the-sky" will not be well received). This fraction can, in principle, vary between -1 and $+1$. When F equals -1, every P is sure he can do better by favoring an alternative policy and they all oppose this one, so "support" equals $-P$. When F equals $+1$, every P is sure he can do no better and all support it. One obvious determinant of F is the per capita gain promised by the policy. If the per capita gain is low, as in the Getty expropriation, F will be low also; as the per capita gain increases, so will F.

Thus it appears that F would rise sharply only when a proposed policy moves toward expropriating the wealthiest 49 per cent for the benefit of the poorest 51 per cent. It requires at least 51 per cent support for a policy to dominate, and maximizing the loot with which to buy the favor of beneficiaries requires taxing the rich to pay the poor. While I will immediately consider some forces—the costs of redistribution—that will eliminate this sort of discontinuity, the reader should be forewarned that the Robin Hood feature of this and similar models[16] will be retained. In this stylized democratic process, the rich are taxed to keep down the numerical opposition to redistribution.

The costs of redistribution will limit the appeal of the massive, 49-paying-51, type of redistribution. The costs I focus on are those imposed on private markets by redistribution, rather than, say, the direct costs of running government programs. The P's and Q's deal with each other in goods, labor, and capital markets, so a tax on the Q also decreases the

16. For example, Thomas Romer, Individual Welfare, Majority Voting, and the Properties of a Linear Income Tax, 4 J. Pub. Econ. 163 (1975); Robert Aumann & Mordechai Kurz, Power and Taxes, 45 Econometrica 1137 (1977); and Alan Meltzer & Scott Richard, The Growth of Government (1979) (mimeographed paper at Carnegie-Mellon Univ., Econ. Dep't).

private income of the P. For example, if the Q are major suppliers of capital, a tax on their wealth will discourage saving and so lead to a reduction in the demand for the P's labor services. Thus, any redistribution policy short of pure lump-sum taxes is a mixed blessing for the P; they gain directly but at an indirect cost to their private wealth. This requires two amendments to our story. First, the tax rate levied on the Q to finance any redistributive policy is a political "bad"; the higher it is, *ceteris paribus,* the less attractive the policy is *to the P*'s. Thus, extreme Robin Hoodism (tax rate = 1) is not likely to be politically dominant. In fact, it can easily impose net losses on many or most of the P's.

The second amendment to the story is more technical but helps motivate the subsequent formalism. Specifically, I argue for the Marshallian mistrust of discontinuities: F, the fraction of P who view a policy as "best," will not suddenly leap from -1 to $+1$ for some critical change in policy. The P's are never unanimous about a particular policy, because the importance of private-market links to the Q's will vary among P's. To illustrate, consider a proposed redistributive policy consisting of a per P transfer, g, financed by tax rate R, on Q taxpayers. Now compare this to a proposal for more redistribution, and trace out the effects of the change on F. One possible new proposal is to raise both g and R. Given the varying negative effects of R on the P, some will favor the new proposal, others the old one; F may rise or fall, but is unlikely to go to a corner. Or the proposal might be to raise g but not R. The only way to do this without violating the irrelevance-of-pie-in-the-sky rule is to raise Q. But this also adversely affects P's generally, some more than others. So some will prefer the old policy, others the new. About all we can say at this level of analysis is that, if the old policy involved little redistribution, F (new policy) is more likely to be higher than if there is already much redistribution (and hence much deadweight loss).

The different responses among the P to any program play a crucial role in the theory. To elaborate, let us first recapitulate the discussion so far:

1. A politically dominant redistributive policy maximizes

(1) $M = P \cdot F -$ numerical opposition,

where

   P = number of beneficiaries of the policy
   F = fraction of P who prefer this policy over all others.

2. F depends on at least two parameters of the policy; the payment per $P(g)$ and the tax rate levied to raise the funds (R):

(2) $\begin{aligned} F &= F(g, R) \\ F_g &> 0, F_R < 0. \end{aligned}$

3. Beyond some point, F_g can be < 0, and in general, $F_{gg} < 0$. The reason, to repeat, is that if g is increased, *given R*, more people are being taxed. This is a "bad" for the P which can more than offset the direct benefit of the increased g for at least some of them. Moreover, pushed far enough, proposals to increase g will become too risky for politicians to support even if the proposals would benefit P's on balance. Since such proposals involve adding hostile taxpayers, the politician advocating them increases his risk of losing an election. He or his constituents may prefer to cast their lot with a more modest proposal.

I have argued that any proposal for a dominant policy will involve taxing the rich to benefit the poor. This is because any g can be raised this way at the smallest cost in terms of numerical opposition and at the smallest R for a given numerical opposition. I now want to argue that the income of beneficiaries is also relevant to the likely success of a proposal. One reason for this may be diminishing marginal utility of income, so that the perceived benefits of any g are smaller the higher the private incomes of beneficiaries. But I focus here on the deadweight losses of redistribution borne by the P. These losses are likely to increase with income, at least in absolute dollar terms. Consider, for example, a general reduction in the demand for labor as a result of an increase in R. Surely the dollar loss will be higher the higher the pre-tax labor income of a P. If the tax discourages nonhuman-capital formation, the relative loss to higher income P's will also be greater. If their high income is partly a return on human capital, the rise in the human/nonhuman capital ratio lowers the rate of return to human capital. Those P with a trivial human-capital investment can escape this cost. Put briefly, a P with trivial private income has little at stake in private dealings with the Q and is therefore less resistant to a large tax than a P with substantial income.

This hypothesis requires two further amendments:

1. Equation (2) needs to be expanded to

(3) $F = F(g, R, Y), F_Y < 0,$

where Y = per capita income of the P. This says that if Y falls, it has the same effect as if R falls or g rises—it improves the net benefits of any redistributive policy and hence the likelihood of the policy becoming politically dominant.

2. The complement of "tax the richest" is "benefit the poorest." By our logic, if we had to pick 100 individuals from whom to raise any given total tax, they would always be the richest 100. This would minimize R, implying that any proposal to expand the number taxed means adding less wealthy individuals to Q. Similarly, if 100 individuals are to be benefited,

they should be the poorest 100. They will bear the lowest indirect cost of the associated tax and so be the least ambivalent about supporting it. The implication is that Y, the per capita income of the P, is endogenous to the policy: if you propose to increase P, you are proposing to increase Y, because the new members will have higher income than the average of the 100 poorest. So

(4) $Y = Y(P), Y_p > 0.$

To conclude the analysis, we need to elaborate on the opposition to redistribution from those taxed, the Q's. They face a choice complementary to that of the P's, but simpler: all redistributive policies are bad for the Q's, but some are worse than others. Thus, the degree of opposition from the Q's to any proposed policy will depend on how much the policy would hurt them if adopted *and* how much worse or better off they might be under alternative policies. A simple general statement about the numerical opposition (ϕ) to a proposed policy would be

(5) $\phi = Q(1 - E),$

where E = the fraction of the Q who tolerate (that is, do not oppose) the policy. In principle, E could range from zero (the policy is so harmful that no alternative is likely to be worse and all Q's oppose it) to $+2$ (the policy is so mild that *any* alternative is likely to be worse, so all the Q's actually favor it). In practice, we ought to be concerned only about policies for which $0 < E < 1$, since no politician is likely to count on the support of those he proposes to tax as his path to victory. Generally, we expect

(6) $E = E(R), E_R < 0.$

That is, the higher the proposed tax rate, the larger the proportion of Q's who will conclude that an alternative will be no worse and therefore oppose the proposal.

I now summarize the discussion by rewriting (1) in a modified form, which makes subsequent manipulation more tractable by avoiding inessential complexity. First, express (1) in exponential form

(7) $M = e^{P+F} - e^{Q-E}.$

All symbols, except M, are now and henceforth to be understood as natural logs. For example, "P" is now ln P, "E" is a transformation of ln $(1 - E)$, and so on. In doing this, we implicitly focus on policies that the P's support and the Q's oppose. That is, the new F is bounded by $[-\infty, 0]$ and the new E by $[0, \infty]$. In the new notation $E = \infty$ means "none of the Q's oppose the policy," so opposition is $e^{-\infty} = 0$; $E = 0$ means "all the Q's oppose the policy." Next, I write

(8) $F = F(g, R)$,

where

$g = G - J$,

$G =$ (log of) *total* government expenditures and taxes (recall that we
    are assuming all expenditures to be on redistribution),

$J =$ (log of) total private income of the P's,

$R = G - I$, the log of the tax rate on Q's total income (I).

In (8), I have simplified (3) to make the critical benefits variable depend on the ratio of the direct transfer to private income rather than on the two separately. This expresses the crucial notion that transfers lose appeal to the P's the higher their private incomes.[17] The discussion leading to (4) implies: $J_p > 1$ (J is determined by P, and the "marginal" P is richer than the average), and $I_Q < 1$ (the "richest-first" tax policy implies that the "marginal" Q is poorer than the average). Finally, with the new notation understood, (6) is left unchanged.

The formal problem emerging from the theory is to find the redistributive policy that maximizes (7) and toward which political platforms will converge, a policy described by specific values of P, Q, and G, and subject to the constraint that benefits equal taxes.[18] The first-order conditions for the solution to this problem ($M_P = M_Q = M_G = 0$) yield the following marginal "revenue-cost" equalities (the gain is on the left-hand side):

(9) $1 = F_g J_p$.

This says that the dominant platform pushes P until the direct gain (always a 1 per cent increase in supporters) is balanced by the added cost, which comes from diluting benefits over a wider and wealthier base of beneficiaries.

(10) $-I_Q [e^{P+F+E-Q} \cdot F_R + E_R] = 1$.

---

17. The simplification costs some detail. The theory implies that a simultaneous increase in G and J can, beyond some point, decrease support. This is because, given R, the increase in G increases Q, which is a "bad" for the P's.

18. Another possible constraint would be something like total voters = beneficiaries + taxed. The motivation for not introducing the constraint is more descriptive than substantive. The subsequent analytical results would hold under such a constraint. However, tax and spending policy are typically kept separate both in political platforms and practice, resulting in a large group which receives substantial benefits and pays large taxes. In terms of the formal model, one can regard a member of this group as facing two decisions—one in the role of a P another as a Q—to which equations like (8) and (6) apply separately.

In (10) the gain from expanding Q by 1 per cent is indirect; the tax base is expanded and permits a lower R, which is valued by both P's and Q's (F_R, $E_R < 0$). The cost is the 1 per cent expansion of numerical opposition.

(11) $\quad F_g = -[e^{Q-E-P-F} \cdot F_R + E_R]$.

Here the gain from expanding G is that a larger proportion of P's will support the policy ($F_g > 0$); the cost is that both P's and Q's do not like the resulting higher taxes.[19]

There are two second-order conditions minimally required for (9)–(11) to describe an interior maximum: diminishing returns to benefits and increasing costs to taxation. I have already discussed the economic rationale behind the former ($F_{gg} < 0$).[20] There is also a mechanical rationale; since F cannot be greater than zero (in logs), beyond some point F_g must diminish. With respect to increasing costs, we have a choice: either $E_{RR} < 0$ or $F_{RR} < 0$. Since E has a finite lower bound, it is more convenient to assume $F_{RR} < 0$. This says that a given tax increase leads the Q's to withdraw more wealth from market exchange with the P's at higher than at lower tax rates. There is no strong economic reason for the deadweight losses to accelerate in this manner. However, if they did not, the model would permit completely confiscatory taxes. To make the subsequent results clear, I do not go beyond these minimal second-derivative conditions.

We can now proceed to derive formally the effects of income distribution characteristics on the equilibrium size of government. First I intro-

19. A more general version of (9)–(11) would begin from something like

$$F = (g', L),$$

where $g' = G - P$ (that is, the per capita benefit instead of the benefit-income ratio)
$\quad L = $ loss to P from taxation $= L(Y, R, I)$.
This L-function summarizes the P's private interest in trading with the Q; this would be related to the P's private income (Y) as well as R *and* I (the tax base). Presumably, the same R on a larger base is worse for the P's private welfare. My more tractable specialization already has $F_Y < 0$ implicitly and $F_R < 0$ explicitly, but does not embody a potential offset to the gain in expanding Q (left-hand side of (10)). When Q is expanded it raises I ($I_Q > 0$) as well as reducing R; the former is "bad" for the P, the latter "good." Allowing the ambiguity, (10) would be

$$-I_Q[e^{P+F+E-Q}(F_R - F_I) + E_R] = 1.$$

Note, however, from (9) that $F_g < 1$ ($J_P > 1$) and, consequently, from (11) that $-E_R < 1$. So the term ($F_R - F_I$) must be < 0, to satisfy (10) in spite of $F_I < 0$. In my specialization I assure this by setting $F_I = 0$. All this says is that there has to be some marginal gain for the P from expanding Q to offset the hostility of the Q's. Given this logical necessity, the specialization $F_I = 0$ is only a simplifying detail.

20. Note that, while this is required for an interior maximum, diminishing returns in logs is not necessarily implied by diminishing returns in natural numbers for this variable.

duce a variable (X) into the two cumulative income functions ($J(P)$, $I(Q)$) which changes them exogenously in some prescribed way. Then I derive the total effect of this shift on G (that is, dG/dX) from the general relationship

(12) $[di/dX] = -[M_{iX}][M_{ij}]^{-1}$,

where

$\quad\quad\quad i, j = P, Q, G,$

$\quad\quad [di/dX] =$ vector of total derivatives,

$\quad\quad\quad [M_{iX}] =$ vector of cross-partial derivative with respect to X,

$\quad\quad\quad [M_{ij}]^{-1} =$ inverse of the matrix of cross-partials.

Consider first an exogenous event that increases every member of P's income by 1 per cent while reducing every Q's income by 1 per cent so $J_X = -I_X = +1$, while $J_{PX} = I_{QX} = 0$. This yields the following sign condition:

(13)   sgn $dG/dX =$ sgn $F_{gg}[1 + I_Q F_g] < 0$.

This is the "Robin Hood" result: as the poor P's get wealthier, the political forces for redistribution weaken. The now wealthier P's have a larger stake in private transactions with the Q's and are therefore less anxious to see the latter's wealth taxed. $J_X > 0$ implies $g_X < 0$; and this lower g reduces support for redistribution, since $F_g > 0$. In effect, the private-market redistribution has substituted for part of the task of the political market.

Now consider what happens when inequality is reduced *within* the beneficiary group, while between-group inequality remains the same. To stylize this event, let the two groups' total incomes remain unchanged ($I_X = J_X = 0$), but let the marginal (wealthiest) beneficiary's income decline, or, more generally, the slope of the cumulative income function decline ($J_{PX} < 0$). Application of (12) yields

(14)   sgn $dG/dX =$ sgn $\dfrac{-[F_{RR} I_Q + F_R(1 + E_R I_Q + F_R I_Q)]}{[1 - I_Q F_g]}$.

Both numerator and denominator are positive, so the right-hand side of (14) is also positive.[21] The former reflects the political costs of taxation and the latter the gains of spending, so (14) is telling us that both are altered in a way favorable to *more* spending when inequality among beneficiaries is *reduced*.

Since this result is important for the empirical work, it deserves some

21. Both F_{RR} and $F_R < 0$. The parenthetical expression in the numerator > 0 in equilibrium (see equation (10) and note that $e^{P+F-(Q-E)}$ must > 1 for an interior solution). Since $F_g < 1$ by (9) and $I_Q < 1$, the denominator must be > 0.

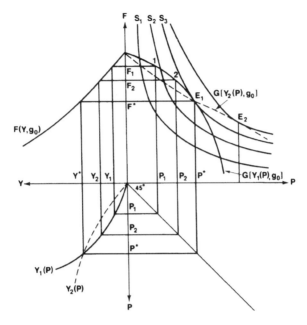

FIGURE 7.1

elaboration. A key element of the result is displayed in figure 7.1, where I have had to suppress parts of the general solution for the sake of exposition, and where, for a similar reason, I temporarily suspend the log notation. Specifically, suppose the per capita transfer to the P's is fixed (at g_0). The political decision in this restricted version of the general problem is the number of P's who will get g_0, so total transfers will be proportional to this number. Recall our crucial assumption that the higher the per capita income of the P's, the less avid their support for any particular redistributive policy. This is shown as $F[Y, g_0]$ in quadrant II of figure 7.1: given g_0, a smaller fraction (F) of P's will support a policy that gives each of them g_0 the higher their average income. Recall also that, since high income dulls the appetite for redistribution, any P chosen will be the poorest P in the population. This enables us to express Y as a function of P as displayed by $Y_1(P)$ in quadrant III. If $P = 1$, Y is the income of the poorest person (0); if $P = 2$, Y = the average income of the two poorest, and so on. So $Y_1(P)$ describes the income distribution of P's; as drawn it is meant to describe a relatively [to $Y_2(P)$, which we discuss later] unequal distribution. There are many poor P's, so Y does not increase much if we propose adding P's to a modest set of beneficiaries. However, if we go further and try to add middle class P's, Y starts increasing sharply, for they are much richer than the poor.

These two functions would, except for one difficulty, enable a politician to answer the question: if I proposed giving g_0 to each of P_0, what fraction of them would find this the most preferred policy? The difficulty is that higher levels of P_0 imply higher taxes and/or more people taxed, which, we have argued, are "bads" for P's as well as Q's. One inelegant way around this problem is to imagine that all of the negative effects of taxation are incorporated into the negatively sloped $F(Y, g_0)$ function. That is, the politician says something like: if I widen P, there are more potential votes for redistribution, but I necessarily raise Y *and* increase R and/or Q. *All* of the latter three effects will offset some or all of the potential political gain from widening P. The crucial notion is simply that there is a trade-off between *increasing* P and *reducing* the fraction of the electorate that supports or tolerates redistribution. For expositional purposes, I will ignore parts of this trade-off—the increased opposition and tax effects—and focus on P-income distribution effects.

All of the above understood, the relevant trade-off available in the political market is $G[Y_1(P), g_0]$ in quadrant I, which shows that if a policy proposes a larger set of P a smaller fraction will support it. It is constructed as follows. Suppose benefits are limited to P_1 people. They will have an average income of Y_1, which I find by (*i*) locating P_1 on the vertical axis of quadrant III by means of a 45-degree line and then (*ii*) reading off from $Y_1(P)$. For $Y = Y_1$, I can determine F_1 from $F(Y, g_0)$ in quadrant II. The resulting combination (P_1, F_1), labeled (1), is one point on this political "transformation" locus, $G[Y_1(P), g_0]$. In a similar fashion, point (2) is generated, starting with P assumed $= P_2$, and the locus of all such points is $G[Y_1(P), g_0]$.

The political objective to be sought in a choice of P is maximum numerical support (again read "support" as "support net of all opposition"). Support is simply the product PF. In quadrant I of Figure 7.1, this objective is characterized by a series of rectangular hyperbolae (S_j), each of which collect the P, F combinations consistent with a given support (S_j). The dominant policy is characterized by (P^*, F^*), or point E, where S is maximized, given $G[Y_1]$.

Imagine the sort of exogenous event that occurs in (14). The average income of the P^*, $Y(P^*)$ is unchanged, but it is more equally distributed among them as represented by the new income function, $Y_2(P)$, in quadrant III. It crosses $Y_1(P)$ at P^* and is flatter at P^* and steeper near the origin. Poor marginal beneficiaries now add more and rich marginal beneficiaries less to the average income of the group. This, in turn, implies a new $G[\cdot]$ which cuts the old one from below at the old equilibrium E_1. The dominant policy is now E_2 which implies a higher P^* and, given g_0, a higher level of government spending.

To understand what is involved here, recall why P^* was an equilibrium when $Y_1(P)$ prevailed. There was a positive probability that the P^* + 1st beneficiary would himself favor extra redistribution. But this small expected gain was insufficient to overcome the adverse effects of the added taxes on the remaining P^*. The gain was small because P^* + 1 is so wealthy that he bears a heavy indirect cost of the added taxes required to pay him g_0. Now P^* + 1 is less wealthy and would bear correspondingly smaller losses to his private wealth if taxes are raised. He is thus more likely to return the favor if a politician proposes to include him among the beneficiaries. Rational politicians will respond by proposing to expand the set of beneficiaries.

The principle that more similar interests in redistribution broaden the support for it could be extended to the direct costs of redistribution, which the formal model ignores. If more diverse interests imply a greater variety of programs (transfers for the poor, state opera for the rich) and each has its own "set-up" costs, the benefits perceived per dollar expenditure will be smaller than otherwise. If we permit benefits to be a fraction of total expenditures to reflect these government "brokerage" costs, it is straightforward to show that the equilibrium expenditure rises as the brokerage costs fall. A corollary to this is that governments will not want to completely offset the effects of divergent within-beneficiary-group interests with different per capita transfers. Equalization of benefit/income ratios among beneficiaries, for example, would be too costly, since it would entail complete exclusion of the poorer beneficiaries from access to some programs. Moreover, even if equalization were feasible, our model implies that an optimal policy redistributes wealth *within* as well as *between* groups.[22] This also has a corollary: the total support produced by any

---

22. This is seen most easily in the following restricted problem (log notation again suppressed): A given G is to be distributed among two equal-sized (P) groups of beneficiaries, who differ only in their incomes (J), to maximize the political support (S) forthcoming from the two groups. Thus, the objective is to maximize

$$S = \overline{P}[F(g_1) + F(g_2)],$$

where F has the same meaning as before and

$$g_i = G_i / J_i, \quad i = 1, 2.$$

given redistribution is enhanced if the pretransfer income differences among beneficiaries narrow.[23] So while we have, for simplicity, ignored problems connected with the distribution of benefits, their resolution reinforces the previous result that homogeneity among potential beneficiaries increases the demand for redistribution.

In any event, the model suggests a distinction between two types of inequality, that *between* beneficiaries and taxpayers and that *within* the former group. It also suggests that a reduction in within-beneficiary-group inequality stimulates the growth of government, whereas reduced inequality between groups retards it. Thus no straightforward connection is implied between any overall measure of income inequality and the size of government. As we shall see, there are formidable empirical problems in disentangling the two types of inequality from the available data.

B. Costly Information

Learning about the effects of a proposed policy or candidate is not, of course, costless, as we have been assuming it to be. There will also be costs of organizing groups to support or oppose adoption of a policy. These costs of access to the political mechanism mean that some voters will be ignorant of the effects of a policy. This section discusses the effects of ignorance on the results just derived.

I will continue to assume that all members of Q are fully informed. This simplification is intended to capture a qualitative difference between them and members of P rather than for descriptive accuracy. Any dominant policy will have to keep Q smaller than P, so Q members will have the larger per capita incentive to become informed about the effects of a policy and organize their interests. Therefore, incomplete knowledge

---

Since $G = G_1 + G_2$, this reduces to selecting the optimum G_1. The solution is to select G_1 such that

$$\frac{F_{g_1}}{F_{g_2}} = \frac{J_1}{J_2}$$

If group 1 is poorer, this ($J_1/J_2 < 1$) and diminishing returns imply $g_1 > g_2$—i.e., the poorer receive higher transfers relative to income.

23. To stylize this, let $J_{1X} = -J_{2X} = +1$, and note that

$$\frac{d_s}{d_X} = \frac{dg_1}{d_X} - F_{g_1} - F_{g_2}).$$

Since group 1 is now richer, the optimal response is to reduce g_1. Since $F_{g_1} < F_{g_2}$ in equilibrium, $d_s/d_X > 0$. So the narrowing of within-group inequality enhances the political payoff to the total transfer expenditure.

should have the strongest impact on the behavior of group P. To get at this differential impact of ignorance, I confine the analytical burden of ignorance to the P group.

I allow for two effects of ignorance. The *direct* effect is simply that only a fraction of the P who would support a policy if all were informed ($P + F$, in logs) will actually know enough to do so. The ignorant remainder either "stay home" or vote randomly. The *secondary* effect is that politicians will try to exclude some of the ignorant from benefits, so as to concentrate benefits on those most likely to reciprocate. To get both effects, I expand (8) as follows

(15) $F = H(g, R, Z)$.

The added variable, Z, is an "exclusion" parameter, which varies between $(0, 1)$ in natural numbers or $(-\infty, 0)$ in logs. The variable P is now to be interpreted as the maximum number of beneficiaries, that is, the number who would share G under "free" information. If Z is at its lower bound (no exclusion), the "free-information" case obtains: all the P are informed and share in G. An increase in Z represents more ignorance, which means a smaller fraction of the P support a policy and a smaller fraction are rewarded. If Z ever attained its upper bound (total ignorance), $e^F = 0$ and no redistribution policy would be politically viable.

The indirect (concentrated-benefits) effect of ignorance can be expressed as follows. Retain the definition of $g = G - J$, but redefine J to be the total income of those actually receiving benefits. So

(16) $J = J(P, Z)$
       $J_z < 0$.

That is, the more P excluded, the lower the total income of *actual* beneficiaries. For simplicity, assume that those excluded are a random selection of the P's, $J_Z = -1$ (Z in logs); that is, if 1 per cent of the P are randomly excluded, those left have 1 per cent less total income.[24]

If we now combine the indirect with the direct effect of exclusion and examine the overall consequences of increasing the exclusion of P's from benefits, we get for the effects of exclusion

---

24. More plausibly $-1 < J_Z < 0$. This would hold if those excluded tend to be a poorer than average subset of the P's, which is what would be implied by the positive correlation between income and likely indicators of the ability to process political information (education).

A counterforce is that high income implies high time costs of acquiring information. The optimal included beneficiary is poor and well educated.

(17) $F_z = H_z + H_g \cdot g_z = H_z + H_g$ (since $g_z = -J_z = +1$).

The second right-hand side term is the indirect effect of exclusion which states that the more concentrated benefits improve support for any given total expenditure. The H_z term will be the resultant of two opposing forces. On the one hand, there are fewer potential supporters, since a sub-set of the P receives no benefits. This would imply $H_z = -1$. On the other hand, the remaining beneficiaries are of higher "quality"—that is, more responsive to any benefits, and this implies $H_z > 0$. Presumably, a rational selection process of excluding the dumbest first will imply diminishing "quality" effects with exclusion, so $H_{zz} < 0$. We also know that beyond some point $H_z < 0$ on balance, since total exclusion implies $e^F = 0$.

As it happens, a first-order condition for the expanded policy choice problem (which now requires selecting Z as well as P, Q, G) is

(18) $H_g = -H_z$.

So $H_z < 0$ in equilibrium. Exclusion is pushed until its direct effects are negative at the margin and counterbalanced by the favorable effects of concentrated benefits. The remaining first-order conditions carry over in-tact from the free-information case ((9)–(11)). As a result, the effects of income-distribution changes on the growth of government are the same in both models. The added insight we gain into the size of government con-cerns changes in the "ability" or quality of voters. The effects of some manifestations of such change can be summarized as follows:

1. An exogenous increase in the average "ability" of the P's ($H_X > 0$ at any Z) increases the equilibrium G.

2. There is no ability counterpart to the within-group income equality effect. Specifically, suppose those individuals at the margin of exclusion suddenly become more able, while average ability is the same. Thus, the difference in ability between the most and least able beneficiary narrows ($H_{ZX} < 0$, $H_X = 0$). This generates two conflicting forces which exactly offset each other: (i) the degree of exclusion is reduced, but (ii) the maxi-mum set of beneficiaries (P) is contracted. This latter occurs to mitigate the otherwise adverse tax and benefit-dilution effects from a net addition of beneficiaries.

3. Similarly, an exogenous increase in the ability of P's to translate marginal changes in g into political support ($H_{gX} > 0$, while $H_X = 0$) has not effect on G. The temptation to expand P is countered by the negative consequences of higher taxes, which lead to increased exclusion.

In short, G will vary directly with average ability of beneficiaries, but only its distribution among beneficiaries is altered by changes in the distribution of ability. If income and "ability" are positively related, it will no longer necessarily follow that the poor*est* citizens will be prime beneficiaries of redistribution. But the corollary (2, above) to this version of "Director's Law" is that, if the poorest become *relatively more* able, the middle class will lose some of its benefits.

The main theoretical results whose empirical content is the subject of the next section can now be summarized.

1. If potential beneficiaries' incomes increase relative to those of taxpayers, G will fall.

2. But if there is a similar increased equality of the ability of the two groups to recognize their interests, G will increase.

3. Anything which increases the efficiency of G in "buying" support can be put under the "ability" rubric. Thus lower costs of collecting taxes, or of transforming them into benefits, increases the gross G.

4. More equal income among beneficiaries increases G, but more equal ability has no effect.

V. EMPIRICAL ANALYSIS

The theory shows how some "pregovernment" distribution of income and ability affects the politically optimal level of government spending. Since no such pristine distributions will ever be found in the world, any attempt to relate empirically the size of government to an actual distribution entails a classic "identification" problem; the distribution can both affect the size of government and be affected by it. Moreover, we would not want to abstract entirely from this feedback effect, even if we could. For example, suppose a progressive income tax is levied and the proceeds are shipped abroad or used to pay for public goods that everyone agrees ought to be bought. Now we want to predict the size of redistributive government spending, the main choice variable in our model. My argument that the stake of potential beneficiaries in private dealings affects optimal redistribution implies that *after*-tax income and its distribution are the relevant variables. On the other hand, it could be argued that the progressive tax is the outcome, not a contributing cause, of the optimal policy. Transfer incomes would seem even more clearly an outcome of the process. But that does not imply that, for example, pretransfer income is the appropriate proxy for the "private" income in our model. Someone with only transfer income might have substituted private income absent the transfer. Government affects the distribution of earned income before as well as after taxes. But how? Presumably progressive taxes lead to more pretax inequality, but egalitarian social policies could offset this, by directly or indirectly shifting demand toward lower-wage labor. This listing of the potential crosscurrents in government's effect on any empirical distribution of income or ability could be extended.

I deal with the lack of any real-world counterpart to the theoretical "state-of-nature" distributions in two ways. First, I ignore the complications and use what is available, assuming implicitly that the crosscurrents cancel each other. I focus mainly on income concepts (for example, earned income) where some of the direct effects of government (transfers) are absent, but ultimately there is no obvious income concept that is more nearly "right" for our purposes.[25] Second, I focus on the growth as well as the level of government spending, assuming a lagged adjustment to any target level of G. In this framework, one can explicitly control for the current actual level of G and implicitly for any effects on other determinants of the target G. To elaborate, consider this version of a familiar lagged adjustment model:

(19) $\Delta G = a(G^* - G)$,

where $*$ = target value and a = fractional adjustment coefficient; and

(20) $G^* = bX$,

where b = vector of constants and X = vector of variables determining G^*. For simplicity, assume only one determinant of G^*, say a summary measure of income inequality. However, the measure ought to be one that would prevail in the absence of at least some effects of the current G, and we cannot observe this directly. Instead, we observe Y, which, for simplicity, can be expressed

(21) $Y = X + cG$,

where c = coefficient (we do not know its sign). Substituting (21) into (20) and (20) into (19), we get

(22) $\Delta G = abY - a(1 + bc)G$.

Here the coefficient of G amalgamates the usual partial adjustment effect, a, and the influence of G on the observed measure of income inequality, c. Empirical implementation of (22) thus entails all the econometric prob-

---

25. Simultaneous equation techniques might appear to offer a way out. But with government spending 40% of GNP and regulating much of the remainder, specifying "exogenous" determinants of, say, the distribution of income involves as much risk as assuming that the distribution is itself exogenous.

lems of partial adjustment models plus that of collinearity between Y and G (if $c \neq 0$).

The model and the preceding discussion of the empirical literature imply that the target level of G or of the G/income ratio is affected by at least three characteristics: between- and within-group income inequality and some average level of "ability." The available data do not always permit anything like this level of detail. Frequently, nothing more than a crude proxy for overall income equality is available, and the model makes clear that this variable has ambiguous effects on G^*. The initial empirical work is an attempt to see if any of the conflicting forces embedded in an overall equality measure dominate; the refinements are dealt with subsequently. To compensate partly for the crudity of the data, I will examine a few distinct sets of data to see if they yield a consistent story. These include British, American, Canadian, and Japanese time series and cross sections of developed countries, U.S. state and local governments, and less developed countries. Most of these data imply that income inequality, on balance, retards growth of government. We shall see, however, that this connection is more complex than just stated.

A. Time Series

1. Britain and the United States.

The historical patterns we seek to explain were described broadly in Section I. In light of our review of the empirical public-goods literature, I focus on the government budget share of GNP as shown in detail in figures 7.2 and 7.3 for the United States and Britain. The history of government's share of GNP is similar for both countries: decline or stability in the nineteenth century and growth in the twentieth. The most notable differences between the two countries seem to be: (1) the earlier completion of the British nineteenth-century decline, (2) the larger ratcheting effect of the two world wars for Britain, (3) the substantial U.S. growth in the 1930s versus none for Britain, and (4) the sharper recent growth for Britain.

Is there some plausible connection between this history and income inequality? In asking this, I ignore for now a host of potential complicating factors such as, for example, the extent of the franchise and changes in political structure. This leaves a major empirical problem of devising a proxy for income equality that can be matched to the data. Nothing like the standard size distributions is available for most of the period covered by the data, although Kuznets has conjectured they would show inequality following a path opposite to that in figures 7.2 and 7.3, with inequality

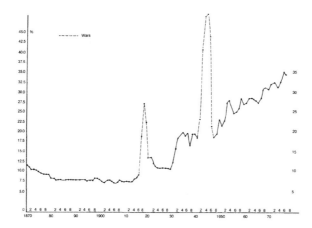

FIGURE 7.2 U.S. government expenditures/GNP. Annual, 1870–1976.

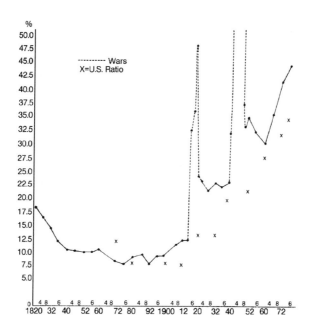

FIGURE 7.3 British government spending/GNP. Five-year intervals, 1829–1974.

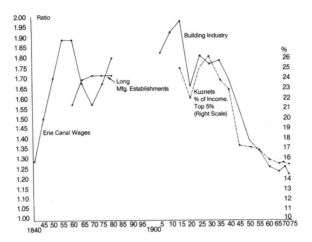

FIGURE 7.4 Skill differentials, United States 1840–1975, and income
share, top 5 percent, 1915–1975.

first widening then narrowing in consequence of the gradual shift of resources from the low-income agricultural sector.[26]

The only inequality-related data of which I am aware that are useful
for a long time series concern intra-industry wage dispersion, specifically
skill differentials (the ratio of wage rates of skilled to unskilled labor). In
a way, this crude measure is better for our purposes than an overall inequality measure, because it should be more closely connected to inequality within the beneficiary group. More recent data, however, imply that it
may be difficult to make the sort of distinctions about inequality required
by the model. Figure 7.4 illustrates the scattered data we have on U.S. skill
differentials over the past 135 years. For the last 60, we also have a series

26. Simon Kuznets, Modern Economic Growth: Rate Structure and Spread (New Haven: Yale Univ. Press, 1966). His argument in its simplest form is as follows. Suppose that
there are no differences in income within either of the two sectors, but that the nonagricultural incomes are higher. Then the variance of logs (VL) of individual incomes (a standard
inequality measure) in the community at a moment in time is

$$VL = a(1 - a)(A - N)^2,$$

where a = fraction of population in agriculture and A, N = log of agricultural and
nonagricultural incomes, respectively. If A and N do not change, the change in VL over
time is

$$d(VL)/dt = (A - N)^2(1 - 2a)\,da/dt.$$

Thus if a starts out high ($>1/2$) and declines steadily ($da/dt < 0$), inequality at first rises, then
falls (when $a < 1/2$). Kuznets's conjecture assumes that this effect dominates any offsetting
changes in $(A - N)$ and within-sector income dispersion.

of the share of national income going to the richest 5 per cent of the population. This is labeled "Kuznets," since the pre-1950 data are his.[27] Since 1915, the Kuznets series and the building industry skill differential (journeymen's wages divided by laborers' in union contracts)[28] have followed the same path (their correlation exceeds .8), even though they measure very different aspects of inequality. These data imply that the forces promoting equality have been pervasive.

The skimpy nineteenth-century American data are from Long's study of wages in manufacturing and Smith's study of Erie Canal wages.[29] The pattern emerging from all these data is one of increasing wage disparity over most of the nineteenth and early twentieth centuries and a long decline from World War I to the present. The two world wars, in particular, have coincided with profound movements toward equality, though some of the change of World War I was offset in the 1920s. These historical patterns are roughly the obverse of the secular path of government. They hint that, on balance and perhaps counter to intuition, income equality stimulates the growth of government. I pursue this hint shortly.

Another kind of inequality deserves mention here, namely, inequality across legislative constituencies. The theoretical discussion abstracts from the legislative mechanism through which conflicting individual interests are actually adjudicated. This is analytically convenient, but risks obscuring some aspects of political choice in a representative system. For one thing, legislators can specialize in collecting and communicating political information and thus a "full-information" model might adequately describe bargaining among legislators. More to the immediate point, bargaining would be more closely focused on the constituencies' average interests than on the interests of income groups who have members everywhere. The legislator will, of course, still have to worry about the disparity of interests within his constituency, but we ought to expect him, all else

27. Simon Kuznets, Share of Upper Income Groups in Income and Savings (New York: Nat'l Bureau Econ. Research, 1953). Post-1950 data are for families—the two series are virtually identical where they overlap—from Historical Statistics of the U.S. and Statistical Abstract.

28. From U.S. Bureau of the Census, Historical Statistics of the U.S. (1975) [hereinafter cited as Historical Statistics]; id., Statistical Abstract of the U.S. (1978); and Harold F. Lydall, The Structure of Earnings (Oxford: Clarendon Press, 1968).

29. Clarence Long, Wages and Earnings in the United States, 1860–1900 (New York: Nat'l Bureau of Econ. Research, 1960); and Walter Smith, Wage Rates on the Erie Canal, 1828–1881, 23 J. Econ. Hist. 298 (1963).

Interpolating over the 1885–1905 gap is likely to be as reasonable a procedure as any. For 1890–1900, we know that the ratio of building trades' wages (where skilled labor is important) to manufacturing wages rose.

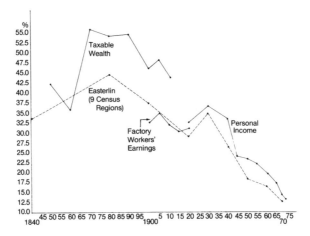

FIGURE 7.5 Coefficients of variation per capita income or wealth. States (United States) 1840–1975.

the same, to ally more easily with a legislator from a district with, for example, a similar average income. Thus, if greater personal income equality facilitates agreement on expanding the size of government, greater interdistrict equality ought to facilitate legislative agreement to implement the expansion.

Given the nature of the American political system at the national level, inequality of average incomes across states can serve as a proxy for the diversity of legislator interests. Figure 7.5 shows the relevant history for the available data,[30] which corresponds roughly to the pattern for skill differentials. But the narrowing of disparities began earlier (around 1890 versus 1915), was hardly affected by World War I, and was more profoundly affected by World War II. Also, unlike the relatively small changes in income equality after World War II, a substantial narrowing of interregional disparities continues to this day.

In the empirical work, I investigate whether this narrowing of interregional disparities has contributed to or retarded the growth of govern-

30. Sources of data are as follows: "Taxable Wealth" from U.S. Bureau of the Census, Wealth, Debt, and Taxation (1915). "Easterlin" from estimates by R. Easterlin of per capita personal income by census region relative to U.S. average as reported and updated in Historical Statistics, *supra* note 28. My calculation assigns each state its region's income relative. "Factory Workers' Earnings" from Paul F. Brissenden, Earnings of Factory Workers (U.S. Bureau of the Census, 1929). "Personal Income" from Survey of Current Business (various issues); 1920 figure is from Maurice Leven, Income in the Various States (New York: Nat'l Bureau Econ. Research, 1925).

TABLE 7.5 Regressions of U.S. Government/GNP on Inequality
Measures, 1870–1975 (5-Year Intervals, 22 Observations)

Regression	Coefficients (t-ratios) of						
	Skill Differential (1)	State Inequality (2)	Trend (3)	Lagged Government/ GNP (4)	R^2	SE	D-W or H
(1)	−21.99	.08	.147		.943	2.28	1.09
	−5.33	.42	3.47				
(2)	−20.90		.132		.942	2.23	1.01
	−6.67		5.82				
(3)	−6.50	.10	1.07	.650	.979	1.48	−2.19
	−1.51	.81	3.24	4.03			
(4)	−5.20		.088	.648	.978	1.46	−1.33
	−1.31		3.74	4.06			
Mean	1.63	30.9		14.85			
SD	.23	9.0		7.92			

Notes: The dependent variable is government spending/GNP × 100. See figure 7.2 and
text for sources. The time interval between observations is five years, and each value is a
three-year average centered on 1870, 1875, . . . To eliminate effects of wars, 1922 replaces
1920 and 1946 replaces 1945 in this sequence.

The skill differential is the series labeled "Long" in figure 7.4 for 1870–1880, the "Building Industry" series for 1905–1975, and a linear interpolation of the two for 1885–1900.

State inequality is the "personal income" coefficient of variation (see figure 7.5) for
1920–1975, the series labeled "factory workers' earnings" spliced to later data at 1920 for
1900–1915, and the series labeled "taxable wealth" spliced to later data at 1900–1910
for 1870–1895. Gaps in this series are eliminated by linear interpolation.

D-W and H are "Durbin-Watson" statistic and Durbin's H. The latter is calculated for
regressions (3) and (4) where D-W is inappropriate. For (1) and (2) the D-W test implies
positive serial correlation with about 5% risk of error. For (3) H implies negative autocorrelation with risk of <5%.

ment.[31] Any connection between the two ought, strictly speaking, to apply
only at the federal level, unless disparities among regions within states
have tended to follow the same path as interstate inequality.

Table 7.5 contains regressions of U.S. government expenditures relative
to GNP on the two crude inequality measures just discussed. A trend variable is included as a proxy for "other forces" which may have produced

31. It is difficult to argue that growth of government is itself responsible for the narrowing, at least directly. For 1970, the coefficient of variation of private income per capita
across states is about 18% versus 14.5% for all personal income. This difference is an exagger-
ated measure of the role of direct government payments, since it assumes that government
workers, for example, would earn zero in the private sector. Yet 18% is still half the 1930
figure. Of course, past government activity—World War II—seems to have had a permanent
effect on interregional inequality.

secular growth of government. Clearly any comprehensive investigation would have to spell out these "other forces," and several are suggested by the theoretical model (for example, mean education, "between-group" inequality). However the limitations of the time series preclude anything more refined than table 7.5. For example, a glance at figure 7.2 indicates that our 105 annual observations are hardly independent. There are really two or three distinguishable episodes, with a few much less important subcycles. Consequently, I draw observations at five-year intervals, which yield only around twenty degrees of freedom, and even this may overstate the number of independent observations. In addition, the trend variable is itself a proxy for some aspects of inequality. The agricultural share of the labor force, for example, crossed 50 per cent at about our starting point of 1870. Thus, on Kuznets's argument,[32] the subsequent further industrialization would have contributed to equality. Even the two inequality measures in table 7.5 are hardly time independent. The correlations with time are $-.75$ and $-.93$ for the skill and state measures, respectively. Table 7.5 thus addresses a limited question: is there any plausible connection between inequality and the size of government?

The answer seems to be a qualified "yes." There is no perceptible effect from the narrowing of cross-state inequality, but in equations (1) and (2) there is a substantial and significant expansionary effect from the narrowing skill differential. To put this effect in perspective, note that from 1870 to 1975, the government/GNP ratio increased by around 23 percentage points, while the skill differential narrowed by about .5. Equation (2) assigns over 40 per cent of this growth (.5 × the 20.9 coefficient = 10.45 percentage points) to the skill differential variable.

The link between inequality and government becomes more obscure, but does not disappear, when we allow for lagged adjustment and the possible effect of government on measured inequality. Equations (3) and (4) in the table are slightly modified versions of (22). The point estimates of the skill-differential effect remain substantial: if we assume no feedback effect ($c = 0$) in (22), then the implied derivative of the target government/GNP ratio with respect to the skill differential—which equals (coefficient of skill differential)/(1 − coefficient of lagged government/GNP)—is on the order of -15 to -20. Indeed, the derivative becomes still larger if we go to the other extreme. Suppose the growth of government is responsible for *all* of the .5 decline in the skill differential since 1870. Then, from (21) and (22), we can estimate c ($\approx -.02$), and the implied derivative (b) is

32. See note 26 *supra*.

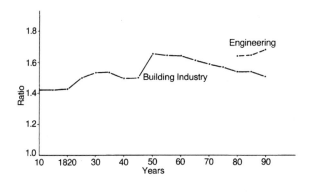

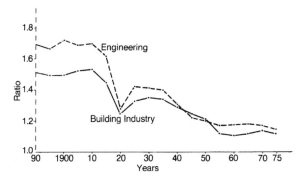

FIGURE 7.6 British skill differentials, 1810–1975.

about −30. However, given the relevant standard errors, we cannot attach much confidence to these calculations. They simply encourage examination of other data.

Figure 7.6 shows the history of British skill differentials since the Napoleonic Wars, mainly for the same industry that dominates our U.S. data.[33] The major difference between the two countries seems to be the earlier peak in the British data, around 1850. Skill differentials in the

33. The "building industry" series is composed of the following: 1810–1880: weekly or hourly rates for bricklayers relative to helpers at London (or Manchester, if rates for London are unavailable) British Labour Statistics: Historical Abstract (1971). 1880–1950: K. G. J. C. Knowles & D. J. Robertson, Differences between the Wages of Skilled and Unskilled Workers, Bull. of Oxford Inst. Stat. 109 (1951). 1950–1975: the London series, with 1970–75 from British Labour Statistics, supra (various years).

The engineering series is also from Knowles & Robertson supra for 1880–1950, then spliced to a series of union pay scales for skilled and unskilled labor in London area engineering industry establishments as reported in British Labour Statistics, annual issues and Historical Abstract.

United States do not clearly peak until World War I. Given the U.S. time-series results, this earlier reversal of the Industrial Revolution's trend toward inequality may help explain Britain's earlier completion of the nineteenth-century decline in the size of government. The twentieth-century pattern for skill differentials in the two countries is, however, broadly similar—a World War I downward jolt that was incompletely offset in the 1920s and a subsequent downward trend that only recently has flattened. As I point out later, this pattern is characteristic of much of the developed world in the twentieth century.

The British data, summarized in table 7.6, show a stronger connection between equality and government than the American data. The effect is numerically larger, completely dominates "trend" effects, and remains significant in the lagged-adjustment formulation. It also holds up in first differences (regression (2), which is motivated by the autocorrelation of the residuals from (1)). Finally, as with the American data, the lagged-adjustment regression implies that, unless growth of government has retarded the decline in skill differentials, the coefficients of this variable in (1) and (2) may actually understate the extent of the relevant relationship.

Putting the data in tables 7.5 and 7.6 together would imply that Britain has a larger government sector than the United States because the movement toward equality has gone farther there and because the British political system seems more sensitive to the resulting pressures (that is, the coefficient of the same skill differential is larger). This may be too sweeping a generalization from very crude data. To see if it is, I ask the following question. Do the historical *differences* in the size of the U.S. and British governments have anything to do with the minor *differences* in their histories of inequality? The answer is hardly obvious from the preceding data. The broad movements in both government and inequality in the two countries are more notable for their similarities than differences, making it more plausible that some common "third" force is pushing on both variables in both countries at any moment. By focusing on relative effects and thereby eliminating this third force, we might easily be left with data reflecting national idiosyncrasies.[34]

34. To put this more formally, suppose the true relationship is

$$g_i = \beta Y + \varepsilon_i,$$

where g_i = country i's government/GNP ratio; Y = the cosmic force determining both g_i and g_j which we do not observe; and ε_i = random error. We do, however, observe X_i, a country-specific variable (skill differentials) which may be related to Y. For example, suppose

$$X_i = Y + u_i.$$

This does not, however, appear to be the case. In table 7.7 the differences between or ratios of the British and U.S. government/GNP are regressed on differences or ratios of their skill differentials. In either form, the results indicate that any other forces propelling the growth of government seem to be enhanced by more equality. Thus a good part of the differences between the development of British and U.S. government seems explainable by different movements in equality. The main qualification comes from regressions (2) and (5) in the table, which allow for lagged adjustment of relative sizes. Collinearity between the two independent variables makes it hard to separate relative inequality and lagged-adjustment effects, but the direction of the inequality effect is consistent with the other results.[35]

To summarize, the British and American data did not allow the separation of the between-group and within-group components of income inequality as our model requires. Instead, we were forced to use skill differentials, which come closer conceptually to the within-group measure but which are also highly correlated, at least in the U.S. data, with a plausible between-group measure (the share of income going to the top 5 per cent). The empirical results all point in one direction: the within-group effects in the model dominate. More equality appears to stimulate expansion of the government sector.

2. Canada

Canada is of interest mainly because of its similarity to Britain and the United States. Her economic development has been intertwined with that

---

u_i = country-specific random measurement error. When we estimate the regression

$$g_i = bX_i + v_i,$$

b will be biased toward zero but will have the same sign as β, because of the correlation between X_i and Y. However, if we estimate

$$g_i - g_j = b'[X_i - X_j] + v_i - v_j,$$

which is akin to what is done in table 7.7, we remove the presumed "cosmic force" (Y) and are left with

$$g_i - g_j = b'[u_i - u_j] + v_i - v_j.$$

Our independent variable would be purely random and $E(b') = 0$ (so long as the country-specific components of X_i really do not matter).

35. The significant trend term in regressions (1) and (2) is better taken as recommending the ratio model than evidence of any unexplained divergence in government growth. The trend term reflects mainly the post-World War II experience, where both government sectors have grown so large that the absolute gap between the two today (about 12 percentage points) is larger than either government sector 100 years ago.

TABLE 7.6 Regressions of British Government/GNP on Skill
Differential, 1820–1975 (5-Year Intervals, 32 Observations)

| Regression | Coefficients/t-ratios of | | | R^2 | SE | D-W or H |
	Skill Differential (1)	Trend (2)	Lagged Government/ GNP (3)			
(1)	−48.63	.001		.898	3.61	.98*
	−9.05	.52				
(2) First	−22.97	.118		.240	3.02	1.83
differences	−3.03	1.08				
(3)	−20.92	.002	.596	.948	2.68	0.76
	−3.03	1.01	5.07			
Mean	1.469		18.27			
SD	.207		10.96			

Sources and Notes: Dependent variable is government spending/GNP × 100 at five-year intervals from 1820–1975. The following replacements are made to eliminate effects of wars: 1898 (instead of 1900), 1913 (1915), 1922 (1920), 1938 (1940), 1947–1948 average (1945); also 1974 (1975) due to data availability.

The numerator is from Organization for Economic Cooperation & Development, National Accounts of OECD Countries for 1955–74. Data for 1820–1950 are from Alan Peacock & Jack Wiseman, The Growth of Public Expenditures in the United Kingdom (1961). They give data at irregular intervals which usually correspond to a year divisible by 5. However, I used their 1822, 1831, and 1841 figures for 1820, 1830, and 1840 respectively. Missing years in the Peacock & Wiseman series were interpolated from percentage changes in British central government expenses (Brian Mitchell & Phyllis Deane, Abstract of British Historical Statistics [1962]).

The denominator is GDP at market prices. Data for 1900–1950 are from The British Economy: Key Statistics, 1900–64 (1965), Organization for Economic Cooperation & Development, National Accounts of OECD Countries; for 1820–1900 from estimates of net national product in Mitchell & Deane, supra, spliced to GDP at 1900.

The skill differential is an average of the two series in figure 7.6 for 1880–1975. The building industry series is spliced at 1880. See text for sources.

* = Significant autocorrelation of residuals.

The coefficient of "Trend" in regression (2) is the annualized constant term in this regression.

of the United States, and her political institutions have been borrowed from Britain. Accordingly, analysis of Canadian government spending should provide a strong check on the findings for Britain and the United States.

The results in table 7.8 generally corroborate and in one respect extend those for Britain and the United States. For Canada, unlike the United States, cross-regional income disparities seem important, and they push in the same direction as personal income equality (column (2), regressions (1)–(3)): both are negatively related to the size of government. This result

TABLE 7.7 Regressions of Relative Size of British and U.S. Government Sectors on Skill Differentials, 1870–1975

| | Coefficients/t-ratios of | | | | | |
| | Relative Skill Differential (1) | Trend (2) | Lagged Relative Size (3) | R^2 (4) | SE (5) | D-W (6) |
Regression						
	Differences					
1	−10.76	.103		.645	3.01	1.69
	−2.19	5.05				
2	−7.59	.076	.226	.608	3.09	*
	−1.28	2.21	.94			
	Ratios					
3	−3.03	.001		.531	.235	1.23
	−4.04	.86				
4	−3.24			.513	.233	1.21
	−4.59					
5	−1.27		.464	.573	.210	*
	−1.24		2.15			
Mean/SD:						
Differences	−.23		5.21			
	.13		4.80			
Ratios	.86		1.33			
	.07		.33			

*= H statistic cannot be calculated because of large standard error of coefficient in column (3).

tends to confirm the importance of the "within-group" inequality effect that has so far dominated the results. Were the "between-group" effect important, large regional inequalities would stimulate rather than retard redistribution in a political system with regional representation. Of course, the inconsistency between the U.S. and Canadian results for this variable ought to give us pause. One possible explanation, elaborated below, is that changes in Canadian regional inequality over the last century have not been nearly as trend-dominated as in the United States, so collinearity problems are less likely to obscure any true effect of regional inequality.

The negative effect of inequality on the size of government persists in the last three regressions, which focus on the relative size of the Canadian and U.S. government sectors. The effect is predictably weaker in these data and seems confined to the personal income-inequality proxy, which again suggests caution in pushing too far the preceding results for regional in-

TABLE 7.8 Canadian Government/GNP Regressions, 1880–1975

Dependent Variable: Government Spending/GNP	Coefficients/t-ratios						
	Skill Differential (1)	Regional Inequality (2)	Trend (3)	G_{-1} (4)	R^2 (5)	SE	D-W
1. Canada:	−12.59	−54.52	.30		.96	2.0	1.08
level	5.02	3.90	16.76				
2. Canada	−9.06	−39.89	.22	.30	.97	2.0	–
level	2.45	2.25	3.39	1.30			
3. Canada: first	−8.71	−51.24	.31[1]		.41	2.1	2.00
differences	2.01	2.84	3.29				
4. Canada/	−1.01	−.31	.41		.30	.173	1.26
U.S.	1.24	1.02	.70				
5. Canada/	−.47	−.14			.28	.171	1.24
U.S.	2.11	.79					
6. Canada/	−.63	−.76[2]			.27	.172	1.20
U.S.	2.30	.65					

Sources of Canadian Data:
1.*Government spending*
1955–1975. Organization for Economic Cooperation & Development, National Accounts of OECD Countries.
1926–1955. Richard M. Bird, The Growth of the Government Spending in Canada (Canadian Tax Papers No. 51, July 1970).
1870–1926. The annual data are estimates from benchmark data in Bird, *supra.* He gives total government spending for 1870 and decennially from 1890, federal spending annually for 1867–1926, and an "Alternative Series" which includes a part of nonfederal expenditures annually for 1900–26. I use year-to-year percentage changes in these two annual series to estimate annual changes in total expenditures between benchmark years.
2. *GNP*
1926–1975. Same as government expenditures.
1870–1926. Annual estimates from decennial benchmarks for nominal and real GNP, 1870–1910, in Bird, *supra.* I assumed that real GNP grew at a constant rate between benchmarks, and I interpolated annual fluctuations in the GNP deflator from the annual wholesale price index in M. C. Urquhart & K. A. H. Buckley, Historical Statistics of Canada (1965) [hereinafter cited as Historical Statistics]. Nominal GNP in nonbenchmark years is the resulting estimate of real GNP × the estimated GNP deflator. For 1910–1920, the interpolation uses an annual national income series and for 1920–1926 a net domestic product series in Historical Statistics, *supra.*
3. *Skill differentials.* 1920–1975. An average of skilled/unskilled hourly wages in the building and printing industries for five cities (Halifax, Montreal, Toronto, Winnipeg, and Vancouver). The skilled wage for the building industry is an average of wages for carpenters, electricians, and plumbers, and the unskilled wages is for "labourers." The skilled printing occupations are compositors and pressmen and the unskilled "bindery girls." The printing skill differential is set equal to the building industry differential at 1920 and the two are averaged thereafter. Building industry data for 1920–1960 are from Historical Statistics; for 1960–1975, from Canada Year Book (Ministry of Trade & Commerce, various years). Printing industry data are from Wage Rates, Salaries, and Hours of Labour (Dep't of Labour, now Labour Canada, various years).

1901–1920. Building industry differential from data in Historical Statistics (see above).

1880–1900. These are estimates, spliced to and extended backward from the 1901 value, taken from Historical Statistics. For 1890–1900, an Ottawa and Toronto sample of wages for carpenters, masons, painters, and unskilled laborers is used. For 1885–1890, I use immigration agents' reports of carpenters' and laborers' wages at Halifax, Montreal, Toronto, and Winnipeg. For 1880–1885, I use similar 1882–1885 data for Montreal, Ottawa, Hamilton, and Winnipeg.

4. *Regional differentials.* This is a standard deviation of the log of wage rates across cities. The cities, except where noted, are Halifax, Montreal, Toronto, Winnipeg, and Vancouver, each of which represents an important Canadian region. The sources are the same as for the skill differentials. For 1900–1920, the variable is an average of that for the four building occupations. For 1920–1975, an average of the three printing occupations is spliced to the building industry average at 1920. For 1885–1890, we have a subsample of the post-1900 building industry data (see above—Vancouver and plumber and electrician data are missing). I spliced data from this subsample to a similar one drawn from 1901 data and estimate the 1895 value by linear interpolation. The 1880 values are set equal to 1885.

Notes:

All variables are, where the data permit, three-year centered averages at five-year intervals from 1880–1975. To remove effects of the World Wars on government/GNP, the following replacements are made. 1923 for 1920, a linear interpolation of 1910 and 1923 for 1915, 1939 for 1940, and 1947 for 1945. In lines 1–3, Canadian data only are used. In lines 4–6, Canadian data are divided by the U.S. counterpart. Sample size = 20 (19 for line 3).

[1]Annualized constant term.

[2]Canadian variable *not* divided by United States.

equality. But it is more interesting that a negative inequality effect remains in these data, which abstract from the shared history of the two countries.[36]

We gain further insight into these results from figure 7.7, which displays the data underlying (4)–(6) in table 7.8. Canada has typically had the larger government sector, but the difference tended to be greater up to, say, 1930. Relative skill differentials have moved in the opposite direction; they are higher for Canada in the most recent fifty or so years. These opposing movements are reflected in the negative coefficients of the relative skill differentials in (4)–(6) of table 7.8.

Figure 7.7 also raises the possibility of lags in the adjustment of government to equality that the regressions have not captured. The relevant labor market history summarized in figure 7.7 is that the United States has a ten-to-fifteen year headstart on Canada in the movement toward equality. Up to World War I, skill differentials tend to widen in both countries. They then begin to decline in the United States, but only do so in Canada with the onset of the Great Depression. Notice, however, that, whereas the effects of the U.S. headstart toward equality on relative skill

36. Note that the standard errors for regression (4)–(6) in table 7.8 are on the order of a fourth smaller than those of the British-U.S. counterparts in table 7.7.

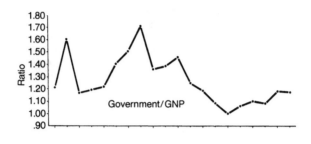

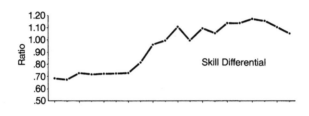

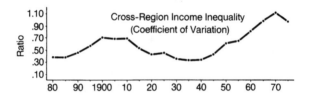

FIGURE 7.7 Canada-United States ratios.

differentials ends around 1930, a major part of the narrowing in the relative sizes of the two government sectors occurs thereafter. Indeed, if the
relative skill differentials in equations (4)–(6) of table 7.8 are lagged by
twenty years, explained variation roughly doubles. The relevant lag may
be even longer. Glancing back at the U.S. data in figure 7.4, another kind
of lag is apparent, that of the skill differential behind the broader ("Kuznets") measure of inequality.[37] Since all of this implies that movements in

37. The relevant regression is

$$\text{Skill differential}_t = \text{constant} + 3.3 \text{ Kuznets}_t$$
$$(t = 4.7)$$

$$+ 2.4 \text{ Kuznets}_{t-1}; \quad R^2 = .97.$$
$$(t = 3.4)$$

the size of government tend to lag behind those of inequality, a model in which the latter "causes" the former gains some credibility. While we cannot pursue the lag structure further with the crude data and small samples, subsequent data reveal lags to be an important part of the story. In fact, the twenty-or-so year lag that is clear in figure 7.7 is close to the order of the lag magnitudes that these data will reveal.

The bottom panel of figure 7.7 reflects a substantial recent divergence between Canadian and U.S. movements in cross-regional equality. From 1900 to World War II, regional disparities narrowed in both countries. Whereas this decline accelerated in the United States, it has actually been reversed in Canada in the postwar period, a fact which may help explain the recent centripetal pressures in that country.[38] However, it is evident from figure 7.7 (and regressions (4)–(6)) that this reversal has not slowed the growth of Canada's government sector. The negative coefficient of regional inequality in regressions (1)–(3) appears to reflect mainly the earlier history. Unlike the United States, Canadian regional disparities widened up to 1900, while its government sector declined or grew slowly. Regional income disparities then narrowed sharply up to about 1930, and this roughly coincides with a period of relatively rapid growth of government.

3. A Note on the Role of Voting Behavior in the Three Anglo-Saxon Countries

I have so far ignored the role of political institutions in the growth of government in the three basically Anglo-Saxon countries. Since the theoretical model suggests that they have a role, it is worth asking if the role is sufficiently important to qualify any of the preceding results. In the theory, political institutions would enter under the rubric of "ability." Anything which makes it easier for beneficiaries to return political support ought to stimulate growth of government. Since all three countries have had democratic structures for the periods studied, we must ask whether differences in the administration of these structures have had perceptible effects. One such difference has been the extent of the franchise. Here, there is a sharp division around 1920 when suffrage was extended to women, and the franchise became virtually universal in all three countries. Although the suffrage of women coincided with the beginning of a continuing expansion in the size of government in all three countries, such a crude correlation should be greeted skeptically. Since women represent a roughly random

---

38. In fact, it is Quebec and the maritime province wages which have lagged the rest of the country, at least up to 1970.

sample from the income distribution, it is unclear that women's suffrage heralded a shift in the demand for redistribution. More to the point, it is doubtful that, with the possible exception of female-headed households, women lacked influence on voting patterns prior to 1920. So we ought to look to the pre-1920 period for unambiguous political effects.

The considerable variety among the three countries prior to 1920 does not seem to explain the role of government.[39] Here we must distinguish voter eligibility from participation. In all three countries, participation rates in national elections have been essentially trendless since at least 1900. They have ranged around 70 to 80 per cent for Canada and the United Kingdom and about 15 points less for the United States.[40] So no change in participation seems connected to the dramatic change in the growth of government experienced by all three countries after World War I. The main differences among the countries occur in pre-1920 eligibility rates (eligible voters/male population over twenty-one). The United States had attained near-universal (90 per cent) male suffrage by 1870. For the United Kingdom, on the other hand, this figure is only one-third. It required an electoral reform in 1884, which doubled eligibility, and another in 1918 for the United Kingdom to close the gap. Canada is the intermediate case. In the immediate aftermath of the British North America Act, it appears that roughly half of Canadian adult males had the franchise. Over the next thirty or so years, most provinces gradually removed property qualifications so that eligibility exceeded three-fourths by 1900. A 1920 federal law made suffrage universal. If the extent of suffrage promotes growth of government, Britain clearly should have had the most rapid growth of government in the nineteenth century, since significant franchise extensions took place in 1832 and 1867 in addition to 1884. But, as we have seen, British government growth was actually negative in the wake of the earlier reforms, and after 1870, all three countries are more notable for their similarities—generally stable government/GNP ratios—than any differences.

These data are too crude to rule out a connection between suffrage and the size of government. They do, however, suggest, that the major changes in the size of government have little to do with extension of the franchise;

39. The data here are from Historical Statistics, *supra* note 28; Howard A. Scarrow, Canada Votes (New Orleans: Hauser, 1962), for Canada; and Stein Rokkan & Jean Meyriat, International Guide to Electoral Statistics (New York: Humanities Press, 1969), for the United Kingdom.

40. There was a perceptible, but temporary, decline in all three countries in the decade or so after women's suffrage.

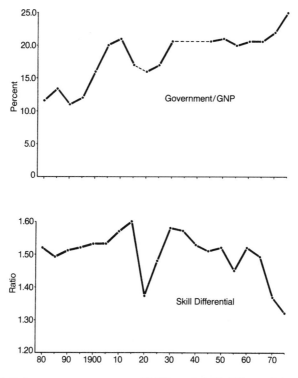

FIGURE 7.8 Japanese government/GNP and skill differential.

otherwise the United States would have had by far the largest government sector in 1870.

4. Japan

Japan provides perhaps a better test of the role of politics than any of the three countries we have looked at so far. The basically democratic institutions that prevailed in these three countries are absent for most of Japan's history. Japanese economic development was also somewhat isolated from the common forces affecting the three Atlantic countries. Japan's particularism is mirrored amply in the growth of its government, which is shown in the upper panel of figure 7.8. Unlike any of the Atlantic triad, the major growth in Japan occurs before World War I. It shares virtually none of their subsequent growth and today has the smallest government sector in the developed world.

To what extent can Japan's singular history be reconciled with the pre-

TABLE 7.9 Japanese Government/GNP Regressions, 1880–1975

	Skill Differential (1)	Regional Inequality (2)	Trend (3)	D (4)	$D \times SK$ (5)	R^2	SE	D-W.
			Coefficients/t-ratios					
1.	11.45	−10.24	.11			.77	1.98	1.22
	1.58	.67	4.75					
2.	11.50		.12			.76	1.95	1.16
	1.68		6.94					
3.	17.87		.14	41.35	−29.66	.82	1.76	1.58
	2.05		6.42	1.89	1.98			

Sources: 1. Data for government spending and GNP 1953–1975, are from Organization for Economic Cooperation & Development, National Accounts of OECD Countries. For 1880–1953, government expenditures are those in the "general account" budgets of national and local governments from Koichi Emi & Yuichi Shinoya, Government Expenditures, vol. 7 Estimates of Long Term Economic Statistics of Japan since 1868 (Kazushi Ohkawa, Miyohei Shinohara, Mataji Umemura eds. 1966). The general account excludes war expenditures which were financed through a "special account" and it excludes operating budgets of, but not subsidies to, nationalized industries. GDP is from Kazushi Ohkawa, Nobukiyo Takamatsu, & Yuzo Yamamoto, National Income, vol. 1 Estimates of Long Term Economic Statistics of Japan since 1868 (Kazushi Ohkawa, Miyohei Shinohara, Mataji Umemura eds. 1965).

2. Skill differential is the ratio of daily wages for skilled workers to day laborers in construction. Data for 1880–1939 are from Ohkawa, et al., *supra;* for 1945–1960 from Koji Taira, Economic Development and the Labor Market in Japan (1970); 1960–1975: Japan Statistical Yearbook (Bureau of Statistics, Office of the Prime Minister, various years).

3. Regional inequality is the coefficient of variation of average wages across 13 cities spliced to series for 46 prefectures at 1940. Data are from Taira, *supra.*

4. $D = +1$ for 1955–1975, 0 otherwise.

5. $D \times SK = D \times$ skill differential.

Note: The dependent variable is government expenditures/GNP, constructed in the same way as for Britain, Canada, and the United States. Since Japan was more frequently involved in wars, there is more extensive adjustment for Japan. Specifically, the following substitutions are made: 1895 (average of 1893 and 1896), 1905 (average of 1902 and 1908), 1915 (1913), 1920 (average of 1921 and 1922), 1935 and 1940 are linear interpolations of 1930 and 1945 (which is set at the 1947–1948 average).

vious findings? The first two regressions in table 7.9 suggest reconciliation may be difficult. The inequality proxy is positively, rather than negatively, related to the size of government, though the coefficient is of marginal significance. (And we cannot replicate the significant effect of regional inequality found in the Canadian data.) A slightly different perspective is gained by looking at the two series in figure 7.8. Except for the "blip" around World War I, the Japanese skill differential shows remarkable stability at least up to 1960. It is within 10 points of its mean of about 150 for the entire period, when the Western differentials tended to lie between 100 and 200. This lack of any pronounced move toward greater equality, a move which is almost universal in the Western world, seems confirmed by other data.[41] A negative corroboration of the previous results may be that Japanese government did *not* grow in the twentieth century because it lacked the crucial stimulant, a decline in inequality. Of course, this leaves us with the need to explain the rapid growth before World War I. It seems reasonable to raise here the issue of costs of tax collection even if we must postpone explicit analysis of it. The important changes in transportation and communication costs, the size of businesses, the extent of impersonal markets, and so forth, which occurred in the West in the nineteenth century and which presumably reduced tax-collection costs, ought to have stimulated growth in government's share of national income there. That this did not occur in the West may imply that, once a fairly rudimentary legal and institutional infrastructure is in place, most important tax-collection economies are achieved. But Japan may not have been so endowed immediately following the Meiji restoration. Its per capita income in the late nineteenth century appears to have been on the order of one-fifth or one-tenth that of the United States, and modern local government institutions did not replace the feudal structures of the Tokugawa era until 1878.[42] Thus it seems risky to dismiss tax-collection costs as a factor in the growth of Japan's government in the early Meiji years as easily as we can for the Western countries.

The post-World War II period in Japan is especially interesting for two reasons. The obvious one is the radical change in its political institutions from dictatorship to democracy, a change that permits a sharper test of the role of political institutions than for the three Western democracies. The second reason has to do with changes in income inequality. As in its economic development generally, Japan seems to have lagged behind the Western world by around thirty years. The bottom panel of figure 7.8

41. See, for example, Akira Ono & Tsunehiko Watanabe, Changes in Income Inequality in the Japanese Economy, in Japanese Industrialization and Its Social Consequences 363 (Hugh Patrick ed.) (Berkeley: Univ. of California Press, 1976). Also Yasukichi Yasuba, Evolution of the Dualistic Wage Structure, in *id.* at 49, calculated coefficients of variation in average wages across operatives in each manufacturing industry for selected years from 1909 to 1951. There is no tendency for the coefficients to decline over time for comparable industries. While such a measure will reflect, *inter alia*, age, sex, and skill mix changes, this stability does seem to conform to the general pattern of comparatively minor changes in inequality before 1960.

42. Koichi Emi, Government Fiscal Activity and Economic Growth in Japan, 1868–1960, (Tokyo: Kinokuniya Bookstore, 1963).

shows a sustained narrowing of skill differentials starting in 1960. I would be reluctant to draw firm conclusions from this brief period's data except that they seem to comport well with other data. Ono and Watanabe, after examining a variety of inequality measures, also date the start of a perceptible decline in inequality at about 1960.[43]

From figure 7.8 it seems clear that neither the political nor income inequality changes have so far produced any dramatic change in the size of Japan's government. But to determine if there are any symptoms of change, line 3 of table 7.9 repeats the basic regression with an intercept and slope dummy variable (columns (4) and (5), respectively) for the period from 1955 (the "democratic" era in Japan). The coefficient of the slope dummy ($D \times SK$) addresses the question: did the process linking inequality to the size of government change when Japan became a democracy? The answer seems to be "yes" and, more interesting, the change is toward the same process that characterized the three other democracies of more equality being associated with bigger government. This regression is, in effect, telling us that the "Robin Hood" motive to redistribution predominates in the nondemocratic era (note the now significantly positive coefficient of the skill differential in column (1), line 3), but that within-beneficiary-group considerations are more important in a democracy.

Moreover, this strengthened importance of within-group equality is predicted by the theory. Refer back to (14), which summarizes the within-group effect. Of the variables in that expression, the one most immediately affected by a shift from dictatorship to democracy would be the variable reflecting the ability of the numerous beneficiaries to give their interests political weight. This is F_g, the marginal political product of the benefit, which should be higher in a democracy. After substitution of some first-order conditions[44] and rearrangement of terms, (14) can be rewritten schematically

$$(14') \quad D = \frac{A + BF_g}{1 - I_Q F_g} > 0,$$

where A and B are positive expressions not involving F_g, and D is the derivative on the left-hand side of (14). Treating the advent of democracy as an event (X) which raises F_g by a unit, the effect on D is summarized

---

43. *Supra* note 41.
44. To eliminate F_R, which may also be affected by the shift to democracy.

(23) $\text{sgn} \dfrac{dD}{dX} = \text{sgn}(B + AI_Q) > 0.$

Note that (23) does *not* say that government will grow if F_g increases, but rather that government growth will be *more responsive* to *changes* in inequality within the beneficiary group, whether the changes push for more government or less. This is precisely what the Japanese findings show: no vast expansion of government, but a larger weighting of the within-group equality effect. Moreover, the model implies no correspondingly unambiguous shift in the importance of the between-group effect, which could have obscured the shift we observe in the Japanese data.[45]

If this analysis is valid (we will subsequently pursue this interaction between equality and political ability), there are profound implications for Japan's future. It appears that the Japanese government sector is on the verge of substantial growth, if its recent move toward greater income equality is as permanent and far-reaching as that experienced in the West some thirty years before. It now has the democratic political structure in which more equality seems to fuel expanding governments. Thus all the conditions now seem in place for Japan to repeat the vast expansion of government which has characterized the Western world since the depression, including perhaps the replacement of its famed intracorporate welfare system with a national social security system.

B. Post-World War II Experience in the Developed World

I now want to see whether the postwar experience among developed countries is consistent with the time-series evidence. While government has grown everywhere, there is enough variety to make the investigation interesting. Table 7.10 provides some relevant data. The general pattern has been that of rapid growth in Northern Europe, slow growth following high

---

45. The reason for the ambiguity here can be seen most easily by focusing on the marginal political product of numbers of beneficiaries (M_p). This is proportional to $1 - F_g J_p$. An exogenous increase in F_g reduces the marginal product of numbers. When P's become more responsive, the first-order response is to cultivate them more "intensively," with a higher g given to fewer P's so that the ambivalence of the highest-income P's about redistribution can be economized. (This is analogous to Ricardo's extensive margin shrinking when the marginal product of labor rose.) This is why a rise in F_g, by itself, will not increase the optimal G. However, if the rise in F_g is compensated by a decline in J_p, the ambivalence of the marginal P's is reduced, and the force shrinking the "extensive" margin is attenuated. Now, when there is an increase in between-group inequality, J_p is unaffected, so there is no necessary reason for a rise in F_g to induce a larger rise in G than would otherwise occur; the same rise in G could be optimal if concentrated on fewer P's. But a reduction in within-group inequality *does* lower J_p. When F_g rises in *these* circumstances, it calls for both more intensive *and* extensive cultivation of the P's and thus an unambiguously larger rise in G than would otherwise occur.

TABLE 7.10 The Size and Growth of Government/GDP 16 Developed
Countries Selected Years, 1953–1974

	Government Spending/GDP			Percentage Increase		
Country	1953–54 (1)	1963–64 (2)	1973–74 (3)	(2)/(1)	(3)/(2)	(3)/(1)
Australia	24.2%	25.4%	30.1%	4.8%	18.5%	24.2%
Austria	31.9	34.8	38.3	9.3	10.0	20.3
Belgium	28.1	31.2	39.5	10.9	26.6	40.4
Canada	26.2	28.0	36.4	6.7	30.1	38.7
Denmark	24.4	30.3	46.6	24.4	53.8	91.4
Finland	31.1	31.3	38.4	0.6	22.7	23.5
France	35.6	37.8	38.5	6.2	1.9	8.1
Germany	35.5	36.6	41.9	3.0	14.5	17.9
Italy	27.6	31.5	39.6	14.1	25.6	43.3
Japan	21.0	20.9	24.0	−0.2	14.6	14.3
Netherlands	31.8	36.9	50.7	16.0	37.3	59.3
Norway	30.5	36.5	48.7	19.5	33.5	59.5
Sweden	28.0	36.3	49.0	29.5	35.2	75.0
Switzerland	27.8	28.9	35.2	4.1	21.8	26.8
United Kingdom	32.7	33.7	42.0	2.9	24.8	28.4
United States	27.0	28.0	32.2	3.9	14.8	19.3
Average	28.9	31.7	39.4	9.7	24.1	36.9

Sources: See notes to table 7.2 for sources.

initial levels for France and Germany, and slow growth from low or average levels for the non-European countries. There are, of course, some notable exceptions such as Canada recently, Finland for the whole period,
and Britain in the 1950s when it was liquidating its empire. The simple
question I try to answer is: can income inequality differences help rationalize this variety?

Comparing inequality across countries poses important problems. The
data come from a variety of sources in which income concepts, coverage,
and so forth can differ greatly among countries and are susceptible to bias.
For example, many income distributions have been compiled from tax returns, which are heavily influenced not only by coverage and income definition differences but by differences in enforcement of the tax laws. I am
aware of only two attempts to systematically surmount these comparability problems so that a credible ranking of countries by inequality emerges.
The first by Lydall, focuses on pretax wage and salary income.[46] Since it
excludes both transfers and property income, this income concept seems
like a good proxy for the potential beneficiary-incomes of the theoretical

46. Lydall, *supra* note 28.

model. Lydall had to rely mainly on tax-based distributions, which he then tried to adjust to a common basis (adult male full-time workers). He is sometimes cryptic about how these adjustments are made, particularly where resolving conflicts among different data for the same country. His ranking, however, can be useful here, since it is independent of this problem.

The more recent study by Sawyer for the Organization for Economic Cooperation and Development (OECD) has the advantage of drawing its data from household budget surveys, rather than tax records, supplemented by unpublished data designed to mitigate comparability problems.[47] The major drawback, for our purposes, is the inclusion of transfers in the basic income concept (household pretax money income). Sawyer is able to estimate income distributions, standardized for household size,[48] for ten countries in Lydall's sample. For six countries, the two studies are in broad agreement about inequality rankings. For four there are clear discrepancies since the countries wind up in different halves of the two rankings. Columns (1) and (2) of table 7.11 summarize the findings of the two studies.

The four discrepancies are divided equally in direction. They occur with Australia and Germany (lower OECD ranks), on the one hand, and Japan and the Netherlands, on the other. The following two obvious possible sources of these discrepancies cannot explain them.

1. Time Period

Lydall's ranking is for the late 1950s, and Sawyer's is for the late 1960s. However, Sawyer provides data for three of the countries in question (Germany, Japan, the Netherlands) which go back to the Lydall period. In no case is there any change in inequality remotely close to explaining the discrepancy. More generally, Sawyer's retrospective data imply that any 1960 ranking would essentially duplicate that for 1970.

2. Income Definition

The inclusion of transfers in Sawyer's data raises forcefully the issue of the endogeneity of equality. While transfers may affect cardinal measures of

47. Malcolm Sawyer, Income Distribution in OECD Countries, in 19 OECD Economic Outlook, Supp. at 3 (Occasional Studies, July 1976).

48. The standardization is important. Countries with generous pension and unemployment insurance schemes have many one-person households: more retired and young single people find it feasible to set up their own households. These households typically have below average incomes, so their proliferation tends to increase inequality measured over all households.

TABLE 7.11 Countries Ranked by Income Equality—Two Comparative
Studies and Related Data

Country	Rank Order (1 = Most Equal) Lydall (1)	Sawyer-OECD (2)	Coefficient of Variation—Factory Workers (3)
Australia	1	7	—
Austria	10	—	—
Belgium	8	—	13.5
Canada	7	6	15
Denmark	2	—	—
Finland	12	—	—
France	13	10	19
Germany	5.5	9	15
Japan	14	5	—
Netherlands	11	1	4
Norway	5.5	3	10
Sweden	4	2	11
United Kindom	3	4	8
United States	9	8	18.5

Notes: See text for income concepts used, years covered, and so on. A dash indicates
the country is not in the sample.

Norway is here assigned equal rank with Germany in the Lydall sample, partly on the
basis of the OECD data. Lydall is unable to reconcile two sources of data, one of which
would place it "near Germany" (1968, p. 161)—that is, relatively high in degree of equality—and another which would place it much lower. Given the OECD findings, the "tie"
with Germany may still leave Norway's ranking too low.

Column (3) is the coefficient of variation × 100 of average wage rates for production
workers across manufacturing industries *ca.* 1960 from Organization for Economic Cooperation and Development, Wages and Labour Mobility (1965). Industries are approximately
two-digit SIC level. Wages are hourly for males, except: United States and Germany (both
sexes), France (yearly), and Belgium (daily).

inequality, they do not appear to explain the discrepancies in rank. Sawyer
provides decile income shares. If the bottom two deciles—where transfers
are heavily concentrated—are deleted and the countries re-ranked, the
discrepancies remain. Notice that each discrepant couplet contains one
country with extensive transfers (Germany, the Netherlands) and one with
unusually low transfers (Australia, Japan). Similarly, each couplet has one
"big government" and one "small government" country. So government-
induced effects on inequality do not appear to resolve the specific discrepancies, though they still may affect the general pattern of the ranks.

The third column of table 7.11 shows coefficients of variation in average hourly wages across manufacturing industries from another OECD

study. While such a measure will be affected by, for example, differences in skill mix across industries and in national industry definitions, it shares with Lydall the advantage of focusing on income least directly affected by the tax-transfer system. Nevertheless, it would resolve two of the disputed cases (Germany and the Netherlands) in favor of Sawyer. For the remaining seven countries, column (3) basically corroborates both the Sawyer and Lydall rankings.

Since it is beyond the scope of this paper to resolve these differences, I will assume that a "true" ranking of late 1950s earnings inequality is given by: $L + kD$, where L = Lydall rank, k = constant, and $D = -1$ for Japan and the Netherlands and $+1$ for Australia and Germany. Presumably, $k > 0$. The essential question is whether any such ranking scheme can rationalize either the size or growth of government.

The size-growth distinction is especially important in this cross section in light of Lydall's discussion of the recent history of inequality. He finds that the broad outlines of the British, American, and Canadian twentieth-century experience hold almost everywhere in the developed world. Some time around World War I, wage and salary inequality began to decline and some time around 1950, the decline flattened or stopped. Kuznets's data give much the same impression about the upper-tail money incomes.[49] He simply reports what is available in the literature, so comparability across countries is risky. But a clear pattern emerges. Around World War I the top 5 per cent of income recipients in the typical developed country account for around 30 per cent of national income and the fragmentary nineteenth-century data show no clear trend from 1870 to World War I. However, by about 1950 this share falls to just under 20 per cent. Crude interpolation of Sawyer's data for the upper two declines implies that the *circa*-1970 figure is around 17 per cent. In broad outline, the growth of government follows a similar path, in that the aftermath of World War I coincides with a permanent enlargement and sustained growth of government. An important detail, however, is that for many countries a major part of the growth of government has occurred in the last twenty-five years, or after the main force of the trend toward equality had been spent. If equality is indeed a major determinant of the equilibrium size of government, a lagged-adjustment process has been dominating recent experience. Thus recent *growth* of government would be more closely related to the level of inequality than absolute size.

This conjecture is confirmed by the data in table 7.12, where the size

---

49. Kuznets, *supra* note 26.

TABLE 7.12 Regressions of Size and Growth of Government/GDP on Income Equality Measures, 14 Countries, 1958–1959 to 1973–1974

Dependent Variable	Coefficients/t-ratios				
	Lydall Rank (L)	OECD Dummy (D)	1958–1959 Government/ GDP	R^2	SE
Size 1958–1959					
1. Rank (1 = largest)	−.22 −.77			.048	4.24
2. Rank	−.47 −1.32	−3.03 −1.14		.145	4.19
3. Log (Government/GDP)	.27 .67	2.26 .74		.054	4.80
Growth, 1958–1959 to 1973–1974					
4. Rank (1 = most % growth)	.56 2.35			.315	3.60
5. Rank	.56 2.17		.028 .11	.316	3.76
6. Rank	1.20 6.80	7.26 5.55	.226 1.61	.832	1.95
7. Rank	1.10 6.24	6.58 4.97		.789	2.09
8 Log Δ (Government/ GDP) × 100	−1.77 −2.41		.306 .16	.346	11.04
9. Log Δ	−3.43 −6.55	−20.17 −5.06	.151 1.41	.816	6.14
10. Log Δ	−3.31 −6.14	−18.92 −4.66		.780	6.41
11. Δ Government/GDP × 100	−1.28 −4.64	−7.65 −3.67		.673	3.29
Subcategories of Government/GDP, Log Δ × 100					
12. Nondefense	−3.49 −3.36	−5.90 −.76		.561	12.34
13. Government consumption	−2.88 −3.88	−3.09 −.55		.646	8.80
14. Government transfers	−4.35 −4.16	−39.64 −5.02		.711	12.47

Notes: The 14 countries are listed in table 7.11. L = "Lydall" variable in Table 11. D = +1 for Australia and Germany, −1 for Japan and the Netherlands, 0 for all other countries.

Transfers in line 14 include interest on public debt.

The 1958–1959 Government/GDP independent variable is a rank for 5 and 6, and a log for 8 and 9.

of government at the time of Lydall's ranking and its subsequent growth are regressed on his ranking and the correction factor from Sawyer's study. Size of government and inequality were essentially uncorrelated in the late 1950s. But there is a very strong negative correlation between inequality then and subsequent growth. Some combination of the Lydall and Sawyer data can explain most of the recent growth no matter how the growth is measured, whether we include or exclude defense spending, or focus on transfers or on consumption.

A major puzzle in the table, however, is lack of evidence of convergence toward equilibrium. None of the coefficients of the government-size variable have the expected negative sign and two (in 6 and 9) suggest an explosive system. The puzzle did not disappear, though the explosive tendency did, when I replicated the relevant regressions for growth in the last ten years instead of the last fifteen. It seems scarcely credible that the governments of, for example, the Scandinavian countries and Holland will continue to grow substantially faster than the rest of the world, yet that is what table 7.12 implies.[50]

One way to rescue stability from these data is hinted at by the scheme in (19)–(22). Let X in (17) increase with equality, so $b > 0$. From (22) the whole coefficient of the size of government $[-a(1 - bc)]$ can be zero or even positive while $-a < 0$ if $c < 0$. This would mean that increased government spending *reduces* measured equality. Since our basic equality measure is of pretax earnings, less equality may not be so far-fetched. And the simultaneous slowing of the decline of inequality and growth of government is at least crudely consistent with this sort of process. However, crude extrapolation of prewar-inequality trends hardly provides sufficient evidence.

The broad outlines of the results from the international cross section strongly confirm the time-series evidence. At least for developed democracies, reduced inequality of income stimulates the growth of government. The results also imply, much more strongly than do the Canadian and U.S. time series, a considerable lag in response of the size of government to greater equality.

50. The essential results in table 7.12 are reproduced if the arguably atypical years, 1975–76, are substituted for 1973–74. Also, if the OECD dummy is replaced by a synthetic OECD ranking of the fourteen countries which uses the Lydall rank to interpolate the missing data; the counterpart to regression (10) gives about twice as much weight to this variable as to the Lydall ranking, though both are significant. If, as column (3) of table 7.11 suggests, the Sawyer data more accurately measure inequality, we would expect those data to get the larger weight if there is a negative correlation between growth of government and "true" inequality.

The international data seem to say something even stronger. Nothing much besides income inequality is needed to explain the growth of government. We are able to pretty much write the history of government growth in the next fifteen years from what we know about income inequality in 1960. In the next section, we show that the relationship is more complex. Moreover, the complexity is hinted at in the international data. Consider the cases of Finland, France, and Germany which appear not to have been nearly as affected by this century's egalitarian tendencies as, say, Holland or Sweden.[51] Yet, by the early 1950s, their government sectors were all larger than average. To be sure, they have now been surpassed by the more egalitarian countries, but their experience hints that Japan may not be alone in the recent emergence of the stimulative effect of equality on government.

C. State and Local Governments in the United States

An examination of state and local government budgets promises to extend as well as corroborate the previous results. We can employ a fairly extensive sample of comparable data on both government budgets and a diverse set of population characteristics to test parts of the theory that were inaccessible with the preceding data. For example, we can at least hope to exploit cross-sectionally comparable data on income distribution to distinguish "between-" from "within-" group inequality effects.

These virtues are, however, bought at a considerable potential cost. The exigencies of statistical analysis force us to treat the nonfederal jurisdictions as essentially independent observations. Yet they are neither independent of what goes on at the federal level nor of each other. To cite just one problem raised by interdependence, the ability of a local government to serve redistributionist motives is going to be constrained by interjurisdictional competition, both for the tax base and potential supporters. Whereas that possibility did not seem important in the cross-country comparison—small open economies, for example, Denmark, did not appear constrained to have small government sectors—the possibility seems substantially more important across states and localities. Our fears may be partly allayed by data on the actual redistributive impact of governmental tax-spending programs. Reynolds and Smolensky's results indicate that

51. For France, this is confirmed by fragmentary skill differential data in Organization for Economic Cooperation and Development, Wages and Labour Mobility (1965). Unlike Britain, the United States, and Canada, these show no narrowing at all since 1930.

both federal and nonfederal budgets entail substantial rich-to-poor redistribution, and that the nonfederal redistribution is actually the more extensive.[52]

Even if there is considerable redistribution at the local level, a cursory glance at the data suggests another problem. Clearly broad historical forces producing ubiquitous growth of government dominate any local variety. For the period 1942–1972, the average ratio of state and local spending to personal income across forty-eight states was .15 with a standard deviation of only .02. The average change (standard deviation) between these years is .12 (.02). Variation across states is thus much smaller than across countries (see tables 7.2 and 7.10). This small variation left to be "explained" by local factors poses a substantial constraint on the added insight these data may provide.

In table 7.13, I attempt to implement the three main implications of the theory, which are that the size of government responds (*a*) positively to income inequality between prospective beneficiaries and taxpayers, (*b*) negatively to inequality among beneficiaries, and (*c*) positively to the "ability" of beneficiaries to process information. The empirical counterparts to these three notions are:

1. Between-group equality: the share of a state's income accounted for by the richest 5 per cent of the population (SH5).

2. Within-group equality: the standard deviation of the log of income of the group in the twentieth to ninety-fifth percentile of the income distribution in each state (SD2095).

3. Ability: average years of schooling (ED).

The choice of the ninety-fifth percentile as a lower bound for the SH variable was forced by the data. When this bound is lowered, the correlation between the SH and any corresponding SD variable rises dramatically; for example, it is on the order of .8 to .9 if the lower bound of SH is the eightieth percentile and the upper bound of SD is anything up to eighty, compared to .4 when ninety-five is the lower bound. This intercorrelation makes it difficult to distinguish "between-" from "within-" group effects. The motive for excluding the poorest 20 per cent of the population was the model's suggestion of "Director's Law": the very poorest may not have sufficient ability to be included as beneficiaries. The results, however, were basically the same when the lower bound for SD was zero and the

---

52. Morgan Reynolds & Eugene Smolensky, Public Expenditures, Taxes, and the Distribution of Income: The U.S., 1950, 1961, 1970 (New York: Academic Press, 1977).

TABLE 7.13 Regressions of State and Local Government Expenditures/
State Personal Income (48 States, 1942–1972)

Form of Dependent Variable	1942, 1957, 1972 Average		1972	(1972)– ½(1942)	1972–1942	
Model	Complete Adjustment after 15 Years		Complete Adjustment, 30 Years	50% Adjustment, 30 Years	Indefinite Adjustment	
Independent Variables	(1)	(2)	(3)	(4)	(5)	(6)
POP	−.73	−.82	−.41	−.35	−.29	−.14
	2.65	3.21	.31	.29	.25	.12
ED	.35	.47	.35	.35	.34	.13
	.60	.80	.37	.41	.41	.16
SD2095	2.05	2.06	−6.50	−6.56	−6.61	−6.98
	.33	.33	.68	.76	.79	.84
SH5	−8.02		−7.45	1.36	10.18	
	.82		.53	.11	.82	
R^2	.26	.25	.12	.10	.10	.08
SE	1.71	1.71	2.67	2.39	2.32	2.31

Notes: The dependent variables are constructed from the ratio of general expenditures by state and local governments in a state to that state's disposable personal income ($\times 100$). Government expenditures are from the U.S. Bureau of the Census, Census of Governments (various years), while personal income is from U.S. Bureau of the Census, Survey of Current Business (various years). Columns (1) to (5) are variants of the partial adjustment model:

$$g_{72} - g_{42} = k(g^* - g_{42}),$$

where g_t is this ratio for year t, g^* is its target, and k is a fractional adjustment coefficient. This can be expressed

$$g_{72} - jg_{42} = kg^*, \quad j = (1 - k)$$

and the variables in (2) and (5) are constructed accordingly. In column (1), g_{57}, represented by an average centered on 1957 to reduce error, replaces g_{72} and k is set = 1.
Independent Variables
ED: Mean years of schooling attained by population over 27 in 1940 from U.S. Bureau of the Census, Census of Population. State Volumes. For college graduates, I assume 90% complete 16 years and 10% 17 years.
SD2095: Average of 1950 value and ca. 1920–1930 estimate of the standard deviation of log of income of male heads of households in the 20th to 95th percentile of the income distribution. 1950 data are from Census of Population. State Volumes, supra, which gives a distribution by dollar intervals. For each state, a continuous function was fit to these data by method of cubic splices up to the open-ended upper income interval; this latter was approximated by a Pareto distribution. From this, we were able to estimate income $= f(R)$ where R is an individual's ranking in the distribution. For this purpose, each state's population was set = 1000, and we computed SD2095 from $f(200), f(201), \ldots f(950)$.

The 1920 value is estimated from

$$SD2095_{20} = A + \Sigma b_i X_{i,1920},$$

where the X_i are

1. log of per capita income.
2. $\sqrt{[w(1 - w)]}$, w = proportion of population white.
3. $\{\sqrt{[f(1 - f)]}|I_f - I_0|\}$, f = proportion farmers, I_f, I_0 is log of per capita income of farmers and other respectively. (The motivation for the square root constructs is that, if the only source of dispersion in the population is, for example, $I_f \neq I_0$, this formula gives the standard deviation of log income in the population.)
4. SH5 (see below).

With the exception of w, which is from U.S. Bureau of the Census, Historical Statistics of the U.S. (various years), all these variables are from Leven, Income in the Various States (1925). The b_i are coefficients from a regression of the 1950 SD2095 on the 1950 counterparts to X_i (R^2 = .9 and all coefficients were significant).

(The coefficient of $\sqrt{[w(1 - w)]}$ was multiplied by 1.5. In principle, this variable should include an income difference term like that in 3. I had to exclude such a term because the 1920 counterpart does not exist. The 1950 coefficient therefore includes the average racial income difference. For the mid-1930s, when the first racial income data are available, that difference is around 1.5 × that of 1950). A is set so that the mean of the 1920 estimate = .53, which is the value for the first comparable U.S. income distribution (1929).

SH5: share of state income of wealthiest 5%, average of 1950 and 1920. The 1950 value is from $f(R)$, described above, and the 1920 value is from Leven, supra. (It is restricted to nonfarm incomes.)

POP: log of state population in 1942, or (columns (3)–(6)) change between 1942 and 1972. From U.S. Bureau of the Census, Statistical Abstract (various years). The means (standard deviations) of the variables are: Average of $g_{72,42,47}$ = 14.7 (1.9); $g_{72} - g_{42}$ = 11.8 (2.3); ED = 8.40 (.89); SD2095 = .451 (.083); SH5 = .246 (.031).

t-ratios are below coefficients.

upper bound was the sixtieth or eightieth percentile.[53] In light of the results in table 7.4, state population is included as an independent variable.

The dependent variable is the ratio of state and local government expenditures to personal income, or its change, for each of forty-eight states. The data are for 1942, 1957, and 1972. The motive for this lengthy time span was to gain insight into the lag process, which the international cross section and some of the time series suggested was an important part of the story. An initial attempt at implementing a conventional partial adjustment model like (19) failed.[54] Therefore, table 7.13 shows a range of results.

53. Similarly, cutting out either the lower or upper tail of the education distribution made no substantial difference.

54. Entering the lagged dependent variable as an independent variable always yielded absurdly low adjustment coefficients—on the order of .2 for 30 years. The reason appears to be that "state-specific" effects not captured by the model persist over time—for example, New York had unusually large governments in 1942 as well as 1972. Thus, when a 1972 expenditure variable is regressed on its 1942 counterpart, the coefficient of the latter (1 − adjustment coefficient) tends to have a positive bias.

Specifically, the income distribution and ability variables are defined as of *circa* 1940, that is, the start of the thirty-year period.[55] These initial conditions are assumed to determine a target level of the ratio of government spending to personal income. Then a range of adjustment rates to this target is imposed on the data via suitable definition of the dependent variable.[56] The last column of the table departs from the partial adjustment framework in favor of a less specific form: the initial conditions *circa* 1940 simply determine the rate of change over the indefinite future.

The results are uniformly disappointing. None of the coefficients of interest are distinguishable from zero. Some hint of the source of this sharp contrast with previous results is, however, given by the underlying data. The simple correlations between the ability (ED) and within-group inequality (SD2095) variables, on the one hand, and the dependent variable, on the other, always have the "correct" signs (positive and negative, respectively). These correlation coefficients range between .2 and .4 in absolute value, depending on the definition of the dependent variable. While these values are not spectacularly high, they are often significant with only moderate risk of error. (The simple correlation on between-group inequality (SH5) is, however, typically negative, sometimes significant. Yet, when that variable is deleted from the regression, as in column (2) or (6) there is no improvement in the performance of the remaining variables.) There is, however, a substantial negative correlation (around $-.9$) between ED and SD2095, which may be helping to obscure their independent effects.

The negative correlation between education and inequality may be a systematic outcome of the human-capital accumulation process.[57] If this

55. Usable data on income distributions begin with the 1950 census. (There are some in 1940, but always with a frighteningly large group reporting no or trivial income.) But these data are an implausible proxy for initial conditions around 1940. We have seen that there was a sharp narrowing of income dispersions generally beginning around 1930 and ending around 1940, so the 1950 distribution is more likely to typify the end rather than the beginning of our 30-year period.

The way I took out of this difficulty is as follows. For the early 1920s data are available on several important correlates of SD2095 in 1950. The 1920 counterparts are then weighted and summed to generate an estimate of SD2095 for 1920 (see note to Table 13). This is then averaged with the 1950 value to generate the variable used in the regression. In substance, we are assuming that policy decisions made in 1940 respond to about half of the profound change in inequality that occurred during the depression and World War II.

56. This procedure confines any state-specific effect to the residual of the regression, thereby avoiding any obvious bias of the coefficients.

57. In what Gary S. Becker, Human Capital (New York: Nat'l Bureau Econ. Research, 1975), terms the "egalitarian approach" to human capital accumulation, interpersonal differences in the costs of funds are the major determinants of differences in education. So those with a lower cost of funds buy more education and, at least on the margin, earn lower rates of return. *Ceteris paribus,* the income distribution is more equal, the lower the rate of return. Becker cites scattered evidence of a decline over time in rates of return, which, given

is so, it raises not only statistical problems but important interpretive problems for our previous results of a fairly consistent negative correlation between inequality and government/GNP. But if inequality and education are also negatively related, could not part of the negative correlation reflect the effects of increased education (political "ability")? To be sure, increased education may have been partially reflected in the typically positive "trend" components of the time-series regression. Our cross-sectional data, however, raise the possibility that inequality is a better proxy for ability than simple trend. A still more subtle possibility, encountered both in the Japanese data and the theory, is summarized by $(14')$ and (23). Perhaps there is no simple relationship between the size of government, on the one hand, and inequality and ability, on the other. Rather, the latter two interact. Explicitly the general scheme estimated in table 7.13 is

$$(24) \quad g = a \cdot \text{ABILITY} + b \cdot \text{INEQUALITY} + X,$$

where X = other factors influencing the size of government (g)

a, b = constants, $a > 0, b?$

In spite of our attempt to decompose INEQUALITY, measures like SD2095 tend to be highly correlated with any summary measure of the whole income distribution, like SD0100. So, if SD2095 is our proxy for "INEQUALITY," b will absorb both within- and between-group effects. But if increased ability—whether due to a shift to democracy, as in Japan, or to more education—raises the marginal political impact of g, then $(14')$ and (23) tell us that the weight on the within-group effect is increased. Since this effect is negative, (23) would imply the approximation

$$(25) \quad b = b_0 + b_1 \cdot \text{ABILITY}; b_1 < 0, b_0?$$

The second term here approximates the derivative in (23); it says that an increase in ability enhances the stimulative effect of equality on the size of government. (Since b_0 still contains both within- and between-group effects, its sign remains uncertain.) Substitution of (25) into (24) yields

---

the simultaneous spread of education, would seem consistent with the "egalitarian approach." Barry R. Chiswick, Income Inequality: Regional Analyses within a Human Capital Framework (New York: Nat'l Bureau Econ. Research, 1974), shows a strong negative correlation between rates of return and mean education across states, which is also consistent with the egalitarian approach. In his work, this rate of return × standard deviation of education is the crucial systematic determinant of income inequality. Since schooling inequality and mean schooling are uncorrelated, the clear implication is that the negative schooling-income inequality relationship which we observe is driven by the tendency for more schooling to lower rates of return.

TABLE 7.14 State and Local Government Expenditures/Personal Income Regressions

Form of Dependent Variable	1942, 1957, 1972 Average		1972	(1972)–½(1942)	1972–1942	
Model	Complete Adjustment after 15 Years		Complete Adjustment 30 Years	50% Adjustment 30 Years	Indefinite Adjustment	
Independent Variables	(1)	(2)	(3)	(4)	(5)	(6)
POP	−.71	−.75	−.67	−.60	−.53	−.27
	2.69	3.10	.53	.54	0.49	0.24
ED	4.51	4.71	7.27	7.10	6.92	5.81
	2.39	2.59	2.48	2.74	2.75	2.39
SD2095	72.11	74.50	109.88	107.02	104.17	90.65
	2.33	2.47	2.29	2.53	2.54	2.23
ED × SD2095	−9.01	−9.32	−14.98	−14.62	−14.26	−12.60
	2.30	2.45	2.47	2.74	2.75	2.45
SH5	−4.07		−.01	8.62	17.26	
	0.43		0.00	.71	1.46	
R^2	.34	.34	.23	.24	.23	.19
SE	1.63	1.62	2.52	2.22	2.16	2.19

Notes: See table 7.13 and text for definitions and sources of variables.

$$(26) \quad g = a \cdot \text{ABILITY} + b_0 \cdot \text{INEQUALITY} + b_1 \cdot (\text{ABILITY} \cdot \text{INEQUALITY}) + X.$$

The scheme in (26) is estimated in table 7.14, and many of the uncertainties evident in table 7.13 appear to be clarified. The explanatory power of the regressions in table 7.14 (R^2, SE) increases substantially over their counterparts in table 7.13, which lends credibility to the interactive scheme in (26). The precision of the coefficients is correspondingly improved, allowing some conclusions:

1. The coefficient of ED is now always significantly positive, as the theory implies, if ED is a proxy for "ability."

2. There is some evidence for a positive between-group inequality effect. Most of this evidence derives from the significantly positive coefficient of SD2095, which is the counterpart to b_0 in (25). This says that, at low levels of ability, more inequality *increases* the size of government. An effort to further isolate this between-group effect in the coefficient of SH5 yields mixed results. The coefficient varies from insignificantly negative to "suggestively" positive, depending on the form of the dependent variable. If SH5 is deleted, none of the other coefficients changes very much.

3. Most important, the significant negative coefficient of the interaction term corroborates what we found in the Japanese data: The within-group effect gets stronger (and eventually outweighs the between-group effect) the more "able" the populace.

4. We are unable to pin down the relevant lag structure. The various lag structures explain the data about equally well,[58] and the pattern of the coefficients provides no further illumination.[59] Some experimentation with different lags than those assumed in table 7.14 did, however, suggest that very short lags in response were inappropriate.[60]

Table 7.14 shows that the concept of "ability" is important both in its own right and on account of its interaction with equality. I therefore try to improve the simple proxy used in table 7.14 (education). The theoretical concept can, after all, comprehend any factor facilitating the political repayment of benefits. In table 7.15, I consider two additional factors that might have such potential: voter participation and the size of organized interest groups (specifically labor unions and farmer cooperatives). The historical evidence did not imply an important role for voter turnout, but the cross-section data permit a more refined test. There is also a historical motivation for the interest-group variables. The early twentieth-century expansion of government coincides with the emergence of broad-based interest groups, like labor and farm organizations, which successfully exerted influence on the political process. By 1940, the start of our period of analysis for the states, these groups had attained roughly their present size. I want to see if the influence they subsequently exerted at the local level led to a net expansion of local governments. Also, since these groups did not organize primarily for local political action, we can distinguish the impact of organized interests on the growth of government from any

58. Regressions (3)–(5) of table 7.14 purport to explain g_{1972}. When we generate predicted values of this variable and compare them to the actual g_{1972}, we get roughly the same standard errors (2.52, 2.38, and 2.41, respectively). Regression (1) explains a different variable, $\bar{g}_{1942,57,72}$. However, if one (a) assumes that standard deviations of g are proportional to means and then (b) synthesizes a $\bar{g}$ with the same mean and variance as g_{1972}, the standard error of that synthetic variable from regression (1) would also be about the same (2.33) as the others.

59. In the lagged-adjustment model, the implied coefficient of the target g = regression coefficient/adjustment coefficient. Thus, if the regression coefficients increased roughly in proportion to the assumed adjustment coefficient, we would at least know something about the target g, even if we could not specify how quickly the adjustment proceeded. However, the regression coefficients are largely invariant to the assumed adjustment coefficient,

60. For example, when the dependent and independent variables were made contemporaneous, the precision of the regression coefficients and the overall fit of the regression tended to deteriorate, though the overall pattern of the results was the same as in table 7.14.

TABLE 7.15 State and Local Government Expenditures Regressions
with Added Political Ability Variables

Dependent Variables	1942, 1957, 1972 Average		1972–1942 Change	
Independent Variables (Coefficient Symbol, Equation (28))	(1)	Weights for Ability Index (2)	(3)	Weights for Ability Index (4)
POP	−.69		−1.23	
	2.41		1.10	
	[3.05]			
Ability Index (a)	.86		1.09	
	3.95		3.78	
	[4.58]		[4.41]	
VPAR (c_1)		−.77		−.97
		3.05		3.60
FARM (c_2)		.73		−.11
		2.03		.37
LABOR (c_3)		.16		.21
		.60		.98
SD2095 (b_0)	186.95		15.50	
	2.24		0.15	
	[4.37]		[2.21]	
SD2095 × Ability (b_1)	−1.78		−2.23	
	2.24		3.51	
	[4.38]		[4.05]	
SH5	12.00		24.67	
	1.24		1.93	
	[1.30]		[2.41]	
R^2	.51			.40
SE	1.46			1.53

Note: See text and table 7.13 for sources and definitions of variables.
The numbers in brackets are t-ratios calculated on the assumption that the index weights are known beforehand. They are obtained by computing the ability index for each state and substituting the index for ED in ordinary least squares regressions like those in table 7.14.

stimulus to such organization provided by that growth. (For similar reasons, I use voter participation in presidential, rather than purely local, elections.)

The empirical implementation follows (26) except that an index is the proxy for "ability" instead of a single variable. Specifically,

(27)   ABILITY = ED + c_1 VPAR + c_2 FARM + c_3 LABOR,

where the c_i are weights, measured as fractions of the weight on ED, and VPAR = ratio of votes cast in the 1940, 1944, and 1948 presidential elections to the population over twenty-one in each state.

FARM and LABOR equal the ratio of membership in farm cooperatives and labor unions respectively to the population of the state.[61] When (27) is substituted back into (26), we get

$$(28) \quad g = [a \cdot ED + \Sigma a \cdot c_i A_i] + b_0 \cdot INEQUALITY + [b_1 ED \cdot INEQUALITY + \Sigma b_1 c_i A_i \cdot INEQUALITY] + X,$$

where A_i are the three additional components of the ability index. The resulting overidentified scheme is then estimated by nonlinear least squares, where the restrictions in (28) (that the c_i in the two bracketed expressions be the same) are imposed. To facilitate comparisons, ED and the A_i are each entered as standardized variables with the mean equal to 100 and standard deviation equal to 10. Thus $c_i = .5$ would mean that if VPAR is one standard deviation above the mean, ability is enhanced by half as much as if ED is a standard deviation above the mean.

The results, for two forms of the dependent variable, the 1942–1972 average level and 1942–1972 change, are summarized in table 7.15. There is another substantial improvement in explanatory power and in the precision of the ability and inequality coefficients. Our confidence in the crucial result of table 7.14—that ability and within-group inequality interact negatively—is clearly strengthened by table 7.15. In addition, the role of the wealthiest citizens as tempting targets for taxation seems better defined here than in table 7.14; the coefficient on SH5 is consistently positive. All this is compatible with the notion that changes in the political process, as well as in personal capabilities of voters, play a role in the growth of government. But the nature of this role seems peculiar. The role of organized interest seems generally weak, statistically and numerically. The one exception of the large and significant impact of farm cooperatives on the level of government (column (2)) does not carry over to the change (column (4)). The unexpected result of a consistent and strong *negative* effect of voter participation on expenditures deserves more study than I can give it here. It is broadly consistent with certain nineteenth-century historical

61. To avoid distortion by one-party dominance in the South in the 1940s, I calculate VPAR for the 1968 election for the southern states. I then multiply the ratio of VPAR in a state to the national average in 1968 by the national average for the 1940 elections to get estimates of the "true" VPAR in the South for those years.

Data on membership in labor unions and farm cooperatives are unavailable for the early 1940s, so I use the earliest available dates (1960 for cooperatives and 1964 for unions). All data are from Statistical Abstract.

facts. Recall that Britain had a rapidly expanding franchise in the nineteenth century, while the United States did not, and apparently experienced a sharper contraction in the size of government. The result is also consistent with the spirit of bureaucratic-monopoly models, such as Niskanen's or Peacock and Wiseman's,[62] which have at their core the notion of government expansion being antithetical to the interest of the broad mass of citizens. Our result implies that when the masses indicate they have sufficiently overcome their "rational ignorance" to come to the polls, the political process pays more heed to their interest.

There would then remain the question of just whose interest the political process is serving. It could not plausibly be just the bureaucracy's, given the empirical importance of broad measures of education and income equality. But our theory does not require that everyone in a specific income-education range be a beneficiary either. In fact, the technology of government, in which benefits are conferred through specific programs, rather than per capita grants, pretty much rules this out. One plausible interpretation of table 7.15 is that government expands when specific programs attract a sufficiently broad constituency, but this constituency is always smaller than a majority of voters. However, a bigger potential coalition is better than a smaller one, and the chances for forming a successful coalition would be greater the larger the pool of voters who are prime potential beneficiaries. In our analysis, the size of this pool is larger the more educated voters with similar economic interests there are.

I now address the issue of the quantitative, as opposed to the statistical, significance of the ability-inequality nexus uncovered in tables 7.14 and 7.15. Specifically, do the results explain any substantial part of the recent growth of government, or are the ability-inequality effects merely a sideshow on how spending is distributed among locales? This question is relevant for two reasons. First, even if ability, inequality, and their interaction help explain variation in the size and growth of local government, we have already noted there is not much variation to explain. Since the similarity among states is more notable than their differences, our regression can be measuring empirically trivial deviations from an all-important average. Second, the results imply that changes in inequality or ability, standing alone, have no clear-cut empirical implications for the size or growth of local government. This is most clear in table 7.13 and confirmed by measuring the partial effects of either inequality or ability in table 7.14 or 7.15 at the sample means (they are essentially nil). The issue of empirical

---

62. Niskanen, *supra* note 3; and Peacock & Wiseman, *supra* note 1.

significance thus rests on the importance of the interaction effect when there are substantial changes in *both* inequality and ability. Even at this level, the issue has no clear *a priori* answer. The differential form of (26) is

(26′) $\Delta g = \Delta \text{ABILITY} [a + b_1 \cdot \text{INEQUALITY}]$
$+ \Delta \text{INEQUALITY} [b_0 + b_1(\text{ABILITY} + \Delta \text{ABILITY})].$

Since we find a, $b_0 > 0$ and $b_1 < 0$, there is no obvious prediction even for the direction of Δg.

To get at the empirical import of the results, I use the coefficients in tables 7.14 and 7.15 to estimate the effects of the sorts of changes that have characterized the relevant history, namely an increase in education or ability coupled with a decrease in income inequality. Specifically, for table 7.14 I ask: what is the predicted effect on the level (column (1) is the relevant regression) or the change (column (6)) in the size of government if education increases two standard deviations while inequality (SD2095 and SH5) decreases two standard deviations from the sample mean: The effect on the level is +4.28 percentage points and on the change +6.57 percentage points. For table 7.15, we can perform a similar exercise in which the ability index is also increased by two standard deviations. The results are +8.05 for level and +7.36 for change.

There are three points to note about these results.

1. The effects are substantial by any measure, running between 2.6 and 5.5 times the relevant regression standard errors. The effects on the level are between 30 and 60 per cent of the sample mean, and on the change about 60 or 70 per cent of the mean. Put differently, the level regressions purport to describe the change over the fifteen years from 1942 to 1957, while the change regressions pertain to 1942–1972. The 1942–1957 actual change is around +6.0 and the 1942–1972 change around +12.0. If our simulated ability-inequality changes accurately describe what went on in the interwar period, the regression parameters account for over half of the subsequent growth of government.

2. Our simulation roughly corresponds to the relevant historical change. For example, the simulated change in education is a little less than +2 years. Whereas we do not have pre-1940 data on ED, we know that mean schooling has been rising at over one year per decade subsequently (from 8½ years in 1940 to over 12 in 1970). We also know that prior to World War I no more than 5 per cent of seventeen-year-olds were graduating from high school and that secondary school enrollment was also only 5 per cent of elementary school enrollment. So extrapolating the post-1940 experience back to around 1920, as done in the simulations, could

not be far off the mark. Our assumed changes in inequality and the ability index are also reasonably accurate caricatures of the relevant history.[63]

3. The driving force behind our results is the negative effect of the interaction between education-ability and inequality. The combination of increasing education-ability and decreasing inequality decreases their product and thereby accounts for the bulk of the historical growth in government that the cross-section results can rationalize. Consequently, considerable weight must be given to the confluence of these two forces, rather than to either separately, in any explanation of the growth of government.[64]

D. The Less Developed Countries (LDCs)

The less developed countries (LDCs) pose a severe test of our model, perhaps too severe. Quite apart from the data problems, which are discussed subsequently, one can be skeptical whether the same processes that affect the size of government in the developed countries (DCs) carry over more or less intact to societies with markedly different economic and political structures. Yet the severity of the test is also an attraction, one that is enhanced by the diversity of LDCs. While they differ on average from the DCs in most measures of political and economic development, they also span a much wider range—from countries with living standards only moderately below the DCs to those with virtually all the population in subsistence agriculture, from democracies to dictatorships, from income

63. For SD2095 and SH5 our simulations entail decreases of .16 and .06, respectively. The former roughly corresponds to the actual change between 1930 and 1950, so we may be overstating the pre-1940 change. The latter figure describes roughly what occurs between 1930 and 1942; this series is shown in figure 7.4. We have almost surely understated the historical change in the ability index. The relevant history is a change of around $+2$ SD for ED and unionization, $+1$ for farm cooperatives, and 0 for VPAR. If we sum these changes with the weights in columns (2) or (4) of table 7.15, we would get changes in the index of around $+30$ or $+20$, respectively. The simulations entail changes only two-thirds as large.

64. I attempted unsuccessfully to replicate the results in tables 7.14 and 7.15 for the developed country cross section. I first constructed an inequality index $= L + 6 \cdot \varnothing$ which seems to be roughly the weighting scheme implied by the regressions in table 7.12. Then I constructed an ability index: a simple average of standardized indices of newspaper circulation per person over 25 and school attendance per person under 15. When these two variables and their interaction were entered in a regression like 10 in table 7.12, none of the coefficients was significant. However, when the interaction term was dropped, both of the remaining variables had significant *negative* coefficients and the R^2 increased from .8 in table 7.12 to about .9. This implies that the "ability" index may be improving our inequality measure: as in our state and local data, "ability" and inequality are negatively $(-.5)$ correlated in this sample. If our ability measure is partly a proxy for inequality, detection of the interaction effect would be difficult, since inequality would interact with itself rather than with "ability."

distributions more equal than those in the DCs to inequality far exceeding any recorded in the DCs over the last century. This enormous diversity creates a special opportunity to clarify the relative impact of political institutions and personal "abilities" on the growth of government. So far we have been able to treat this issue only in the context of isolated events (for example, the advent of Japanese democracy) or fairly homogeneous populations (for example, education differences across American states).

The basic facts about the size of government in the LDCs can be summarized succinctly. They are neither as large nor growing as rapidly relative to GDP as those in the DCs.

1. In the sample we will analyze (42 LDCs in the decade 1960–1970), the average government/GDP ratio is 17.6 per cent, or about half that of our DC sample (see table 7.2).

2. There is substantially more diversity among the LDCs, at least relative to the lower mean. The standard deviation of government/GDP for the LDCs is 5.1 per cent, which is comparable to that for the DCs, so the coefficient of variation is about double that of the DCs.

3. The average 1960–1970 growth in government/GDP in the LDCs tends to be smaller than for the DCs; the mean change (standard deviation) is $+3.4$ (2.2) percentage points.

This combination of small and slowly growing governments is somewhat reminiscent of the pre-1920 history of the Western DCs (and of Japan for most of the twentieth century). And the crude data on LDC income distributions seem compatible with the explanation offered for DC history. A within-group measure of inequality which we subsequently exploit is the ratio of eighth to third decile incomes. This exceeds 3, on average, for the LDCs versus $2+$ for the DCs. (The same sort of difference holds for the upper tail: the average share of income for the tenth decile is 39 per cent for the LDCs and 25 per cent for the DCs.) But there is considerable overlap in the two samples, and, of course, much more than differences in income inequality distinguish them. So the crude consistency ought to be greeted cautiously. We are on even slipperier ground with the changes in inequality in the LDCs. The earlier history of the DCs, the more recent experience of Japan and Kuznets's elaboration of the conflicting implications of development for inequality are all we have to create a presumption that nothing like the pervasive shrinking of inequality in the DCs has gone on in the LDCs.

My strategy in analyzing the LDC data is to replicate the analysis of the U.S. state and local government data, thereby forcing a comparison between the most and least homogeneous samples. Analogues to the variables in (26) (namely, ABILITY, INEQUALITY) are required, thus entailing considerable compromise with the poor quality of LDC data. For example, while there are published income distributions for most LDCs, there is none of the refinement of their conceptual differences as in the Lydall-Sawyer data for the DCs.[65] Nevertheless, I take from these raw data the ratio of income in the 70–80 percentile of the distribution to income in the 20–30 percentile (R83) as a proxy for "within-group" inequality. (See notes to table 7.16 for details on this and the other variables discussed below.) In preliminary work, I also used the tenth decile share as a proxy for between-group inequality. Since this variable proved even less helpful than its analogue in the state and local data (SH5), none of the results reported here use it.

I supplemented R83 with the same sort of nonmonotonic transform $\sqrt{x(1 - x)}$ of the agricultural share of the population that proved useful in estimating U.S. income distributions and is suggested by Kuznets's work.[66] Here some facts about LDCs are useful. Most have substantial agricultural population shares (about 50 per cent on average), but they span virtually all of the relevant range. In addition, a large share of the typical LDC's farmers are in a "traditional" or subsistence sector where income differences with the rest of the economy are especially great. Accordingly, I use for "x" above the share of the population in this traditional sector as estimated by Adelman and Morris.[67] I then simply average indexes of this variable and R83 to construct an index of INEQUALITY (see below for refinements).

An ABILITY proxy for the LDCs should make use of the considerable variety of their political institutions as well as of relevant population characteristics. Therefore, I constructed an ABILITY measure which weights the two kinds of ability equally. "Political ability" is an average of two indexes constructed by Adelman and Morris of the "strength of democratic institutions" and of the "degree of freedom of political opposition and press."[68] These indexes contain large subjective elements but are at least independent of this study and may shed light on a major unresolved question: does more active representation of broad groups of potential beneficiaries ("democracy") stimulate the growth of government? Data on

---

65. Sawyer, *supra* note 47; Lydall, *supra* note 28.

66. See text at note 26 *supra.*

67. Irma Adelman & Cynthia Taft Morris, Society, Politics, and Economic Development: A Quantitative Approach (Baltimore: Johns Hopkins Univ. Press, 1969). Data on income differences between sectors are unavailable.

68. See *ibid.*

TABLE 7.16 Government Expenditures/GDP Regressions 42 Less
Developed Countries, 1960–1970

Form of Dependent Variable	1960–70 Average	1970	1970– ½(1960)	1970–1960
Model	Complete Adjustment, 5 Years	Complete Adjustment, 10 years	50% Adjustment, 10 Years	Indefinite Adjustment
Independent Variables	(1)	(2)	(3)	(4)
POP	−.28	−.30	−.17	−.05
	.69	.67	.58	.20
MODERN	.18	.18	.10	.01
	2.61	2.40	1.88	.21
MODERN 2	−.10	−.10	−.05	−.01
	.93	.86	.69	.10
ABILITY	−.06	−.04	.01	.05
	.56	.30	.07	.78
INEQUALITY	−.26	−.32	−.22	−.13
	2.90	3.23	3.37	2.47
R^2	.54	.55	.54	.30
SE	3.66	4.08	2.72	2.08

Notes:

Definitions and Sources of Variables

Independent variables are derived from the 1960 and 1970 ratios × 100 of current government revenue from domestic sources to GDP, from United Nations Yearbook of National Account Statistics (various years). Revenue rather than expenditures is used, because data on capital expenditures are sketchy and, where available, they imply that capital expenditures are financed mainly from current revenues. In the rare case where current expenditures exceeded current revenues, the former is used.

For some countries, either 1960 or 1970 government revenue data are unavailable. If data over an interval of at least 5 years are unavailable, the country is excluded. Otherwise, I computed the ratio of government revenue to government consumption in the first or last available year and multiplied government consumption in the terminal year by this ratio. In two cases (Israel and South Vietnam), I extrapolated the 1960–1966 growth in government/GDP to 1970 to eliminate the effects of post-1966 wars.

Independent Variables

POP: Log of 1960 population. Statistical Yearbook, *supra.*

ABILITY: Average of four indexes, each normalized to mean = 100, standard deviation = 10. The components are:

1) *Democracy:* An index of the "strength of democratic institutions" which ranges 0–100 from I. Adelman & C. T. Morris, Society, Politics, and Economic Development: A Quantitative Approach (1971) (hereinafter cited as AM). Their sample covers about three-fourths of mine. For the remainder (non-AM countries) I first regressed the AM index on a set of dummy variables which were based on my reading of each country's political history in Political Handbook of the World: 1975, (Arthur S. Banks ed.) (New York: McGraw-Hill, 1975).

(a) Degree of party competition: +1 if, *ca.* the early 1960s, a democratically elected parliament wielded effective political power; −1 if power was held by one person or party and rivals were outlawed; 0 for intermediate cases.

(b) Post-World War II history of party competition: +1 if a multiparty democracy had prevailed for the whole period; −1 if the country had always been a dictatorship; 0 if some party rivalry had occurred for some of the period.

(c) Press freedom: +1 if, up to the early 1960s, the press was largely free of government control; −1 if the press was government controlled; 0 for intermediate cases.

(d) Military coups: −1 if a military coup has been attempted since World War II; +1 if a military coup has never been attempted up to 1965; 0 for doubtful cases (for example, civilian disturbances with military participation).

(e) Coups in one-party states: −1 if a coup had *not* been attempted in a one-party state, 0 otherwise. The notion here is that military opposition to a dictator means more "democracy" than a totally unopposed dictatorship.

(f) Log of GDP per capita in 1963 in U.S. dollars, to capture any positive income elasticity of democracy. The regression ($R^2 = .7$) coefficients were then used to generate an estimate of the "democracy index" for non-AM countries.

2) *Freedom of Political Oppression and of Press:* Index from AM with estimates for non-AM sample from regression technique described above. The independent variables for the estimating regression are the same as above ($R^2 = .5$).

3) *Extent of Mass Communication:* Index from AM, for non-AM countries a regression estimate of the AM index is used. The independent variables in the estimating regression ($R^2 = .95$) were the logs of per capita newspaper circulation and radio ownership (from UNESCO, Statistical Yearbook, various years)—that is, the AM index is essentially a weighted average of newspaper and radio use.

4) *Literacy:* Percentage of population literate *ca.* 1960 (UNESCO, Statistical Yearbook, various years).

MODERN: Weighted average of two AM indexes. The level of modernization of techniques in (1) agriculture and (2) industry. The weights are the percentage of population in agricultural and nonagricultural sectors. For non-AM countries, a regression estimate of the AM index (on log per capita GDP, $R^2 = .6$) is used.

MODERN 2: MODERN = MODERN if this difference > 0; 0 otherwise.

INEQUALITY: This is an average of two standardized (Mean = 100, S.D. = 10) indexes based on:

1) R83, the ratio of the share of income in the 8th to the share in the 3rd decile of the income distribution. The main data source is Shail Jain, Size Distribution of Income: A Compilation of Data (World Bank, 1975), which gives decile share estimates for most published income distributions. Where possible, I use a national household distribution *ca.* 1960. (Alternatives in order of preference are national population, urban households, national income recipients. For the latter 0.3% is added to the 3rd decile share, because this was the average (significant) difference between income recipient and household 3rd decile shares where both are available for the same countries. No other similar difference among distributions was found.) For some countries data are from a similar, partly overlapping, compendium in Irma Adelman & Cynthia T. Morris, Economic Growth and Social Equity in Developing Countries (1973) (hereinafter cited as AM2). They provide five points on the cumulative income distribution, rather than decile shares. To estimate the relevant decile shares, I first regressed the logs of the shares in Jain on the logs of the five values in AM2 for the 16 cases where both summarize the same distribution ($R^2 > .9$, SE < .05 for both decile shares), then I used the regression coefficients as weights to estimate 3rd and 8th decile shares from the AM2 data for other countries. The Jain and AM2 data cover about three-fourths of our sample. For the remainder, I averaged available estimates of R for countries in the same region at roughly the same level of per capita GDP.

2) $\sqrt{[t\,(1-t)]}$, where t = percentage of population in traditional agriculture, as estimated by AM. For non-AM countries, estimates are based on weights from a regression of the AM estimate (on the percentage of the population in agriculture and log per capita GDP, R^2 = .8). The sample comprises the following 42 countries:

Argentina	Israel	Singapore
Barbados	Jamaica	South Africa
Bolivia	Jordan	South Vietnam
Burma	Korea (Republic of)	Southern Rhodesia
Chile	Malaysia	Spain
Colombia	Malta	China (Taiwan)
Costa Rica	Nicaragua	Tanzania
Dominican Republic	Nigeria	Thailand
Ecuador	Panama	Togo
Greece	Paraguay	Trinidad
Guatemala	Peru	Tunisia
Guyana	Philippines	Turkey
Honduras	Portugal	Uruguay
India	Sierra Loene	Venezuela

educational attainment, the personal-ability proxy used in table 7.14, are too fragmentary to permit a direct analogue. Accordingly, I used an average of two proxies for personal ability, the fraction of the literate population and an Adelman-Morris index of the "effect of mass communication" (essentially a weighted average of newspaper circulation and radio ownership per capita).[69] The ABILITY measure is the average of the "political" and "personal" ability indexes.

My only substantive departure from the analysis of U.S. local governments is to add variables reflecting the level of economic development and, implicitly, tax collection costs. The motive is to use this diverse sample to elaborate on two aspects of the earlier data: Japan's atypical pre-World War I growth of government and the general absence among DCs and U.S. states of any correlation between per capita income and the relative size of governments. Taken together, these two factors seemed to imply that major income-related reductions in revenue-raising costs occur only fairly early in the development process. To verify the implication, I use two variables. One is an index of the extent to which the economy has adopted "modern" techniques,[70] which presumably entail monetary exchange, modern record keeping, and so forth and hence serve as a proxy

69. In the subsample of countries where median schooling attainment is available, the simple correlation with either proxy is about .9.

70. This is a weighted average of two Adelman-Morris indexes, *supra* note 67: the "level of modernization of industry" and of agriculture, with urban-rural population shares as weights.

for tax collection costs. The second is simply this variable less its sample mean for countries with above average modernization. If tax-collection-cost economies diminish with development, the first variable should have a positive partial correlation and the second a negative partial correlation with the size of government.

All of these variables are defined *circa* 1960 and are used to explain the size and growth of government in the subsequent decade, which is about as long a period as the data permit.[71] Our sample consists of forty-two LDCs for which government budget data are available and which were substantively independent political entities around 1960.[72] The analogues to the regressions in table 7.13, which implement equation (24), are in table 7.16. One notable difference from table 7.13, where essentially nothing but population worked,[73] is the consistently negative correlation between inequality and either the size or growth of government. We also find a pattern of coefficients for the tax-collection-cost proxies (MODERN, MODERN 2) consistent with the hints in the Japanese, DC, and state data. That is, lower collection costs stimulate the growth of government (the coefficient of MODERN is positive), but at what appears to be a diminishing rate (the negative coefficient of MODERN 2 is insignificant). Table 7.16 duplicates the insignificant ABILITY effect of table 7.13.

We learned from table 7.14, however, to mistrust the too easy inference that effects of ability play no role in determining the size or growth of government. Accordingly, table 7.17 implements the interaction model of equation (26) on the LDC data, yielding a remarkable consistency with the results for U.S. states in table 7.14: (1) The ABILITY and INEQUALITY variables both tend to have significantly positive coefficients as in table 7.14. (2) The interaction effect (coefficient of ABILITY × INEQUAL-ITY) tends to be significantly negative as in table 7.14. (3) There is a sub-

71. Pre-1960 budget data are unavailable for most LDCs, and the gaps and reporting lags get more serious the closer we approach the present. In addition, the sharp rise in oil prices post 1973 leads to major departures from trend for revenues of some of the governments in our sample.

72. That is, if the country was *de jure* a colony for a substantial part of the period, it had to have been granted at least local autonomy by around 1960 to be included in the sample. The *de facto ca.*-1960 status was determined from the country narratives in Political Handbook of the World: 1975 (Arthur S. Banks ed.) (New York: McGraw-Hill, 1975).

73. The role of population here is less clear-cut than for U.S. states. In the public goods framework, there are both "set-up-cost" and density economies, and among U.S. states population and density are positively correlated. However, in this sample the smallest entities include some of the most densely populated (Barbados, Malta, Singapore). I include the population variable here only for the sake of completeness.

TABLE 7.17 LDC Government/GDP Regressions, with Ability-
Inequality Interaction

Form of Dependent Variable	Average, 1960–70	1970	1970– $\frac{1}{2}(1960)$	1970–1960
Model	Complete Adjustment, 5 Years	Complete Adjustment, 10 Years	50% Adjustment, 10 Years	Indefinite Adjustment
Independent Variables	(1)	(2)	(3)	(4)
POP	.06	.04	−.00	−.05
	.16	.09	.01	.19
MODERN	.18	.19	.10	.01
	3.06	2.72	2.03	.21
MODERN 2	−.13	−.14	−.07	−.01
	1.40	1.25	.93	.10
ABILITY	3.29	3.31	1.68	.05
	3.29	2.89	2.09	.08
INEQUALITY	3.16	3.10	1.48	−.12
	3.10	2.65	1.82	−.18
ABILITY × INEQUALITY	−.034	−.034	−.017	−.001
	3.37	2.93	2.09	.01
R^2	.65	.64	.59	.30
SE	3.23	3.71	2.60	2.11

Note: See notes to table 7.16 for definitions and sources of variables.

stantial improvement in the fit of the table 7.17 regressions over their table 7.16 counterparts, again duplicating the pattern for U.S. states.

The only exception to these conclusions is in column (4) of table 7.17, where the interaction model clearly fails to work. However, the indefinitely long adjustment process implied by column (4) seems to be an inappropriate characterization of the growth of LDC governments.[74] And this, too, appears reasonable. The rationale for a long drawn-out adjustment process is strongest when the determinants of the size of government have

74. We can use the same test as for the state data (see note 58 *supra*). Note that columns (2)–(4) of Table 17 purport to explain Government/GDP for 1970. When we compute the standard error of the value of this variable predicted by each of these regressions we get 3.70 for (2), 3.87 for (3), and 4.82 for (4). So (2) and (3) do about equally well in explaining the data, but (4) is clearly inferior. Column (1) describes a different dependent variable (1960–70 average). To compare that regression with the others, we compute the standard error of this regression after adjusting the dependent variable to the same mean and variance as the 1970 variable. This turns out to be 3.93, or about the same as for (2) and (3).

changed profoundly over a relatively short interval. This was true of the
developed world, especially with respect to inequality, up to about 1950,
but it is not obviously true of the LDCs. Although table 7.17 does not
permit pinning down the adjustment lag for the LDCs to anything closer
than a five- to twenty-year range, it does rule out much longer lags. The
LDCs thus appear to have adjusted faster to their smaller gap between
actual and "desired" size of government than the DCs.

Finally, note that table 7.17 is slightly more emphatic about the diminishing effect of tax-collection costs. If we take the results for the MOD-
ERN variables at face value, they imply the marginal impact of "modernization" is only about one-fourth as great for the more developed LDCs
as for the least developed. The implication for the historical experience is
that Japanese government grew rapidly prior to World War I while Western governments did not, because Japan was then developing the sort of
revenue-raising infrastructure that the others had achieved much earlier.

The results in table 7.17 raise two questions:

(1) What is the relative importance of political ability (democracy, and
so on) and personal ability (literacy, and so on)? An attempt to use the
technique of table 7.15 failed for the LDC data.[75] However, experimentation with different weights on the "political" and "personal" components
of the ABILITY index revealed that both are important and that it is
tolerably accurate to give them equal weight.[76] So these LDC results are
consistent with both the Japanese results, which isolated a political ability
effect (the shift to democracy), and the U.S. state results, which isolate
personal ability effects (education).

75. In an attempt to estimate the weights of the components of ABILITY and IN-
EQUALITY, the nonlinear-least-squares regression failed to converge.

76. For example, consider the following weighting schemes for the political (average of
"democracy" and "freedom" indexes) and personal (average of "literacy" and "mass communications") components and the resulting R^2s for regressions otherwise identical to (2),
table 7.17

ABILITY =	
j POLITICAL + k PERSONAL	R^2
$j = 0, k = 1$	.607
$j = \frac{1}{4}, k = \frac{3}{4}$	.628
$j = \frac{1}{2}, k = \frac{1}{2}$ (as in Table 17)	.644
$j = \frac{3}{4}, k = \frac{1}{4}$	.648
$j = 1, k = 0$	.641

They suggest only that very low weights on the political variables are inappropriate. I
conducted a similar exercise for the components of INEQUALITY (see note to table 7.16).
Here, too, nothing much improved on the equal weighting in table 7.17, and only low weights
on the $R83$ component could be ruled out.

(2) Is the ability-inequality nexus important empirically? The LDC data suggest an even more positive answer than the state data. One useful formulation of the problem is to see if the results in table 7.17 can rationalize any of the substantial difference in size of government between LDCs and DCs. Recall that the average DC government sector spends fully twice as large a fraction of GDP as the average LDC government. Therefore, I plugged values of the independent variables appropriate to the DCs into table 7.17 regressions to obtain estimates of what the size of the average LDC government sector would be if these countries had the characteristics of DCs.[77]

For regression (1) table 7.17, the results of this exercise were:

1) Average government/GDP, 1960–70, for LDCs	17.62%
2) Predicted change, if LDC industry became as modernized as DCs (MODERN = 100, MODERN 2 = 42)	+3.55
3) Predicted change, if LDC ABILITY and INEQUALITY = DC average	+12.49
4) Predicted government/GDP for LDC with DC characteristics (1 + 2 + 3)	33.7%
5) Actual average for 16 DCs, 1960–70	33.4

For regression (2), which describes 1970 data, the counterparts to lines (1), (4), (5) above were:

1) Average government/GDP, LDCs, 1970	19.2%
4) Predicted 1970, DC characteristics	36.9
5) Actual average, 1970, DCs	36.7

(The relative magnitudes of the counterparts to lines (2) and (3) were roughly the same as above.)

The essential result is that we are able to rationalize *all* of the differences between DCs and LDCs, virtually to the decimal point. These remarkable[78] results suggest that the large behavioral differences between these two groups are really the outcomes of precisely the same process,

77. Specifically, the characteristics assumed for a *DC* are: (1) A fully modernized industrial structure. MODERN = 100. (2) A democratic society with no restraints on opposition or the press, that is, "democracy" and "freedom" indexes = 100. (3) A fully literate society. (4) A "mass communications" index as implied by the AM index and the average values of radio ownership and newspaper circulation for the DC sample of table 7.12 (see note to table 7.16). This index = 106. (5) A nominal .01 share of the population in subsistence agriculture. (6) The average value of $R83$ for the DCs in Sawyer's data (*supra* note 47)

78. There is one catch. The predicted values, line (4), are for an *equilibrium* size of government. But our analysis of DCs suggested that the *actual* values around 1970 or 1965 were subequilibrium.

one which is dominated by the ability-inequality nexus (compare lines (2) and (3) on previous page).

If that is so, there are some strong implications for the future growth of government in the LDCs. As (if) the LDCs' overall level of economic development, their degree of income inequality, and the "personal" characteristics of their populations approach those of contemporary DCs, the recent slow growth of LDCs' government sectors will accelerate. Whether the gap between them and contemporary DC governments closes completely depends on political developments that are difficult to predict. If there is no corresponding move toward more democratic political institutions at all, a nontrivial gap will remain.[79]

VI. CONCLUDING REMARKS

The broad conclusion to which our diverse data point is that governments grow where groups which share a common interest in that growth *and* can perceive and articulate that interest become more numerous. The view that sharp differences are (should be?) an important source of government-sponsored redistribution seems to carry less weight. Our results do detect a stimulative role of inequality but only where the population is least capable of articulating support for more government spending.[80] As this capability increases, homogeneous interests become a more important source of government growth. Our results imply that the *leveling* of income differences across a large part of the population—the growth of the "middle class"—has in fact been a major source of the growth of government in the developed world over the last fifty years. On our interpretation, this leveling process, which has characterized almost every economically developed society in the latter stages of industrialization, created the necessary conditions for growth of government: a broadening of the political base that stood to gain from redistribution generally and thus provided a fertile source of political support for expansion of specific programs. At the same time, these groups became more able to perceive and articulate that interest (as measured by, for example, educational attainment). On our interpretation, this simultaneous growth of "ability" served to catalyze politically the spreading economic interest in redistribution.

The counterintuitive result that, on balance, more equality breeds a

79. If one carries out the extrapolation above, keeping the levels of "democracy" and "freedom" at the LDC sample mean, the predicted size of government is on the order of 5 percentage points less than on line (4).

80. In both the U.S. state and LDC data, the net effect of more inequality on the size of government is positive only at below average levels of ability.

political demand for still more income equalization runs through virtually all our data and proves capable of rationalizing a wide variety of experience—for example, why Britain's government declined in the early nineteenth century and grew in the twentieth, why Sweden's government has grown faster than ours, why the developed world has larger and more rapidly growing government sectors than the underdeveloped. The role we assert for "ability" as a catalyst for equality-induced growth also has a broad base of support, and the concept appears to comprehend attributes of both the political system and its constituency. We were able to see the catalyzing process at work in Japan, when it became a democracy, in the U.S. states with above average levels of education, and in less developed countries that were both more democratic and had better-educated populations than is typical of that group. It is, in fact, the enormous diversity of experience that the ability-equality nexus proves capable of rationalizing, rather than any single result, that provides the main empirical message of this paper. This common process seems capable of rationalizing a substantial part of the differences among and between constituencies as diverse as local school boards, European welfare states, and traditional agricultural societies.

A caveat is in order, lest my conclusion be read as implying that all or even most members of groups which contribute support to growth of government have benefited from that growth. The "bourgeoisification" of Western societies widened the political base from which support for expansion of government could be drawn. But the particular programs that expand will, at least in each instance, benefit a subgroup. It is at least arguable, and compatible with "rational ignorance" in politics, that the net result is for a minority of the population to receive large per capita net benefits at the expense of the majority. Our one result relevant to this issue—that large voter turnout retards the growth of government—tends to support this view.

If the foregoing analysis is correct, it points to a future somewhat different from the recent past. In developed countries, the leveling process in the labor market has been far more gradual in the last quarter century than the preceding. At the same time, the scope for increased educational attainment of their population, at least in the United States (and Canada, Australia, and—to some extent—Britain) has narrowed. A high school education has become the norm, and the waves of the unschooled immigrants who produced the high school and college graduates of a subsequent generation have long since crested. If the twin forces of increased equality and increased education are indeed petering out, our analysis implies that the pressure for further growth of government is likely to abate in the developed world. It would be imprudent to try to be precise about this prediction, especially in light of our evidence that these forces can take considerable time to work themselves out and of our lack of success in pinning down just how long it is before they are spent. Nevertheless, it would be fair to infer from the evidence here that the next quarter century will witness a perceptible, perhaps substantial, deceleration of the relative growth of government in the developed world. If anything, this ought to be more profound in the United States than in Continental Europe, where there still may be some scope for the spread of education. The one exception is Japan, where the emergence of a broad middle class as a concomitant of a mature industrial economy seems to be a comparatively recent phenomenon, and where, in consequence, we are led to predict a narrowing in the gap between the size of its government sector and that of the Western democracies. With less confidence, we can also predict a narrowing of differences between the developed and less developed worlds.

The larger message of this paper is that there is nothing inevitable or inexorable about the growth of government, nor is there some arbitrarily limiting ratio of government to GNP.[81] Instead, our argument is that the size of government responds to the articulated interests of those who stand to gain or lose from politicization of the allocation of resources. The balance of those interests can make for declining governments, as they appear to have done in the last century, as well as for the growth we have experienced more recently.

81. Not even 100 per cent. Government transfers, for example, can be taxed, retransferred, retaxed, and so on, so that the annual government budget can be a multiple of GNP. In fact, this ratio exceeds 1 in Israel currently.

Current Developments in the Economics of Regulation

The economics of regulation seems to have arrived at a crossroads. Activity in the field is burgeoning and threatening to burst the boundaries established by theoretical insights that just yesterday seemed adequate to guide research for some time. My task here will be to step back and try to set some of the new work in a longer perspective, a perspective which I think indicates that we ought to be cautious about what to expect from it.

I find it useful, like so many who are charged with summarizing the work of academic conferences, to proceed taxonomically. So, I will organize my remarks around three principles that I believe are suggested by the history of the economics of regulation. The first of these is that the theory seems to move in waves, in the sense that once-respected theoretical insights seem easily superseded by new ones. This partly reflects the muddled state of the field, where normative and positive issues tend to get indiscriminately run together and a common theoretical bond is lacking. The first identifiable wave, which held center stage up to about 1960, is sometimes called the "public-interest" view. It can be found in one form or another in the seminal work of Hotelling (1938) and in generations of text books on public utilities. The focus is on market failure, typically of the natural monopoly variety, as the stimulus for regulation. While the public-interest view of regulation as guardian against monopolistic inefficiency always viewed itself as more proscriptive than descriptive, it did claim some practical insights. Surely a finding that, for example, electric rates were not held down by regulation would represent a loss of innocence.

When the work initiated by Stigler and Friedland (1962) began revealing that regulation did not work as the public-interest view held that it should or did, the way was prepared for a new generalization: the cartel

This article was prepared for a 1977 conference on public regulation sponsored by the National Bureau of Economic Research. The conference papers, including this article, were published in Gary Fromm, ed., *Studies in Public Regulation* (Cambridge: MIT Press, 1981), 371–384. Reprinted by permission.

or "capture" view of regulation, whereby compact interest groups, usually of producers rather than consumers, were held to dominate regulatory decisionmaking. The public-interest view became more clearly a normative paradigm. Its underlying welfare economics remained a valid way of organizing discussion about what regulators ought to be doing, but any belief that regulators often did what they should was now severely tempered. For about a decade the capture model provided a major framework for the positive analysis of regulatory behavior. This work is not yet complete, as evidenced by Leone and Jackson's intriguing attempt to bring out the rent-generating elements for producers in pollution-control regulation (a form of regulation that appears, on its surface, to cut against the producer's interest). Nevertheless, the simple, straightforward view of regulation as a cartel enforcement device now is coming under serious question. Perhaps this is due partly to the lavish growth of forms of regulation that, like pollution control, seem to require much excavation before any cartelizing element emerges. More likely, it is due to a growing recognition that very substantial rent-dissipating elements (such as the perpetuation of excess capacity in railroads, which Levin's article documents so well) were an integral part, and not merely a sideshow, of regulatory activity in areas where the producer-protection model seemed most fruitful (for example, transportation).

While it may be premature to call it a new wave, this conference seems to confirm what is at least a new ripple. For want of a better term, I will call it "creeping realism" ("creeping" both because it is not a radical break with either the public-interest or producer-interest models and because, as I will argue, its analytical structure is so unevenly balanced that walking straight will be difficult). What it seems to me the creeping-realism literature is trying to do is to integrate some of the newer economics of political decision making with some of the elements of the older normative economics of regulation. The older welfare economics is invoked to rationalize one or another form of regulatory intervention, but the resulting real-world institution then must bend to the realities of politics. And politics means coalition building and logrolling, so that nothing so simple as a "public" interest or a "producer" interest is going to predominate.

It is best to let a more precise characterization of this literature emerge from a few examples provided by this conference. The article of Leone and Jackson is a good starting point. Somewhere in freshman or sophomore economics the normative rationale for pollution control is typically spelled out, and then later our charges are told that the way regulators actually do things leaves much to be desired. Leone and Jackson see more here than a confused attempt to control pollution. If this were the whole story, we should see congressmen from districts with large paper mills (an industry with large pollution-control costs) opposing increased restrictions. They do not. Why not? Possibly they are implicitly bought off by the design of the regulation, the very design that seems laden with inefficiency to the conventional analyst. Leone and Jackson then find empirical support for this possibility. In effect, the regulators levy a higher implicit tax on new entrants than on established mills. With just a little growth in demand, the net effect of the regulation is to generate nontrivial rents for established mills. Thus, a potentially antagonistic and powerful interest is brought within the coalition served by the regulators. Of course, potential entrants are hurt, but you will not find the Association of Potential New Entrants listed in the Washington telephone directory.

Sometimes creeping realism means a partial revival of a public-interest, or at least a non-producer-interest, view. For example, minimum capital requirements have long been recognized as a potential restriction of entry. Munch and Smallwood and their discussants focus on the possible benefits of such requirements for consumers of insurance, who might otherwise be left stranded in a bankruptcy. In effect, the minimum capital requirement substitutes for the high costs facing the untutored consumer in evaluating the financial capacity of the insurer.

The last example I want to cite is the article of Willig and Bailey. Their wholly normative paper breaks with the venerable tradition of separating allocative from distributive issues. They want to guide a regulator who wishes to set prices that take simultaneous account of efficiency and income distribution norms. What about the old story that redistribution is better done by explicit money transfers than by the Public Service Commission? Willig and Bailey are silent on this. Though I am persuaded by Gary Becker's (1976) argument that the old story is wrong, I suspect that Willig and Bailey's silence is deliberate. For all our past hand-wringing about how messy it is, regulators persist in allowing distributive considerations to intrude on, and even dominate, their pricemaking. Even the pure theorist, Willig and Bailey seem to be saying, had better adjust to this reality.

The approach of Willig and Bailey illustrates my second principle of the economics of regulation, which is that practice leads theory. The full-blown development of the welfare economics of natural monopoly lagged the growth of electricity and telephone regulation. The capture models lagged the most notable empirical counterparts—ICC regulation of trucking, organization of the Civil Aeronautics Board, oil import quotas, and so on. The creeping-realism literature seems to be lagging two events, one practical and the other intellectual. The practical antecedent seems to be the growth of the whole panoply of safety, environmental, and consumer-information regulation, whose very existence or whose practice has often proved difficult to rationalize theoretically. The intellectual precursor seems to be the perceived difficulties with earlier models about which one or another theory did seem to have a lot to say. For example, if, as the capture model holds, the ICC is in business to organize a trucking cartel and enforce rate-making collusion among the railroads, why does it harm both captors by perpetuating excess railroad capacity?

Of course, intellectual and real-world developments are related here. The newer forms of regulation, such as consumer protection and pollution control, began their great growth at about the same time the capture model was making its biggest splash in academia. However, the Second Principle was at work, and most students of regulation did not rush to apply the capture model to the new regulations. Instead, they seemed willing, for a time, to try to understand the new regulations within the framework of the older public-interest model. When it became clear that the newer agencies were no more dedicated to Pareto optimality than their ancestors, the first reaction in the literature (still the dominant one) was to tell the new regulators to mend their ways. Kneese's 1971 work on the potential gains from effluent fees comes immediately to mind. The next reaction was more analytical. Much of what I have called creeping realism seems to be focusing on the new regulation. It seems to say that if the public-interest model doesn't explain how the new regulation works and if the capture model has been found wanting in explaining important aspects of the behavior of those agencies to which it seems most applicable, we now have all the more reason to develop a new synthesis.

However, we ought to embrace any new model of regulation with some caution. Implicit in much of what I have so far said is, perhaps, another principle of the economics of regulation: that the currently fashionable theory is usually wrong, or at least misleading. This conference provided more examples of this Third Principle than I have already touched upon. For example, none of the literature spawned by Stigler and Friedland argued very strenuously against the notion that natural-monopoly problems were an initial impetus to regulation of utilities. The story seemed to be that once the clamor for regulation had been heeded, the industry was able to assert itself in the mundane activity of the new agencies. However, Jarrell (1978) argued that the facts are more compatible with the view that industry interest was present at the creation of these agencies as well. The article of Fuss and Waverman, though working from a much different perspective, also ends up questioning the natural-monopoly rationale for telecommunications regulation. The elaboration of the producer interest in pollution regulation by Leone and Jackson serves to update this story.

As I have pointed out, the producer-protection model has met its own share of skepticism, both at this conference and elsewhere. Levin's article adds new insights into work begun by Keeler (1974), Friedlaender (1971), and others. But, these have a common theme. The ICC's attempt to preserve excess capacity in railroading is an integral part of its history, and not some aberration of a cartel manager manque. It constitutes a huge tax on the wealth of railroad owners for the benefit of a few shippers. Moreover, Keeler pointed out that U.S. railroads are not alone in facing such a tax. Similarly, Munch and Smallwood's discussion of the potential benefits to at least some consumers of capital requirements was echoed at the conference in discussions of similar benefits from more explicit entry control, like licensing. Occupational licensure may have been the first form of regulation to which economists applied the producer-protection model. Adam Smith deserves paternity here, as in much else. His descendants, like Friedman and Kuznets and Kessel, gave the model considerable empirical content. However, the realist challenge intrudes here too. The potential empirical importance of a consumer interest in shaping licensing regulation was debated at the conference and is the subject of ongoing work by Holen, Leffler, and Gaston and Carroll. It is, however, too early to tell whether this work will end up confirming my Third Principle, which is that the predominant licensing-as-cartel model is wrong.

However, if that principle has any validity, I believe that its lesson may be especially important for the new realist literature, as well as for some of the more institutionally innocent work that seeks new applications for market-failure models. The realist literature seems to be organizing around the following pattern: Select an area where producer protection has seemed important (for example, licensing, minimum price, or entry regulation); then show that there is a potential market failure that makes it credible for a coalition of producers and consumers, not merely the producers alone, to seek regulation. Or, reverse the pattern: Select an area, such as pollution, where market failure had seemed the most compelling force for regulation; then show how regulation of the market failure can be structured to serve a producer interest at the same time, and thereby enhance the political survival value of the regulatory institutions. This is an interesting research strategy that, I believe, deserves encouragement. Indeed, I have argued elsewhere (1976 [chap. 6]) that diversification of the interest groups served by a regulatory agency, rather than specialization, ought to be the common pattern.

There appears to be a dangerous asymmetry in the way this research is carried out: One part of the model (the cartel element) gets serious analytical treatment, while the other (market failure) is hardly developed beyond the point of vague possibility. Needless to say, the danger of this asymmetry increases with the emphasis placed on market failure as the source of regulation.

I can best elaborate on this sweeping claim by making another: Conjuring up rationales for regulation is too easy a sport; perhaps it deserves a Pigovian tax. On a few minutes' notice, any competent economist could apply an externalities model to fashions in clothing, a natural-monopoly model to stereo equipment (after all, don't they advertise amplifiers powerful enough to drive all the speakers on your block?), or a producer-protection model to laws against heroin. The only reason for taking some applications more seriously than others is our sense of their empirical importance. This, I would argue, is precisely what led us ten or fifteen years ago to take producer protection seriously as an important element in regulatory behavior. From the beginning the focus of that literature was on the importance of the measurable features of that phenomenon, not simply on the legal possibilities embedded in, say, the Civil Aeronautics Act or the Interstate Commerce Acts; so the literature developed by estimating the number of firms excluded from one or another market (for example, Jordan's work [1970] on airlines), the size of rents to existing firms (Friedman and Kuznets [1954] on the AMA), the gap between competitive and regulated prices (Keeler [1972] on the CAB). The range of sophistication in this literature is, to be sure, very wide, but most of it seemed to point in the same direction of pinning down the empirical magnitudes. And the increased technical virtuosity seems to have resulted in better or more credible estimates of the size of the regulatory effects. Perhaps the air-transportation literature, starting from Keyes's (1952) work, best illustrates these points. By now any new entrant to any part of the capture literature is conditioned to worry not only about the potential or directional effect of regulation, but about its size. Note, for example, the procedure of Leone and Jackson. After stating the rather novel possibility that the EPA is creating positive rather than negative producer rents, they immediately give a crude estimate of magnitudes (capital gains of $200 million versus losses of about 1 percent of this). Had the numbers been reversed, I doubt that the theoretical possibility would be given much attention.

This degree of concern for empirical relevance does not, however, seem to carry over to our treatment of market-failure issues. To be sure, some of the relevant issues have received analytically sophisticated treatment attentive to empirical importance. A case in point is the treatment of scale economies in two of the articles presented here. Levin's on railroad costs makes precise the nature of economies of scale in this industry, and then proceeds to measure the magnitude of the costs of excess capacity resulting from restrictions on exit when there are traffic-density economies. The compelling result is not the theoretical possibility of suppressed density economies, but their very large magnitude. Similarly, the main motive to Fuss and Waverman's work seems to be concern with the extent of scale economies in telecommunications; that is, with how the economies can be measured in the multiproduct-firm, and how big the economies are. Again, the interesting result is the sense of empirical proportions conveyed by the work—the suggestion that scale economies may not be so extensive as heretofore believed. Both these articles add to previous work. Examples that come to mind are Keeler's (1972) and Friedlaender's (1971) work on railroad costs, in the case of Levin, and Christensen and Greene's (1976) work on electric utilities, in the case of Fuss and Waverman. However, even in the economies-of-scale literature no one will accuse us of great haste in this search for empirical relevance. Public utility commissions were being created for almost a century before this empirical literature became established, textbooks were written about their operation, and Hotelling made it evident in the title that his classic article on optimal pricing applied to railroad and utility rates. This whole enterprise was based on a presumed but undemonstrated belief in the importance of scale economies in particular activities.

Much of the current discussion of newly fashionable market failures seems to be at a similar stage of development. To be sure, vague beliefs are now enshrined in jargon and clothed in formal models which give them the correct ritual flavor and exclude the uninitiated. Perhaps a card-carrying member of the profession should not oppose this too loudly or even be entirely cynical about it. There is, after all, a gain in precision in talking about failure of information and insurance markets instead of about the cheated consumer. My worry is that the professional discussion here does not seem to be leading toward the next question: How important are the problems being discussed? Here, I would refer the reader back to Noll and Joskow's summary of the literature on health, safety, and performance standards. They review a welter of possible problems with unregulated markets that have cropped up in this literature, and a modest number

of attempts to evaluate the effects of regulation. But they are as struck as
I am by the lack of work on the empirical importance of the theoretical
problems. At this stage in the development of economics, one would have
hoped that the empirical question would be given priority. It does, after
all, matter for how seriously we want to pursue the theoretical enterprise
whether 1 percent or 50 percent of the sales of some product generated
negative consumer surplus, just as it ought to have mattered to the early
public-utility economists whether the output elasticity of total costs was
0.95 or 0.25. Nor do I mean to imply by this lapse into jargon that the
theoretical enterprise has to be held captive to a sophisticated technology
of data production and analysis. Precise point estimates are not required
for getting at gross magnitudes. But, at least in the safety-health literature,
we have not begun to find out if the theoretical problems we explore are
worth talking about.

The literature on environmental externalities also falls into the "newly
fashionable" category, and the situation here is a little better than in safety
and health. The work by Lave and Seskin (1970) on health effects of pollution and that of Ridker (1967) and Crocker (1971) on land values is a start
at defining the scope of the problem. But, again, compare the attention to
this basic part of the problem with that given to theoretical problems
which implicitly assume that there is a substantial problem. I refer here to
the literature cited by Noll and Joskow on such matters as optimal control
mechanisms for pollution and the attendant general equilibrium consequences. Similarly, the bulk of applied research on pollution control tends
to avoid the issue of how important pollution externalities are, choosing
instead to focus on such matters as the costs of various abatement policies.
If someone today asserted that any substantial reduction in pollution
would have trivial benefits, or that the resources spent in the name of
pollution control had trivial effects on pollution, there would be no substantial concrete basis for laughing him out of court. Given this state of
affairs, we may be seriously compromising our knowledge about pollution
regulation. For all we know, this regulation may be only the disguised form
of entry control Leone and Jackson describe, or a WPA project for the
suppliers of control equipment, or something else that would call for a
fundamentally different analytical framework than we have so far brought
to bear on pollution regulation.

My point here is not to propose radically alternative models, since that
would implicitly decide the crucial empirical issues. Instead, I am suggesting that, before we push our normative models into the newer areas
of regulation or try to marry the normative models with economic analy-

ses of politics, we not rush past an essential question: Are the welfare problems we are invoking trivial or sizable? We may well conclude that there is more reason to spend analytical energy on the externalities of automobile pollution than, say, those of automobile colors, in much the same way that we were able to conclude that there were at least some interesting scale-economy problems in regulated utilities. However, the justification for taking this sort of risk is much weaker today than it was fifty or one hundred years ago, when the tools of empirical analysis were far less developed.

I do not want to minimize the difficulties inherent in assessing the magnitude of the problems on which we focus our analysis. One need only read the discussion surrounding the Fuss-Waverman paper to see that there are still many difficulties to the measuring of scale economics. The corresponding measurement problems in the newer areas of regulation are going to be even more formidable, because we will not typically have something like balance sheets and income-expense accounts to start from. However, the biggest challenge, I suspect, will be to our imagination and flexibility in using analytical tools that we already have. If this is right, then I am more optimistic than Noll and Joskow, at least about the potential for success.

To be more concrete, let me give a couple of examples of how we might frame questions that could get us closer to discovering the size of some of the problems I have mentioned.

- Are consumers behaving in a way consistent with the story that a big problem exists? For at least some goods there will be some objective measure of performance: accident frequencies of cars, failure propensities of insurers, injury frequencies of various occupations. Given these (or, more precisely, the relevant exogenous components), we can ask whether the good products or jobs sell at a premium to the bad and by how much relative to an independent estimate of the extra costs of the bad product. We will have an interesting problem if this premium is small, or if the good products do not drive out the bad.

- Does the political process act as if the problem is large or small? By now we are sufficiently wary not to take at face value the nominal intent of regulation. Nor can we easily interpret departures from this intent. Thus, suppose we found that, long after the establishment of a well-financed and amply empowered Consumer Protection Agency, as many consumers were being cheated or maimed as before. This could mean that the cheating and maiming was so small as to be practically irreducible. It could also mean that the title of the agency was hiding its objectives. If we found a large physical reduction in consumer fraud or injury, we would still have to evaluate its economic significance.

No study of the political process or the markets it regulates can escape such interpretive problems. Still, I believe we can gain something by looking for consistencies or regularities in political behavior, because the political process should not be expected to be indifferent to dead-weight losses in unregulated markets. These may be tolerated or even encouraged because they help "buy" another objective, but no rational model of political behavior would hold the dead-weight losses to be a good in and of themselves. Thus, if the dead-weight losses are large enough and inherent in unregulated markets, we ought to expect a consistent political response.

To uncover this consistency, I believe that the economics of regulation will have to give up some of its provincial focus on American institutions. The simple fact that many jurisdictions seem to persist in leaving large parts of transportation unregulated is telling (if crude) evidence that unregulated markets do not systematically generate large dead-weight losses. This is not to say that if regulation were ubiquitous the converse would be demonstrated. It could be that the forces making for regulation in the United States are so universally powerful that they can always overcome dead-weight losses of their own making. However, ubiquitous regulation would, I think, force us to take more seriously than otherwise the potential problems with unregulated transportation markets raised by advocates of regulation. My suggestion is that international comparisons of regulatory institutions can be a useful check or a crude screening device for selecting problems that may be worth pursuing. For example, we will take the possibility of market failure in electricity and telecommunications more seriously if every important country intervenes in these markets with seemingly appropriate institutions; we will be more skeptical if there is the same variety as in transportation. In view of the potential payoff to a modest analytical effort, there seems to me to be considerable scope for pursuing international institutional comparisons. If I am right, this strategy can also have obviously valuable spinoffs—for example, comparisons of the effects of apparently similar institutions.

These examples are more illustrations of a point than an agenda. The point is that deficiencies of data or analytical technique are not great enough to justify our neglect of the crucial empirical issues which have so far been ignored in analyses of the newer regulatory institutions. If this is so, perhaps we ought to impose that Pigovian tax on further proliferation of normative models or on their incipient marriage to the economics of politics until we begin redressing this neglect.

Such a reallocation of effort is not, of course, a substitute for a generally useful theory of regulatory behavior. It is entirely possible that when that theory is written it will so restructure our analysis of the regulatory process that the welfare problems that now tend to hold center stage will be pushed off to the side. We might, in hindsight, regret the time spent in worrying about their size. However, even though such a theory does not yet exist, research on specific forms of regulation has to look for some theoretical grounding. This is now being done by extending traditional normative models to the newer forms of regulation and by implicitly inserting specific allocative outcomes into the relevant objective function of regulators. Meanwhile, a good deal of the theoretical work on regulation has a similar motivation.

The promise of these analyses, either in enhancing our current understanding of regulation or in leading to a richer theory, rests on the importance of the problems around which they are organized. This is why I believe it is especially timely to divert some analytical energy to discovering the importance of these problems.

The increasing scope and spread of regulation and its impact on academic research make it almost obligatory for me to discuss policy issues. While my primary purpose in criticizing some of the focus of current research is to point out the unmet intellectual challenge, there are also related policy issues. At least some of the recent research seems to want to breach the wall between allocative and distributive issues that has stood so long in academic discussions of regulatory issues. The reasons for this are debatable, but, whatever their source, the infirmities of "make price equal marginal cost and send a check to the losers" advice are heeded at several points in these articles. Willig and Bailey discard this paradigm at the formal level, since their model starts with a marriage of allocative and distributive objectives as a given for the regulator. If one thing is clear from the discussion of excess capacity in railroads, it is the practical failure of our traditional advice. Finally, one of the motives to the marriage of the economics of regulation and the economics of politics is recognition of the practical link between economics and politics in regulatory policy.

The inference I choose to draw from the practical failure and the perhaps impending intellectual disintegration of the traditional policy advice of regulatory economists is that policy advice is not our strong point. An earlier generation of economists, with fewer policy problems tempting them, might have told us to stick to organizing the facts of the world intelligibly and systematically. If we follow this advice well, our impact on policy may increase. Since the impact is so small now and since "Policy Implications" is likely to remain the traditional conclusion to papers on regulation, this is a fairly safe prediction. Here again we are forced to proceed on less firm theoretical ground than we would like. This means that one day we may find out that the very categories in which we communicate with policymakers have little relevance for them. However, for now, any economist who wants to do "policy-relevant" work is forced to run that risk. If costs and benefits of the type we usually focus on are relevant for policy, the policymakers will inevitably have to deal with their magnitudes. Here I believe, economists have started to develop a methodology that can substantially reduce these policy-information costs.

In many cases the policymaker will, at least crudely, "know the score" without our help. Bankruptcies of short-haul, low-density railroads will, for example, get part of Levin's message across. However, consider the position of a politician whose constituency is not directly affected by the problems of short-haul, low-density railroads. He or she may be reluctant to vote for subsidizing these railroads, but fearful that without a "yea" vote a massive disaster will befall a political ally from another district. For such a swing voter, the sort of information provided by Levin's work, which pins down the consequences of the existing policy, can be far more valuable than *a priori* arguments about the desirability of free entry and exit. The other side of this is that policymakers looking for the "facts" will have to rely heavily on economists in these matters. The sport we have developed of debunking purely technical attempts at getting the "facts" is symptomatic. No competitor has succeeded in challenging our ability to organize data around a consistent theoretical superstructure in matters relevant for social policy.

Perhaps a better example of the policy payoff of our giving empirical content to theoretical issues is the current state of airline regulation. Congressional acceptance of deregulation and increased implementation of the basic principles of competition by the CAB provide a rare example of political endorsement of the professional consensus. But the professional consensus, backed by *a priori* arguments about lack of scale economies in the business and perhaps a few casual observations about experience in deregulated markets, was achieved well before policy began changing. What I want to suggest is that it took the weight of a fairly extensive empirical literature, able to generalize from the experience of deregulated markets and make precise the range of effects to be expected from deregulation, before policy changed—or at least before politicians felt able to use the work of economists to press for a change in policy.

Let me quickly recognize some of the risks of generalizing from this correlation between the flowering of an empirical literature and a shift in policy:

- The number of "swing" legislators susceptible to academic evidence is probably unusually large in the particular case of airlines, since the industry interest is not great in many congressional districts.
- The literature here is unusually well developed. One thinks immediately of the work of Keyes (1952), Caves (1962), Jordan (1970), Eads (1975), Keeler (1972), Douglas and Miller (1974), and the CAB's own economics staff, and fears that the list is incomplete. The quantity is matched by quality, and this combination may well be unmatched in the literature on the economic effects of regulation.
- There is probably by now a professional consensus, backed by a growing empirical literature, that regulation of exit from railroading is very costly. However, there has been little change in policy.
- Policy has changed in the same direction as a professional consensus, which had no strong empirical base. I am thinking here of the deregulation of stock-brokerage commissions. My casual judgment is that most economists would have "voted" with the Securities and Exchange Commission on this in the belief that the industry was structurally competitive. However, even if this is so, the direct role of economists in the process was peripheral.

In view of all these crosscurrents, I am left less with any strong conclusions than with a tentative hypothesis: that the impact of economists on policy is indirect, and that the empirical support for their arguments weighs more heavily on policymakers than the arguments themselves. The justification for providing some future historian of ideas with more data with which to test this hypothesis is partly to make the sample more representative, but mainly because I think the choices are limited. The gap between theoretical possibility and empirical grounding has become so great in so much of regulatory economics that achieving a professional consensus, not to mention professional development, is going to compel us to look harder and harder at just how the world really works.

References

Becker, G. 1976. Comment. *Journal of Law and Economics* 19: 245–248.

Caves, R. 1962. *Air Transport and Its Regulations: An Industry Study.* Cambridge, Mass.: Harvard University Press.

Christensen, L., and Greene, W. 1976. "Economies of Scale in the U.S. Power Industry." *Journal of Political Economy* 84: 655–676.

Crocker, T. 1971. "Externalities, Property Rights and Transaction Costs." *Journal of Law and Economics* 14: 451–464.

Douglas, G., and Miller, J. 1974. *Economic Regulation of Domestic Air Transport.* Washington, D.C.: Brookings Institution.

Eads, G. 1975. "Competition in the Domestic Trunk Airline Industry: Too Much or Too Little?" In A. Phillips (ed.), *Promoting Competition in Regulated Markets.* Washington, D.C.: Brookings Institution.

Friedlaender, A. 1971. "The Social Costs of Railroad Regulation." *American Economic Review* (Papers and Proceedings) 61: 226–234.

Friedman, M., and Kuznets, S. 1954. *Income from Independent Professional Practice.* New York: National Bureau of Economic Research.

Fuss, M., and Waverman, L. 1981. "Regulation and the Multiproduct Firm: the Case of Telecommunications in Canada." In G. Fromm, (ed.), *Studies in Public Regulation.* Cambridge: MIT Press.

Gaston, R., and Carroll, S. 1981. "Occupational Licensing and the Quality of Service Received." *Southern Economic Journal.*

Holen, A. 1977. The Economics of Dental Licensing. Center for Naval Analyses. Washington, D.C. Mimeographed.

Hotelling, H. 1938. "The General Welfare in Relation to Problems of Taxation and Railway and Utility Rates." *Econometrica* 6: 242–269.

Jarrell, G. 1978. "The Demand for State Regulation of the Electric Utility Industry." *Journal of Law and Economics* 21: 269–296.

Jordan, W. 1970. *Airline Regulation in America: Effects and Imperfections.* Baltimore: Johns Hopkins University Press.

Joskow, P., and Noll, R. 1981. "Regulation in Theory and Practice: An Overview." In G. Fromm, (ed.), *Studies in Public Regulation,* Cambridge: MIT Press.

Keeler, T. 1972. "Airline Regulation and Market Performance." *Bell Journal of Economics and Management Science* 3: 399–423.

———. 1974. "Costs, Returns to Scale and Excess Capacity." *Review of Economics and Statistics* 56: 201–208.

Kessel, R. 1958. "Price Discrimination in Medicine." *Journal of Law and Economics* 1. 20–53.

Keyes, L. 1952. *Federal Control of Entry into Air Transportation.* Cambridge, Mass.: Harvard University Press.

Kneese, A. 1971. "Environmental Pollution Economics and Policy." *American Economic Review* (Papers and Proceedings) 61: 153–166.

Lave, L., and Seskin, E. 1970. "Air Pollution and Human Health." *Science* 169: 723–730.

Leffler, K. 1978. "Physician Licensure: Competition and Monopoly in American Medicine." *Journal of Law and Economics* 21: 165–186.

Leone, R., and Jackson, J. 1981. "The Political Economy of Federal Regulatory Activity: the Case of Water-Pollution Controls." In G. Fromm, (ed.), *Studies in Public Regulation.* Cambridge: MIT Press.

Levin, R. 1981. "Regulation, Barriers to Exit, and the Investment Behavior of Railroads." In G. Fromm, (ed.), *Studies in Public Regulation,* Cambridge: MIT Press.

Munch, P., and Smallwood, D. 1981. "The Theory of Solvency Regulation in the Property and Casualty Insurance Industry." In G. Fromm, (ed.), *Studies in Public Regulation*, Cambridge: MIT Press.

Peltzman, S. 1976. "Toward a More General Theory of Regulation." *Journal of Law and Economics* 19: 211–260 (chap. 6 of this volume).

Ridker, R. 1967. *Economic Costs of Air Pollution*. New York: Praeger.

Stigler, G., and Friedland, C. 1962. "What Can Regulators Regulate: The Case of Electricity." *Journal of Law and Economics* 5: 1–15.

Willig, R., and Bailey, E. 1981. "Income-Distribution Concerns in Regulatory Policy Making." In G. Fromm, (ed.), *Studies in Public Regulation*, Cambridge: MIT Press.

The Economic Theory of Regulation
after a Decade of Deregulation

What has come to be called the economic theory of regulation, or ET, began with an article by George Stigler in 1971.[1] The most important element of this theory is its integration of the analysis of political behavior with the larger body of economic analysis. Politicians, like the rest of us, are presumed to be self-interested maximizers. This means that interest groups can influence the outcome of the regulatory process by providing financial or other support to politicians or regulators.

Simultaneously with Stigler, Richard Posner provided an important critique, and several years later he gave the theory its grandiose name. The major theoretical development of the ET has been an article by Peltzman in 1976 and one by Gary Becker in 1983.[2] By conventional measures the theory has been an academic success. In this paper I evaluate that success in light of the changes in regulatory institutions that have occurred since the ET's early development.

The most notable changes have meant a reduction or substantial elimination of regulatory constraints whose scope is unprecedented in modern American history. The challenge posed by these changes for the ET seems obvious. One strand in the theory is that the producers' interest in restricting competition dominates the political system. But deregulation was sweeping aside many long-standing legal barriers to competition even as

First published in *Brookings Papers on Economic Activity: Microeconomics* (Washington, D.C.: Brookings Institution, 1989), 1–41. Reprinted by permission.

I am grateful to Gary Becker and George J. Stigler for their valuable comments. I am also grateful to the Center for the Study of the Economy and State, Graduate School of Business, University of Chicago, for financial support.

1. George J. Stigler, "The Theory of Economic Regulation," *Bell Journal of Economics and Management Science*, vol. 2 (Spring 1971), pp. 3–21.

2. Richard A. Posner, "Taxation by Regulation," *Bell Journal of Economics and Management Science*, vol. 2 (Spring 1971), pp. 22–50, and "Theories of Economic Regulation," ibid., vol. 5 (Autumn 1974), pp. 335–58; Sam Peltzman, "Toward a More General Theory of Regulation," *Journal of Law and Economics*, vol. 19 (August 1976), pp. 211–40 (chap. 6 of this volume); and Gary Becker, "A Theory of Competition among Pressure Groups for Political Influence," *Quarterly Journal of Economics*, vol. 98 (August 1983), pp. 371–400.

the ink was drying on the theory. Doesn't deregulation then decisively falsify the theory?

One easy answer would be that the deregulation movement was a special case—a one-shot response to the peculiar macroeconomic and political conditions of the late 1970s. That was a time of increased concern about inflation and of disillusion with the efficacy of government intervention generally. It was also a time when most of the ultimately successful legislative initiatives toward deregulation bore fruit. It is hard to treat the conjunction of the rightward shift in the political mood and deregulation as entirely coincidental. But it is also hard to push this, or any, special-purpose explanation too far.

This particular special-purpose explanation has factual problems. For example, the deregulation movement was selective. Many areas of regulation escaped essentially unscathed; others, such as the regulation of labor contracts and health care, even prospered. Because of this selectivity, the plausible role of deregulation in the fight against inflation is largely symbolic. No serious investigation could attribute to deregulation more than a microscopic effect on the overall inflation rate. Also, the timing of the political change is not quite right. The culmination of the rightward shift in American politics and of the inflationary spiral occurred in the same year (1980) that saw the end rather than the beginning of de jure deregulation.[3]

Ultimately, however, I eschew a special-purpose absolution of the ET on methodological grounds. The theory purports to be a general model of the forces affecting regulation; that is, it suggests the common elements underlying regulatory change. In evaluating the theory, one must weigh the importance of these common elements before considering what might be special about the 1970s.

Seen in this light, if the theory implied that every restriction of competition was permanent, one could easily dispose of the ET as a useful model for the deregulation movement. But that is, I will argue, too simple a characterization of the theory. One complication is that the theory does not speak with one voice on the subject of entry into and exit from regulation.

---

3. My focus here is on de jure deregulation—that is, the institutional changes which would require new legal initiatives to reverse. The plausible role of arguably exogenous or temporary political shifts would grow if the administration of basically unchanged legal institutions were part of the inquiry. Changes in administration and, consequently, administrators can change the regulatory "output" temporarily. It remains uncertain how many of Reagan's purely administrative initiatives, such as the reduced enforcement of the antitrust laws and of occupational health and safety laws, will survive the Bush administration. Evaluation of those initiatives is therefore premature.

Another is the lack of a satisfactory alternative theory. Not one economist in a hundred practicing in the early 1970s predicted the sweeping changes that were soon to happen. Most believed that, however desirable, events like the demise of the Civil Aeronautics Board (CAB) and the shriveling of the Interstate Commerce Commission (ICC) were unlikely to occur soon. This was hardly the first or last forecasting failure in economics, and the methodological pitfalls of evaluating theory by forecasting ability are well known. Nevertheless, the fact that deregulation was such a surprise partly reflects, I will argue, some general problems in the theory of regulatory entry and exit. I will also argue that no version of that theory, including the ET's, is sufficiently well developed to generate sharp predictions about where and when entry or exit will occur.

It is possible, nevertheless, to take advantage of the hindsight afforded by the experience of the past decade in order to evaluate the ET. Though the ET is not a full-blown theory of institutional change, it does suggest circumstances under which such change is more or less likely to occur. Accordingly, one may ask whether the circumstances surrounding the changes of the last decade are broadly consistent or inconsistent with those emphasized by the ET. This is the procedure I follow. To see the underlying motivation, consider entry and exit theory in the more familiar context of ordinary markets. The theory says distressingly little about the speed or timing of entry or exit. But one would recognize a serious shortcoming of the theory if, for example, it frequently took a long time for entry to respond to profits. And it would be hard to take the theory seriously at all if new firms usually entered in the wake of losses and exit followed profits. Here I will ask, in effect, if the ET's version of "losses" in the political market had any plausible connection to the deregulation that took place. Perhaps unsurprisingly, my overall answer is positive. But the exit-follows-profits phenomenon is not entirely absent.

In the first section of the paper I summarize the development of the ET and the historical background in which it occurred. I then discuss the shortcomings of the ET as a theory of entry. Finally, I review some of the important changes in regulation that occurred after the theory was developed and evaluate each of them against the relevant elements of the theory.

The Economic Theory in Historical Perspective

The ET made its debut in 1971 after a decade of unusual ferment in the economic analysis of regulation. Until the early 1960s the prevailing theory of regulation was what Joskow and Noll have called the "normative analysis as a positive theory" (or NPT).[4] This theory, which has been around in one form or another since Adam Smith, regarded market failure as the motivating reason for the entry of regulation. Once established, regulatory bodies were supposed to lessen or eliminate the inefficiencies engendered by the market failure. The ingenuity of economists ensures that the list of potential sources of market failure will never be complete. But in the early 1960s the most popular culprit was natural monopoly followed at a distance by externalities.

The main problem with the NPT was that until the 1960s it was not systematically tested. To be sure, some economists had expressed dissatisfaction with its predictions in such industries as truck and air transportation where the natural-monopoly rationale for entry and rate regulation did not seem readily applicable.[5] But these were exceptions to a general belief that most regulatory activity was compressing the gap between price and marginal cost that would otherwise exist. Perhaps the first formal test of that belief was, appropriately enough, Stigler and Friedland's analysis in 1962 of the effects of regulation of electricity rates.[6] At the time, nothing seemed more settled in the economics of regulation than the presumptive effects of such regulation. Surely restricting entry and imposing maximum rates in this quintessence of a natural monopoly would make rates lower than otherwise. The authors concluded, however, that regulation had not resulted in lower electricity rates.

The importance of the Stigler-Friedland article lies less in this particular result than in its catalytic role. It stimulated an ongoing empirical literature on the effects of regulation. The seeds of the ET were planted by the pattern of results emerging from the first decade of that literature.

That pattern was uncongenial to the NPT. Indeed, it suggested a synthesis that was the exact opposite of the NPT. In 1972 William Jordan provided a good summary of this new synthesis, sometimes called the capture theory of regulation, or CT.[7] After surveying the extant literature on the effects of regulation, he concluded that Stigler and Friedland's finding of ineffective regulation did not hold for all forms of regulation. But the

4. Paul L. Joskow and Roger G. Noll, "Regulation in Theory and Practice: An Overview," in Gary Fromm, ed., *Studies in Public Regulation* (MIT Press, 1981), pp. 1–65.

5. See, for example, John R. Meyer and others, *The Economics of Competition in the Transportation Industries* (Harvard University Press, 1959); and Richard E. Caves, *Air Transport and Its Regulators: An Industry Study* (Harvard University Press, 1962).

6. George J. Stigler and Claire Friedland, "What Can Regulators Regulate? The Case of Electricity," *Journal of Law and Economics,* vol. 5 (October 1962), pp. 1–16.

7. William A. Jordan, "Producer Protection, Prior Market Structure and the Effects of Government Regulation," *Journal of Law and Economics,* vol. 15 (April 1972), pp. 151–76.

available examples in which regulation did affect prices shared striking similarities. All were found in naturally competitive or nonmonopolistic industries like surface and air transportation, and in all these instances the effects of regulation were to raise prices and reduce the number of competitors. By contrast, regulation did not change prices in natural monopoly industries, where, Jordan argued, the NPT led us to expect that regulation would have suppressed monopoly power. Thus the correct generalization seemed to be the CT—that regulation served the producer interest either by creating cartels where they would otherwise not exist or by failing to suppress monopoly.

Stigler

The capture theory was not new by the early 1970s. Well-known versions had appeared earlier.[8] What was new was its broad appeal to economists based on the accumulating evidence of empirical research within their discipline. However, this new version of the CT shared a conceptual problem with the NPT. Both were empirical generalizations without a theoretical foundation. Neither had a ready answer to the question "why should regulation be expected to encourage or suppress monopoly?" Stigler's version of the ET sought to fill that theoretical lacuna.[9] The specific conclusions Stigler reached bear the imprint of the then accumulating evidence in favor of some form of the CT. Indeed, his article comes across as an effort to rationalize those results. And Stigler had important predecessors. The notion that ordinary voters are "rationally ignorant," which is associated with Anthony Downs, and the free-rider obstacle to collective action, which appears in Olson, are prominent features of Stigler's theory.[10] But as with the Stigler-Friedland article, the lasting significance of Stigler's 1971 article is less in its specific conclusions or elements than in the question it poses—the why of regulatory behavior—and in the structure of its answer.

As mentioned earlier, in Stigler's formulation political actors are presumed to be self-interested maximizers. Just what is in their objective function is not completely spelled out, but surely it includes securing and maintaining political power. For clarity and simplicity, Stigler ignores both the

8. For example, Marver H. Bernstein, *Regulating Business by Independent Commission* (Princeton University Press, 1955).

9. "Theory of Economic Regulation."

10. Anthony Downs, *An Economic Theory of Democracy* (Harper & Row, 1957); and Mancur Olson, *The Logic of Collective Action: Public Goods and the Theory of Groups* (Harvard University Press, 1965).

fact that regulators are usually agents of an executive or legislature rather than agents of voters and the many problems of stability and existence of equilibrium in political modeling. He assumes that regulators do the bidding of a representative politician who has the ultimate power to set prices, the number of firms, and so on.[11]

Stigler's next step is to specify the concrete objects of choice in this politician's utility function. These come down to two—votes and money. That is, one consequence of a regulatory decision is that members of groups affected by the decision will be moved to vote for or against the representative politician. Because his ultimate goal is securing and enhancing his power, the politician prefers decisions that directly elicit favorable votes. Regulatory decisions can also elicit campaign contributions, contributions of time to get-out-the-vote, occasional bribes, or well-paid jobs in the political afterlife. Because the more well-financed and well-staffed campaigns tend to be the more successful and because a self-interested politician also values wealth, he will pay attention to these resource (money) consequences of regulatory decision as well as to the direct electoral consequences. Accordingly, groups that may themselves be too small to offer many votes directly in support of a regulatory policy can nevertheless affect that policy by delivering other valuable resources. This notion is another durable feature of the ET literature.

Another durable aspect of Stigler's contribution is his emphasis, already implicit in the preceding, on the distributional aspects of regulatory decisions. Self-interested politicians and constituents exchange objects of utility—a price or entry certificate for votes and money—and what matters to each actor is their wealth or utility, not the aggregate social wealth. Aggregate welfare does matter, in the sense that slices of a pie tend to be larger if the pie is larger. But Stigler's criticism of the NPT is simply that aggregate welfare as such is not what a politician plausibly maximizes.

The results of any analysis of utility-maximizing behavior usually hinge more critically on its specification of the constraint than on the objective

---

11. In a recent attempt to extend the ET by filling in some of the missing institutional structure, Weingast and Moran argue that, at the federal level, congressional oversight committees are the crucial intermediary between the regulatory agency on the one hand and the congressmen and their constituents on the other. They show that policy changes by the Federal Trade Commission were related to changes in the policy preferences of the oversight committee. This evidence, according to the authors, is inconsistent with the view that agencies are essentially unconstrained by legislatures and thus can pursue their own policy agenda. Barry R. Weingast and Mark J. Moran, "Bureaucratic Discretion or Congressional Control? Regulatory Policymaking by the Federal Trade Commission," *Journal of Political Economy*, vol. 91 (October 1983), pp. 765–800.

function. This is true for Stigler. Though he makes no formal analysis of a constrained maximization problem, one clearly emerges from the discussion. If regulators bestow benefits in exchange for votes and money, the latter must be delivered. (Whether this is done before or after a regulatory decision is one of those suppressed details of the machinery of politics.) Because the benefits typically accrue to groups rather than individuals, the technology for delivery entails group organization. Stigler's results follow more or less directly from his specification of this technology.

Stigler emphasizes two related kinds of costs that constrain a group's ability to deliver votes and money: information and organization costs. Groups must organize to lobby and to deliver campaign contributions, and their members must know enough to vote "right" on election day. Because knowledge and organization consume resources, low-cost groups tend to be favored at the expense of high-cost groups. And more important, if, as is typical in regulatory issues, the relevant groups are of widely different size, the numerically larger group will tend to be the loser. To see why, consider a decision on how high or low a price should be set or on how many firms should be allowed in. In the relevant range, having more firms and lower prices benefits buyers and harms sellers. Though Stigler alludes to complexities, such as the potentially disparate interests of subgroups, the main issue is whether the buyers or the sellers win a more-or-less fixed prize. Since the number of buyers is usually manyfold greater than the number of sellers, the buyers will probably face prohibitively high costs of organization. The number of collections required and the incentives to free riding will ensure this. Moreover, because each buyer's stake in the outcome is trivial compared with that of the typical seller, it is unlikely that all buyers will know enough to reciprocate any benefits (or punish costs) at the polls unless considerable resources are spent on educating them. The larger per capita stakes yield a saving of information costs to the smaller group (consider the odds that a typical taxpayer knows more about the National Science Foundation's budget than a typical economist), and their smaller numbers make for lower organization cost. Thus the main conclusion of Stigler's analysis is that the producer interest will win the bidding for the services of a regulatory agency. More generally, in any similar political contest between groups of disparate size, the compact organized interest (say, farmers in a developed economy) will usually win at the expense of the diffuse group (taxpayers).

The general framework developed by Stigler, with its emphasis on self-interested political behavior and the importance of organization and information costs, became a hallmark of the subsequent ET literature. But it quickly became apparent that the generalization that regulation served the producer interest had moved too far from the NPT. Indeed, in the same issue of the *Bell Journal* in which Stigler's article appeared, his colleague Richard Posner demonstrated some of the infirmities of the CT as empirical generalization.[12] He did so by emphasizing the phenomenon of "internal subsidization" (sometimes called cross-subsidization), the enforced provision of service to selected consumer groups at especially low, often below-cost, prices. Those consumers are "subsidized" out of potential producer rents generated elsewhere in the regulated industry. Posner's argument was that cross subsidies are so pervasive and important that no fig-leaf modification of the CT can cover them. Consider just one of many examples offered by Posner: the pre-Amtrak perpetuation of railroad passenger service by the ICC. In CT revisionism, the ICC's raison d'être is to cartelize surface transportation. But how can such devotion to the producer interest be reconciled with the preservation of money-losing passenger service? The simple answer, repeated for many other examples, is that it cannot. The losses were too great and the efforts of the railroads to escape them were too strenuous for any CT explanation to be plausible.

Posner's discussion of cross subsidies illustrates a more general point. Viewed from afar, a particular type of regulation often seems to fit the CT or NPT mold. But a closer look usually uncovers too many exceptions for this dichotomy to be plausible. Consider, for example, areas of regulation like antitrust or health-safety-environmental regulation. If these had been put to the vote in a two-theory election, most economists would have voted for the NPT even after the ascendancy of the CT. But when economists analyze these modes of regulation more closely, they turn up at least as many exceptions to the NPT as confirmations and even a healthy dose of CT-like results.[13]

Peltzman

The notion that no single economic interest captures a regulatory body plays a prominent role in the 1976 article by Peltzman.[14] He derives an equilibrium in which the utility-maximizing politician allocates benefits

---

12. "Taxation by Regulation."

13. Most economists, for example, favor increased use of taxes and tradable pollution rights in environmental regulation and regard the reluctance of the regulators to adopt these techniques as an exception to the NPT. The history of antitrust is replete with restrictions— on price discrimination, vertical mergers, resale price maintenance, and so on whose anticompetitive potential was first recognized by economists and more recently by judges and the enforcement agencies.

14. "Toward a More General Theory of Regulation" (chap. 6).

across groups optimally—that is, in accord with the usual *marginal* conditions. Thus as long as some consumers can offer some votes or money for a small departure from the cartel equilibrium, pure producer protection will not, in general, be the dominant political strategy. Two factors work against such a solution. First, the organization and information costs emphasized by Stigler make it unlikely that the producers will withdraw all their support for the regulatory system for a small reduction in cartel rents. Second, those rents need not be spread to all consumers. Subgroups can organize (or be organized by the regulator) with the appropriate characteristics for efficiently reciprocating a regulatory benefit. Considerations like these led Peltzman to a general characterization of the politician's problem that is distinctly familiar to economists. Economic benefits to any group are reciprocated according to a technology of diminishing returns with the usual continuity properties. As a result, politicians normally hire the services of all groups. A similar general statement applies within groups. Given the usual constraints on discrimination, regulators will allocate benefits across consumer and producer groups so that total political utility is maximized.

This result—that all groups will share in the rents at the regulators' disposal—is as essentially empty as any similar result of constrained maximization analysis. It is the analytical equivalent of results such as "consumers buy food as well as clothing" or "firms hire capital as well as labor." And like these results, Peltzman's gives no guidance on expenditure shares, that is, whether the producers, the consumers, or neither group typically gets the lion's share of the rents. The interesting results in Peltzman come, as is usual in constrained maximization problems, from the comparative static analysis of the constraints on the utility function rather than from any worry over the detail of what is in that function.

In that formulation, the regulator wants to make everyone (with any marginal political weight) as happy as possible, but he is constrained by the demand and cost functions of the regulated industry. Peltzman then investigates the effect of changes in (or different types of) demand and cost conditions on the nature of the resulting equilibrium. Though some of the results are standard CT, or second-best welfare-economics fare (such as less elastic demand or supply functions imply higher prices), two predictions deserve special mention. They are the tendency toward systematic, cost-based cross subsidization and the tendency for regulation to offset the effect of market forces on the division of rents between producers and consumers.

A simple example helps illustrate these results. Suppose a regulated firm, X, sells to two customers, A and B. Suppose further that A and B have equal demands and equal political weight (that is, their utility enters the regulator's utility function in the same way), but that the marginal cost (MC) is higher for serving A than for serving B. Now recall the general result that X will not get maximum profits; for simplicity call this "tax" on maximum profits, T, and assume it is fixed. Since X cares only about the size of T, not its distribution among A and B, and since A and B are politically equal, the regulator has only one remaining task: to make the price (P) to A and B (P_A and P_B), and thereby A's and B's consumer surplus, as nearly equal as possible, given T. The result will be a lower P_A/MC_A than P_B/MC_B. If T is big enough to permit it, the regulator will completely ignore the fact that $MC_A \neq MC_B$ and set $P_A = P_B$. While there are the inevitable complications and ambiguities, this tendency for the high-cost customer to get the low P/MC is common. It rests on the lack of any general connection between the cost differences and the political importance of the two buyers. And it is a result that does not obtain in CT or NPT regulation or unregulated markets.

The regulator-as-buffer result can be illustrated by a cost or demand change that would leave prices unchanged in the absence of regulation— say a change in fixed cost. This change would, however, alter the distribution of rents between sellers and buyers. Since the regulator is seeking to maintain a politically optimum distribution, he will change prices to offset the distributional effect of the cost or demand change. Thus an increase in fixed cost does not come entirely out of X's hide, as in standard monopoly analysis; it gets translated into higher P_A and P_B to recover some of X's lost rents. Later I give examples of both results—the cost-based cross subsidization and the regulator as buffer—in the discussion of specific cases of regulatory change.

Becker

Results like these come from a view of regulation in which industry wealth (producer and consumer rents) is the prime political currency to be disposed of in ways that best suit the regulator. This view provides a link between the ET, with its emphasis on redistribution, and the NPT, with its emphasis on efficiency. That link has been most extensively developed by Gary Becker, first in his comment on Peltzman's paper and then in his 1983 article.[15] His setup is similar to Peltzman's: groups organize to exert

15. Gary Becker, "Comment," *Journal of Law and Economics,* vol. 19 (August 1976), pp. 245–48, and "Theory of Competition among Pressure Groups."

pressure on the political process to grant them benefits or exempt them from paying for others' benefits. And the equilibrium represents a balancing of marginal pressure exerted by winners and losers. Becker's central argument is that in a setup like this deadweight losses are a constraint on inefficient regulatory policies. The reason is simple: as the regulator moves output away from the efficient level, the deadweight loss increases at an increasing rate. (The marginal deadweight loss is the difference between the heights of the demand and the supply function, which gets bigger the further quantity is pushed from the efficient level.) Deadweight loss is nothing more than the winner's gain less the loser's loss from the regulation-induced change in output. These gains and losses are what motivate the competing pressures on the political process. So rising marginal deadweight loss must progressively enfeeble the winners relative to the losers. The pressure the winners can exert for each extra dollar's gain must overcome steadily rising pressure from the losers to escape the escalating losses.

Becker's formulation produces a political equilibrium with some deadweight loss. It does, however, suggest a bias against the unbounded deadweight losses implicit in the CT. Among the concrete manifestations of this bias is what Becker calls the "tyranny of the status quo." Most structurally competitive industries, for example, are not subject to price or entry regulation, even though the producers have Stiglerian organization and information cost advantages. But rising marginal deadweight loss can offset the producers' other advantages unless the demand and supply functions are sufficiently inelastic to attenuate it. The other side of this avoidance of inefficiency is a search for greater efficiency. Becker argues that the political process will be drawn toward efficient modes of redistribution in general and to efficiency-enhancing regulation in particular. The reason is simply that neither winners nor losers would rationally oppose changes that eliminated some deadweight loss. This is an important point for at least two reasons.

First, economists have a well-honed instinct for separating allocational from distributive issues. So there appears to be an obviously more "efficient" way of accomplishing the redistribution that the ET ascribes to regulation: why not directly pay off the winners without messing up a nice $P = MC$ equilibrium? In a world of competing pressure groups, however, no redistributive mechanism, not even the proverbial lump-sum tax, is without its deadweight cost. Payers and payees will incur costs to generate pressure and to alter their behavior so as to maximize the benefits or minimize the costs meted out by the political process. Given this situation, it is no longer obvious that all the costs associated with tax-transfer redistribution will be smaller than the costs of comparable redistribution through regulation. In fact, if regulatory redistribution survives, the presumption must be that it is the less costly mode. Otherwise both winners and losers would press for a change.

Second, market failure, the standby of the NPT, creates incentives for regulation. If regulation can reduce the resulting inefficiency, there will be more wealth available for distribution. This extra wealth can induce greater pressure for regulation from winners and can attenuate the opposition of losers. In contrast to the NPT, the ET says that the regulation will not maximize the extra wealth, because buyers and sellers are not in general equally well organized politically. But faced with a portfolio of potential areas to regulate, the political process will tend to be attracted to industries where it can increase wealth as well as to those where deadweight losses are small.

Summary of ET Findings

A useful way to summarize the foregoing discussion is to list some of the important characteristics of regulation that emerge from the literature on the economic theory of regulation.

- Compact, well-organized groups will tend to benefit more from regulation than broad, diffuse groups. This probably creates a bias in favor of producer groups, because they are usually well organized relative to all consumers. But the dominant coalition usually also includes subsets of consumers.
- Regulatory policy will seek to preserve a politically optimal distribution of rents across this coalition. Thus, over time, the policy will tend to offset changes in this optimal distribution arising from shifts in demand or cost conditions. At any one time, the price structure will cross-subsidize high-cost consumers from rents generated by prices to other groups.
- Because the political payoff to regulation arises from distributing wealth, the regulatory process is sensitive to deadweight losses. Policies that reduce the total wealth available for distribution will be avoided, because, other things being equal, they reduce the political payoff from regulation.

The Academic Effect of the ET

While some of these features of the ET literature have received more attention than others, the literature as a whole has made its mark on academic

TABLE 9.1 Number of Citations to Selected Articles, 1972–86

	Economic Theory of Regulation Articles[a]			Other Articles[b]	
Year	Stigler	Peltzman	Becker	Coase	Averch and Johnson
1972	16[c]	...	...	61	21
1973	7	...	...	59	22
1974	18	...	...	58	20
1975	17	...	...	81	27
1976	27	...	...	66	30
1977	16	6[c]	...	53	30
1978	29	11	...	56	19
1979	28	19	...	74	32
1980	48	33	...	90	25
1981	42	43	...	84	14
1982	53	46	...	102	28
1983	60	34	...	100	29
1984	67	48	12[c]	86	21
1985	79	62	23	88	13
1986	77	70	31	93	26
Annual average					
1972–86	38.9	36.0	22.0	76.7	23.8
1980–86	60.9	46.3	22.0	91.9	22.3

Source: *Social Science Citation Index.*
   a. George J. Stigler, "The Theory of Economic Regulation," *Bell Journal of Economics and Management Science,* vol. 2 (Spring 1971), pp. 3–21; Sam Peltzman, "Toward a More General Theory of Regulation," *Journal of Law and Economics,* vol. 19 (August 1976), pp. 211–40 (chap. 6 of this volume); and Gary Becker, "A Theory of Competition among Pressure Groups for Political Influence," *Quarterly Journal of Economics,* vol. 98 (August 1983), pp. 371–400.
   b. Ronald H. Coase, "The Problem of Social Cost," *Journal of Law and Economics,* vol. 3 (October 1960), pp. 1–44; and Harvey Averch and Leland L. Johnson, "The Behavior of the Firm under Regulatory Constraint," *American Economic Review,* vol. 52 (December 1962), pp. 105–69.
   c. Includes previous (publication) year.

analyses of regulation. Table 9.1 summarizes one measure of this impact, the number of citations to the three articles I have just summarized. To put this number in perspective, I have included citation counts for two recognized classics in the same general area—Coase's 1960 article on social cost and Averch and Johnson's 1962 article on rate-of-return regulation. By now all three ET articles have passed Averch-Johnson in the citation derby. The two mature ET articles—Stigler and Peltzman—have run considerably ahead of Averch-Johnson and below Coase in recent years.

Stigler has been getting about two-thirds and Peltzman about one-half the citations accruing to Coase. Moreover, interest in this literature seems to be growing. Note the jump in the Stigler and Peltzman citations from 1980 on and the rapid growth in the Becker citations since publication. Becker's article is getting about twice the citations of its two predecessors at a comparable post-publication stage. Though citation counts are an obviously crude index, the data suggest that academics have been treating the ET as an important piece of intellectual capital that is not yet fully depreciated.

I leave an assessment of the reasons for this impact to others. Here I evaluate whether this academic success is somehow justified in light of recent real-world developments. Many of these involve deregulation—that is, exit from regulation. Exit is the logical and chronological successor to entry. So, before discussing the ET's success in coping with exit, I evaluate its utility as a theory of entry into regulation. I argue that as entry theories both the ET and its competitor, the NPT, have specific weaknesses that affect their ability to cope with deregulation.

ENTRY IN THE THEORY OF REGULATION

Most of the development of the ET concerns the behavior of established regulatory bodies: whom they will favor and how and why their policies will change. But the question of why the body was established in the first place cannot be ignored. The ET's answer to that question is about what one would expect from a maximizing theory of institutional behavior: politicians seek politically rewarding fields to regulate and avoid or exit from the losers. The difficulty with the ET as an entry theory is precisely that it never gets much beyond this level of generality.

Consider Stigler's version. In some absolute sense, the lopsided advantages that producers have over consumers are essentially universal. This fact suggests that regulation which generates rents for producers should also be universal. To the non-Marxist, or anyone concerned with making distinctions, such a formulation obviously says too much. Accordingly, Stigler implicitly imposes a budget constraint on the entry problem. To find the prime candidates for regulation, he looks for industries where the producers' advantage is unusually large. Operationally this means searching for a link between the probability that an industry is regulated and variables like the geographic concentration of sellers which are proxies for organization or information cost advantages of producers. Stigler has only limited success with this strategy, nor has it led to a literature with much stronger results. Given the lack of explicit attention to constraints on entry, one leaves Stigler's model with the nagging question of why minimum rate or entry regulation of structurally competitive industries is comparatively rare.[16]

Peltzman's version is hardly an improvement. Given its emphasis on the optimal allocation of wealth among potentially conflicting interests, almost anything that makes the wealth pool "large" or its allocation politically nonoptimal should induce regulatory entry. Thus *both* naturally competitive and naturally monopolistic industries ought to attract regulation (they are at a "corner" and hence farthest from the optimal rent distribution). Growth in demand, technological progress, inelastic supply and demand curves (all of which generate large or growing wealth), and unexpected disturbances in supply and demand (which upset the optimal wealth distribution) are all mentioned as conducive to regulation. This list is still reasonably compact, but it is unclear that the extra variables buy much more explanatory power. That is, Peltzman's model, like Stigler's, seems incapable of explaining why substantial and continual regulation of important structural or behavioral characteristics seems concentrated in a few industries.

In this respect, Becker's article marks an advance. In its full generality—efficiency in producing pressure for regulation generates regulation—Becker's formulation shares the infirmities of its two predecessors. But the specific emphasis on economic efficiency leads Becker to emphasize correction of market failure as an important motive for regulation. If market failure is comparatively rare, Becker's version of the ET gives some insight into the pattern of regulation. Consider a political decision on whether industries $A_1, A_2, \ldots, A_n$ or B should be regulated, where the A_i are all structurally competitive and B is ridden with market failure. The proregulation pressure group in each of the A_i is handicapped by the regulation-induced deadweight losses, and the group in B is helped by the potential efficiency gains. If regulation is not universal, B would, all else the same, end up as the only regulated industry.

Read this way, the ET comes close to merging with the NPT's entry story—entry occurs only to correct market failure. Shouldn't we then just invoke Occam's razor and prefer the NPT? The answer, given our present state of knowledge, is a resounding maybe. If there is an empirical basis for

---

16. There are, of course, modes of intervention other than rate or entry regulation that, in principle, are within the purview of the ET. Such measures as tariffs, taxes, subsidies, and product standards have distributive implications that generate incentive for political pressure. On the broadest view, therefore, every industry is "regulated" to some degree. This view, however, still begs a question about magnitudes: a handful of structurally competitive industries seem singled out for unusually large departures from competitive equilibrium.

the NPT's continuing attraction for economists, it is probably its apparent success as an entry theory. Consider Hotelling's classic statement in 1938 of the natural monopoly version of the NPT.[17] In this purely theoretical piece, railroads and utilities are presumed, without much evidence, to be the main real-world examples of natural monopoly. They also occupied most of the regulatory (including public ownership) effort when Hotelling wrote. This correspondence between the NPT and the real-world allocation of regulatory effort seems striking. Now consider the postwar expansion of regulation. In terms of the resources involved, the biggest single chunk is probably accounted for by environmental regulation, where the externalities aspect of the NPT scores another success. As for much of the impossible-to-catalogue remainder—health, safety, old-age security, and so on—the NPT becomes frayed at the edges. To be sure, a good economist needs no more than fifteen minutes' notice to produce a market failure to "explain" any of these interventions. But credulity is strained when the list of market failures grows at roughly the same rate as the number of regulatory agencies. And even in Hotelling's time the regulation of trucks and airlines, agriculture, labor markets, and many professions was already taxing the NPT's explanatory power. In sum, if the ET overpredicts the incidence of regulation, the NPT underpredicts it. If a case exists for favoring the NPT as a general entry model, it would be that underpredicting a comparatively rare phenomenon produces a smaller average error than overpredicting it.

REGULATORY CHANGE IN THEORY AND PRACTICE

The topography of American regulation has changed considerably in the last two decades. Some types of regulation have grown or consolidated their position: regulation of the environment, product and workplace safety, the medical industry (such as prices and entry of hospitals), the disclosure of financial information, the operation of financial institutions (such as the de facto nationalization of distressed banks and savings and loan associations), and labor contracts (especially race and sex pay differentials). The avidity with which particular administrations pursue these areas may vary, but the strength of the governing institutions has grown or remained unchallenged. Here I focus on a historically more interesting change: the substantial reduction or elimination of the regulation of entry/exit or rates, or both, in a number of industries. These comprise surface

17. Harold Hotelling, "The General Welfare in Relation to Problems of Taxation and of Railway and Utility Rates," *Econometrica*, vol. 6 (July 1938), pp. 242–69.

and air transportation, long-distance telecommunications, securities brokerage, and bank deposits. In one important case—oil—maximum price regulation came and went within a decade. For nearly a century it had appeared that each new peacetime regulatory initiative was essentially permanent. That historical pattern was now decisively broken.

These deregulation initiatives are particularly interesting to economists. Had they been put to a vote of the American Economic Association membership, all the initiatives would have passed with large majorities. Probably not since the rise of free trade in the nineteenth century has so broad a professional consensus been so well reflected in policy. The reason for this consensus is economists' belief that deregulation enhances efficiency. This naturally raises a question about the current status of the NPT. Has it been resuscitated because of deregulation? Though the full answer requires evaluation of the alternative ET, deregulation hardly seems like a striking confirmation of the NPT. The main reason has to do with timing. The P, or positive, part of the NPT implies two reasons for deregulation: (1) technological or demand changes eliminate the market failure, or (2) regulation is revealed to have been a mistake by the light of the N, or normative, part of the theory. Most of the examples of deregulation would fit into the second category. The difficulty for the NPT is that these were recognizable as mistakes long before deregulation corrected them. The most obvious problems for the NPT are those cases not discussed here, because deregulation has not yet occurred. For example, the continued licensing of a myriad of professions, such as barbers and beauticians, looks like a continued mistake by the light of the theory. Of the cases I discuss, at least two, ceilings on bank deposit rates and minimum brokerage rates, were normative mistakes from the start, about forty years before deregulation. In transportation, the normative argument for truck regulation had also been dubious from the beginning (1935). As for rail and air transport, the normative case for at least some easing of regulatory constraints on competition goes back at least to the early 1960s. When the exit required by the theory takes twenty or forty years or has yet to occur, the theory can hardly be deemed powerful. Among the cases I discuss, the only one where deregulation seems to have followed reasonably promptly after the normative basis of the regulation became obsolete is long-distance telecommunications.

The relevant question is whether the ET looks any better than the NPT from today's vantage point. My overall answer is that it does, though the ET has its share of failures and unanswered questions. I should point out that the same question and roughly the same answer can be found in an article by Theodore Keeler.[18] His analysis is more narrowly focused on transportation than mine, and it is couched in terms of a synthesis between the NPT and ET. So, though I place more emphasis on the differences between the two theories than he does, there is inevitable overlap. I begin this evaluation of the ET by first summarizing what the theory says about deregulation. Then in the following sections I proceed case by case to summarize the "facts" surrounding deregulation and show how these facts are or are not consistent with the ET explanation of deregulation. I then try to draw general conclusions about the state of the political economy of deregulation.

My discussion of the entry model implicit in the ET points to two general sources of pressure for deregulation: changes in the "politics" and changes in the "economics" of the regulated industries. Political change includes such things as shifts in the relative political power of contending groups and changes in the underlying organization and information technologies. Anything that, for example, made it cheaper to organize or inform the broad mass of consumers about the adverse consequences of regulation in a structurally competitive industry would increase the political payoff to deregulation. Here I ignore these political factors, partly because economists have so far had limited success in pinning them down, but mainly because the more familiar terrain of the economic factors is sufficiently fertile. In the Peltzman and Becker versions of the ET, two kinds of economic change are conducive to deregulation: (1) the gap between the regulated equilibrium and the one plausibly characterizing deregulation of the industry narrows, so continued regulation becomes pointless, or (2) the wealth available for redistribution becomes too small to provide the requisite political payoff to regulation.[19] These two forces can be related. For example, a lower demand for the regulated industry's product may bring the regulated price closer to marginal cost, and it will

18. Theodore E. Keeler, "Theories of Regulation and the Deregulation Movement," *Public Choice*, vol. 44, no. 1 (1984), pp. 103–45.

19. The first type of change—convergence of the regulated and deregulated equilibriums—would also produce deregulation in the NPT. The difference between the two theories rests on how the convergence occurs and where the regulatory equilibrium is. In the NPT, convergence would occur because the source of market failure is removed by a change in technological or demand conditions. Then the market could be relied on to prevent a wedge between price and marginal cost. Since the ET equilibrium entails a *regulated* wedge between price and marginal cost, convergence occurs because the wedge that optimally allocates available rents differs trivially from the unregulated wedge.

lower the potential producer rents from regulation. However, I argue that the second force—decreases in available wealth—is empirically more important.

To see how a reduction in available wealth can lead to deregulation, consider the simple case of a constant-cost industry that experiences increased input prices. That reduces the available sum of producer and consumer surplus. In Peltzman's analysis the first-order regulatory response is to distribute the loss across producers and consumers with a price increase less than the cost increase. But this reduces the producer rents that must pay the organizational and information costs that politically support regulation. If the cost increase is large enough, the producer rents may no longer be sufficient to generate the requisite political support for continued regulation.[20] In Becker's framework the loss of rents reduces the pressure for continued regulation of this industry relative to other industries, and the higher price increases the counterpressure from consumers. Suppose further that the cost increase has in fact been induced by regulation. Then the deadweight losses emphasized by Becker become especially important. There is now not only attenuated support for continued regulation but also the potential for major gains in political utility from deregulation. These would come from the elimination of the cost increase attributable to regulation. For a structurally competitive industry, the lower costs would translate into higher producer and consumer surplus in the short run and higher consumer surplus in the long run, thus raising the possibility that the coalition pushing for deregulation would include some producers.

Railroads

Since the railroad industry was already mature and arguably overbuilt when the Interstate Commerce Act of 1887 was passed, the important features of regulation are control of rates and exit from the industry. The industry technology exhibits increasing returns to density and length of haul, which is also important in understanding the regulatory history.

The regulatory system that was to govern the industry until the late 1970s not fully developed until the Transportation Act of 1920. That act, as implemented by the Interstate Commerce Commission, had the following results:

- A rate structure characterized by cross-subsidies to the high-cost,

20. The producers will continue to support regulation, because it promises some rents. But if the rents are too small to finance *politically effective* support, the political process will seek greener pastures. Producer requests for a free or even cheap lunch will not be honored.

light-density, and short-haul shippers from long-haul shippers on high-density routes. As nonrail passenger modes developed and rail passenger densities fell, the cross-subsidy was extended to rail passenger service.

- Commodity-based price discrimination was superimposed on this rate structure. Goods with a high value per ton and presumably less-elastic demands for freight (because transportation costs represented a smaller share of final product cost) tended to have the higher rates. Railroads could also collude on rate proposals.

- Exit control. Abandonment of freight and passenger service required ICC approval, and the ICC acted to slow the process—even to the point of discouraging applications—more than the industry would have liked.

This structure is not, of course, wholly consistent with the earliest version of the ET, which mainly emphasized the producer interest. That interest is recognizable here only in the value-of-service rate structure (supplemented by collective ratemaking). But the basic structure of railroad regulation provides a good illustration of what is central to later versions of the ET—the spreading of rents to nonproducer groups. Producers got something—protection from competition and (at least temporarily) profitable price discrimination. Then these gains were partly shared with other groups through cross-subsidies. Because these cross-subsidies would otherwise induce exit from the industry, implementation of the scheme required restrictions on exit.

However, if this structure represented an equilibrium balance of forces in 1920, that equilibrium came under pressure almost immediately. Unregulated nonrail alternatives became increasingly viable as the highway and inland waterway networks spread. Trucks, in particular, began drawing some of the railroads' high-value, high-rate, primarily manufactured goods traffic. The resulting erosion of the rents that funded the political equilibrium was, of course, greatly exacerbated by the Great Depression. The first line of political defense was to bring the trucks under the regulatory tent in 1935.

The Motor Carrier Act of 1935 established minimum rate and entry controls on common-carrier trucks. If the first effect of this was to slow the erosion of railroad rents, subsequent developments rendered the regulatory system a mixed blessing for the railroads. The system now had two producer interests to contend with, and the trucking interest was soon to be aided by the unionization of the vast majority of common-carrier truck drivers. Though the contribution of regulation is debatable, the fact is that the shift of traffic, particularly the high-margin manufactured goods, from rails to trucks continued over the ensuing decades. The corresponding shift in the political weights of the two ICC constituencies gradually weakened the railroads' stake in continued regulation. Empirically, their best response to the declining demand conditions they faced would have been exit.[21] But maintenance of excess capacity was necessary to preserve the politically optimal system of cross-subsidies. So, here, continued regulation could only hurt the railroads. Another margin of response to declining demand was price reductions. These sometimes elicited political opposition from the motor carriers, and this opposition now had to be paid heed. Thus important elements of the regulatory system undermined the railroads' battle to preserve their eroding rents.

Those rents would have been eroding without regulation, given the decline in demand and the long-lived, specialized nature of railroad capital. The plausible effect of regulation was to alter the time profile of the declining rents in a way that ultimately undercut the basis for the regulation. The elements of producer protection—the value-of-service rate structure, the constraints on intramodal competition—worked to make the initial level of the rents higher than otherwise. But the wealth-spreading elements, manifested by the slowing of exit in the face of declining demand, and the need to serve the increasingly important producer interests of other modes, speeded the rate of decline of the rents. Over time the second effect came to predominate, so that the net effects of regulation on rail owners became unfavorable.[22]

In retrospect, the turn of the political tide toward deregulation can be traced to a spate of railroad bankruptcies in the early 1970s. The bankrupt roads were located in the Northeast, which bore heavily the cross-subsidy to short-haul and passenger traffic, and in the upper Midwest, where the cross-subsidy to light-density traffic was important. These bankruptcies were a signal that the rents required to support the system created in 1920 were no longer available. The first political response was to nationalize the

21. Richard C. Levin, "Regulation, Barriers to Exit, and the Investment Behavior of Railroads," in Fromm, ed., *Studies in Public Regulation,* pp. 181–224.

22. Levin provided one measure of the magnitude of the unfavorable effect. He estimated that unrestricted abandonment would increase 1975 railroad profits by $1.4 billion. This was about one-tenth of industry revenues at the time, or roughly the same fraction of revenue as *total* industry profits in the best postwar years. He also estimated that, even with these added profits, the industry's rate of return on assets would be less than 9 percent, a figure that is still plausibly lower than the (deregulated) industry's cost of capital. Thus, even after the response to unrestricted abandonment is complete, continued secular decline in the industry's capital stock can be expected. Ibid., p. 192.

cross-subsidies through Conrail and Amtrak. Given the railroads' continued secular decline, the choice facing Congress and the railroads was now clear: further nationalization or deregulation of exit and rates. The railroads chose deregulation and they essentially got it by 1980.[23]

This brief history fits the ET's deregulation scenario very well. The rents supporting the political equilibrium eroded, partly because of the incentives created by the value-of-service rate structure and partly because of the enforced provision of below-cost service. Support for the regulation eroded along with the rent. The organized producer interest ultimately favored and got deregulation. And the deregulation occurred not long after the economic and political forces turned decisively against regulation.

A major unanswered question in this story—which I return to but do not answer in my discussion of air transport—concerns labor rents. As an organized producer interest, it is plausible that unionized railroad workers shared in any rents generated by regulation.[24] The magnitude of these rents and the degree, if any, to which they were eroded before or after deregulation remains uncertain. This uncertainty should not, however, obscure the basic message provided by the industry's financial difficulties: the old coalition of producers and consumers was no longer sustainable under the established regulatory framework.

Trucking

If rail deregulation is a victory for the ET, truck deregulation is a resounding defeat. In generating producer rents, trucking regulation was a signal and long-lasting success. Comparing wages of unionized workers in trucking with the wages of nonunionized trucking employees, Thomas Moore estimated a wage premium due to regulation exceeding 30 percent and showed that the premium was growing over time. From the analysis of transactions in operating rights, he was able to estimate that the total value of operating rights represented rents roughly equal to those of workers. Using more sophisticated statistical techniques than Moore, Nancy

---

23. This came in two stages, the Railroad Revitalization and Regulatory Reform (4R) Act of 1976 and the Staggers Rail Act of 1980. These eased constraints on mergers and abandonments and provided a wide band (a variable-cost) floor and (1.8 × variable cost) ceiling within which individual railroads could set rates to all but "captive" shippers without regulatory review. The net effect is to allow much more room for the railroads to abandon money-losing traffic and to compete with trucks and barges.

24. See Theodore E. Keeler, *Railroads, Freight, and Public Policy* (Washington, D.C.: Brookings, 1983).

Rose basically confirmed the magnitude of the regulation-induced wage premium.[25]

Where would the ET have us look for sources of pressure for regulatory change in this industry? The answers would include the following.

- Growing labor rents. These may have been symptomatic of a drift away from the political equilibrium. The cost of that drift would include the accelerating deadweight losses emphasized by Becker.
- Dissipation of owner rents. The operating rights were not output quotas. On multifirm routes the minimum price regulation gave each firm an incentive to expand its market share, which led to cost-increasing service rivalry. Also, the entry control led to circuitous routing: a firm denied permission to enter the A-B market could get in if it bought an A-C and a C-B operating right, but then it had to move the freight through C. (Since these cost-increasing elements of the regulation raised the demand for labor, they would not be inconsistent with growing labor rents.)
- Deregulation of the railroads. This had the potential for lowering the present value of rents in trucking by more than the corresponding gain in total railroad surplus. The difference would be due to the inefficient traffic allocation engendered by rail deregulation when truck prices remained regulated: that is, rails could draw traffic when their marginal cost exceeded the truck cost by less than the regulated price-cost markup in trucking.

None of these possibilities can save the ET here. The reason is empirical rather than logical.

- The growing rents would suggest perhaps some easing of entry control to restore equilibrium. Instead, the regulatory rents have been entirely eliminated. The still-required operating rights are worthless, and according to Rose's estimate, the labor rent has vanished.
- According to Moore's comparison of the price effects of regulation with the observed rents, no more than one-fourth of the potential industry rent was being dissipated by such things as service rivalry and route circuity. And even if that estimate is not exactly right, the dissipation had to be far from complete, since operating rights of substantial value became worthless overnight because of deregulation.

25. Thomas Gale Moore, "The Beneficiaries of Trucking Regulation," *Journal of Law and Economics*, vol. 21 (October 1978), pp. 327–44; and Nancy L. Rose, "Labor Rent Sharing and Regulation: Evidence from the Trucking Industry," *Journal of Political Economy*, vol. 95 (December 1987), pp. 1146–78.

- The importance of rail regulation as a source of rent for the regulated truckers has long been debated. And the excess capacity maintained by rail regulation worked to reduce rents in trucking. All this aside, however, there is a crude test that shows why rail deregulation cannot have been an important reason for truck deregulation. If it had been important, the trucking industry would have split politically. Those owners and Teamster locals facing especially close rail competition would at least have supported rate deregulation once rail deregulation was in the wind. That did not happen. The opposition of the American Trucking Association and the Teamsters to deregulation seems to have been monolithic and vigorous to the bitter end (too vigorous in the case of the president of the Teamsters, who was jailed for attempted bribery of the chairman of the Senate committee considering the deregulation bill).

Here then is an industry in which substantial and sustainable rents received the fullest measure of organized support from the beneficiaries. There is simply no way I know of to square the wholesale elimination of these rents by political action with any current version of the ET.

Airlines

The formal structure of airline regulation was essentially identical to that of trucking. Minimum rate and entry controls were combined with wide latitude for concerted industry action. But in terms of generating producer rents, airline regulation did not work as well as trucking regulation, and it worked conspicuously less well in the period just before deregulation. Table 9.2 provides some background. It shows the industry's operating cash flow (operating profits plus depreciation) as a percentage of revenues. In the parlance of the empirical industrial organization literature, it is an estimate of the industry's price-cost margin. I use cash flow rather than, say, accounting profits to allow for the possibility that rents may have been hidden in depreciation charges.[26] Though any such accounting data are always to be treated gingerly, the story they tell is not fundamentally different from that found in more detailed analyses, such as those by Keeler, Douglas and Miller, and Jordan.[27]

26. The airlines had the usual tax incentives to overdepreciate. These were enhanced by the CAB's use of rate-of-return targets as part of its rate regulation procedures.

27. Theodore E. Keeler, "Airline Regulation and Market Performance," *Bell Journal of Economics and Management Science,* vol. 3 (Autumn 1972), pp. 399–424; George W. Douglas and James C. Miller III, *Economic Regulation of Domestic Air Transport: Theory and Policy* (Washington, D.C.: Brookings, 1974); and William A. Jordan, *Airline Regulation in America: Effects and Imperfections* (Baltimore: Johns Hopkins University Press, 1970).

TABLE 9.2 Airline Operating Cash Flow per Revenue Dollar, 1950–86[a]
Cents per Dollar

Period	Operating Cash Flow/Revenue[b]	Period	Operating Cash Flow/Revenue[b]
1950–54	23.2	1970–74	13.3
1955–59	18.2	1975–80	9.8
1960–64	14.9	1980–86	7.1
1965–69	17.7		

Sources: U.S. Bureau of the Census, *Historical Statistics of the United States: Colonial Times to 1970*, vol. 2 (Department of Commerce, 1975), p. 770; and *Statistical Abstract of the United States, 1976*, p. 612; *1986*, p. 616; and *1988*, p. 592.

a. Operating cash flow = operating profits (that is, before interest expenses and taxes) + depreciation.

b. Depreciation of ground assets is not reported before 1961. I estimated this at 4 percent of revenues for 1950–60, the difference between the reported 1960 and 1961 ratios of depreciation to revenues. Data are for domestic operations.

These authors did not have the benefit of hindsight. However, if one takes the 1980s' data as typifying an unregulated equilibrium, the evidence suggests that regulation was generating some producer rents—maybe 10 cents per dollar of revenues—until the late 1960s. Then a process of erosion set in lasting up to the dawn of deregulation in 1978. In fact, erosion of potential rents seems to have had a longer history. Keeler estimated that around 1970 the average ratio of price to "competitive marginal cost" was about 1.5 for thirty routes. That translates into a price-cost margin of 33 percent. Note that the figures in table 9.2, which make no allowance for capital costs, never approach that height. Why not, and why the decline in the decade preceding deregulation? The answer seems to lie in cost-increasing service rivalry induced by the structure of regulation. The industry's technology is characterized by economies (in terms of costs per quality-constant passenger mile) in distance and route density. The Civil Aeronautics Board fare structure imperfectly reflected the distance economy and ignored the density economy. Thus it contained elements of cost-based cross subsidization—from the low-cost, high-density long-haul markets to the low-density short-haul markets. But even many of the latter were potentially profitable.

Cost-increasing service rivalry, most notably from increased flight frequencies, had always been a source of rent erosion on nonmonopoly routes. It became increasingly important in the 1960s after the widespread introduction of jet-powered aircraft. This technology widened the scope for nonstop service in long-haul markets. The regulated fare structure made securing nonstop authority in such markets lucrative, especially in the high-density markets.

Throughout its history the CAB had assiduously resisted all pressure for entry by outsiders. But it was now faced with a shift in the distribution of wealth among its constituents that favored those with long-haul, nonstop authority. It responded in a manner consistent with Peltzman's wealth-spreading result. The poorer constituents were cut in on the lucrative routes. As a result, by the late 1960s most important routes were served by several carriers. Service rivalry thus grew more pervasive, so that wealth dissipation became the handmaiden of wealth spreading. One symptom of this phenomenon was the behavior of load factors. In the 1950–59 decade the average domestic load factor was 63 percent. In the next decade it was 53 percent. By the early 1970s (1970–73) this figure had fallen to 48 percent. By this time, it appeared that most of the industry rents had been dissipated by the quality competition.[28]

The CAB responded to these events with a celebrated domestic passenger fare investigation. This led to a number of administrative steps in the early 1970s, such as elimination of the distance cross subsidy, toward greater efficiency. In hindsight, these can be seen as the precursors of deregulation in 1978. As far as consistency with the ET is concerned, the story here was roughly the same as for the railroads, except that the dissipation of rents was more clearly related to the working of regulation. By the 1970s the regulation had rendered too many routes too competitive for minimum rates to generate the rents required to sustain support for regulation—a fact clearer in hindsight than it was when deregulation became live politically. Most of the industry opposed deregulation, but important fissures developed. For example, the largest airline (United), which had borne a heavy cost from the CAB's wealth-spreading policy on internal entry, supported deregulation.

As with railroads and trucks, an important question about the effect of regulation concerns labor rents. These played no important role in the academic literature on the subject.[29] But the air transport unions opposed deregulation, and deregulation has brought visible pressure on union wages. This casual evidence suggests that regulation may have been sustaining labor rents. Less casual, but very crude, evidence is not so clear. Table 9.3 shows the evolution of wages in the three transportation indus-

28. See, for example, Keeler, "Airline Regulation and Market Performance."
29. Keeler calculated his competitive marginal cost on the assumption that unregulated carriers would face the same labor costs as regulated firms. Ibid.

TABLE 9.3 Wages in Transportation Relative to Those in
Manufacturing, 1980, 1984

Industry	Relative Wage (1975 = 100)[a]		Percent Change, 1980–84
	1980	1984	
Railroads	109	116	6
Trucking	101	92	−9
Air transport	108	109	1

Source: Bureau of the Census, Statistical Abstract of the United States, 1986, pp. 412, 414, 620.
a. For railroads, trucking, and all manufacturing, the wage is average hourly earnings; for air transport it is the Air Transport Association labor cost index.

tries, relative to the average manufacturing wage, over the period spanning deregulation. From 1975 to 1980 wages in all three industries were rising at least as fast as wages elsewhere. But only in trucking was that tendency decisively broken in the early 1980s. In this respect, the crude data are consistent with what we already know from Rose's work about the demise of labor rents in trucking from deregulation. They are not consistent with a similarly pervasive erosion of labor rents due to deregulation of air and rail transport.[30]

Pending more systematic evidence on labor, it is best to be somewhat tentative about the details of the effects of airline regulation on producer rents. What can be said is that at least one side of the producer interest—the owners—had essentially lost their stake in continued regulation. And the deadweight losses of regulation had opened the possibility that they could now gain from deregulation.[31]

Long-Distance Telecommunications

Up to the 1960s intercity telephone service was provided by a regulated monopoly, AT&T, whose subsidiaries also provided most of the local service. The prevailing wisdom was that both types of service were natural monopolies, and though the regulatory authority was fragmented, both were regulated accordingly. The formal structure was maximum rate-of-

30. Card's analysis of airline mechanics' wages also finds little obvious impact of deregulation on this worker group. David Card, "The Impact of Deregulation on the Employment and Wages of Airline Mechanics," Industrial and Labor Relations Review, vol. 39 (July 1986), pp. 527–38.

31. That possibility appears to have been realized. According to Morrison and Winston, deregulation has produced gains of $2.5 billion a year for the owners. Steven Morrison and Clifford Winston, The Economic Effects of Airline Deregulation (Washington, D.C.: Brookings, 1986).

return regulation. Since local and long-distance service shared common facilities, any statement about cross subsidies is tenuous. But two kinds of cross subsidy seemed to emerge from the regulation. Long-distance rates subsidized local service, and long-haul, high-density intercity service subsidized thin short-haul service.[32] The latter is another example of cost-based cross subsidies, since the traditional long-distance technology is subject to substantial economies of density and distance. This rate structure combined with new technology to undermine the regulation.

Microwave technology developed rapidly after World War II. Unlike in the traditional technology, there are no important density economies in microwave technology. In addition, microwave costs came down over time, and by the 1960s they were below those of the traditional technology over a wide range of output. Thus comparatively small microwave systems were now cost-competitive with AT&T, and the rents built into long-distance rates provided a further lure for actual competition.[33] The first symptom of growing competition was the growth of private microwave systems, which carried signals for their owners. These private systems did not by themselves siphon off enough long-distance volume to threaten the continued viability of regulation. But the threat was obvious. Consider XYZ, Inc., which operated a private microwave system between its facilities in A and B. It was now possible for XYZ and even its employees and their friends in A to place a local call there to be transported by XYZ's microwave system to B, where another local call would carry it to anyone in B. The total cost of this maneuver, including the two (subsidized) local calls, would be less than AT&T's high long-distance rates. Thus the regulated rates and the new technology were providing an incentive for large users to build their own systems. They were also providing an incentive for these private systems to arbitrage the difference between AT&T's rates and the private system's costs for third parties.

How far and how quickly such arbitrage would have spread in the absence of regulatory change is debatable. Until 1969 it was illegal for private microwave systems to offer long-distance service to the general public. Thus the relevant counterfactual (what would have occurred if regulation had not changed) turns on the costs of getting around this legal restriction.

32. Leonard Waverman, "The Regulation of Intercity Telecommunications," in Almarin Phillips, ed., *Promoting Competition in Regulated Markets* (Washington, D.C.: Brookings, 1975).

33. Waverman compares an estimated microwave cost function to AT&T's cable costs. He finds that microwave average costs flatten at an output that is a trivial fraction of total output on typical high-density routes. He also finds that the minimum cost for microwave dominates the average cost of cable at any cable output level. Ibid.

Had these been suitably modest, a fairly rapid unraveling of the regulated rate structure becomes a credible part of the counterfactual. This scenario—a rapid dissipation of rents through competition from private networks—would then provide a basis for deregulation consistent with the ET.

This scenario never took place. And that fact, in my view, is not congenial to an ET-based explanation of the actual events. What happened was that the owner of a private microwave system, MCI, applied for permission to provide public long-distance service by interconnecting with the local networks. This permission was granted in 1969. That decision was the beginning of the end of regulation in long-distance telecommunications. There are now essentially no regulatory constraints on entry, and much of the proverbial cream has been skimmed from long-distance rates. Some formal rate regulation still exists, largely in the form of the rates charged the long-distance carriers for access to the now independent local networks.

The difficulty in viewing this history through the lens of the ET lies in the heavy weight one must give to the foresight of the regulators. One has to argue that they saw as imminent such a rapid erosion of the long-distance rents from the new technology that the present value of the political gains derivable from those rents had, in some sense, become negative by 1969. This kind of argument does not sit well with the experience in airline and railroad deregulation, already reviewed, or in financial services, discussed below. In all those industries considerable actual rent dissipation preceded deregulation. Also, though we will never know the counterfactual time path of the long-distance telecommunication rents, we do know that the United States is still, twenty years after the crucial regulatory change, the main exception to a worldwide rule of entry restriction in this market. That fact at least suggests that U.S. regulators could have resisted new entry for some time after they permitted it. Accordingly, if one had to choose between the ET's explanation and the NPT's—that deregulation follows the demise of natural monopoly conditions—the latter is simpler and thus more appealing.[34]

Stock Brokerage

Though the history is somewhat murky, it appears that until twenty years ago a cartel of New York Stock Exchange (NYSE) members had been

---

34. The role of numbers, which Stigler emphasized and which I have so far ignored, may be more important here than in the other cases. Stigler argued that the politically dominant group would be neither too small to count politically nor too big to overcome free riding

setting minimum brokerage rates since 1792. In the 1930s this cartel came within the ambit of the Securities and Exchange Commission (SEC). However, the SEC sanctioned minimum rates at least up to 1968. The interaction between the SEC and the NYSE cartel never acquired a formal institutional structure. But the rates bore the familiar imprint of cost-based cross subsidization: brokerage costs per share (or dollar) decrease as the size of the transaction increases, and these economies of size were incompletely translated into rates. The result was that profits on large transactions subsidized losses on small transactions.[35]

Gregg Jarrell has already invoked the ET in explaining the industry's transition to deregulation, and I can do little more than paraphrase him here.[36] The precursor to deregulation was the rise of institutional trading in the 1960s. These large-block traders doubled their share of NYSE trading volume between 1960 and 1976, accounting for nearly half the volume at the latter date. Given the rate structure, this event increased the potential rent available to NYSE members. But that potential was not realized. The rent dissipation took many shapes, the most obvious being nonprice competition in the form of "free" ancillary services (research) provided to large institutional traders. Also, institutional traders began arranging trades off the NYSE floor, either through their own newly formed brokerage subsidiaries or through specialists that were not NYSE members. These leakages created a split within the cartel. The larger NYSE member firms, which wanted to compete for institutional business, were increasingly hobbled by the need to use inefficient methods to counteract the straight discounts offered by nonmembers. They ultimately supported rate deregulation (and, according to Jarrell, benefited from it).

Formal deregulation of brokerage rates came through congressional action in 1975. But beginning in 1968, a series of regulatory changes pushed in the same direction—more competition and consequently lower rates on large transactions. So far, the brokerage story resembles the airline or railroad story: potential rents from regulation eroded to the point where the supporting coalition was undermined. There is, however, a twist in the story congenial to the ET. It lies in the growth of institutional trading, which touched off the forces leading to deregulation. The institutions

---

and rational ignorance. Depending on one's view AT&T may have been too small (one firm) or too big (3 million stockholders) to dominate the compact group (large users and private system operators) that would benefit from deregulation of entry. See Stigler, "Theory of Economic Regulation."

35. See Gregg A. Jarrell, "Change at the Exchange: The Causes and Effects of Deregulation," *Journal of Law and Economics,* vol. 27 (October 1984), pp. 273–312.

36. Ibid.

had the attributes making for political success in Stigler's explanation—compact numbers with large per capita stakes. Jarrell, however, emphasized the purely economic aspects of the institutions' growth as embodied in Peltzman's version of the ET. The institutions were the relatively elastic demanders of NYSE brokerage services, especially after they began integrating vertically and arranging off-board trades. In Peltzman's multi-interest model, higher demand elasticities shift the equilibrium toward lower prices. So even if the consumers' political ability had not increased, the SEC would have faced pressure to weaken regulation.

Bank Deposits

The formal regulation of deposit rates is one of the series of regulatory reforms enacted in the wake of the widespread bank failures of the 1930s. But it took another thirty years for the regulation to have any substantial effects. The original regulation prohibited payment of interest on demand deposits and set a 2.5 percent maximum rate on time deposits in commercial banks. The latter was nonbinding for many institutions until the 1950s, and then was raised to 3 percent in 1957, the first move in a delicate balancing act that was to be played out in the ensuing years.

From the onset of regulation, ninety-day Treasury-bill yields never averaged over 4 percent in any year until 1966. In such a world the marginal effect of the interest ceilings was modest. They moved in the direction of providing some rents to the commercial banks and fostering the growth of savings and loan associations, whose rates were not then regulated. In this sense the regulation served some important organized interest groups—the commercial banks and the S&Ls and their allies, the home-building industry. The banking rents were partly dissipated by various forms of nonprice and near-price competition, such as forgone service charges on demand deposits and competition in locational convenience (branching). But regulation of bank entry, state restrictions on branching, and prohibition of S&L competition for demand deposits all acted to restrain the competitive rent dissipation.

This equilibrium could not withstand the dramatic increase in the level and volatility of interest rates that began in the late 1960s and became especially important in the inflation of the 1970s. The first symptom that the equilibrium was unraveling was the extension of maximum rates to the S&Ls in 1966. As interest rates rose, the unregulated S&Ls began drawing time deposits from the commercial banks. In 1966 the S&Ls were allowed to pay only a fixed premium above the maximum rates for bank time deposits. This attempt to preserve the distribution of rents did not, however, work well. In the interest-rate environment of the time, fixed rate differentials exacerbated the volatility of the flow of funds between institutions.

Even more important cleavages were created by the unregulated capital markets' response to the regulation in this interest-rate environment. This response acquired a generic name—disintermediation. When market interest rates could quickly exceed the regulated rates by 500 basis points, depositors were motivated to look for close substitutes for deposits, and suppliers were encouraged to offer them. The first to benefit were the large depositors. Their major close substitute heretofore had been Treasury paper. Now, in the late 1960s and early 1970s, the commercial paper market grew rapidly and non-U.S. banks (joined by offshore subsidiaries of U.S. banks) began issuing dollar-denominated deposits, all at rates beyond the reach of the regulators. By 1970 it was clear that rate regulation on large time deposits was no longer viable, and these were deregulated. As monetary instability grew, the stage was set for new competition for the smaller depositors' business. Mutual funds arose that held the unregulated large-denomination deposits (and/or T-bills, commercial paper, Eurodollar deposits, and so forth) and sold shares to the broad public. The average fee for this service is about 70 basis points per dollar of deposit, which was no longer enough to stifle their growth given the interest rates of the 1970s. When short-term rates rose into double digits, these funds came of age. From next to nothing in 1978, their assets grew to more than $200 billion by 1982 (or to roughly 15 percent of total time deposits of all financial institutions). An interesting wrinkle was that these funds typically allowed shares to be "sold" by a check drawn on the fund's bank account. The implications for the future of non-interest-bearing checking accounts were clear.

The rise of the money market funds made it clear that monetary instability and technology had rendered interest-rate regulation obsolete. It also tore apart what remained of the political coalition supporting the regulation. There had long been a large bank–small bank conflict about the regulation. On balance, the larger institutions were net losers because the regulation hindered their ability to compete against money market instruments for large time deposits. Now their "retail," or smaller deposit, base was being eroded by the growth of the money market funds. More important, the rate regulation was a threat to the future growth of the larger institutions. The same technology—telephones, computers, advertising, and so on—that permitted the funds to gather $200 billion in a few years made it clear that the geographic balkanization of financial markets was ending. Many of the larger institutions saw their future in the retail market linked to geographic expansion. This meant ultimately attracting the customers of the smaller institutions as well as the relatively sophisticated and demonstrably mobile patrons of the money market funds. Much of the retail base of the smaller institutions consisted of customers who wanted locational convenience and who preferred an insured bank account to the new, unfamiliar money funds. They could be attracted, but not if the large banks had to pay the same rates as small banks. Accordingly, the large banks now openly supported deregulation.

In 1980 and 1982 Congress enacted legislation that, details aside, provided for phased deregulation of all deposit rates except business checking accounts. Given the history just outlined, the life of the latter anomaly may be brief. That history repeats a familiar scenario. A regulation once capable of generating rents was undermined by incentives—in this case to product innovation—created by the regulation that resulted in dissipation of the rents.

Oil

The history of oil-price regulation is brief and complex. I will ignore the complexities and, in the process, shove some arguably important interest groups into the background. Stripped to essentials, the facts are these. Maximum prices were set on domestically produced oil in the early 1970s. Price increases initiated by the Organization of Petroleum Export Countries (OPEC) in 1973 and 1979 pushed world prices substantially above the regulated domestic prices—roughly by a factor of two. The price ceilings were eliminated in 1980, and a windfall profits tax was imposed in their place. This excise tax was a specified fraction of the difference between the transaction price and some stipulated base price for the oil. The tax was to be phased out beginning in 1988, but the base prices have exceeded market prices since 1985. So the effective tax has been zero since then.

The way in which the rents captured from domestic oil producers were distributed is a matter of some controversy, which I will not join. It is sufficient to say that some were captured by intermediaries (refiners, wholesalers), some were captured by certain consumers, and some were dissipated in inefficiency induced by the detail of the regulation (most notably in the building of small, "tea-kettle," refineries). The weaseling here about consumers has to do with the uncertain effects of the regulation on product prices at those times—the majority—when there was no obvious queueing, and the uncertain benefits of the queue-inducing prices to typical consumers. To simplify, then, I will henceforth call all the downstream users of oil and refined products "consumers."

These consumers lost their benefits in 1980, but the industry was not deregulated. Instead, a new, arguably more efficient, method of collecting producer rents with a new beneficiary—the Treasury—replaced the old method. Accordingly, my focus here is not on the change in 1980, important as that may be in its own right, but on the larger question of why the producer rents were taxed in the first place.

The answer to that question, within the context of the ET, is fairly simple. It is to be found in the earlier history of regulation of the industry. Until the 1970s federal regulatory policy created producer rents. It sanctioned output quotas in the 1930s and enforced import quotas beginning in the 1950s. Both policy initiatives occurred in the wake of events (the Depression, the discovery of prolific fields in the Middle East) that reduced producer rents. Thus the producer interest had received its most active political support at times when rents were threatened. This is consistent with the aspect of the ET that emphasizes the role of regulation as a buffer against shifts in the distribution of wealth. Until OPEC increased prices in the 1970s, the important shifts were going against producers, and these were, as the theory predicts, offset by political action.

OPEC's actions, of course, resulted in a dramatic shift in the opposite direction. The rise in world oil prices generated a massive increase in the demand for domestically produced oil. In the absence of intervention, that would have generated a correspondingly large shift of wealth toward producers, thereby upsetting the politically optimum distribution of wealth. In these circumstances the theory predicts an offsetting tax on producer wealth, which is precisely what happened. The price ceilings and windfall profits tax would, in this theory, help to restore the politically optimum distribution as did the oil import quotas and production quotas in their day.

Thus the ET seems capable of telling a coherent story about regulatory policy both before and after the price increases. The about-face from generating to taxing rents did not represent some unintelligible loss of political power by the producers. (They were left with considerable rents from the OPEC price increases.) Instead, regulatory policy had to accommodate to a large outside shock, and the accommodation required just the sort of change in policy that occurred. The importance of this rent-buffering aspect of regulation is attested to by the fact that when price deregulation occurred, it was accompanied by an explicit tax on the resulting rents. The action of other countries in this period also tends to corroborate the importance of political rent-buffering. Those countries that had negligible domestic production (continental Europe, Japan), and consequently no domestic producer interest, allowed domestic prices to rise to world levels. Those that had substantial domestic production (Canada, Mexico), and would consequently, according to the ET, face the need to balance the interests of producing and consuming sectors, did just what the United States did. They kept domestic prices below world prices during the 1970s.

If the ET provides a unified explanation for oil regulation, it also suggests a corollary for the future. The current real price of oil remains about double the pre-1973 level. Any substantial decline to or below that level should produce pressure for revival of rent protection—through import quotas, tariffs, or other means. Any substantial increase, say to or above the 1973 or 1979 levels, would produce pressure for renewed taxation of the rents.

SUMMARY

The ET was born in a wave of enthusiasm for the notion that regulatory agencies are captured by producers. That notion left little room for deregulation: as long as an industry is viable producers can benefit from regulatory restraints on competition. The ET, however, has evolved away from those origins toward an emphasis on the coalitional aspects of politics. Here the need to balance pressures emanating from competing interests plays a central role. This formulation leaves much more room for deregulation. As long as deregulation benefits some part of the relevant coalition, it cannot be ruled out as a viable policy option. When the deregulation benefits become large relative to the associated losses, the probability that the option will be exercised rises. This situation is more likely to occur if the regulation itself has generated inefficiencies, so that shedding the inefficiency through deregulation provides a potential source of benefits.

Indeed, if there is a model of regulatory entry and exit implicit in the ET, a few simple notions can provide its outlines. Regulation occurs when there is a wide discrepancy between the political balance of pressures and the unregulated distribution of wealth. The regulation (of, say, price) then creates incentives for wealth dissipation (through, say, cost increases), which ultimately make restoration of the preregulation status quo more attractive than continuing regulation. In such a model deregulation is not the correction of some belatedly recognized policy error. It is the last stage in a process about which, in principle, all the actors could have had perfect foresight at the beginning. In practice, of course, there can be mistaken entry into regulation, but none of the industries I have discussed are obviously in this group. Airline regulation, for example, lasted four decades, and the others lasted longer. Few private sector enterprises would be deemed mistakes, even in hindsight, if they survived so long. The point here is that erosion and ultimate elimination of profits, either of the political or monetary kind, is not a reasonable criterion for evaluating the success of a venture. Some attention has to be paid to how durable the profits are and how quickly any requisite exit from the activity occurs. Indeed, if a model with "endogenous deregulation" proves a useful extension of the ET, it may help illuminate the selective character of entry into regulation. One reason for not regulating an industry would be the prospect that, for example, quality competition would erode rents so quickly that the upfront investment in political pressure required to implement regulation is not worthwhile.

Whether the deregulation is the predictable consequence of regulation or not, any explanation for deregulation derived from the ET has to look for some dissipation of the wealth upon which the political equilibrium in the theory is based. If there is only trivial wealth to redistribute, the ET finds no rationale for continued regulation.

I have examined some of the notable recent examples of deregulation to see how closely they fit the scenario implicit in the ET. Specifically, is there evidence of erosion of the wealth base on which the regulatory equilibrium was plausibly based? I also paid attention to magnitude and timing. Is the erosion plausibly large enough to suggest a crisis in which continued regulation would be unviable? Did the deregulation occur more or less promptly after the crisis?

The answers to these questions were mixed, but in the main followed the pattern implied by the ET. Two cases did not follow this pattern. Trucking was de facto deregulated when substantial rents were being earned by owners and workers who formed the heart of the relevant political coalition. Not only were the rents substantial, but there was no evidence of any serious erosion of them. Entry into long-distance telecommunications was deregulated after the technological threat to existing rents became clear but before substantial erosion took place. This is a less spectacular failure of the ET than trucking, but it has to be counted a failure nevertheless.

All the other cases follow more or less closely the pattern suggested by the ET. The railroads were deregulated after a long decline in demand that eroded the rents spread among producers and high-cost shippers. The precipitating crisis was the widespread bankruptcy and subsequent nationalization of important parts of the industry. Airline deregulation was preceded by a dissipation of regulatory rents because of service competition induced by the regulation. The dissipation followed promptly upon increased internal entry in the 1960s and was fairly complete by the 1970s when deregulation occurred. In the stock brokerage business, a sharp increase in institutional trading in the 1960s created the crisis leading to deregulation in 1975. This shift in trading patterns provoked increased service rivalry and bypassing of the stock exchange, which dissipated rents and upset the intraindustry allocation of rents. In banking, the inflation of the 1970s bred the crisis leading to deregulation of deposit rates. The accompanying rise in nominal interest rates and in their variability allowed good substitutes for bank deposits to draw funds from the banks, and, as with the brokerage industry, exacerbated a divergence of interests within the industry. The last case I examined, petroleum, is somewhat special in that price deregulation was supplanted by an excise tax, which I interpreted as the last in a series of moves consistent with maintaining the optimum distribution of rents. Accordingly, I argued that obituaries for petroleum regulation may be premature.

Even though the ET can tell a coherent story about most of the examples of deregulation, it still cannot answer some important questions about them. Specifically, some of the examples raise questions about the design of institutions and their adaptability that have so far eluded the grasp of economists. Airline regulation is probably the best case in point. When it became clear in the early 1970s that service rivalry was dissipating rents, the CAB encouraged limited, voluntary output quotas. This tentative move was quickly abandoned. A more vigorous, possibly compulsory, system of quotas seems never to have been discussed, though it held the potential for preserving some rents and enhancing efficiency at the same time. The same ends could have been served earlier by a less relaxed policy on internal entry combined with more flexibility on interfirm transfers of operating rights than the CAB evinced. (Interfirm route transfers could be accomplished only through merger.) The then flourishing lightly regulated market in truck operating rights provided a potential role model. In short, obvious measures to stem the forces leading to deregulation seemed available but went unused.

Similar questions are raised by the history of railroad regulation. Here the government provided a flexible political response to the crisis of the 1970s. It nationalized the bankrupt railroads and passenger service and replaced the previous cross subsidies with substantial explicit subsidies.

These can be viewed as a substitute for regulation in distributing wealth. For railroads, subsidies are in fact the mode of choice in most of the world for achieving roughly the same distributive goals as American railroad regulation did. But, except for passenger subsidies, the American rail subsidies were terminated by the end of the 1970s. If the ET succeeds in explaining the end of railroad regulation, it is obviously not sharp enough to explain why the alternative is deregulation here and subsidies in other countries.

These examples illustrate why the deregulation wave came as such a surprise to most economists. It was one plausible response to forces that called for regulatory change. But it was not, in many instances, the only plausible response. Indeed, in some cases, like those just cited, more or different regulation would have been an equally plausible response. To show the difficulty here, one need only consider an important contemporary regulatory problem—how to respond to the massive losses in the savings and loan industry. It is utterly implausible that the dissipation of upward of $50 billion in public funds on unproductive investments and random transfers to impecunious borrowers is the low-cost method of serving this industry's political constituency. Accordingly, it requires only modest courage to predict that the current regulatory system will not survive much longer. Given our current state of knowledge, however, it requires a courage bordering on foolhardiness to predict the precise nature of the regulatory change that this particular crisis will breed. Policy options ranging from less regulation (such as reducing the scope of deposit insurance) to more regulation (such as increased capital requirements or restrictions on assets) would be consistent with resolving the crisis.

Twenty years ago economic theory faced the challenge of providing a basis for understanding the behavior of regulatory agencies. The ET was a modest step toward meeting that challenge. I have argued here that it also gives some insight into the forces that strain the institutional underpinnings of regulation. But so far a full analysis of the scope and form of these institutions remains unwritten.

TEN

George Stigler's Contribution to the Economic Analysis of Regulation

George Stigler changed the way economists analyze government regulation. This enormous legacy is essentially embodied in two articles: his 1962
analysis of electricity rates with Claire Friedland and his 1971 theoretical
piece. There were, to be sure, precursors and successors in his own work.
But none of them so profoundly affected the course of intellectual inquiry
as these two.

The importance of both articles rests more, I believe, with the questions each posed than with the answers. Even by the standards of the day,
neither piece evinced the sort of technical sophistication that the profession has come to admire. Neither produced conclusions that were impervi-
ous to all serious subsequent challenges. But both produced insights that
have altered the course of research in the area to this day.

To understand Stigler's contribution, it is best to proceed chronologi-
cally and to begin with the state of the field around 1962. There is room
here only for caricature rather than extensive survey. However, I think it
is fair to say that the field derived its main energy from the normative
economics of marginal cost pricing. The proper role of government was
to correct the private market failures that prevented attainment of marginal cost pricing. Applied economic analysis of regulation was then
largely descriptive, and its main tendency was to show how the regulatory
institutions constrained departures from marginal cost pricing.

Monopoly was viewed as the main barrier to marginal cost pricing,
and the "natural monopoly" occupied center stage in the economics of
regulation.[1] The prime examples of natural monopoly were supposed to
be the public utilities. The main role of utility regulators was held to be
prevention of private exploitation of the market power that would inevit-

First published in *Journal of Political Economy* 101, no. 5 (1993): 818–832. © 1993 by
The University of Chicago.
    1. Man-made monopolies were the main subject matter of industrial organization.
Stigler's profound influence on this field is summarized by Harold Demsetz's (1993) article.

ably flow from natural monopoly cost conditions. And the broad professional consensus was that utility regulation succeeded in this task.

It was understood that regulation did not succeed completely in forcing price down to marginal cost. Political and legal constraints on public subsidization of the difference between marginal and average cost forced the regulators to set something approximating average cost prices.[2] But it was regarded almost as given that without regulatory intervention utility rates would be substantially higher than they were.

The main problem with this professional consensus was that it had never been subject to empirical verification prior to 1962. In this fact lies the main contribution of the Stigler-Friedland paper. As put succinctly by Joskow and Rose in their 1989 review of the subsequent literature, "Systematic empirical analysis of the effects of economic regulation originated with Stigler and Friedland's 1962 paper which sought to measure the effects of state commission regulation of franchised electric utilities. . . . Since 1962 there have been several hundred scholarly studies of the effects of economic regulation" (p. 1495).

As the quote implies, the intellectual contribution here goes quite beyond primacy in the study of the specific effects of utility regulation. The tendency of economists to accept without examination the effects of a wide range of government regulation was pervasive before 1962. This was changed permanently by the Stigler-Friedland paper. It launched an intellectual enterprise that is still in business.

The substance of the Stigler-Friedland article is a regression estimate of the reduced form

(1)   price $= f(D,S,\text{regulation})$,

where D is demand shifters (urbanization and income) and S is nonregulatory supply shifters (fuel price and share of output from [low-cost] hydro power). The sample is a cross section of states in the early 1920s; regulation is represented by a binary dummy. This setup took advantage of the uneven spread of state regulation of the industry prior to 1920, which left about one-third of the states unregulated. The main result was a statisti-

2. The typical electricity rate structure was, and is, full of nonlinearities. They usually make the marginal price facing a customer less than the average price, thereby mitigating the inefficiency from simple average cost pricing. A good part of the applied analysis of utility rates was then, and is today, concerned with refining the complex rate structures that were understood as necessary components in the regulators' striving for efficiency.

cally weak and small (under 5 percent) difference between prices in regulated and unregulated states. (A similar result was obtained for output.)

The impact of the Stigler-Friedland article on the profession owed as
much to this then startling result as to the methodological innovation of
estimating the effect of regulation from an explicit statistical model.[3] Had
the result merely confirmed the conventional wisdom, economists might
have been less eager to pursue the effects of regulation. It is, in this connection, ironic that the original result is wrong about the magnitude (but not
the statistical significance) of the effect of regulation. A miscoding of the
dummy variable for regulation (regulated states = +10) and the use of
common instead of natural logs caused the estimated effect of regulation
to be dramatically understated.[4] Table 10.1 sets the historical record
straight by repeating the key regressions on the original data set (provided
by Claire Friedland). There are a number of minor discrepancies, but the
most important result is the size of the coefficients of the correctly coded
dummy variables in columns 3 and 6. They imply that regulation lowered
price by about a fourth and thereby caused output to rise by over half.

These specific results were superseded by subsequent work.[5] The more
important outcome of the article was that economists began eagerly estimating effects of many kinds of regulation. They also began to confront a
number of previously neglected theoretical questions.

One of these questions concerned the prior beliefs that economists
should bring to any study of the effects of regulation. If Stigler and
Friedland were right about the inadequacy of the view that electricity regulators prevented the depredations of monopoly, what should one expect
from this form (and from other forms) of regulation? As is implied by
their title, Stigler and Friedland grappled with this question and thought
they had an answer: that demand and cost functions were sufficiently elastic to preclude a substantial effect of regulation. Perhaps the industry was
a natural monopoly in some narrow technical sense. But both customers and capital were sufficiently mobile to leave little pricing discretion
for regulators.

3. In an earlier version of the paper, the estimate of (1) included a quantity term on the
right-hand side. When this version was presented to the Industrial Organization Workshop
at Chicago, Stigler was forcefully criticized by Dale Jorgenson, then a faculty member in the
Economics Department. Jorgenson pointed out that Stigler had estimated a demand function in which no clear meaning could be assigned to the insignificant coefficient of the regulation dummy. This was the only time I ever saw Stigler rendered utterly speechless.

4. Claire Friedland brought this to my attention, and she credits Kevin J. Murphy with
first having uncovered the coding error.

5. Joskow and Rose (1989) have a good summary.

TABLE 10.1 Original and Corrected Regressions, Electricity Price and Output, 1922

	Dependent Variable					
	Price			Quantity		
Independent Variable	As Reported (1)	Rerun, Dummy Corrected (2)	Natural Logs (3)*	As Reported (4)	Rerun, Dummy Corrected (5)	Natural Logs (6)*
Urban population	−.0592	−0.43		.395	.292	
	(2.39)	(2.28)		(7.60)	(6.71)	
Cost of fuel	.0604	.068		−.577	−.670	
	(.36)	(.41)		(1.65)	(1.87)	
Per capita income	.230	.204		.718	1.057	
	(1.13)	(1.00)		(1.68)	(2.50)	
Proportion of	−.498	−.490	−1.13	.491	.395	.910
horsepower hydro	(6.00)	(5.92)		(2.82)	(2.19)	
Regulation	−.0109	−.111	−.257	.0172	.204	.469
	(1.60)	(1.63)		(1.20)	(1.41)	
R^2:						
With regulation	.567	.563		.694	.693	
Without regulation	.540	.534		.684	.674	

Note: Cols. 1 and 4 come from Stigler (1962), table 3. Price (average revenue per kilowatt hour), quantity (kilowatt hour), urban population, cost of fuel, and per capita income are in common logs for cols. 1, 2, 4, and 5 and in natural logs for cols. 3 and 6. Urban population is zero for Vermont, North Dakota, Mississippi, Idaho, Wyoming, New Mexico, and Nevada. Claire Friedland informs me that they were set equal to 100 to permit the use of logs. This procedure is followed in the reruns. The regulation dummy was initially miscoded as equal to 10 for regulated states and zero otherwise. For cols. 2, 3, 5, and 6, this is corrected to equal one for regulated states and zero otherwise. For cols. 1–3, the sample size is 47 states (District of Columbia, Maryland, and Delaware are combined); for cols. 4–6, the sample size is 43. Data for Arizona and New Mexico are unavailable. Montana and Utah, and Vermont and Rhode Island are combined. Fuel cost, hydro, and income variables are estimated as population weighted averages for the combined states. Absolute t-ratios are in parentheses.
*Entries in this column are the same as in col. 2 except where noted.

Stigler and Friedland did not try to generalize this assertion.[6] However, to his colleagues and students of the early 1960s, Stigler did press the case for a basically competitive economy with substantial long-run resource mobility in which regulation was bound to be mainly ineffective. Some of his published work of the period reflects this view.[7] But he gradually abandoned it.

Stigler did this under the accumulating weight of the evidence spawned

6. No evidence was offered in its support.
7. See Stigler (1964), which argues the ineffectiveness of securities regulation, and Stigler (1966) on the failure of the antitrust laws to affect industrial concentration.

by the Stigler-Friedland article. Much of this found regulation to be effective but in ways opposite to what the traditional "public interest" model of regulation would suggest. A clear statement appears in Jordan's (1972) survey of this first wave of post-Stigler-Friedland empirical studies. He finds that "the essential thrust [of the evidence] has been consistent with implications derived from a producer protection hypothesis once the effects of prior market structure were taken into consideration" (p. 174). As Jordan saw it, where the prior (i.e., ex-regulation) market structure was monopoly, as in electricity, regulation was found to be ineffective. Where competition would otherwise prevail (his prime examples pertained to transportation), regulation typically lowered output, raised price, and generated monopoly rents. Since effective regulation of a natural monopoly would be inconsistent with the interests of sellers, the single story consistent with the whole pattern of mixed results on the effects of regulation was, according to Jordan, one in which regulators preserved or promoted the interests of sellers rather than consumers.

Jordan's formulation is symptomatic of a revisionism that, by the early 1970s, was exercising considerable influence over the profession. Within a decade, the benign view of regulation as promoter of the general interest had been mainly abandoned. The ascendant image was of the regulator captured by the regulated.

While this image was hardly new (see, e.g., Bernstein 1955), the willingness of many economists to embrace it on the basis of mounting evidence was new. As with much else in economics, evidence preceded theory. In this case, the evidence of capture seemed to ask for an explanation of why regulation had come to work in this seemingly perverse way. The answer provided in Stigler's (1971) article on the theory of regulation stands as his second major contribution to the economics of regulation.

As with the Stigler-Friedland article, it is necessary to distinguish the methodological contribution of the 1971 article from its specific result. The specific result is a theoretical rationale for capture of regulatory agencies by producer interests. In subsequent development of Stigler's theoretical apparatus (e.g., Peltzman 1976 [chap. 6]; Becker 1983), regulators serve a broader constituency than regulated producers. In time, Stigler came to accept these generalizations. So, his capture result needs to be taken in its historical context. In 1971, the wave of professional enthusiasm for evidence of capture was just cresting.

What survives from Stigler's 1971 article is an integration of the economics of regulation and the economics of politics in which transactions between self-interested suppliers and demanders determine the regulatory outcome. Because of this supplier-demander framework, the body of theory pioneered by Stigler has come to be called the "economic theory of regulation." In any market, transactions are costly, and his 1971 article is the first serious inquiry into the costs of expressing a politically effective demand to regulators. This yielded an emphasis on the importance of organized interest groups that remains an important part of contemporary analyses of regulation.

The suppliers in Stigler's theory are unspecified political actors. No distinction is made among legislators, executives, and their regulator-agents. What they have to sell is power: tangibly, power over, say, prices and entry, but ultimately over the wealth of a regulated industry's buyers and sellers. These two groups compete for access to this power, and the high bidder wins. The currency with which the demanders bid is obviously a bit more complex than the stuff reported in the monetary aggregates. It includes votes delivered in support of politicians, campaign contributions, jobs in the political afterlife, and so forth. The prototypical result of the competition is the triumph of the cohesive producer interest over the diffuse consumer interest. This is manifest in regulatory decisions on prices and entry that transfer rents from consumers to producers. More generally, the political equilibrium in Stigler's model is one in which cohesive minorities tax diffuse majorities.

To get this result, Stigler drew on several strands of the then emerging public choice literature. His basic assumption of political utility maximization was an important ingredient of James Buchanan and Gordon Tullock's (1962) influential work. Anthony Downs (1957) had argued that voters would be "rationally ignorant" about most public policies because of weak incentives to acquire information. For this reason, Stigler argued, consumers were an unreliable ally of the rational regulator. Their stake in the regulatory outcome was typically too small to make them informed supporters of proconsumer policies or opponents of anticonsumer policies. By contrast, the producer stake was typically large enough to overcome rational ignorance. But knowledge needs to be translated into power, and in politics this requires organizing to bring pressure to bear on the political process. Here the compact producer groups also have the advantage, because they can more easily overcome the "free-rider" deterrent to collective action emphasized by Mancur Olson (1965). In short, producers have decisive information and organization cost advantages over consumers.

An important reason for the lasting influence of Stigler's 1971 article— one recent review (Noll 1989) calls it "the watershed event" in the literature on the politics of regulation—is primacy. While the components of Stigler's theory were not new, the application to regulation was new. And it occurred at an appropriate time. Prior to 1960, economists essentially ignored the political context within which regulation occurs even as the economic analysis of politics was making important strides. By 1970, economists were seeking a rationale for the seemingly perverse effects their empirical research had uncovered. Stigler's theory provided it in a form bound to appeal to economists: a model of rational choice. Whatever the subsequent modifications of the theory, the emphasis on regulators as rational actors has remained a durable part of the economics of regulation. So too has the emphasis on the role of organized interests in regulatory politics. In this way, the economics of regulation has been decisively changed. The pre-1960, benign view of the effects of regulation has not been entirely superseded. But it is no longer simply assumed. Arguments that regulation enhances efficiency now must show what is "in it" for the political actors when they move in that direction.

This theoretical transformation came to have consequences not only for the study of regulation but also for economists' views on public policy. I would credit the line of work begun by Stigler's theory with a catalytic role in shifting the professional center of gravity toward skepticism about the social utility of regulation. Economists venerate efficiency. When they became convinced that regulation was not in fact primarily efficiency enhancing, their ardor for it cooled. When they became convinced that the primary goal of regulation was not, even in principle, likely to be efficiency maximization, their ardor cooled further.[8] To be sure, regulation does not yet occupy the same place as, say, tariffs. Economists are almost unanimously convinced (without much evidence) that tariffs decrease welfare, though they admit the contrary as a theoretical possibility. Regulation elicits a more diverse reaction, both across types and across economists. But this difference has narrowed considerably, because economists now understand that regulation and tariffs share a common political susceptibility to the influence of organized interests.

Stigler's theory has also affected the course of empirical research on regulation. His 1971 article contains some direct applications of the the-

8. I use efficiency here in the traditional sense of net surplus maximization. Becker's (1983) development of Stigler's theory argues that regulators will be drawn to efficient modes of redistribution, because deadweight losses reduce potential political utility. But even Becker's equilibrium generally has positive deadweight losses because producer and consumer interests do not systematically receive equal weight and because of the transaction costs of the competition for political influence. Accordingly, regulation cannot systematically be expected to increase a conventional welfare measure.

ory. Measures of regulatory decisions (e.g., weight limits on trucks) are regressed on measures of the strength or stakes of affected interest groups (the investments of farmers in trucks). However, the main influence of the theory lies in a direction different from such direct applications. It has been to sensitize researchers to look toward interest group pressures for an understanding of the effects of regulation. I can illustrate this by comparing styles of pre- and post-1971 empirical research on regulation. Consider, as an example of the former, the Stigler-Friedland article. The main line of inquiry here is, Did regulation accomplish its stated goal (lower rates)? The Stigler of 1962 armed with his theory of 1971 might have asked instead, Which influential interest groups would the utility commission plausibly serve? And he might then have gone on to inquire about the effects of regulation on, say, workers, large users of electricity, suppliers of fuel and equipment, and so forth.[9] Questions like this are commonplace after 1971. There is room here only for illustrative examples. One would be the literature on the effects of regulation on wages.[10] The stated goals of ordinary rate entry regulation are silent about the welfare of workers. But economists came to understand that workers had a concentrated, often organized, interest in regulatory decisions. So they were drawn to investigate, with some success, the connection between regulation and wages. Another example would be the literature on the effects of the convoluted regulation of oil prices following the rise of OPEC (e.g., Kalt 1981; Smith, Bradley, and Jarrell 1986). This regulation had minor effects on the prices paid by consumers of refined products, and a pre-1971 type study might have stopped after demonstrating that. Or it might have puzzled over the apparent perversity of the numerous inefficient refineries induced to enter by the regulation. The actual literature focused on the transfer of rents among interest groups (refiners gained and producers lost). Stigler's theory provides no clear insight about which interest group triumphed here. But it created the intellectual background in which the search for the distribution of rents among these interests becomes a primary focus of research.

George Stigler had an abiding faith in the progress of economics. It is, I believe, appropriate to conclude this review of his work in the spirit of

9. The limited discussion of such matters seems naive in light of the later theory. For example, Stigler and Friedland inquire into the residential/industrial price ratio because "as a political matter, the numerous residential users might be favored relative to industrial users" (p. 9).

10. This literature was essentially nonexistent prior to 1971. It includes Hendricks (1977), Ehrenberg (1979), and Rose (1987).

that faith by indicating some areas in which progress in the economics of regulation remains to be made.

Which Industries Are Regulated?

There are, by my count, over 1,500 entries under "Associations" in the District of Columbia Yellow Pages. Obviously, lobbying groups could not survive without obtaining something for their members. Yet only a handful obtain the important transfers that Stigler taught us to associate with entry and rate regulation. This is so in spite of the apparent information and organization cost advantages that many industry groups would appear to have over consumers. It will take a more precise theory to explain why, for example, the trucking industry seemed able to extract so much more rent from regulation than a myriad of interest groups with apparently similar characteristics. The deregulation of that industry illustrates the complementary problem: Why did this well-organized producer interest so suddenly and completely lose political support for the regulatory rents?[11]

The Timing of Regulatory Innovation

Stigler's "central thesis" was "that, as a rule, regulation is acquired by the industry and is designed and operated primarily for its benefit" (1971, p. 3). This metaphor of government as order-taker is useful in highlighting the importance of interest groups. But it may obscure some interesting regularities on the supply side of this market. One is the pronounced cyclical character of regulatory innovation. Consider the pattern of establishment of new agencies and of enactment of laws affecting their operation for the 20 presidential terms from 1900 to 1980.[12] Over this whole period, 49 agencies were established and 334 regulatory laws were enacted. Only 10 agencies were established in the eight pre–New Deal administrations, but Woodrow Wilson's first term accounts for four of them. The concentration of legislation is less pronounced, but Wilson's two terms still account for 41 percent (19 of 46) of the pre–New Deal laws. The next burst of activity occurs during Franklin Roosevelt's first term. It accounts for over half the agencies (6 of 9) and laws (30 of 57) in the four terms to which he was elected. One might be tempted at this point to conclude that

11. I have argued elsewhere (Peltzman 1989 [chap. 9]) that an interest group theory of regulation can accommodate deregulation when economic change, including change induced by the regulation, weakens the interest group's stake in continued regulation. This does not appear to have occurred prior to deregulation of trucking.

12. These data, from Penoyer (1980, 1982), do not extend beyond 1980.

newly elected Democrats tend to foster regulation. But the postwar period belies this. Here a Republican administration, Richard Nixon–Gerald Ford, dominates regulatory innovation as completely as Wilson's did in the pre–New Deal period. It accounts for over half the new agencies (19 of 30) and just under half the new laws (106 of 231) in the 1948–80 period. Time may be as important as party. For example, of the laws not enacted during the Nixon-Ford years, around two-thirds (78 of 125) were produced in the two surrounding Democratic administrations.

These are crude measures, and they need to be interpreted cautiously.[13] But they leave a clear overall impression of long, quiet periods punctuated by relatively brief eruptions of activity. Post-1980 data would surely strengthen this impression.[14] On its face, these pronounced waves of regulatory innovation are hard to reconcile with the passive role of government in Stigler's theory. The growth and decline of pressure groups, changes in the technology of political pressure, and so forth would seem to imply a smoother time path. In my development of Stigler's theory (Peltzman 1976 [chap. 6]), I showed how large economic shocks, such as the Great Depression, could produce unusual pressure for regulatory innovation. But the macroeconomy of the 1970s was hardly so unusual as to satisfactorily account for the regulatory boom of the Nixon-Ford years, when around one-third of all the 1900–1980 regulatory innovation occurred. It is hard to avoid a suspicion that supply conditions play a role here. For example, even if a Democratic presidency is not a necessary condition for a regulatory boom, a sizable Democratic majority in the Congress seems to be. In the four terms with the most regulatory innovation (Wilson I, Roose-

13. They weight equally the Federal Reserve Act and the Bald Eagle Protection Act; laws can reduce regulation as well as increase it, etc.

14. Consider the following data on growth of real regulatory expenditures and agency employment (from the Center for the Study of American Business, Washington University, St. Louis):

Administration	Annual Percentage Change in	
	Spending	Employment
Nixon-Ford (from '70)	9.6	7.5
Carter	6.0	3.1
Reagan I	−1.6	−4.4
Reagan II	3.8	.6
Bush (est.)	4.2	4.6

No subsequent administration comes close to matching the growth rates of the Nixon-Ford years.

velt I, Nixon, and Nixon-Ford), the Democrats' average share of House
seats (64 percent) exceeded comfortably[15] their average share (53 percent)
in the remaining 16 terms. But large Democratic majorities are hardly
sufficient, given their domination of Congress over the whole post–New
Deal period.

Who Demands Regulation?

Another problem for the theory of regulation concerns the nature of the
commodity being transacted. The putative buyers in Stigler's theory sometimes seem overly reluctant. For example, the primary beneficiaries of the
Motor Carrier Act of 1935 were the truck owners and unionized workers.
But the industry was ambivalent about the law, and the union had not
yet been organized in 1935. Anecdotal examples of industry resistance to
regulatory innovation abound: the securities industry's resistance to the
Securities and Exchange Commission, the drug industry's opposition to
the 1962 Drug Amendments, and the broad opposition of manufacturers
to increased pollution regulation, to name a few. More systematic evidence
is provided by Binder (1985). He examines the stock market's response to
20 regulatory changes from 1889 to 1978 (of which 16 involve increased
regulation). He finds no systematic tendency for increased industry wealth
around these changes.

Of course, industry interests were not subsequently ignored. The truckers did get entry control, the 1962 Drug Amendments did create a barrier
to entry, the Securities and Exchange Commission did sanction a brokerage rate cartel, and established polluters did get a cost advantage over
new plants. Nevertheless, the Stiglerian metaphor of government as order-
taker seems to obscure a more complex interaction between regulators
and regulated. Their relationship is not concretized at conception, but
rather seems to evolve over a time during which the industry interest has to
be defined, possibly reshaped by the regulatory institutions, and asserted.[16]

Waste

In Stigler's theory, deadweight loss is one of the costs of the political competition for regulatory rents. This was a major theoretical advance. Pre-

15. But not significantly, given the small samples.
16. For example, the 1962 Drug Amendments substantially increased the concentration
of innovation (Grabowski 1976). This was a result of exit from innovation consequent on
regulation-induced increases in costs. Thus the increased concentration helped some firms
and hurt others. Even if these effects could have been anticipated in 1962, it is unclear that
they are consistent with the interest of the "industry" as it was structured in 1962. However,
a proposal to substantially lower regulatory barriers to entry might well meet with resistance
from the industry as structured today. Today, incumbent firms are presumably the low-cost

viously, economists mainly imprecated against the numerous instances of inefficiency created by regulation. Now, when one was faced with something like backhaul restrictions in trucking,[17] there was a new intellectual challenge: were there really cheaper methods of preserving the truckers' rents in a world in which access to political power was costly? The recent growth of health, safety, and environmental (HSE) regulation poses the problem that the answer seems too often to be "yes."

The main problem here is one of magnitude. The important institutional innovations occurred in the late 1960s and early 1970s and contributed significantly to the aforementioned regulatory boom of the Nixon-Ford years. The design of automobiles and other consumer products, safety in the workplace, and, most important, the condition of the environment became subject to federal regulation. Since then the economic costs of HSE regulation have come to dwarf those of the older forms of regulation. This is driven mainly by the costs of environmental regulation, which imposes direct costs exceeding $100 billion per year and entails forgone output at least this large (Crandall 1992).

One approach economists took in analyzing HSE regulation, inspired by Stigler, was to look for the rent creation and distribution elements in it. This search did not go unrewarded (see Gruenspecht and Lave 1989, pp. 1530–31). The tendency for HSE regulation to create entry barriers and shelter high-cost firms and workers from competition proved not so different from more traditional modes of regulation. This line of research will likely continue to be fruitful. But it is unlikely to provide a very powerful explanation for HSE regulation, because the costs of environmental regulation are just too large. For example, they are roughly double the total profits of the whole manufacturing sector. Surely there are cheaper ways to create rents.

Another line of inquiry, inspired by the traditional efficiency rationale for regulation, has been to look for HSE benefits that might offset the costs. This has been mainly unsuccessful. While this is not the place for a survey of the relevant literature (see Gruenspecht and Lave 1989), it is safe to say that finding benefits that come close to offsetting the costs has proved elusive. Low benefit/cost ratios are a common finding in the empirical literature.

Mainly economists have found waste, not simply in the elusive or low benefits, but more notably in terms of cost effectiveness. Most HSE regulation has evolved into highly detailed rules about design and process. The

---

adapters to the regulatory system, and entry might jeopardize their accumulated regulatory capital.

17. Whereby a truck carrying freight from A to B had to return empty to A.

sobriquet economists award this mode of regulation—"command and control"—bespeaks, in its evocation of Stalinist central planning, a negative reaction. Our professional instinct is that such a system must violate the marginal conditions for cost minimization. And the evidence tends to reinforce this strongly. For example, a survey of recent HSE rules found a range of $100,000 to $72 billion in cost per statistical life saved across 24 adopted rules (Viscusi 1992, p. 264). The precise meaning of this enormous range is surely debatable,[18] but the broad implication that value maximization cannot be high on the HSE regulation agenda is not. This is confirmed by the literature that estimates the difference between the lowest cost of achieving a given pollution reduction objective and the cost of current regulatory methods. The typical finding is that this difference is substantial, often accounting for over half the current costs (Tietenberg 1988, p. 346). The literature leaves the clear impression that a large chunk of what is by far the most expensive regulatory enterprise in history is being wasted.

A recent review of the literature I have just alluded to chastises economists: "When a movement as sweeping and important as the environmentalist-consumerism movement occurs, economists should not be complaining two decades later that government programs are not efficient; we should have done more to show how to improve the efficiency and effectiveness of these social programs" (Gruenspecht and Lave 1989, p. 1544). This criticism is misplaced. Economists know what steps would improve the efficiency of HSE regulation, and they have not been bashful advocates of them. These steps include substituting markets in property rights, such as emission rights, for command and control, emphasizing performance (lives saved) over design (thicker guardrails); subjecting rules to cost/benefit tests; and so forth. The real problem lies deeper than any lack of reform proposals or failure to press them. It is our inability to understand their lack of political appeal.

George Stigler will be remembered for extending the economists' rational behavior paradigm to regulation. He argued eloquently against our tendency to treat public policy "as a curious mixture of benevolent public interest and unintentional blunders" (Stigler 1982, p. 9). In so doing, he sensitized us to the political utility of seemingly inefficient policies. However, consider, for example, the literature on tradable emission rights versus command and control. It finds potential efficiency gains so large that

18. For example, these are average, not marginal, costs; the exotically high figures may imply trivial total costs (divided by minuscule benefits).

the political transaction costs of changing present policies must be a small fraction of them. Neither Stigler's theory nor, of course, the "benevolent public interest" model he criticized would lead us to expect perpetuation of present policies in these circumstances. There is, to be sure, halting movement toward more efficient policies.[19] But even instant elimination of the inefficiencies would leave a considerable historical puzzle. Perhaps it will be resolved by showing that economists have greatly overstated the inefficiencies of current policies. Otherwise, as George Stigler would undoubtedly remind us, inefficiency is just a synonym for our ignorance. When our ignorance can be measured in billions (of dollars of seemingly pointless expenditures), the challenge to progress in the intellectual enterprise that owes so much to George Stigler becomes clear.

REFERENCES

Becker, Gary S. "A Theory of Competition among Pressure Groups for Political Influence." *Q.J.E.* 98 (August 1983): 371–400.

Bernstein, Marver H. *Regulating Business by Independent Commission.* Princeton, N.J.: Princeton Univ. Press, 1955.

Binder, John J. "Measuring the Effects of Regulation with Stock Price Data." *Rand J. Econ.* 16 (Summer 1985): 167–83.

Buchanan, James M., and Tullock, Gordon. *The Calculus of Consent: Logical Foundations of Constitutional Democracy.* Ann Arbor: Univ. Michigan Press, 1962.

Crandall, Robert. *Why Is the Cost of Environmental Regulation So High?* St. Louis: Washington Univ., Center Study American Bus., 1992.

Demsetz, Harold. "George J. Stigler: Midcentury Neoclassicist with a Passion to Quantify." *J.P.E.* (October 1993): 793–817.

Downs, Anthony. *An Economic Theory of Democracy.* New York: Harper & Row, 1957.

Ehrenberg, Ronald G. *The Regulatory Process and Labor Earnings.* New York: Academic Press, 1979.

Grabowski, Henry G. *Drug Regulation and Innovation: Empirical Evidence and Policy Options.* Washington: American Enterprise Inst., 1976.

Gruenspecht, Howard K., and Lave, Lester B. "The Economics of Health, Safety, and Environmental Regulation." In *Handbook of Industrial Organization,* vol. 2, edited by Richard Schmalensee and Robert D. Willig. Amsterdam: North-Holland, 1989.

Hendricks, Wallace. "Regulation and Labor Earnings." *Bell J. Econ.* 8 (Autumn 1977): 483–96.

Jordan, William A. "Producer Protection, Prior Market Structure and the Effects of Government Regulation." *J. Law and Econ.* 15 (April 1972): 151–76.

---

19. Under the Clean Air Act of 1990, a tradable emission right system for sulfur oxide emissions is to be implemented in 1996.

Joskow, Paul L., and Rose, Nancy L. "The Effects of Economic Regulation." In *Handbook of Industrial Organization,* vol. 2, edited by Richard Schmalensee and Robert D. Willig. Amsterdam: North-Holland, 1989.

Kalt, Joseph P. *The Economics and Politics of Oil Price Deregulation: Federal Policy in the Post-Embargo Era.* Cambridge, Mass.: MIT Press, 1981.

Noll, Roger G. "Economic Perspectives on the Politics of Regulation." In *Handbook of Industrial Organization,* vol. 2, edited by Richard Schmalensee and Robert D. Willig. Amsterdam: North-Holland, 1989.

Olson, Mancur. *The Logic of Collective Action: Public Goods and the Theory of Groups.* Cambridge, Mass.: Harvard Univ. Press, 1965.

Peltzman, Sam. "Toward a More General Theory of Regulation." *J. Law and Econ.* 19 (August 1976): 211–40 (chap. 6 of this volume).

———. "The Economic Theory of Regulation after a Decade of Deregulation." *Brookings Papers Econ. Activity* (suppl., 1989), pp. 1–41 (chap. 9 of this volume).

Penoyer, Ronald. *Directory of Federal Regulatory Agencies.* 2d ed. St. Louis: Washington Univ., Center Study American Bus., April 1980.

———. *Directory of Federal Regulatory Agencies: 1982 Update.* St. Louis: Washington Univ., Center Study American Bus., June 1982.

Rose, Nancy L. "Labor Rent Sharing and Regulation: Evidence from the Trucking Industry." *J.P.E.* 95 (December 1987): 1146–78.

Smith, Rodney T.; Bradley, Michael; and Jarrell, Gregg. "Studying Firm-specific Effects of Regulation with Stock Market Data: An Application to Oil Price Regulation." *Rand J. Econ.* 17 (Winter 1986): 467–89.

Stigler, George J. "Public Regulation of the Securities Markets." *J. Bus.* 37 (April 1964): 117–42.

———. "The Economic Effects of the Antitrust Laws." *J. Law and Econ.* 9 (October 1966): 225–58.

———. "The Theory of Economic Regulation." *Bell J. Econ. and Management Sci.* 2 (Spring 1971): 3–21.

———. *The Economist as Preacher, and Other Essays.* Chicago: Univ. Chicago Press, 1982.

Stigler, George J., and Friedland, Claire. "What Can Regulators Regulate? The Case of Electricity." *J. Law and Econ.* 5 (October 1962): 1–16.

Tietenberg, Thomas. *Environmental and Natural Resource Economics.* 2d ed. Glenview, Ill.: Scott, Foresman, 1988.

Viscusi, W. Kip. *Fatal Tradeoffs: Public and Private Responsibilities for Risk.* New York: Oxford Univ. Press, 1992.

INDEX

Abrams, Burton, 70
Adelman, Irma, 260
Airline industry: with dissipation of regulatory rents, 322; international, xii; rate structure, 183–85; regulation of, 309–11; support for, and opposition to deregulation, 311–12
Americans for Democratic Action (ADA) ratings, 4, 17–18, 20, 30
Arcelus, Francisco, 78
Averch, Harvey, 298

Bailey, E., 273, 281
Banking industry deposit rates, 316–18
Barriers to entry: created by health, safety, and environmental regulations, 335; in current telecommunications market, 314; in regulatory process, 158
Becker, Gary, 273, 286, 295–97, 299, 303, 328
Beneficiaries of regulation: under regulated prices, 176–86; regulator choice of, 158–67; in theory of politically dominant policy of income redistribution, 202, 204–5; of trucking industry under Motor Carrier Act, 334
Bernstein, Marver H., 328
Binder, John J., 334
Bloom, Howard, 70
Borcherding, Thomas E., 197–98
Bradley, Michael, 331
Brazer, Harvey, 196
Brokerage rates: deregulation of, 315, 322; NYSE rate-setting cartel, 314–15
Buchanan, James, ix, 36, 329
Budget, government: governor's influence over state-level, 117; political effect of, 117; president's influence on federal, 117; voter response to federal government spending, 118–34; voter response to increased spending at state level,

118, 135, 138–47. *See also* Spending, government
Bureaucracy model (Niskanen), 194
Business cycles, political, 70 n. 1

Campaign funds voting behavior model, 7, 14
Canada: growth of government spending in, 228–33; role of political institutions in, 233–35
Capture theory (CT) of regulation: conceptual problem of, 290; cross-subsidization (Posner), 293; introduction of, 289–90; producer interest group decision making, 271–72; theoretical rationale for, 328
Caves, R., 283
Christensen, L., 277
Coase, Ronald H., 298–99
Committee on Political Education (COPE) ratings, 17, 19–20, 30
Competition: among political actors, 329; deadweight loss as cost of political, 334–35; effect on airline regulatory rents, 322
Constituencies: characteristics of legislator's, viii, 11–14; characteristics related to voting behavior, 14–31; diversity of economic interests across, 44–45; inequality across legislative, 221–22; interests correlated with contributors, 30–31; voting behavior of, 79, 93–96, 99–100
Consumers: as diffuse majority, x, 156–57, 329; regulatory weighting toward protection of, 172–73
Contributors to campaign funds: interests correlated with constituents, 30–31; political party as interest group, 33–34
COPE. *See* Committee on Political Education

339